£55·00

KV-398-020

Sale and Supply of Goods

Sale and Supply of Goods

Second Edition

Iwan Davies LLM PhD (Wales)

Barrister, Director, Centre for Instalment Credit Law,

University of Wales, Swansea

LAW & TAX

© Pearson Professional Limited 1996

Iwan Davies has asserted his right under the Copyright,
Designs and Patents Act 1988 to be identified as the
author of this work

ISBN 075200 2236

Published by
FT Law and Tax
21–27 Lamb's Conduit Street, London WC1N 3NJ

A Division of Pearson Professional Limited

Associated Offices
Australia, Belgium, Canada, Hong Kong,
India, Japan, Luxembourg,
Singapore, Spain, USA

A CIP catalogue record for this book is available from the
British Library

Printed in Great Britain by Bell & Bain

Contents

Preface

The purpose of this book is to consider the law relating to domestic sale and supply of goods. An attempt has been made to make the book as comprehensive and self-contained as possible as well as to specifically address conceptual notions and practical problems.

There have been significant recent legal developments in this area including three amendments to the Sale of Goods Act 1979. The Sale of Goods (Amendment) Act 1994 abolished the ancient doctrine of market overt, and the Sale and Supply of Goods Act 1994 introduced new provisions aimed at bolstering the position of consumers. The Sale of Goods (Amendment) Act 1995 attempts to deal with the issue of identification of goods for the purpose of the passing of property in part of a bulk and it is therefore still necessary to seek a potential solution in equity to protect prepaying buyers in unidentified goods. Further there have been important developments emanating from Europe with the Regulations implementing the Unfair Contract Term Directive and also the General Product Safety Regulations.

The substitution for the merchantability test of that of satisfactory quality has potential significance and there is considerable scope for a new body of case law to emerge if the courts treat this new terminology as a legislative signal to adopt a more purposive application of the quality test. Whilst the adoption of satisfactory quality does have the advantage of communicating to consumers the standard required in a more meaningful way than did merchantability, nonetheless, the effect of the reform is to confirm a bifurcation between consumer and commercial transactions: satisfactory quality is not an appropriate standard for commercial transactions in the sense that the goods may still be commercially useful. In any case, the introduction of the satisfactory quality test could be premature because it is likely that further legislative intervention will be necessary to implement the European Commission proposals in their Green Paper on Consumer Guarantees which deals with the extent and nature of manufacturers' liability. All in all the time may have come for a thorough review of the law of sale and supply which clearly separates commercial from consumer transactions as the task of putting further patchwork in this area of law can no longer be reasonably sustained.

It is a pleasure for me to record my gratitude to Mr Andrew Petersen, undergraduate student at the University of Wales, Swansea who checked the case notations. I would also like to thank Mr Walter Rainbird and his able team for their sympathetic understanding during the time of the preparation of this manuscript. Finally I should like to record my gratitude to my wife and also our children, Elidir and Osian, who are a constant source of joy.

A determined attempt has been made to state the law from material available to me up to and including 31 December 1995.

Iwan Davies
Swansea
January 1996

Table of Cases

Table of Statutes

Table of Statutory Instruments

Table of European Provisions

Abbreviations

APR	annual percentage rate
CCA	Consumer Credit Act 1974
cif	cost, insurance and freight
CPA	Consumer Protection Act 1987
DTI	Department of Trade and Industry
FA	Factors Act 1889
fob	free on board
FTA	Fair Trading Act 1973
GPSR	General Product Safety Regulations 1994
NHS	National Health Service
OFT	Office of Fair Trading
SGA	Sale of Goods Act 1979
SGSA	Supply of Goods and Services Act 1982
SI	Statutory Instrument
SOGIT	Supply of Goods (Implied Terms) Act 1973
TDA	Trade Descriptions Act 1968
UCC	Uniform Commercial Code (US)
UCTA	Unfair Contract Terms Act 1977

Part I

Contract Formalities and Obligations

Chapter 1

Sources of the Law of Sale and Supply

An important issue which arises from contracts for sale and supply of goods is the interaction of legislation and the common law. Some of the statutes are essentially 19th Century in orientation, the most notable being the Factors Act 1889 (FA) and the Sale of Goods Act 1979 (SGA), which consolidates the original Act of 1893 with the subsequent amendments made especially in the Supply of Goods (Implied Terms) Act 1973 (SOGIT), now substituted by the Consumer Credit Act 1974 (CCA). There are also other statutes of relatively recent origin which follow the tradition adopted under the SGA 1979 as seen, for example, under the Supply of Goods and Services Act 1982 (SGSA). More recently the trend has been to amend the SGA and the SGSA through further legislative intervention. The Sale of Goods (Amendment) Act 1994 abolished the ancient doctrine of market overt, and the Sale and Supply of Goods Act 1994 introduced new provisions aimed at bolstering the position of consumers. The Sale of Goods (Amendment) Act 1995 deals with the issue of identification of goods for the purpose of the passing of property in part of a bulk, the motivation for this reform being to protect the commodity trading market in the UK.

For the most part, the SGA 1979 and the SGSA 1982 reflect an attempt to re-form the shape and organisation of common law rather than effect a reform of the substantive law. Certainly Chalmers, the draftsman of the SGA 1893, considered that each provision in the Act should have a common law history, an approach which influenced the formation of the statutory implied terms in contracts of hire under the SGSA 1982. Consequently, when, subsequent to the passage of the SGA 1893, Chalmers wrote his various *Digests*, his purpose was not merely to annotate the Code with cases decided under it: 'Our common law is rich in the exposition of principles, and these expositions lose none of their value now that the law is codified. A rule can never be appreciated apart from the reasons on which it is founded' (see Chalmers, *The Sale of Goods Act 1893*, 4th ed (1899) at p x). The underlying approach of codification in re-forming the law has stressed the mechanistic nature of legal reasoning as essentially a syllogistic exercise. The language of the Code is taken to constitute the major premise so that Lord Herschell said in *Bank of England v Vagliano Brothers* [1891] AC 107: '[T]he law should be ascertained from interpreting the language used instead of, as before, roaming over a vast number of authorities in order to discover what the law was . . .' (p 145).

At the same time, codification was seen as a starting point for finding and applying common law rules. This point was expressed by Lord Herschell in *Vagliano* as follows:

> I am of course far from asserting that resort may never be had to the previous state of the law for the purpose of aiding in the construction of the provisions of the code. If, for example, a provision may be of doubtful import, such resort would be perfectly legitimate . . . (p 145).

Because Chalmers saw codification as an improvement in the *form* of the law, resurrection of old authorities is easy. This approach is assisted by the common law saving provision found in s 62(2) of the SGA 1979 which states:

> The rules of the common law, including the law merchant, except in so far as they are inconsistent with the provisions of this Act, and in particular the rules relating to the law of principal and agent and the effect of fraud, misrepresentation, duress or coercion, mistake, or other invalidating cause, apply to contracts for the sale of goods.

Indeed in *Cehave NV v Bremer Handelgesellschaft* [1976] QB 44, the Court of Appeal considered that it had been intended to re-state the pre-existing sales law and that this intention translated itself into a canon of statutory interpretation. Nonetheless, some speeches in the House of Lords in *Ashington Piggeries Ltd v Christopher Hill Ltd* [1972] AC 441 would suggest an important gloss to this approach. In particular, in the interpretation of provisions of the SGA 1979 relating to implied terms, Lord Diplock said (at p 501) that the Act 'ought not to be construed so narrowly as to force on parties to contracts for the sale of goods promises and consequences different from what they must reasonably have intended'.

The value of the unamended SGA and SGSA was often said to be their general applicability to all products and transactions. In fact this was not the case. For example, the disposition of motor vehicles developed its own legislative scheme seen in Part III of the Hire Purchase Act 1964, which has been re-enacted under the Consumer Credit Act 1974. The changes made, especially by the Sale and Supply of Goods Act 1994, are such that it has to be asked whether consumer and commercial law can now exist in the same statute. The 1994 reform appears to confirm the trend of recent years of discriminating between consumer and non-consumer transactions: see the Unfair Contract Terms Act 1977 (UCTA) and most notably now the Unfair Terms in Consumer Contracts Regulations 1994 (SI 1994 No 3159). As it stands, the SGA as amended is a patchwork of various styles of draftsmanship emanating from the 19th Century to the modern Parliamentary draftsman. In general, the recent reforms reflect the unease felt about the SGA 1979, with its echoes of 19th Century sales practice where the distinction between retail and wholesale sales was not as acute as it is today.

An important phenomenon behind recent legislation in the area of sale and supply of goods is the role of the European Community. Part I of the Consumer Protection Act 1987 (CPA) is the response of English law to the European Community Directive (85/374/EEC) on the approximation of the laws of the member states relating to liability for defective products. More recently the

General Product Safety Directive (92/59/EEC) has been implemented in the UK by the General Product Safety Regulations 1994 (SI 1994 No 2328). In addition, the European Community Directive on Consumer Credit was agreed in 1986 (87/102/EEC). To a great extent this is based on the Consumer Credit Act 1974 (CCA) although it is not as extensive. There is also a further Directive on the calculation of APRs (90/88/EEC). The Directive on Doorstep Selling (85/577/EEC) implemented by the Consumer Protection (Cancellation of Contracts Concluded Away From Business Premises) Regulations 1987 (SI 1987 No 2117) regulates most contracts, whether for cash or credit, where negotiations have been conducted away from business premises. Perhaps the most significant reform in terms of its impact upon substantive common law doctrine is the Unfair Terms in Consumer Contracts Directive (93/13/EEC) which has now been implemented in the UK (see Chapter 5). The general theme behind the European Community intervention is to protect consumers within the European Union the theory being that harmonising the law will stimulate inter-Member State consumer transactions by increasing consumer confidence, while at the same time assisting suppliers in their task of selling goods and services within the European Union.

The CCA 1974 came about in the wake of the Crowther Committee Report on *Consumer Credit* (1971) Cmnd 4596. The Report made serious and far-reaching criticisms of the previous law which regulated transactions on the basis of legal form rather than commercial reality. Furthermore, the Report contains a full historic, economic and social critique of consumer credit and proposed a new legal framework. This has been largely achieved under the 1974 Act. Unfortunately, the second strand to the Report that a Lending and Security Act be implemented to regulate commercial transactions has yet to be successful. The Government's response in the White Paper on *Reform of the Law on Consumer Credit* (1972) Cmnd 5427, para 14 stated:

> The Government accept that there are aspects of the existing law in this field which cause difficulty, but they do not have sufficient evidence either of a need for such major recasting of existing law on new principles or of general support for the particular solution proposed by the Committee.

Even so, renewed impetus for reform along Crowther lines was provided by Professor Diamond's DTI Report, *A Review of Security Interests in Property* (1989). The attempt here was to highlight the inadequacy of the present legal approach where it is assumed that selling on credit, or leasing for the useful life of the equipment is not lending, and that reservation of title on sale does not constitute the creation of a security interest but is merely an agreement as to the time at which the property should pass to the buyer. In this respect, as the Crowther Committee pointed out (para 5.5.6), art 9 of the US Uniform Commercial Code (UCC) is 'in concept and in structure an admirable prototype for a modern law of personal property security'. Such a scheme would, if implemented, introduce into English law two key features, namely, a functional classification of security interests and a priority system based on the order of registration of those interests. A filing mechanism cuts down debtor misbehaviour, because the availability of reliable information about the debtor's property reduces the debtor's incentive to misbehave by removing the opportunity to do so. Furthermore, one set of filing rules to replace the many chattel security files which now exist in England, would allow for secured financing of stock-in-trade through the simple priority rule of first-to-file.

Chapter 2

Definition and Nature of Contracts for the Supply of Goods

There is no doubt that sale of goods is the principal method by which legal ownership in goods can be transferred for value. There will be a strong emphasis on sale in this work because it provides the model for other supply contracts. The purpose of this chapter is to define the contract of sale and highlight its similarities and differences as compared with other supply contracts. The reference made throughout to the SGA 1979 and the SGSA 1982 will incorporate the amendments made by the Sale of Goods (Amendment) Act 1994, the Sale and Supply of Goods Act 1994 and the Sale of Goods (Amendment) Act 1995.

Definition of sale contract

The statutory definition of 'sale' in s 2 of SGA 1979 contains a number of ingredients which distinguish sale from other transactions. It is worth setting out the definition in full:

(1) A contract of sale of goods is a contract by which the seller transfers or agrees to transfer the property in goods to the buyer for a money consideration, called the price.

(2) There may be a contract of sale between one part owner and another.

(3) A contract of sale may be absolute or conditional.

(4) Where under a contract of sale the property in the goods is transferred from the seller to the buyer the contract is called a sale.

(5) Where under a contract of sale the transfer of the property in the goods is to take place at a future time or subject to some condition later to be fulfilled the contract is called an agreement to sell.

(6) An agreement to sell becomes a sale when the time elapses or the conditions are fulfilled subject to which the property in the goods is to be transferred.

In order to satisfy the SGA 1979, the definition requires that the following components be present:

Contract for the sale of goods

It should be noted that within the definition of a contract of sale a distinction is drawn between an executory sale or agreement to sell, and an executed transfer. The distinction is important because the executory contract creates only personal rights between the parties themselves whereas the executed contract

7

gives the buyer an interest in the goods. Nevertheless, the inclusion of both the executed and executory agreement within the statutory definition does emphasise that delivery of the goods is not an essential element of a sale contract. Even so, there must be a contract, a requirement that can prove particularly problematic in supply situations where the contract element is missing, for example, drugs prescribed under the NHS.

The statutory definition of 'goods' in s 61(1) of SGA 1979 includes the following:

> 'goods' includes all personal chattels other than things in action and money, and in Scotland all corporeal moveables except money; and in particular 'goods' includes emblements, industrial growing crops, and things attached to or forming part of the land which are agreed to be severed before sale or under the contract of sale.

From this definition, assignments of choses in action are excluded and this is also the case with money. Of course, where the money is no longer legal tender (for example, the half-crown coins and sixpences in *R v Thompson* [1980] QB 229, or where it is being transferred because of its curiosity value (*Moss v Hancock* [1899] 2 QB 111), or because of its inherent value such as Krugerrands) 'money' can be considered to be 'goods' for the purposes of the statutory definition. The definition of 'goods' also embraces *fructus industriales* including industrial crops and *fructus naturales* such as grass. In *Kursell v Timber Operators and Contractors Ltd* [1927] 1 KB 298, a contract for timber to be felled by the buyer at a future date was treated as a sale of goods. Minerals may also be included within the definition as being things 'forming part of the land'. However, much will depend upon the circumstances so that profits à prendre cannot be considered as a contract for the sale of goods, being simply a privilege to work the land in question.

An important point is whether computer software may constitute 'goods' within the meaning of the Act. There is no doubt that software when it is supplied in a tangible form such as a disk will constitute 'goods', but the thorny issue is whether the software itself can be regarded as part of the goods so that the purchaser can gain the implied terms protection of the SGA. In *St Albans City and District Council v International Computers Ltd* (1994) *The Times*, 11 November, Scott-Baker J concluded that a contract of sale of both hardware and software as a system was goods for the purposes of the Act. A significant problem relates to the demateriality of the software medium where, for example, it is transferred over a telephone line via a modem. Even where it is transferred by a disk it is anomalous to consider that it is the quality of the disk that the law is concerned with and not the program itself. In this regard, Scott-Baker J adopted the description of a computer system applied by Rogers J in the Australian case of *Toby Construction Products Ltd v Computa Bar (Sales) Pty Ltd* [1983] 2 NSWLR 48 at p 50:

> A computer is a device designed to accept data, manipulate or process it in accordance with instructions, being the programs, and generate a useful output. Both input and output need physical devices such as readers, teletype printers, video display tubes and disks. The heart of the computer is the central processing unit which performs the actual processing. All these items are tangible, physical

objects. By itself, hardware can do nothing. The really important part of the system is the software. Programs are the instructions or commands that tell the hardware what to do.

It is sometimes suggested that an appropriate analogy may be drawn with misleading or absent written instructions which have been held to constitute part of the definition of 'goods' (see *Wormell v RHM Agriculture (East) Ltd* [1987] 1 WLR 1091). The analogy is flawed, however, because software can hardly be equated with a manual since it does in a real sense 'inform' the hardware. As Scott-Baker J held:

> [Software] is not simply abstract information passed by word of mouth. Entering software alters the content of the hardware.

The usefulness of the disk depends upon the software being appropriate. The correct analogy here is with *R v Whitely* (1991) *The Times*, 6 February, where the deletion of files on computer disks was held to be criminal damage under the Criminal Damage Act 1971, s 10(1) which requires damage to 'property of a tangible nature'. The argument that all the defendant had done was to alter the magnetic particles on the disc and no damage to the disk had been occasioned was rejected because the usefulness of the disk had been severely affected.

The parties to the contract

The two parties envisaged under the SGA 1979 are the seller and the buyer. The seller is defined as a 'person who sells or agrees to sell goods' and the buyer is defined in similar terms (s 61(1)). Clearly, if a person has contracted to buy his own goods from someone else, the contract can be set aside on the basis of mistake and any money paid over will be recoverable because of total failure of consideration. At the same time, s 2(2) of SGA 1979 does specifically contemplate the sale by one part owner to another (but compare *Graff v Evans* (1882) 8 QBD 373; *Davies v Burnett* [1902] 1 KB 666) and there appears to be nothing wrong, as a matter of legal principle, in treating this as a sale. In this situation the buyer, as owner of the goods, will be able to recover them from a person having a legal authority to sell them, for example, a sheriff acting in execution of a writ of fi fa to which the SGA 1979 will apply.

The proliferation of retention of title clauses requires a sharp distinction to be drawn between contracts of sale and agency. Essentially, the issue here concerns the capacity in which the transferee is holding the goods (see Chapter 11). In addition, a franchise agreement to sell goods may also create an agency to which the SGA 1979 is inapplicable. However, the agency tool has been utilised by the CCA 1974 as a consumer protection measure, so that the negotiator or dealer under a regulated consumer credit agreement (see below) is deemed, in certain circumstances, to be the agent for the financier (CCA 1974, s 56). Under s 57 of CCA 1974, the negotiator is the agent for the purpose of receiving a notice of withdrawal (including rescission) or cancellation under the CCA 1974 (see Chapter 3). Moreover, the deemed agency device is used as far as receiving knowledge relating to undertakings of fitness for purpose is concerned (see Chapter 5), and also for any representations made by the dealer to the consumer in the course of negotiating a regulated consumer credit transaction (CCA 1974, s 56(2)).

Property passing

The object of a contract of sale is 'to transfer the property in the goods' from the seller to the buyer. The SGA 1979 defines property as meaning the general property as distinct from special property (s 61(1)). A hirer has a special property in the goods bailed and it follows that the assignment of such an interest is not a sale. The meaning of general property will be discussed at length in Chapter 7. It is sufficient at this stage to note that the SGA 1979 does not necessarily contemplate the sale of absolute ownership (*National Employers Mutual General Insurance Association Ltd v Jones* [1988] 2 WLR 952) and that relativity of title is the key to the understanding of the property passing provisions under the SGA 1979.

Under s 5(1) of SGA 1979 it is envisaged that future goods, ie 'goods to be manufactured or acquired by the seller', can form part of a contract of sale. However, since no interest in the goods passes to the buyer at the time of the contract this will be an agreement to sell. There may also be a contract of sale with respect to a future contingency so that s 5(2) of SGA 1979 states:

> There may be a contract for the sale of goods the acquisition of which by the seller depends on a contingency which may or may not happen.

Again, this can only be an agreement to sell and the contract will fail if the contingency fails to occur within the stipulated time, or if there is none within a reasonable time (compare the sale of a chance or *spes*).

Price

The statutory definition of sale requires that the transfer of property be for 'a money consideration called the price'. Open price contracts are specifically provided for in ss 8 and 9 of SGA 1979 which state:

> **8**—(1) The price in a contract of sale may be fixed by the contract, or may be left to be fixed in a manner agreed by the contract, or may be determined by the course of dealing between the parties.
>
> (2) Where the price is not determined as mentioned in sub-section (1) above the buyer must pay a reasonable price.
>
> (3) What is a reasonable price is a question of fact dependent on the circumstances of each particular case.

> **9**—(1) Where there is an agreement to sell goods on the terms that the price is to be fixed by the valuation of a third party, and he cannot or does not make the valuation, the agreement is avoided; but if the goods or any part of them have been delivered to and appropriated by the buyer he must pay a reasonable price for them.
>
> (2) Where the third party is prevented from making the valuation by the fault of the seller or buyer, the party not at fault may maintain an action for damages against the party at fault.

Insofar as ss 8 and 9 represent a codification of the common law rules they will also be applicable to other supply contracts, although in the case of regulated agreements under s 61(1) of CCA 1974 there is a requirement to state the price in writing (Sched 6).

The determination of the price is very important since the lack of this may be an indication that the contract has not been concluded. This is especially so where such expressions as 'Our offer is made on the basis of our current price list' are used. Nevertheless, especially in the case of executed contracts, the courts are anxious to uphold contracts between businessmen (*Foley v Classique Coaches Ltd* [1934] 2 KB 1). Indeed, this approach finds statutory expression in s 9(1) of SGA 1979.

A different problem concerns attempts by suppliers to control minimum resale prices where there are statutory controls under the Resale Prices Act 1976. Detailed discussion of restrictive trade practices which are regulated by anti-trust laws such as the Fair Trading Act 1973 and the Competition Act 1980 are beyond the scope of this work. It is sufficient to note here that under ss 1, 2 and 4 of the Resale Prices Act 1976, collective agreement between manufacturers and dealers to withhold supplies from those who do not observe laid down resale prices or charges for hiring, hire purchase, or conditional sale are unlawful. There are similar provisions in relation to individual restrictions regulating minimum resale prices or charges as between a manufacturer and a retailer. Exemptions may be granted on specified grounds with respect to a particular 'class of goods' (Resale Prices Act 1976, ss 14–21).

Supply contracts for consideration other than money

Exchange

Despite the fact that implicit in any definition of money is the element of exchange, English law has traditionally distinguished between sale and exchange disregarding the equivalence of economic function. When the practical rules applicable to sale and exchange are interchangeable, to distinguish between them is little more than a scholastic exercise. Under s 1(1) of SGSA 1982 it would seem that an exchange contract comes within its purview since it generally applies to contracts where 'one person transfers or agrees to transfer to another the property in goods'. The SGSA 1982 incorporates into such a contract terms almost identical to those applying in the sales contract (see Chapter 5). Following on from this there should be no difficulty in categorising transactions where gift tokens or coupons are exchanged wholly for a product as transactions under the SGSA 1982 (compare *Davies v Customs and Excise Commissioners* [1975] 1 WLR 204). Where the price of the goods is more than the value of the token, the inclusion of a money consideration would suggest that the transaction is a sale of goods. In one sense, the characterisation of the transaction as being either sale or exchange may be important because the remedy for defective performance in exchange is not for the price, but rather a claim for unliquidated damages for non-delivery.

In the case of a part exchange transaction there is no difficulty in categorising the supply of new goods as a sale simply because the supplier will be receiving a composite consideration. Thus in *Aldridge v Johnson* (1857) 7 E & B 885 there was an agreement to transfer 32 bullocks valued at £192 in return for 100 quarters of barley valued at £125, the set-off of £23 to be paid in cash; this was construed as a reciprocal sale (see also *Forsyth v Jervis* (1816) 1 Stark 437; *Sheldon v Cox* (1824) 3 B & C 420). Surprisingly, there appears to be only one English decision which deals with the trading-in of motor vehicles in part exchange, even though it is such a commonplace everyday experience. The facts in this case, *GJ Dawson (Clapham) Ltd v H and G Dutfield* [1936] 2 All ER 232, are worth elaboration. The plaintiffs were dealers in secondhand lorries and agreed to transfer to the defendants two lorries for £475 and take in exchange two other lorries valued at £225, provided they were delivered within one month. The defendants paid in cash the balance of £250 but did not deliver the lorries. It was held that this was a contract for sale and the plaintiffs were therefore able to sue for the price. The decision would have been otherwise if no value had been assigned, as in the Irish Supreme Court decision in *Flynn v Mackin* [1974] IR 101. This is particularly significant in relation to Part III of the Hire Purchase Act 1964 (as substituted) which does not apply to exchanges of motor vehicles (see Chapter 10).

Whether the transaction is to be categorised as a sale or exchange is a question of contractual intention. This may be important if credit finance for the new article purchased with a part exchange is declined by the financier. In these circumstances, it is probable that both transactions will be regarded as interdependent so that the part exchange element may be construed as a sale subject to a condition subsequent, thereby making it determinable if the financier does not accept the transaction. This analysis will have relevance as far as the passing of property and risk is concerned (see Chapter 9) where the goods are damaged in the meantime (*Clarke v Reilly* (1962) 96 ILTR 96). Moreover the exception to the *nemo dat* principle discussed in Chapter 10 will be significant here especially if it is considered that the dealer has bought or has agreed to buy the goods under s 9 of FA 1889. There is also special provision under s 73(2) of CCA 1974 for a part exchange allowance in respect of a cancelled regulated agreement where property has been transferred (see Chapter 3).

Free gifts

The requirement of consideration distinguishes a sale from a gift. Nevertheless, as we shall see in Chapter 5, a wide definition is given to the term 'supply' in a contract of sale so that an insertion accompanying goods will be considered as having been supplied under the contract, thereby attracting the implied terms under the SGA 1979. Sometimes the so-called 'free gift' will constitute a collateral contract, the consideration for which being the entry into the main contract of sale. This issue was discussed by the House of Lords in *Esso Petroleum v Customs and Excise Commissioners* [1976] 1 WLR 1 in relation to a promotion scheme. Here Esso petrol stations gave motorists buying their petrol, coins of little intrinsic value which depicted members of the England 1970 World Cup Squad. The Commissioners claimed purchase tax on these coins, but the House of Lords held that there had been no sale. Lord Dilhorne and Lord Russell both thought that there was nothing more than a gift, whereas Lord Fraser, dissenting, considered that there had been a sale of both articles (ie the petrol and the coins) in one transaction. The *via media* was adopted by Lord Wilberforce and Lord Simon of Glaisdale, namely, there was a contract for the supply of the coins but it was a collateral contract. Following this last approach, s 1(1) of SGSA 1982 would apply giving the transferee the benefit of the implied terms in ss 2–5 (see Chapter 5).

If the free gift is supplied as a genuine gift without the transferee being under any obligation to do anything, there will be no contractual relationship between the transferor and transferee. The significance here is that all the implied obligations under the SGA 1979 and SGSA 1982 will be avoided, although there may be liability in negligence including product safety legislation (see Chapter 6). Where the requirements of the Unsolicited Goods and Services Act 1971 (as amended) are satisfied, the recipient of unsolicited goods can treat those goods as an unconditional gift. The relevant circumstances are set out in s 1(2) of that Act which states:

> The circumstances referred to in the preceding subsection [the extinguishment of any right of the sender to the goods] are that the goods were sent to the recipient with a view to his acquiring them, that the recipient has no reasonable cause to believe that they were sent with a view to their being acquired for the purposes of a trade or business and has neither agreed to acquire nor agreed to return them, and either—
> (a) that during the period of six months beginning with the day on which the recipient received the goods the sender did not take possession of them and the recipient did not unreasonably refuse to permit the sender to do so; or
> (b) that not less than thirty days before the expiration of the period aforesaid the recipient gave notice to the sender in accordance with the following sub-section, and that during the period of thirty days beginning with the day on which the notice was given the sender did not take possession of the goods and the recipient did not unreasonably refuse to permit the sender to do so.

Where a person does not have reasonable cause to believe that there is a right to payment in these circumstances, it is an offence under s 2 of the Act as amended to demand such payment. Indeed, the scope of s 2(2) is extensive in this respect:

> A person who, not having reasonable cause to believe there is a right to payment, in the course of any trade or business and with a view to obtaining any payment for what he knows are unsolicited goods sent as aforesaid—
> (a) threatens to bring any legal proceedings; or
> (b) places or causes to be placed the name of any person on a list of defaulters or debtors or threatens to do so; or
> (c) invokes or causes to be invoked any other collection procedure or threatens to do so,
> shall be guilty of an offence and shall be liable on summary conviction to a fine not exceeding [level 5 on the standard scale].

The Secretary of State for the purposes of the Act (as amended) may make under s 3A 'regulation as to the contents and form of notes of agreement, invoices and similar documents' (the Unsolicited Goods and Services (Invoices, etc) Regulations 1975 (SI 1975 No 732)).

Trading stamps

The Trading Stamps Act 1964 (as amended), is of much less importance now that trading stamps are available in so few shops. There is uncertainty as to whether the exchange of trading stamps for goods is a sale or an exchange. Notwithstanding this, the Act (as amended) grants the holder elaborate rights of redemption for cash (s 3) as well as non-excludable implied terms under s 4(1) (as substituted by SSGA 1994, s 7 and Sched 2) against the promoter of the trading stamp scheme.

Transfers of goods and services

The law has traditionally distinguished between contracts for the supply of goods and contracts for the supply of services. With the repeal of the rule that certain sales had to be evinced in writing, and following the enactment of the SGSA 1982, the importance of the distinction is less acute. Nevertheless, there still appear to be notable differences, for example, with regard to the passing of property (see Chapter 7) and also the effects of frustration (see Chapter 9).

The approach of the law is to distinguish the following transactions, namely, a contract for the sale of goods with a severable contract for services, a sale of goods, a contract for work and materials, and lastly, the supply of services. These categorisations are only important insofar as they sound in different legal treatments. Under the SGSA 1982, in any contract of supply the seller's or supplier's duties will normally be strict and excludable only in limited circumstances (see Chapter 5), whereas, in contracts for the supply of services, the supplier's duties will be duties of care which will be excludable subject to the reasonableness requirement of the UCTA 1977, although the terms of such a contract may fall within the provisions of the Unfair Terms in Consumer Contracts Regulations (SI 1994 No 3159). In defining 'satisfactory quality' for the purposes of the SGA reference is made to a 'safety' requirement, and there is overlap here with Parts I and II of the CPA 1987 and also the General Product Safety Regulations 1994. The major difficulty is that the SGSA 1982 has not sufficiently delineated the boundary between the situation where the supply of goods was incidental to the supply of services, so that liability at common law is not strict, with the converse case. At common law, the position is that if the article in question is a standard product like a meal in a restaurant (*Lockett v A and M Charles Ltd* [1938] 4 All ER 170) this is a sale of goods so that liability is strict. On the other hand, the supply and installation of roofing tiles has been held to involve a contract for work and materials (*Young and Marten Ltd v McManus Childs Ltd* [1969] 1 AC 454; compare *Phillip Head and Sons Ltd v Showfronts Ltd* [1970] 1 Lloyd's Rep 140). Where the article is a unique or one-off product such as the commissioning of a portrait from an artist, the court is likely to construe this arrangement as a contract of work and materials notwithstanding the incidental supply of the canvas (*Robinson v Graves* [1935] 1 KB 579; compare *Isaacs v Hardy* (1884) Cab & EL 287).

Where the skill of the transferor is so important and the materials used insignificant, this is treated as a contract for the supply of services. Thus in the medical field, especially with interventionist techniques involving implantation of human products, for example blood or biologics, this may be considered a supply of services because the courts will be reluctant to regard matter of human origin as 'goods' (see *Perlmutter v Beth David Hospital* (1955) 123 NE 2d 792). It follows that the surgeon will not be strictly liable for the products used, his obligation being to exercise reasonable care and skill (*Bolam v Friern Hospital Management Committee* [1957] 1 WLR 582). On the other hand in *Dodd v Wilson & McWilliam* [1946] 2 All ER 691, the plaintiff contracted with a veterinary surgeon to inoculate his cattle with a serum and it was held that the surgeon impliedly warranted the vaccine to be fit for the purpose for which it was supplied. This may be considered to be the more appropriate standard in *contracts* between patients and doctors where artificial products, such as manufactured heart valves, are used for implantation. However, it is very important to take a balanced approach here because value judgments are often made with regard to the comparative worth of the skill of the professional, versus the materials used. For example, it is unlikely that *Lee v Griffin* (1861) 1 B & S 272 would be followed today. In that case the supply of dentures was considered to be a sale, and it was clear that the court paid scant regard to the dentist's skill, providing some indication of the dentist's standing in the 19th century.

Bailment and hire

Bailment is the delivery of goods to another on condition, express or implied, that they shall be returned to the bailor or dealt with according to his instructions. The purpose of bailment and sale is different because, in the case of an ordinary contract of hire, it is not intended that general property in the goods will pass to the bailor/hirer. Sophisticated credit instruments are predicated upon this legal analysis (including equipment leases discussed in Chapter 12). At the same time, contracts in the form of a bailment do raise interesting sale versus security issues (which will be discussed in the context of retention of title clauses in Chapter 11).

A contract of hire is a species of bailment and although it is readily distinguishable from sale in that general property is not intended to pass to the hirer, there are important public policy issues in a consumer hire context, which dictate that the owner be subject to similar liability to that visited upon the seller. This has in large measure been achieved under the SGSA 1982 (see Chapter 5). Nevertheless, there are some important differences which attach to the categorisation of the transaction as a contract of hire:

(1) The hirer is not a person who has 'agreed to buy' for the purposes of s 9 of the FA 1889.

(2) Chattel mortgage legislation does not apply to a genuine contract of hire even in the case of a sale and leaseback.

(3) It is not until the termination of the hiring that the owner has a sufficient interest in the goods to maintain an action for wrongful interference with goods under s 1 of the Torts (Interference with Goods) Act 1977. This action is available if, at the time of the conversion, the plaintiff was in possession of the goods (*The Jag-Shakti* [1986] 1 AC 337) or had an immediate right of possession of them. One significant feature of the 1977 Act is that under s 8 the *jus tertii* may be pleaded, thereby, giving the court power to settle competing claims in one set of proceedings.

(4) Because the essence of a bailment is the transfer of possession, the hiring with its obligation to pay rent does not commence until delivery and the bailee is under a *prima facie* duty to return the goods when the agreement comes to an end.

The CCA 1974 applies statutory control to a regulated consumer hire agreement. This is defined under s 15(1) as:

> A consumer hire agreement is an agreement made by a person with an individual (the 'hirer') for the bailment or (in Scotland) the hiring of goods to the hirer, being an agreement which—
> (a) is not a hire purchase agreement, and
> (b) is capable of subsisting for more than three months, and
> (c) does not require the hirer to make payments exceeding [£15,000].

This is a wide definition and would include leasing of business equipment and vehicles (see Chapter 12), the general effect being to equate consumer hiring with instalment sales and hire purchase agreements (see below). However, in some important respects there are differences in treatment the most notable being as follows:

(1) The hirer is granted a more limited right of termination under s 101(1) of CCA 1974.

(2) The 'protected goods' rules (s 90) do not apply here (see Chapter 12).

(3) The financial relief accorded to a hirer under a consumer hire agreement following the owner's recaption of the goods may be different because under s 100 of CCA 1974 there are limitations placed on recovery of money following termination in the case of conditional sale and hire purchase. However, it is probable that under the common law a minimum payment clause stipulating for future rental payments would be void (see Chapter 12). In any case, under s 132 of CCA 1974 the court has powers to grant the defaulting hirer financial relief in respect of sums paid and payable.

Conditional sales and hire purchase

The right of security is intimately connected with property. Herein lies the reason for the distinction drawn under the common law between credit sales (where the property in goods passes on or before delivery), conditional sales and hire purchase. In *Helby v Matthews* [1895] AC 471, the House of Lords decided that a hirer under a hire purchase agreement who was entitled to terminate the hiring agreement at any time, was not a person who had agreed to buy the goods within the meaning of s 9 of FA 1889, so confirming the *nemo dat* rule (see Chapter 10). Their Lordships distinguished *Lee v Butler* [1893] 2 QB 318 where there was a conditional sale agreement on the basis, in that case, that there was a binding obligation to sell the goods to the buyer.

During the course of the 20th Century, the general statutory approach has moved towards the gradual assimilation of conditional sales and hire purchase. In this respect, although conditional sales are regulated for the purposes of the *nemo dat* exceptions in s 25(2) of SGA 1979, and hire purchase under Sched 4 of CCA 1974, the two sets of provisions are virtually identical. Moreover, the limited exception to the *nemo dat* rule created for dispositions of motor vehicles to 'private purchasers', does not distinguish between a conditional buyer or a hirer under a hire purchase agreement (see Chapter 10). The legislature through the SGA 1979, SOGIT 1973, SGSA 1982 and CCA 1974 has also assimilated sale, conditional sales and hire purchase in relation to the statutorily implied terms as to title, description, quality and fitness for purpose (see Chapter 5). The real dilemma with hire purchase which we will discuss in Chapter 12 is that of deciding the extent of the hirer's proprietary interest in the goods. This is of a peculiarly uncertain nature since the supplier, by lawfully terminating the agreement, will automatically bring the hirer's interest to an end.

Consumer credit

The CCA 1974 was inspired by the American Uniform Commercial Code (UCC). The Crowther Committee on *Consumer Credit* (1971) Cmnd 4596, recommended that transactions should be dealt with not according to their legal form, but according to their economic substance. Under the CCA 1974, there is a recognition that legal rights and duties of a consumer should not necessarily turn upon whether the consumer has borrowed money to buy goods, bought them on credit, or acquired them under a hire purchase contract (ie the traditional distinction drawn between lender credit and vendor credit). Thus the Hire Purchase Acts 1938–1965 have been almost entirely repealed by the CCA 1974, and the rights and duties of the parties involved in a hire purchase contract are similar to those of parties to a sale of goods, in which the consumer has obtained credit, whether from the seller or a third party.

Consumer Credit Act terminology

The CCA 1974 contains new functional terminology so that, as such, there are no references to hire purchase or conditional sales. The central new terms are as follows:

Restricted and unrestricted-use credit
    A restricted use credit is defined in s 11(1):

A restricted-use credit agreement is a regulated consumer credit agreement—
(*a*)   to finance a transaction between the debtor and the creditor, whether forming part of that agreement or not, or
(*b*)   to finance a transaction between the debtor and a person (the 'supplier') other than the creditor, or
(*c*)   to refinance any existing indebtedness of the debtor's, whether to the creditor or another person,
and 'restricted-use credit' shall be construed accordingly.

The issue here is that the debtor has no control over the use to which the credit is put. In contrast, unrestricted-use credit is where the debtor has the control over the application of the loan, and this is so even if it is a term of the loan contract that he must apply the money to a specified purpose (CCA 1974, s 11(3)).

Debtor-creditor-supplier agreements

This is where there is a special relationship between the creditor and the supplier who may even be one and the same person (s 12(*a*)). By definition, this type of contract will always involve restricted-use credit. More difficulty is posed with the party arrangements. In the case of restricted-use credit the CCA 1974 treats what under the common law would be two contracts, one of supply and the other of credit, as one composite agreement, if the credit is given under pre-existing arrangements with the supplier, or in contemplation of future arrangements between them, for example with credit card transactions (s 187(2)). It is possible for there to be unrestricted-use three party debtor-creditor-supplier agreements, but the requirements are more exacting as seen under s 12 (*c*):

an unrestricted-use credit agreement which is made by the creditor under pre-existing arrangements between himself and a person (the 'supplier') other than the debtor in the knowledge that the credit is to be used to finance a transaction between the debtor and the supplier.

Debtor-creditor agreements

All credit agreements that are not debtor-creditor-supplier agreements are debtor-creditor agreements (s 13). Such agreements are likely to be unrestricted-use credit although this may not always be the case, for example where a financier who has no arrangement with the seller insists on paying the money directly to him (s 13 (*a*)).

Fixed-sum and running-account credit

This is the distinction between a hire purchase agreement for a fixed amount (s 10 (*b*)) and a credit card agreement where the debtor enjoys a credit facility that he can draw upon from time to time often subject to a credit limit (s 10 (*a*)).

Connected lender liability

One element of the Consumer Credit Act 1974 (CCA) which has attracted recent attention is s 75. The Crowther Committee first introduced liability for both lender and supplier in their Report published in 1971. The Committee's 'connected lender' concept appeared in s 12, CCA, which introduced the concept of debtor-creditor-supplier agreements (d-c-s). In turn s 75 was passed indicating the liability of creditors for breaches by suppliers. Indeed the section has been seen more recently as a 'form of insurance' transferring risk especially from credit cardholders to credit card-issuers. Section 75 relates to the situation where the creditor and the supplier are different people and the credit will inevitably take the form of a loan.

The supplier must establish a claim based on a breach of contract, and this may include a claim for breach of express or implied terms, including breach of satisfactory quality under the SGA 1994, or a misrepresentation. The section provides the creditor and supplier with equal responsibility for any breach of contract or misrepresentation if the following conditions are fulfilled:

(a) The purchase price charge of the supplied item is over £100 but less than £30,000 (including VAT).

(b) The agreement is 'regulated'. Currently this is an agreement limiting the amount of credit extended to an individual to £15,000.

(c) The business of the creditor is granting credit and the agreement has been made in the course of that business thereby excluding all non-commercial agreements.

(d) There must be a pre-existing arrangement between the creditor and the supplier. This rules out charge card agreements (see Art 3(1)(a)(ii) of the Consumer Credit (Exempt Agreements) Order 1989, SI 1989 No 869). Similarly there is no s 75 liability for debit cards which operate an Electronic Funds Transfer at Place of Sale transaction (EFTPOS) (see s 187(3)(a)).

If these conditions are met, and the debtor has a claim against the supplier, then he will have a *like claim* against the creditor. This means that he can choose to sue the supplier, the creditor, or both, for the full amount of the claim. It should be noted that the debtor does not have to sue the supplier first.

The debtor is the only person who can make a claim under s 75. Claims by authorised users of cards and claims by members of the debtor's family will be excluded. Under the Office of Fair Trading's (OFT's) Proposals of March 1994, *Connected Lender Liability*, the only person who can make a claim is the debtor (which they have insisted is the principal cardholder) as defined in s 189(1). For any claims arising from second authorised users an agency connection must be established. As regards pre-existing arrangements and the dispute over four party transactions (where there is more than one party from within, eg the Visa network involved in a purchase transaction), there is currently in place a method of resolving claims on an *ex gratia* basis, a situation which the OFT in March 1994 described as 'unsatisfactory'. However, *domestic* four-party transactions remain a d-c-s agreement under s 12 and card issuers continue to meet claims up to the full amount and including consequential losses.

An interesting point arises under s 75 regarding rescission of a contract. If a contract is rescinded, the debtor has a right to seek a return of the cash price paid for the goods, and liability to return this falls upon both supplier and creditor. However, it is not clear to whom the goods must be returned. It would seem that current contractual provisions indicate that the supplier is entitled to the goods. This is particularly important when the supplier becomes insolvent, as regards the subsequent position of the supplier's creditors; indeed on the supplier becoming insolvent it may mean that the creditor becomes solely liable for the goods.

The extent and interpretation of equal liability has resulted in a number of important areas being recently examined culminating in two reviews and an extensive consultation exercise being carried out by the Director General of the OFT. The first report *Connected Lender Liability* published in March 1994 resulted in a public hearing in September 1994. Then in May 1995 the DG published a second report where a number of recommendations were made. These were:

1   Equal liability [OFT terminology] should remain, but the card issuers should only be liable for the amount of credit involved in the transaction (the voucher price). So-called 'second in line liability' is not to be enshrined in law, however, the OFT do suggest pursuing a claim against a supplier first.

2   The lower and upper monetary limits should be defined in terms of the amount of credit extended by the creditor (the voucher amount). This would involve changing the wording of s 75(3)(b) from 'cash price' to 'the amount of credit extended'.

3   As regards actual monetary limits the lower limits of £100 should remain, but may in the future be reconsidered (£150 was suggested in March 1994). However, the upper limit should be amended to be the same as the limit for an agreement to be regulated by the Act (currently £15,000, but suggested to be increased to £25,000 in March 1994).

4   A right of subrogation should be introduced to give card issuers the same rights to claim against a scheme as a consumer.

5   As regards overseas transactions, an agreement has been reached which will guarantee consumers protection under s 75 until at least 1996. The voluntary agreement secured with the Association for Payment Clearing Services (APACS) and the Credit Card Research Group (CCRG) will operate as though the recommendations set out above are law, and consequently overseas transactions will only be covered *ex gratia* and be limited to the amount of credit extended.

6   Implementation of the recommendations should be made through the European Communities Act 1972. This would not require separate primary legislation and would also involve fulfilling the UK's obligation under the 1987 Consumer Credit Directive. Section 75 of the CCA could then be revoked under the Deregulation and Contracting Out Act 1994.

Although these recommendations have not yet been implemented the OFT sent their proposals to the Department of Trade and Industry (DTI), and it would seem, bearing in mind the voluntary agreement secured regarding overseas transactions, that reform of the section is inevitable.

In recognising the extremely important consumer protection measure and the initial concerns of the Crowther Committee resulting in the implementation of s 75, the Director General of Fair Trading concluded that s 75 does indeed apply jointly and severally to suppliers and creditors in regard to applicable credit card transactions both in the UK and overseas. This is recognition that s 75(2) and (5), and the card issuer's right to 'charge-back' any successful claim agains them to the supplier or his merchant acquirer, provides lenders with more than adequate protection. This was demonstrated in the public hearing when card issuers recognised the practical problems for consumers associated with second in line liability and conceded that there were far greater concerns requiring change in this area. Currently the creditor grantor's liability is un-limited, and this clearly involves a massive reduction of liability as the total amount of credit available under the Act is currently £15,000 (Consumer Credit (Increase of Monetary Limits) Order 1983 (SI 1983 No 1878)). This would also rule out any claims for consequential losses, for example, negligently made products or travel claims. Defining the monetary limits in terms of 'amounts of credit extended' will affect all transactions that are currently covered by the CCA.

Overseas transactions were one of the few areas that instigated the current review of s 75. It has been claimed by card issuers that s 75 did not apply to them at all as regards overseas transactions, yet at the same time they effec-tively advertised their cards could be used all over the world. By the time of the May 1995 review, card issuers had recognised that s 75 did apply to over-seas transactions, but disputed the extent that it applied. They argued for a reduction in liability, and it would seem they achieved more than a reduction by their agreeing to a 'sensible balance between the interests of consumers and of credit card issuers', which put cardholders in the same position *now* regard-ing overseas transaction as they will be in for *all* transactions when the OFT's proposals become law. The policy applies to overseas transactions provided that:

   (i) the claim would be valid if governed by UK law;

   (ii) the cost of the item charged to the account is more than £100 but not more than £15,000 (see recommendation for reform to s 75 in general, *above*);

   (iii) the policy is not retrospective and only applies to purchases that took place after 15 May 1995.

In the March 1994 Report, the OFT recommended that transactions by authorised second users of a single account should be treated as agents of the principal cardholder and that any claim should be brought by the principal cardholder. Card issuers have in some instances insisted that authorised users are not covered by the Act and ignored the agency connection, a practice the OFT has insisted must stop. Now card issuers should meet claims arising from transactions of authorised second users. However in itself this is a contentious point, because a claim can then only be brought concerning the losses to the principal of the product in question. It may be that this is the total of the card issuers' liability anyway, following the recommendations set out above, and once again major card issuers have succeeded in reducing their liability.

The OFT has recognised that it is not in the interest of anyone to be reliant on essentially informal understandings in the long term, and has called for the recommendations made in May 1995 to be implemented as quickly as possible.

The ambit of the Consumer Credit Act

The CCA 1974 applies to regulated credit agreements. In order to satisfy this, four conditions must be satisfied:

(1) The transaction must have been entered into on or after 1 April 1977 (Consumer Credit Act 1974 (Commencement No 2) Order 1977 (SI 1977 No 325)).

(2) The debtor must be an individual, not a company (s 8(1)). This will be discussed in greater detail in Chapter 12.

(3) The amount of credit given must not exceed £15,000 (Consumer Credit (Increase of Monetary Limits) Order 1983 (SI 1983 No 1878)). The credit here denotes not the total amount the debtor has to pay but the element of financial accommodation. The relevant formula would appear to be:

Credit = Total price – any deposit payable (s 189(1)) + the total charge for credit (s 9(4)).

In seeking to define what items are to be included as part of the total charge for credit, s 20 emphasises that what matters is the cost to the debtor rather than the net return to the lender (see Directive 90/88/EEC and also Consumer Credit (Total Charge for Credit) Regulations 1980 (SI 1980 No 51), Pt 2 (as amended)). In the case of hire purchase transactions, hire rent is treated as credit by virtue of s 9(3) of CCA 1974 (see Sched 2 to CCA 1974, Example 10).

(4) It must not be an exempt transaction. A number of agreements otherwise falling within the ambit of the CCA 1974 are exempted under s 16 of the Act. Most of these relate to mortgages of land and are of no concern here. However, two types of exempt agreements are of significance. The first is in relation to debtor-creditor-supplier agreements where the amount owed is to be paid off in a few instalments. Thus, the Consumer Credit (Exempt Agreements) Order 1980 (SI 1980 No 52) (as amended) which implements s 16(5)(a) of CCA 1974, provides, in the case of fixed sum credit, that the agreement is exempt if no more than four payments are involved, whereas, in the case of running-account, credit exemption is provided if full settlement is made at the end of each period of account. The same statutory instrument implements s 16(5)(b) which exempts debtor-creditor agreements on the basis of the rate of interest charged. Following on from this, a debtor-creditor agreement will be exempted if the annual percentage rate does not exceed the higher of either 13 per cent or 1 per cent more than the base rates of lending banks.

Sale and loans on security

Continental law, with its emphasis upon a unitary concept of *dominium* in which possession is central (*possession vaut titre*), is reluctant to recognise a non-possessory security right except insofar as it has been introduced by statute. It is little wonder therefore that the failure by the SGA 1979 to reconcile 'property' and 'title' have been criticised in a Scottish context. Indeed, the extension of the Sale of Goods Bill 1892 to Scotland is often portrayed as being 'hasty' and 'ill-considered' (see T B Smith, *Property Problems in Sale* (1979)). Despite this, the SGA 1979 does make some attempt to deal with the Scottish dilemma vis-à-vis non-possessory security interests through the insertion of s 61(4) of the 1893 Act (now s 62(4) of the 1979 Act), a provision specifically drafted for Scotland but which also applies to England.

Section 62(4) of the 1979 Act expressly excludes from its application: '. . . a transaction in the form of a contract of sale which is intended to operate by way of . . . security'. This section undoubtedly reflected the Scottish case of *M'Bain v Wallace* (1881) 8 R 330, aff'd (1881) 8 R, HL 106. In this case, the view was taken that so long as the 'sale' was correctly carried through, the arrangement's function as a security did not overturn the transaction. From this it follows that s 62(4) applies to transactions where the sale is a complete sham, ie where the owner purports to sell goods to a creditor in order to raise secured finance while retaining possession. Thus, the Scottish Law Commission in para 5:23 of their Memorandum 25, observed that s 62(4):

> . . . is of importance since the introduction of the rule that property in sale might pass without delivery would otherwise have been possible by resort to transactions in the form of sale to circumvent the rule that a security over moveables may not generally be constituted without transfer to them.

In a similar vein, Lord Moncrieff held in *Robertson v Hall's Trs* (1896) 24 R 120 (at p 134):

> [Section 62(4) of SGA 1979] is in effect a statutory declaration that a pledge of, or other security over moveables, cannot be created merely by completion of what professes to be a contract of sale. The form of the transaction is not conclusive, the reality of the transaction must be enquired into.

The difficulties involved in determining the 'true intentions' of the parties anticipated in s 62(4) are particularly acute in sale and leaseback provisions (see for example *Ladbroke Leasing (South West) Ltd v Reekie Plant Ltd* [1983] SLT 155). There is no doubt that the purpose here is to evade the technical requirements of the Bills of Sale (1878) Amendment Act 1882 which regulates non-absolute sale transfer transactions under which a grantee is given a licence to seize. Any mortgage bill of sale falling within the 1882 Act is void against all persons unless the strict form set out in the Schedule to the Act is adhered to (s 9). Nevertheless, it is the policy of the courts in England where there is security with recourse to property which can be effected by means other than a transaction of loan or charge, not to treat it as registrable under s 395 of the Companies Act 1985. This is so even though the exact economic effect might be carried out through a transaction which, in form, was registrable as a security interest in the goods. In this respect, a document purporting to be a sale of hire purchase agreements was construed by Eve J at first instance in *Re George Inglefield* [1933] Ch 1, as a charge on book debts whereas, in the Court of Appeal (at p 27), it was held to be a sale: '[There is] no reason whatever for attempting to drag the transaction within the operation of the section [s 395 of the Companies Act 1985] by calling it something which in truth it is not.'

A similar issue arose in *Lloyds and Scottish Finance Ltd v Cyril Lord Ltd* (1979) 129 NLJ 366. In this case, the plaintiffs were a finance house and the defendants were a company in liquidation and liquidators of that company. The company before going out of business entered into a 'block discounting' agreement with the finance house. Book debts arising from these credit sales were to be assigned, in blocks containing substantial numbers of such debts, to the plaintiffs in return for a lump sum calculated so as to provide a discounting charge to the plaintiffs. It was argued that these assignments were by way of charge. However, this argument was rejected in the House of Lords and Lord Wilberforce (at p 372) said that to:

> . . . suppose that the assignments were made not by way of sale but by way of security would be to impose upon the parties a form of transaction totally different from that which they had selected — namely, one of sale — and of which there was no evidence whatsoever that either of them desired . . . [The plaintiffs] had no intention of creating any charge over book debts or merely making a series of loans.

His Lordship thought that it would be a strange doctrine of 'looking for the substance' or looking through the documents which would produce a contractual intention so clearly negated by the documents and by oral evidence.

The relationship between sale and security is particularly acute in the retention of title context. The dilemma posed here is the relationship between s 17 (where property passing is linked to contract rather than conveyance) and s 62(4). This is discussed below in Chapter 11.

Chapter 3

Formalities and the Formation of Sale and Supply Contracts

Even though Pt II of SGA 1979 (ss 2–15) is entitled 'Formation of the Contract', there is nothing in it which regulates the actual formation of the contract of sale of goods. The common law saving provision will apply and it is possible to infer from s 62(2) of SGA 1979 that the ordinary principles of contract formation are therefore applicable here. Presumably, this will also apply by analogy to other supply scenarios, even though the major statutes regulating the supply of goods (SOGIT 1973, CCA 1974, SGSA 1982, and the Consumer Protection Act 1987) are entirely silent on the matter.

The modern position regarding the formalities attendant with the SGA 1979 is encapsulated in s 4(1) of the Act which states:

> Subject to this and any other Act, a contract of sale may be made in writing (either with or without seal), or by word of mouth, or partly in writing and partly by word of mouth, or may be implied from the conduct of the parties.

It follows that nearly all contracts of sale and supply can be made by word of mouth, subject to the normal common law rules of contract formation.

Formation

The contract of supply must be a complete agreement (see *Scammell and Nephew Ltd v Ouston* [1941] AC 251), although this does not necessarily mean that every part of the contract has been worked out in meticulous detail. Indeed, as already mentioned (see Chapter 2), the SGA 1979 has special provisions with regard to the determination of price where this is not fixed in the contract of sale (s 8). In general, the courts are concerned to enforce contracts between businessmen, especially executed agreements even where the uncertain terms may be meaningless (*Nicolene Ltd v Simmonds* [1953] 1 QB 543). The common law requirements of contract formation are adequately dealt with in standard works on contract. It is sufficient here merely to note the importance of the objective test for agreement, the relevant question being whether the offeree has accepted the offer in the sense in which a reasonable person would have understood it.

Contract and the doctrine of mistake

Where one party is aware that the offer or the acceptance of the other party does not represent his true intentions but still deals with the other party without disclosing the mistake, the law will abandon the objective interpretation of the first party's intentions. Thus in *Hartog v Colin and Shields* [1939] 3 All ER 566, it was held that the plaintiff could not sue on a contract for the sale of hare skins at so much per pound when he knew that the offeror really meant to sell at that price per piece. Problems with mistake have arisen with hire purchase proposal forms where dealers have manipulated figures on proposal forms. The common law position appears to be that a dealer is not normally the agent of the finance company, and a customer is bound by the terms of the document, unless the finance company knows that it does not accord with the customer's intentions (*United Dominions Trust Ltd v Western* [1976] QB 513). In the case of regulated agreements, the common law rule has been overturned so that s 56(2) of CCA 1974 provides that antecedent negotiations shall be deemed to be conducted by the dealer, 'in the capacity of agent of the creditor as well as in his actual capacity'. The effect of this is that the finance company would be regarded as knowing what its agent knows, namely that the proposal form does not represent the customer's intended offer. The issue of connected lender liability is discussed on pp 18–22.

In cases of mistaken identity, the issue is with whom did the offeror actually intend to contract, as seen in the infamous case of *Cundy v Lindsay* (1878) 3 App Cas 459. Essentially, there is no real answer to this question because, in most cases of fraud, the transferor actually believes that the transferee is the person he is pretending to be. The legal position appears to be (see *Thomas v Heelas* 27 November (1986) CAT No 1065; *Lewis v Averay* [1973] 1 WLR 510; compare *Ingram v Little* [1961] 1 QB 31) that where a sale is made *inter praesentes*, it will be treated as a voidable sale, thereby championing the security of transactions principle discussed in Chapter 10. Less problematic are cases of mistake relating to the quality of the goods. Of course, the relevant question here will often be the extent to which the *caveat emptor* doctrine has been abrogated through legislative intervention in contracts of supply (see Chapter 5). Even so, as Lord Atkin pointed out in *Bell v Lever Bros Ltd* [1932] AC 161 (at p 218), a contract may be set aside for mistake as to the quality of the goods if 'it is the mistake of both parties, and is as to the existence of some quality which makes the thing without the quality essentially different from the thing as it is believed to be'. (See also *Associated Japanese Bank (International) Ltd v Crédit du Nord SA* [1989] 1 WLR 255).

In most cases, a mistake as to quality will be treated as a breach of one of the implied obligations under the SGA 1979. A distinction should be drawn here with the case where the mistake relates to the terms of the sale itself. Thus in *Smith v Hughes* (1871) LR 6 QB 597, it was held that the seller of oats could not hold the buyer to the contract of sale if the seller was aware that the buyer was intending to accept an offer to sell oats warranted to be old, where, in fact, the seller was not intending to give any such warranty.

Formalities

It has already been noted that as far as contracts of supply are concerned, required formalities are the exception. Nevertheless, in the following situations certain formalities have to be satisfied:

(a) Auction sales;

(b) Regulated consumer credit agreements;

(c) Sales of interests in land because the s 61 (SGA 1979) definition of 'goods' as including *fructus naturales* (see Chapter 2) may have to satisfy the requirements of s 2 of the Law of Property (Miscellaneous Provisions) Act 1989. On the other hand, where severance of the subject matter is envisaged under the contract and property is to pass at this time, it is possible to argue that this is only a sale of goods (see *Kursell v Timber Operators and Contractors Ltd* [1927] 1 KB 298);

(d) The Bills of Sale Act 1878 will apply to genuine sale transactions so that a sale of goods evidenced in writing, by virtue of which the seller remains in possession, is void against execution creditors and trustees in bankruptcy unless it is registered in compliance with the Act (Bills of Sale Act 1878, s 8). (Compare non-absolute transfers, or sales by way of mortgages which are outside the scope of the SGA 1979 but must nevertheless comply with the Bills of Sale (1878) Amendment Act 1882);

(e) Sales of certain capital assets such as ships and aircraft which have their own registration formalities;

(f) Some dangerous goods are subject to special statutory regimes, for example, under the Firearms Acts 1968 and 1982 (as amended), the Crossbows Act 1987.

It is sufficient for our purposes to elaborate upon the first two categories.

Auction sales

Auction sales give rise to some particular problems which are specifically regulated in s 57 of SGA 1979. Under s 57(1), where goods are put up for sale by auction in lots, each lot is *prima facie* deemed to be the subject of a separate contract of sale. Section 57(2) goes on to state that a sale by auction is complete when the auctioneer announces its completion by the fall of the hammer, or in some other customary manner. Until this time, any bidder may retract his bid, and this was settled in the 18th Century case of *Payne v Cave* (1789) 3 TR 148. Moreover, it was held in *Harris v Nickerson* (1873) LR 8 QB 286, that an auctioneer will not be liable to a person who, on the strength of an advertisement, attends a place in the hope that an auction will take place. In these circumstances, advertisements will be construed as a declaration of intention to hold an auction and not a contract.

Where the auction is expressly advertised subject to a reserve price, s 57(6) expressly preserves the seller's right not to sell below the reserve price. If the auctioneer, by mistake, forgets that there is a reserve price and knocks down the goods at less than the reserve price, there is no sale. This is because the auctioneer has no express, implied or apparent authority as an agent to sell the goods below the reserve price (*McManus v Fortescue* [1907] 2 KB 1). It would seem that the bidder, in these circumstances, has no remedy against either the seller or the auctioneer because the sale was expressly subject to a reserve price and the auctioneer's authority was known to be so limited.

Where the seller instructs the auctioneer to place a reserve price which is not publicised, the auctioneer may still refuse to accept any bid below the reserve price since bids constitute only offers. However in this situation the auctioneer may not accept a bid on behalf of the seller; s 57(4) and (5) provide:

> (4) Where a sale by auction is not notified to be subject to a right to bid by or on behalf of the seller, it is not lawful for the seller to bid himself or to employ any person to bid at the sale, or for the auctioneer knowingly to take any bid from the seller or any such person.
> (5) A sale contravening sub-section (4) above may be treated as fraudulent by the buyer.

In this case, the contract may be set aside and the buyer will be able to sue for damages. Even where a reserve price is notified, the owner is not entitled to bid unless this is specifically reserved. If, in the absence of this, he does bid and the reserve price is reached then this may be treated as fraudulent by the buyer. Furthermore, where a sale is announced to be without reserve and the seller intervenes, as distinct from withdrawing the goods from the auction, he has no right to bid so that the highest *bona fide* bidder will be able to treat the transaction as fraudulent (*Green v Baverstock* (1863) 14 CBNS 204).

If the auctioneer is a party to the seller's conduct then he may also be sued. The auctioneer may be held liable in any case on the basis that he had contracted to sell the goods to the highest bidder (see *Warlow v Harrison* (1859) 1 E & E 309). Nonetheless, the auctioneer does not, in the absence of a contrary agreement, warrant the vendor's title. In *Benton v Campbell, Parker and Co Ltd* [1925] 2 KB 410, it was held that the auctioneer was not liable to the purchaser for the sale of a car when it transpired that the person who put the car into the auction was not the owner. The extent of the warranty of title implied at common law is that the possession given to the purchaser will be undisturbed by the vendor or auctioneer and that the latter knows no defect in the vendor's title (see Chapter 7).

An attempt to conduct a mock auction is proscribed under s 1(1) of the Mock Auctions Act 1961. Essentially, this is a consumer protection device making it a criminal offence to sell, by way of competitive bidding, prescribed articles listed in s 3(2):

> . . . any plate, plated articles, linen, china, glass, books, pictures, prints, furniture, jewellery, articles of household or personal use, or ornament or any musical or scientific instrument or apparatus.

The following techniques are outlawed under s 3: restricting the right to bid to more than one article; goods being knocked down for a price less than the highest bid; or where there are 'free' gifts.

There are also statutory provisions governing undesirable auction practices by buyers under the Auctions (Bidding Agreements) Acts 1927 and 1969. At common law it appears to be doubtful whether an agreement for a 'knockout', ie a contract between interested bidders to refrain from bidding against each other, was illegal. These Acts apply to prevent dealers from agreeing to abstain from bidding at a sale unless there was a genuine prior agreement to purchase on joint account, and a copy of this agreement lodged with the auctioneer. Section 3 of the 1969 Act provides that the seller may avoid the contract, recover the goods and, in default, any loss he has suffered, the parties to the ring being jointly and severally liable to him (s 3(2)). The major difficulty in practice is that of proving the existence of such 'rings'.

Formation of regulated consumer credit agreement

The consumer credit agreement must contain certain information which is set forth in a prescribed manner laid down by the Consumer Credit (Agreements) Regulations 1983 (SI 1983 No 1553). A failure to comply with this entails that the agreement is improperly executed and cannot be enforced without a court order (s 65 of CCA 1974). The following paragraphs focus upon the right to cancel for failure to comply with the requisite formalities, as this is likely to be most important in practice.

The consumer must be provided with copies of the consumer credit agreement but this requirement will vary. Where the consumer is accepting an offer by the creditor, the copy of the agreement must be given to him immediately (s 63(1)). On the other hand, if the consumer is making an offer, he is entitled, for record purposes, to a copy of the agreement there and then but also to a second copy, which must be sent to him when the creditor accepts his offer, within seven days of the conclusion of the contract (s 63(2)). Failure to comply with these rules means that the credit agreement will be improperly executed and will require a court order to be enforced under s 127 of CCA 1974.

A very important protection afforded by the CCA 1974 in the case of a regulated agreement, is the right to cancel. This can be exercised during the 'cooling-off' period where the debtor did not sign the agreement at the business premises of the creditor, a party to a linked transaction, or a negotiator in antecedent negotiations (s 67(b)). In addition, it can be exercised where, during antecedent negotiations, there were oral representations made irrespective of whether they were concluded on or off business premises (s 67).

The right of cancellation is subject to various exceptions which should be noted:

(a) Exempt agreements (see Chapter 2) and also some small agreements in the case of credit sales where the credit does not exceed £50 (s 74(2)(A)). This provision was inserted by reg 9 of the Doorstep Selling Directive (85/577) implemented by the Consumer Protection (Cancellation of Contracts Concluded away from Business Premises) Regulations 1987 (SI 1987 No 2117) (as amended). This lays down cancellation provisions (reg 4) similar to those applied under the CCA

1974 in relation to supplies by a trader of goods or services to a consumer which are made during an unsolicited visit to the consumer's home, or that of another consumer, or the consumer's place of work (reg 3) for a VAT inclusive payment of £35 or more (reg 3(2)(f));

(b) Certain agreements secured on land, house purchase money or bridging loans (s 67);

(c) Regulated agreements which are not caught by Pt V of CCA 1974 as laid out in s 74 of CCA 1974, for example non-commercial agreements, or small agreements (s 17(1)), or running-account credit such as bank overdrafts or other overdrafts exempted by the Director if this is not against the interests of the debtor. This is also the case with agreements to finance payments on death (ss 74(3) and 183);

(d) Unexecuted agreements signed by the debtor or hirer at 'business premises' which does not include the business premises of the debtor or hirer (s 67(*b*)).

The 'cooling-off' period in the case where the debtor makes an offer, allows the debtor the opportunity to cancel up to five days from receipt of the second copy of the agreement which must be sent to him (s 68(*a*)). Where the debtor accepts an offer made to him, a special notification of the right to cancel must be given to him and the debtor can cancel at any time up to five days from receipt of that notification (s 68(*a*)). A notice of cancellation sent by post is deemed to be served at the time of posting (s 69(7)). However, in cases where the Director General of Fair Trading has dispensed with that notice (usually in the case of mail order consumer credit agreements), the 'cooling-off' period runs until 'the end of the fourteenth day following the day on which he signed the unexecuted agreement' (s 68(*b*)). In circumstances other than where the Director General of Fair Trading has dispensed with a notice of cancellation in relation to certain mail order consumer credit (s 64(4) of CCA 1974 as implemented by the Consumer Credit (Notice of Cancellation Right) (Exemptions) Regulations 1983 (SI 1983 No 1558), time runs from receipt by the debtor or hirer of a second copy or notice. If this is never received, a fresh copy or notice must be served within seven days, and if this is not done, although the agreement remains binding and enforceable, it is perpetually cancellable under s 68. It should also be noted that the right of cancellation is in addition to any common law right of rescission or statutory right of termination.

Duties following cancellation

Where notice has been given, in the case of hire purchase or conditional sale transactions, s 72 generally places upon the debtor a legal duty to redeliver the goods subject to a lien for any part exchange goods tendered by him (s 73(5)). Under s 73(2) the primary entitlement of the debtor or hirer is to recover the 'part exchange allowance'. In the case of loan finance in a regulated debtor-creditor-supplier agreement, the creditor and the supplier are jointly and severally liable to him (s 70(3)). Within a period of ten days from the date of cancellation, the duty to pay the part exchange allowance will be discharged by the return of the part exchanged goods where they are in substantially the same condition as originally delivered to the negotiator (s 73(2)). If both sides agree, any deterioration or delay regarding the return of the part exchanged goods can be ignored (s 173(2)). As far as the debtor's obligations are concerned, he must retain possession of the goods and make them available for the creditor to collect, taking reasonable care of them in the meantime (s 72(4)). The duty to take reasonable care is confined to the period of 21 days after cancellation (s 72(8)); thereafter he usually becomes an involuntary bailee with a duty to refrain from wilful damage.

Where money has been paid over to the debtor before the end of the 'cooling-off' period, the CCA 1974 gives the debtor a choice: first, to take a month's free credit before repaying the credit already advanced (s 71(2)(a)); or secondly, with regard to money already spent, he can repay the money with interest, as provided for in the credit agreement, so that the effect of the cancellation only relates to the linked supply transaction (s 71(3)). Cancellation of a credit agreement also entails the cancellation of linked transactions (s 69(1)) as this has no effect until the principal agreement is made (s 19(3)). Here again the debtor must allow the goods to be collected and take reasonable care in the meantime, whilst sums paid out by him must be repaid. Cancellation of a directly financed transaction will leave the sale from dealer to financier still outstanding; this though is normally covered through a contractual repurchase provision.

Chapter 4

Express Undertaking as to Quality and Description

One important consequence of the mass production of goods has been the rise of extensive media advertising by manufacturers. Such a practice invites scrutiny of the different legal effects concerning express statements. These expressions may constitute either a promise by which the maker of the statement intends that he should be bound, or a representation which is not intended to operate as a promise but is made with the intention and does have the effect of persuading the other party to enter into the contract.

Advertising by manufacturers has become notorious for the extravagant but contractually ineffective commendation of goods. The statements made which have no legal effect are often described as being mere 'puffs' (*Carlill v Carbolic Smoke Ball* [1893] 1 QB 256). The law is concerned only with statements which take the form of remarks which are significant and are representations of present or future fact. Modern advertisements which are specific in detail, for example, advertisements for cars which specify exact performance information, may be sound in legal contractual liability. The scenario envisaged here is that a buyer of a car will have a contract not only with the supplier, but also a collateral contract with the manufacturer on the basis of the terms contained in a precise advertisement, the consideration for which being the entry into the main contract of supply (see *Shanklin Pier Ltd v Detel Products Ltd* [1951] 2 KB 854; *Andrews v Hopkinson* [1957] 1 QB 229). In the case of misleading advertisements, criminal liability is envisaged under legislation such as the Consumer Protection Act 1987 (see Chapter 6).

The basic distinction at common law is between statements which are intended to be terms of the contract of supply, ie promissory in nature, and statements which are representational in nature.

Specific undertakings

Representations

At common law, a mis-statement of fact which induced a contract is a misrepresentation. The common law refused to grant damages for innocent misrepresentation but would do so in the tort of deceit if the representation was fraudulent, although this is notoriously difficult to prove (*Derry v Peek* (1889)

14 App Cas 337). It was because of this that it became so important for a buyer to establish that the seller's representation amounted to a contractual term so that full damages would then be available. However, in *Hedley Byrne and Co Ltd v Heller and Partners* [1964] AC 465, the House of Lords recognised that there could be liability in tort for negligent misrepresentation dependent upon the establishment of a duty of care between the parties. Inherent in this requirement is the establishment of a 'special relationship' between the parties and in *Esso Petroleum Co Ltd v Mardon* [1976] QB 801, the Court of Appeal recognised that a duty of care is owed by a seller who has special expertise.

The Misrepresentation Act 1967 provides considerable protection for the buyer. Where the negligent misrepresentation induces a contract between the parties, it may be more advantageous to proceed under s 2(1) of the 1967 Act, not least because it reverses the onus of proof by placing it upon the seller (see *Howard Marine and Dredging Co Ltd v A Ogden and Sons (Excavations) Ltd* [1978] QB 574). In the case of an innocent misrepresentation, s 2(2) of the 1967 Act gives the court discretion to award damages in lieu of rescission. It provides:

> Where a person has entered into a contract after a misrepresentation has been made to him otherwise than fraudulently, and he would be entitled, by reason of the misrepresentation, to rescind the contract, then, if it is claimed, in any proceedings arising out of the contract, that the contract ought to be or has been rescinded, the court or arbitrator may declare the contract subsisting and award damages in lieu of rescission, if of the opinion that it would be equitable to do so, having regard to the nature of the misrepresentation and the loss that would be caused by it if the contract were upheld, as well as to the loss that rescission would cause to the other party.

The effect of this is that the representee must be entitled to rescind at the date of the court hearing (see *Alton House Garages (Bromley) Ltd v Monk* (1981), unreported). The provision reflects that the normal remedy for misrepresentation is rescission but the excessiveness of this remedy is mitigated by the subsection. Here we find similarities with the position in breach of contract where the courts have recognised the innominate term as a method of reducing the hardship of categorising terms of the contract, irrespective of the consequences of the breach, as conditions (see below).

The right to rescind will be lost where *restitutio in integrum* is impossible, for example where the goods have been consumed or services provided. In addition, rescission is forfeited where the buyer has accepted the goods which is illustrated in *Leaf v International Galleries* [1950] 2 KB 86. In this case, the plaintiff purchased a painting of Salisbury Cathedral from the defendants who innocently misrepresented that it had been painted by John Constable. Five years later, the plaintiff, having been informed that the painting was not a Constable, returned it to the defendants and asked for his money back. The Court of Appeal held that even if there had been a right of rescission it was barred by lapse of time. Essentially, this is a question of fact which will vary from case to case although *prima facie* with innocent misrepresentation, time will run from the date of execution of the contract; in the case of fraud however, it will run from the date of reasonable discovery. It appears from this case (see also *Long v Lloyd* [1958] 1 WLR 753) that the rules of acceptance are substantially the same as those applicable in cases of breach of condition (see Chapter 8). However, in two important respects the Misrepresentation Act 1967 has removed some bars to rescission so that s 1 provides that, whether or not the representation has become a term of the contract or that the contract has been fully performed, the right to the rescission remedy is not lost. In *Leaf v International Galleries*, Denning LJ (as he then was) expressed the view that the right to rescind for misrepresentation cannot survive beyond the point of time when a right to reject for breach of condition is lost. This reasoning no longer applies following s 1(*a*) of the 1967 Act, which permits rescission for a misrepresentation even where the misrepresentation has become a term of the contract. It would be anomalous if the right to rescind was lost at an earlier date when the misrepresentation does not become a term of the contract.

The principal weakness of the rescission remedy and the statutory alternative of damages in lieu of rescission, is that they do not provide for consequential loss, for example, profits on resale. Even though equity together with rescission gives an indemnity, this is limited in scope to cover only expenditure *necessarily* incurred as a result of entering into the contract (*Whittington v Seale-Hayne* (1900) 82 LT 49). In order to get full compensation the buyer will have to look to tort, as in the case of fraudulent misrepresentation, or sue for breach of contract. It would seem from this that the issue of whether the representation has become a term of the contract cannot be avoided, especially if the buyer seeks compensation for loss of profits since expectation damages are linked to breach of contract.

Express terms

Unless there is a written contract (which is rare in most consumer sales) there is the possibility that the parol evidence rule may prevent the successful incorporation of extrinsic evidence. Nevertheless, the rule is subject to so many exceptions that they have practically destroyed the rule. Thus, it does *not* apply where the evidence establishes the existence of a collateral contract; where it can be shown that the document was not intended as a complete record of the contract terms; where its existence or operation was dependent upon some prior unexpected stipulation; or where it was procured by some illegality or misrepresentation. It is not surprising, therefore, that the Law Commission has recommended no reform of the parol evidence rule, declaring that the 'rule' is not as extensive as traditionally expounded (see *Law of Contract—The Parol Evidence Rule*, Law Commission No 154 (1986)).

The question of whether a statement made during the course of negotiations remains a mere representation or becomes a contractual term, turns on the intention of the parties. Such a criterion is notoriously elusive, but in determining the precise legal status of a statement some reliance has been placed upon the *point* during the negotiations at which the statement was made. The further away from the making of the contract it was made the more likely it is to be considered as a misrepresentation. In *Routledge v McKay* [1954] 1 WLR 615, the seller of a motorbicycle incorrectly told the buyer that it was a 1942 model, but the contract was not concluded until one week later and the Court of Appeal held that this statement was not, thereby, a term. In the same way, if after an oral representation, the terms of the sale are reduced into writing which does not include the representation, this may indicate that it did not form part of the agreement. However, in this circumstance, the court will readily infer a collateral contract as illustrated by the case of *Couchman v Hill* [1947] KB 554. Here, a statement at an auction by the auctioneer that a heifer was 'unserved' was held to amount to a collateral warranty, for breach of which the auctioneer was liable even though the main contract excluded liability for fault, imperfections and errors of description.

In *Oscar Chess Ltd v Williams* [1957] 1 WLR 370, Denning LJ suggested that a binding promise might be inferred from the circumstances if the seller stated a fact which was or should be within his own knowledge, and of which the buyer was ignorant, intending that the buyer should act upon it, and with the result that the buyer did act upon it. In this case the seller, as a private individual, had no special expertise and the representation made as to the age of the car being traded-in to the dealers, was held by the Court of Appeal not to be contractual. Where the representation was made by a knowledgeable seller, such as a car dealer, a different result will ensue as in *Dick Bentley Productions Ltd v Harold Smith (Motors) Ltd* [1965] 1 WLR 623. Here the fact that the statement as to mileage done by the second-hand car was not included in the written contract of sale, did not prevent its being treated as a term of that contract.

One particular problem with incorporation of terms has emerged in the context of the so-called 'battle of forms'. Classical theory, as applied in *Butler Machine Tool Co Ltd v Ex-Cell-O Corpn (England) Ltd* [1979] 1 WLR 401, would suggest a mirror image rule, namely, each proffering of standard terms is a counter-offer, and it is the last document proffered which embodies the final offer when the recipient accepts by acting upon it. Of course, in theory, the mirror image rule makes printed forms matter since it encourages or even forces parties receiving documents to read them carefully. However, with standard form contracts directed at consumers, the legislature has interfered because of the imbalance in bargaining power, and this forms the basis of the Unfair Terms in Consumer Contracts Regulations 1994. At the same time the UCTA 1977 regulates the application of exemption clauses especially as against consumers (see Chapter 5).

Resolution of the question whether a statement is a representation or a contractual term, does not resolve the issue as to the legal effect of the statement made between the parties. Express contractual undertakings will have different consequences depending upon the significance given to the particular term ascribed by the law. There has been much confusion here mainly because the SGA 1979 uses the words 'condition' and 'warranty' as technical expressions, the breach of which gives the right to treat the contract as at an end in the case of a condition (s 11(3) of SGA 1979), or in the case of a subsidiary term like a warranty, the breach of which only sounds in damages (s 61(1) of SGA 1979).

Whether a term is a condition or a warranty depends upon the construction of the sale contract (s 11 of SGA 1979). Moreover, s 11(2) of SGA 1979 provides that conditions may be waived, or a breach of a condition may be treated by the buyer as a breach of warranty and not as a ground for treating the contract as repudiated. Section 11(3), on the other hand, emphasises that a stipulation may be a condition even though it is called a warranty in the contract. In Chapter 14 the circumstances under s 11(4) of SGA 1979, where the Act compels a buyer to treat a breach of condition as a breach of warranty, will be considered.

The binary approach to contractual obligations, as anticipated under the SGA 1979, has provoked considerable dissatisfaction. The reason for this is that it permits buyers to set aside a bad bargain following the seller's breach of condition where only slight consequences have ensued. However, a new approach to the question of remedies available for breach was occasioned by Diplock LJ in *Hong Kong Fir Shipping Co Ltd v Kawasaki Kisen Kaisha Ltd* [1962] 2 QB 26 (at p 70):

> There are . . . many contractual undertakings of a more complex character which cannot be categorised as being 'conditions' or 'warranties', if the late 19th Century meaning adopted in the Sale of Goods Act, 1893, and used by Bowen LJ in *Bentsen v Taylor, Sons & Co* be given to those terms. Of such undertakings all that can be predicated is that some breaches will and others will not, give rise to an event which will deprive the party not in default of substantially the whole benefit which it was intended that he should obtain from the contract; and the legal consequences of a breach of such an undertaking, unless provided for expressly in the contract, depend upon the nature of the event to which the breach gives rise and do not follow automatically from a prior classification of the undertaking as a 'condition' or a 'warranty'.

This approach allows for greater flexibility by concentrating on the nature of the consequences of the breach. Nevertheless the language used in the SGA 1979 does not easily admit of Diplock LJ's *tertium quid* where terms are defined as 'conditions' or 'warranties'.

In *Cehave NV v Bremer Handelgesellschaft* [1976] QB 44, Diplock LJ's analysis in the *Hong Kong Fir Shipping* case was extended to sale of goods and this was approved by the House of Lords in *Bunge Corpn v Tradax Export S A* [1981] 1 WLR 711. The *Cehave* case involved a sale of citrus pulp pellets where it was a term in the contract that the goods be shipped 'in good condition'. By the time the citrus pellets were delivered, the market price had fallen. The buyers argued that they were entitled to reject the goods primarily on the basis of breach of the express condition since they were slightly damaged, even though they could be satisfactorily used. The Court of Appeal indicated that the language of the SGA 1979, especially in view of the fact that s 62(2) preserves the rules of the common law, did not preclude the status and effect of a term being regarded, as Ormrod LJ put it, in the light of 'the events resulting from the breach, rather than the breach itself' (p 83). This approach was mirrored in the Law Commission Working Paper No 85 on the *Sale and Supply of Goods* (1983) where a recommendation was made to abolish the automatic classification of statutory implied terms as conditions, the buyer in a consumer sale being given the right to reject for any breach of the implied terms unless the consequences and nature of the breach were trivial so that rejection would be unreasonable. Significantly, the Law Commission Working Paper No 160 did not adopt this approach preferring, in the case of consumers, to maintain the present categorisation of implied terms as conditions (para 4.15). This has now been implemented in s 15A of the SGA 1979, but crucially where the buyer does *not* deal as a consumer, the right to reject for a breach of the statutory implied terms, seen in ss 13–15 of SGA 1979, is limited where 'the breach is so slight that it would be unreasonable for [the buyer] to reject [the goods]'.

It is important not to take a dogmatic stance with regard to the categorisation of terms as always concentrating on the nature of the breach. The need for certainty in commercial transactions is self-evident and the parties' categorisation of terms as conditions will obviously be relevant (see for example the discussion at pp 286–7 below of *Lombard North Central plc v Butterworth* [1987] QB 527). The House of Lords in *Bunge Corpn v Tradax* (1981) tabulated several factors which are relevant in the determination of the classification of a term as being a condition:
  (1) There are enormous practical advantages in certainty especially in string contracts where today's buyer may be tomorrow's seller. Businessmen must be able to do business with confidence in the legal results of their actions.
  (2) Difficulty of assessment of damages is an indication in favour of categorising a term as a condition.
  (3) To make 'total loss' the only test of a condition is contrary to authority, for example, terms as to the time of shipment, delivery and payment have been traditionally regarded as conditions, irrespective of the fact that failure to comply with them does not always have serious consequences. Besides, it is a cardinal principle of law that an innocent party may choose to accept repudiation and sue for damages for breach of contract, or he may choose to refuse to accept the repudiation so that the contract will remain in full effect. How could this right of election be anything other than a fiction if the breach of the term in all circumstances deprives the innocent party of substantially the whole benefit which it was intended that he should receive?

Exclusion and limitation of liability

A contract of supply may state expressly that the supplier is to be exempt from performance of some terms of the contract of supply, or that liability may be restricted in some way or other. The validity and application of such exclusion and limitation clauses have raised many difficult problems, as well as prompting statutory intervention principally through UCTA 1977. This legislation prohibits or restricts the exclusion of terms that would otherwise be implied in contracts of supply. The approach of English legislative intervention has been to police certain categories of exclusion clauses. Significantly, the Unfair Terms in Consumer Contacts Regulations 1994 represent a conceptual shift, in that the way is now open to develop a substantive doctrine of fair terms in consumer contracts (see Chapter 5).

Where an exclusion or limitation clause is permitted, the question then arises as to its effect as a matter of law. For our purposes, it is sufficient to note that the doctrine of fundamental breach, as a rule of law, has finally been laid to rest by *Photo Production Ltd v Securicor Transport Ltd* [1980] AC 827, and it would now appear that fundamental breach is relevant only as a factor to be considered in the construction of the contract, which may therefore be relevant in terms of the fairness criterion under the Unfair Terms in Consumer Contracts Regulations 1994. In no small measure, the issue of incorporation of terms is pertinent which includes the question of notice, such as a previous course of dealings (compare *Olley v Marlborough Court* [1949] 1 KB 532), or trade usage (s 55(1) of SGA 1979), or where reasonable steps have been taken to bring the exclusion clause to the attention of the contracting party (*Interfoto Picture Library Ltd v Stiletto Visual Programmes Ltd* [1989] Q B 433). Where the exclusion clause is embodied in a signed contract, the general rule is that the signatory is bound by the contents of the document regardless of whether he has read or understood them (*L'Estrange v Graucob Ltd* [1934] 2 KB 394) in the absence of a plea of *non est factum* (*Saunders v Anglia Building Society* [1971] AC 1004).

The effect of exclusion clauses is principally a matter of construction of the contract. The strict approach, whereby in construing the effect of a purported exclusion clause everything was construed against the party in whose favour a term was included in the contract, the *contra preferentem* rule is still relevant in determining the issue of fair terms in consumer contracts. At the same time the UCTA 1977 provides the courts with a statutory weapon for controlling exclusion clauses in general (see p 71). In *George Mitchell (Chesterhall) Ltd v Finney Lock Seeds Ltd* [1983] 2 AC 803, the House of Lords endorsed a balanced approach to the construction of exclusion clauses. The facts are well known and involved the defendant seed merchants who agreed in December 1973 to supply the plaintiff farmers with 30 pounds of Dutch winter cabbage seed for £192. An invoice which accompanied the seed when it was delivered, and which was treated as forming part of the contract, contained a limitation clause restricting liability to the price of the seed. It went on to exclude 'all liability for any loss or damage arising from the use of any seeds or plants supplied by us and for any consequential loss or damage arising out of such use . . .'. The plaintiffs planted 63 acres with the seed which turned out to be the wrong kind and unmerchantable, the crop being a total failure. In the Court of Appeal the majority held that, as a matter of construction, the clause did not apply. It was not clear enough to protect the sellers from the consequences of their own negligence and it did not apply when the sellers had delivered something wholly different in kind from that which had been ordered. Significantly, in the House of Lords the limitation clause was as a matter of construction upheld to apply to the circumstances of the case although, in the event, their Lordships affirmed the unanimous judgment of the Court of Appeal in holding that the clause was rendered unenforceable by statute because it would not be 'fair or reasonable to allow reliance' on it.

The approach taken by the House of Lords in *George Mitchell* draws a distinction as a matter of construction for the purposes of the UCTA, between exclusion and limitation clauses evident in their earlier decision in *Ailsa Craig Fishing Co Ltd v Malvern Shipping Co Ltd* [1983] 1 WLR 964. In the case of limitation clauses, the construction given is according to ordinary and plain meaning whilst exclusion clauses, especially those of fundamental breach, are construed more strictly against the party relying on them. However the distinction can be a narrow one especially since some limitation clauses are effectively exclusion clauses where, for example, the limitation of liability is to a trivial sum. Moreover, the approach taken by their Lordships in *George Mitchell* does seem at variance with the *Photo Production* case where it was held that artificial distinctions should be rejected in favour of construction according to plain and natural meaning.

The doctrine of waiver

An indulgence constituting a common feature of commercial life is that of waiver which is essentially acceptance of a substituted performance. This is embodied in s 11(2) of SGA 1979 which reads:

> Where a contract of sale is subject to a condition to be fulfilled by the seller, the buyer may waive the condition, or may elect to treat the breach of the condition as a breach of warranty and not as a ground for treating the contract as repudiated.

The efficacy of waiver is open to the technical objection that it is unsupported by consideration and, as such, it draws heavily on equitable doctrine. It is clear that a waiver is of no effect unless it is unequivocal and only where the representee acts on it to his detriment. The relationship between waiver and equitable estoppel is obvious, as Denning LJ pointed out in *Charles Rickards Ltd v Oppenheim* [1950] 1 KB 616 (at p 623):

> If the defendant, as he did, led the plaintiffs to believe that he would not insist on the stipulation as to time, and that, if they carried out the work, he would accept it, and they did it, he could not afterwards set up the stipulation as to the time against them. Whether it be called waiver or forbearance on his part, or an agreed variation or substituted performance, does not matter. It is a kind of estoppel. By his conduct he evinced an intention to affect their legal relations. He made, in effect, a promise not to insist on his strict legal rights. That promise was intended to be acted on, and was in fact acted on. He cannot afterwards go back on it.

Both waiver and equitable estoppel share some common elements. The principal similarity is that both appear to require that the party seeking to rely on it must show a clear and unequivocal representation, by words or conduct, by the other party that he will not exercise his strict legal right to treat the contract as repudiated.

In *Motor Oil Hellas Refineries v Shipping Corporation of India, 'The Kanchenjunga'* [1990] 1 Lloyd's Rep 391, Golf LJ clearly distinguished between estoppel and waiver. In the case of the latter the party who has to make the choice must either know or have obvious means of knowledge of the facts giving rise to the right, and possibly the existence of the right. However, in the case of estoppel neither knowledge of the circumstances nor of the right is required on the part of the person estopped. Furthermore, waiver has a permanent effect, while estoppel may be suspensory only and may be revoked following reasonable notice. Finally, estoppel requires that the party to whom the representation is made must rely on that representation so as to make it inequitable for the representor to renege upon his representation. There is no such requirement in the case of waiver.

The case of *Charles Rickards* is a convenient illustration of the effects of the doctrine of waiver. In this case, the defendant ordered a Rolls Royce chassis from the plaintiffs who agreed to build a body on it by 20 March. After the plaintiffs had failed to complete the work by that date, the defendant continued to press for delivery but, on 29 June, gave notice that, if the work was not completed within a further four weeks, he would cancel the order. The Court of Appeal unanimously held that the time of delivery was of the essence of this contract, but that this stipulation was waived by the defendant's requests for delivery after the due date, which would have estopped him had there been delivery within the extended time. However, the notice given on 29 June granted a final indulgence of four weeks and constituted reasonable notice (see *Tool Metal Manufacturing Co Ltd v Tungsten Electric Co Ltd* [1955] 1 WLR 761) that time was once more of the essence of the contract, and that failure to deliver would amount to a breach of condition entitling the defendant to rescind the contract. From this it would appear that a party can be considered to have waived his rights without full knowledge of the facts. Nevertheless, the Court of Appeal in *Proctor and Gamble Philippine Manufacturing Corpn v Peter Cremer GmbH and Co (The Manila)* [1988] 3 All ER 843, pointed out that promissory estoppel may be relevant here if there is a representation which carries a strong implication that the representor did have full knowledge of the facts.

The issue of waiver is particularly important where a buyer rejects the goods for a wrong reason. The argument here is that the buyer can rely on the seller's breach as a waiver of performance so as to justify refusal to accept delivery. It is a long-established rule of law that where a contracting party refuses to perform his contractual obligations by giving a wrong reason, this does not subsequently deprive him of a justification which in fact existed at the time of refusal (see *Taylor v Oakes* (1922) 27 Com Cas 261; *Braithwaite v Foreign Hardwood Co Ltd* [1905] 2 KB 543; and *Fercometal SARL v Mediterranean Shipping Co SA* [1989] AC 788 discussed in Chapter 14). Lastly, it should be noted that a party who reserves legal rights following breach can still, as a matter of law, be regarded to have waived the breach. The reason for this is that following the breach of condition which leads to termination, the innocent party has alternative remedies: he can either affirm or terminate the contract. By reserving his rights he does not achieve a legal impasse, and indeed, if this is the goal, he should be advised to terminate the contract and re-negotiate it in the light of the new circumstances.

Chapter 5

Implied Undertakings as to Quality and Description

Historically the doctrine of *caveat emptor*, or let the buyer beware, had little place in English law. This is not surprising in a society where there was Christian influence and the concept of sin was so acute. Thus in *Summa Theologica*, Saint Thomas says that if a defect is known to the vendor, it is a sin not to disclose it and the sale is void. Even if the defect was unknown to the seller he had to recompense the buyer. Standards were kept in fairs and markets so that in the *Assize of Bread and Beer* (1256) a mechanism of complaint was instituted against poor loaves or insufficient gallons of beer. Moreover, there were customs in markets which aimed to protect standards and the emphasis was upon maintaining honesty and standards in trade.

The doctrine of *caveat emptor*, with the adoption of the Latin tag, does have an authentic ring to it although it is alien to the spirit of the civil law. Indeed, Ulpian puts the case of a seller of a female slave who knowingly allows the buyer to believe that she is a virgin when she is not (D.19.1.11.5), a defect which is treated as being strictly liable so that the buyer can return the slave. It is uncertain, therefore, how *caveat emptor* was adopted in English law. Certainly it could not find a place within the great authoritarian scheme by which Christian society was ordered. The emergence of *caveat emptor* is probably explained in terms of it being a shorthand expression to cover the case where no writ or redress was available and this was transmogrified into a legal principle in the 18th and 19th centuries. After all, this was the age of the triumph of the mercantile viewpoint which was quite at variance with any concept of asceticism. The common sense of individualism voiced by Adam Smith won for it judicial acceptance, the high point being *Smith v Hughes* (1871) LR 6 QB 597 where Cockburn J said (at 603):

> The question is whether, under such circumstances, the passive acquiescence of the seller in the self-deception of the buyer will entitle the latter to avoid the contract. I am of the opinion that it will not . . . I take the true rule to be that where a specific article is offered for sale, without express warranty, or without circumstances from which the law will imply a warranty . . . and the buyer has full opportunity of inspecting and forming his own judgment, the rule *caveat emptor* applies.

The SGA 1893 marked the legislative beginning of the movement away from *caveat emptor* where a number of implied terms were laid down. Today s 12 of SGA 1979 provides the implied undertaking as to title (see Chapter 7).

41

Sections 13, 14 and 15 of SGA 1979 include four major implied conditions which relate to conformity with description, and in a supply transaction in the course of a business that the goods are of satisfactory quality, are fit for their purpose and conform to any sample provided. These implied terms have been substantially reproduced in the SGSA 1982. The movement towards *caveat venditor*, at least in consumer sales, was confirmed by the Sale and Supply of Goods Act 1994, which implements the recommendations of the Law Commission Report No 160 on *Sale and Supply of Goods* (1987). A distinction is drawn between consumer sales, where the four major implied conditions remain, whilst in non-consumer sales a *de minimis* principle is introduced under s 15A(1) where breach is treated as sounding only in damages.

Supplies by description

Section 13(1) of SGA 1979 lays down that:

> Where there is a contract for the sale of goods by description, there is an implied condition that the goods shall correspond with the description.

This undertaking can also be found in the case of a contract of supply (s 3(1) of SGSA 1982) and in the case of a bailment (s 8(1),(2) of SGSA 1982) as well as in a hire purchase arrangement (s 9(1) of SOGIT 1973 as substituted by the CCA 1974).

In a sense the inclusion of an implied term of correspondence with description is a little surprising. It was accepted quite early on that a seller would be bound by any description by which he had sold specific goods (*Shepherd v Kain* (1822) 5 B&A 240). Elementary description had a natural place particularly where 'errors of description' had been excepted and the courts tended to discover some measure of description by which the goods had been sold (see for example *Taylor v Bullen* (1850) 5 Ex 779). However, it is wrong to assume that s 13 of SGA 1979 somehow converts all statements made as to description into contractual terms, and the Court of Appeal decision in *Harlingdon Ltd v Hull Fine Art Ltd* [1991] 1 QB 564 confirms that the normal contractual principles as to incorporation of terms still subsist (for example *Dick Bentley Productions Ltd v Harold Smith (Motors) Ltd* [1965] 1 WLR 623). The significance of s 13 is that matters of description are treated as conditions and not as innominate terms, subject in non-consumer supply to s 15A(1) of the SGA (as amended).

The meaning of description

If goods sold by description are defined in terms of being identified or earmarked, then in the case of a contract for the sale of specific goods, noncorrespondence with description ought logically to be impossible, since s 61(1) of SGA 1979 defines 'specific goods' as including those identified and agreed upon at the time of the contract of sale. In *Varley v Whipp* [1900] 1 QB 513, the facts concerned the sale of a secondhand reaping machine which the buyer had not seen and the court interpreted the concept of sales by description to cover all sales of specific goods where the buyer was relying on the description. However, over time it came to be recognised that a sale can be by description even though the buyer has seen the goods. As Lord Wright said in *Grant v Australian Knitting Mills Ltd* [1936] AC 85 (at p 100):

> It may also be pointed out that there is a sale by description even though the buyer is buying something displayed before him on the counter: a thing is sold by description, though it is specific, so long as it is sold not merely as the specific thing but as a thing corresponding to a description, eg woollen undergarments, a hot-water bottle, a second-hand reaping machine, to select a few obvious illustrations.

This is now given statutory effect by s 13(3) of SGA 1979 which provides:

> A sale of goods is not prevented from being a sale by description by reason only that, the goods being exposed for sale or hire, they are selected by the buyer.

It is important to differentiate between which goods are being sold and what they are. With regard to the former, the approach typically involves an existing subject matter by reference to its position in time and space. Essentially, it is a process under which goods are ascertained by being identified. Nonetheless, care should be taken here to distinguish words which can be considered to be merely useful information, from words which go to the identity of the goods sold. In *Reardon Smith Line Ltd v Hansen Tangen* [1976] 1 WLR 989, shipbuilders contracted to build a vessel to a certain specification at Yard No 354 at Osaka Zosen, but the ship was in fact built at a different yard; the House of Lords did not consider these words of location as being part of the identity of the vessel. Indeed, Lord Wilberforce pointed out that only words whose purpose is to identify an essential part of the description, attract the implied condition of s 13.

There is no doubt that statements relating to the nature of the goods supplied, for example, that a car is a vintage Bentley Speed Six 'Old No 1' is a matter of identity which goes to the heart of description. A striking case in this context is *Beale v Taylor* [1967] 1 WLR 1193, where the seller advertised a car as 'Herald, convertible, white, 1961'. The buyer subsequently discovered that the rear half of the car was a 1961 Herald but the front half was part of an earlier model, the two halves having been welded together. In delivering the judgment of the Court of Appeal, Sellers LJ said that, even if there were no other terms as to the state of the goods, fundamentally the seller was selling a 1961 Herald.

Most of the problems with s 13 relate not to the question of which goods are being sold but rather to what they are. Where goods have deteriorated there must come a point in time where they have become so different in quality from what might have been anticipated, that they are no longer goods answering to the contract description at all. In this context, we are concerned with distinguishing identity from attributes which is notoriously difficult. The leading case here is *Ashington Piggeries Ltd v Christopher Hill Ltd* [1972] AC 441 where the facts concerned a consignment of mink food made up, amongst other things, of herring meal. The manufacturer of the food obtained the herring meal from a Norwegian company. Unknown to anyone the herring meal contained DMNA, a substance which was poisonous to mink. As a result of the damage caused to the owner of minks to which the food had been given, the latter counterclaimed when the supplier of the food sued for the price of the food that had been sold and delivered. As between the parties themselves the questions related to quality and fitness for purpose. However, the food supplier brought in as third party the Norwegian company which had provided the herring meal. One issue between these parties was whether the herring meal supplied corresponded with the description.

In discussing the meaning of s 13, the House of Lords focused upon the question of identification so that, as Lord Hodson said (at pp 466–7): 'The language used [in s 13 of SGA 1979] is directed to the identification of goods . . . The essential point is that identification of the goods is that with which the section is concerned.' Lord Wilberforce pointed out that the problem was not to be dealt with as though it were a philosophical question which distinguishes identity from attributes:

> I do not believe that the Sale of Goods Act was designed to provoke metaphysical discussions as to the nature of what is delivered in comparison with what is sold. The test of description, at least where commodities are concerned, is intended to be a broader, more commonsense, test of a mercantile character. The question whether that is what the buyer bargained for has to be answered according to such tests as men in the market would apply, leaving more delicate questions of condition, or quality, to be determined under other clauses of the contract or sections of the Act (p 489).

Thus in the *Ashington Piggeries* case it was held that herring meal containing the poison DMNA had not lost its identity as herring meal 'fair average quality' of the season, since this was a statement of quality and not description.

If goods are sold by description, that is by prescribing the characteristics they are to possess, then, as Salmond J pointed out in *Taylor v Combined Buyers Ltd* [1924] NZLR 627, every element of the description, whether it relates to number, quality, kind, state, should in theory form part of the description. The reasoning here is that such goods are only capable of being identified through defining their characteristics. This phenomenon is particularly prevalent in the case of unascertained future goods where a strict approach is often evidenced. As Lord Blackburn said in *Bowes v Shand* (1877) 2 App Cas 455 (at p 460): 'If the description of the article tendered is different in any respect it is not the article bargained for and the other party is not bound to take it.' The leading case is *Arcos Ltd v EA Ronaasen and Son* [1933] AC 470 where the buyers agreed to buy a quantity of staves of half an inch thickness for making cement barrels. Only five per cent of the staves were of the correct thickness but the rest were nearly all less than nine-sixteenths of an inch thick. It was found as a fact by the arbitrator that the goods 'were commercially within and merchantable under the contract specification'. Despite this, the House of Lords rejected any concept of commercial equivalence so that Lord Atkin held:

> It was contended that in all commercial contracts the question was whether there was 'substantial' compliance with the contract: there must always be some margin and it is for the tribunal of fact to determine whether the margin is exceeded or not. I cannot agree. If the written contract specifies conditions of weight, measurement and the like, those conditions must be complied with. A ton does not mean about a

ton, or a yard about a yard. Still less when you descend to minute measurements does half an inch mean about half an inch. If the seller wants a margin he must, and in my experience does, stipulate for it . . .

No doubt there may be microscopic deviations which businessmen and therefore lawyers will ignore . . . But, apart from this consideration, the right view is that the conditions of the contract must be strictly performed (pp 479–80).

An even clearer illustration of the above can be seen in *Re Moore and Co and Landauer and Co* [1921] 2 KB 519. In this case, tins of fruit conformed with the description in every respect except that some of them were packed in cases of 30 tins instead of 24. The packing made no difference to the market value, but the Court of Appeal held that the tins failed to comply with the description and could be rejected. In the light of the excessive technicality seen here, it is little wonder that Lord Wilberforce in *Reardon Smith Line Ltd*, and the House of Lords in *Ashington Piggeries* proposed giving a narrower scope to s 13, confining it to matters of identification. As Lord Diplock said in *Ashington Piggeries*:

The 'description' by which unascertained goods are sold is, in my view, confined to those words in the contract which were intended by the parties to identify the kind of goods which were to be supplied. It is open to the parties to use a description as broad or as narrow as they choose. But ultimately the test is whether the buyer could fairly and reasonably refuse to accept the physical goods proffered to him on the ground that their failure to correspond with what was said about them makes them goods of a different kind from those he had agreed to buy. The key to s 13 is identification (pp 503–4).

The problem with this approach is that it begs the question concerning the nature of identification in unascertained future goods.

Although Lord Wilberforce in *Reardon Smith Lines* called for a review of cases based upon excessive technicality, his Lordship's views are *obiter*, but it would appear that s 15A(1) of the SGA (as amended) has dealt with the mischief alluded to, that is, a non-consumer buyer can no longer avoid an improvident bargain by merely relying upon a technical breach of s 13. However, it is otherwise where the commercial context as defined by the contract requires strict compliance. Indeed in *Moralice (London) Ltd v ED and F Man* [1954] 2 Lloyd's Rep 526, it was held that where the price is payable by means of a bankers' commercial credit against the shipping documents, the *de minimis* maxim has no application as between the seller and the bank.

Goods sold by description and reliance

If the description has a special trade usage, the goods may have to comply with the specialised meaning if this is part of the contractual intention. This is illustrated by *Grenfell v EB Meyrowitz Ltd* [1936] 2 All ER 1313, where the defendants were held not to be in breach of s 13 when they supplied goggles of 'safety glass' which subsequently had acquired a technical meaning and the goggles conformed to this design (see *R v Ford Motor Co* [1974] 1 WLR 1220 as to the meaning in the motor trade of a 'new' car). It is worth noting that under the

Trade Descriptions Act 1968 and the Consumer Protection Act 1987, it is an offence to apply a false or misleading description. It is therefore unlikely that the *Grenfell* decision would be the same today in the light of this consumer protection legislation (see Chapter 6).

The buyer must contract to buy the goods by description. If there is no reliance then, notwithstanding the fact that the goods were offered for sale by description, the buyer has bought the goods on other terms. Even so, proof of reliance is not difficult especially in view of s 13(3) of SGA 1979, which provides that ordinary articles of commerce as specific goods are expressly included in the definition of sale by description. In *Harlingdon and Leinster Enterprises Ltd v Christopher Hull Fine Art Ltd* [1991] 1 QB 564, the Court of Appeal considered the issue of reliance on description and it is worth dwelling upon the facts. The defendants were art dealers who carried on business from a London gallery owned and controlled by the principal of the defendants, Mr Christopher Hull. In 1984, Mr Hull was asked to sell two oil paintings which had been described in a 1980 auction catalogue as being by Gabriele Munter, an artist of the German expressionist school. Mr Hull specialised in young contemporary British artists and had no training, experience or knowledge which would have enabled him to conclude from an examination of the pictures whether they were by Munter. He took the paintings to Christie's who expressed interest in them and, at the same time, he contacted the plaintiffs who carried on business as art dealers at a London gallery specialising in the German expressionist school. He told the plaintiffs that he had two paintings by Munter for sale and accordingly an employee of the plaintiffs visited the defendants' gallery to view the paintings. Mr Hull made it clear that he did not know very much about the paintings and that he was not an expert in them. The plaintiffs' employee agreed to buy one of the paintings for £6,000 without asking any questions about the provenance of the paintings, or making any further inquiries about them. The invoice for the painting described it as being by Munter, but it was later discovered to be a forgery. The plaintiffs claimed repayment of the purchase price on the basis that the contract was for the sale of goods by description within s 13(1) of SGA 1979 and could, therefore, be avoided on the grounds of misdescription.

The judgment for the majority in the Court of Appeal (Stuart Smith LJ dissenting) was given by Nourse LJ who held that there had not been a sale 'by' description. In this respect considerable reliance was placed upon Lord Diplock's *dictum* in *Gill and Duffus SA v Berger and Co Inc* [1984] AC 382:

> . . . while 'description' itself is an ordinary English word, the Act contains no definition of what it means when it speaks in that section of a contract for the sale of goods being a sale '*by* description'. One must look to the contract as a whole to identify the kind of goods that the seller was agreeing to sell and the buyer to buy . . . where, as in the instant case, the sale (to use the words of s 13) is '*by* sample as well as *by* description', characteristics of the goods which would be apparent on reasonable examination of the sample are unlikely to have been intended by the parties to form part of the 'description' *by* which the goods were sold, even though such characteristics are mentioned in references in the contract to the goods that are its subject matter. (Lord Diplock's emphasis at p 394)

The conclusion arrived at was that the requirement 'by description' had to be determined by reference to the contract as a whole, that is, whether the characteristics had become terms in the contract. Moreover, where there was no reliance upon the description it was unlikely that this could be considered to be an esential term in the contract. Since Mr Hull had made it plain that he was not qualified to give an opinion about the painting's authorship, the plaintiff's employee must have realised that in proceeding with the purchase he was relying on his own skill and judgement.

The issue of reliance has been considered more recently by the Court of Appeal in *Don Commercials Ltd v Lancaster Trucks Ltd* (1994) unreported. This case concerned a sale to the plaintiffs of a secondhand consignment of tractor units taken by the defendants in part exchange as part of a deal with a third-party purchaser. The tractor units were inspected by the plaintiff's managing director and a dispute subsequently arose in relation to one unit which was described in the invoice as 'Make – DAF Model FTG 2800. Reg. No. B30 ANO'. At first instance it was found that:

> B30 was a pig in a poke. It was a FTG 2800 in appearance but its engine, although of the same size and internal bore and stroke, was from a much older four-wheel vehicle and was not one usually inter-cooled. Its torque characteristics were different. It developed less brake horsepower. The B30 was not a FTG 2800 as such. It could do the work that a FTG 2800 could do, but its performance was different. There is no suggestion that the defendant knew this. The defendant was in the habit of buying from a customer which it valued called Canute, the condition of whose vehicles was less than the best.

In the Court of Appeal, Balcombe LJ cited with approval Slade LJ's *dictum* in *Harlingdon* (*above*) where he said:

> While some judicial dicta seem to support the view that there can be no sale by description unless there is actual reliance on the description by the purchaser, I am not sure that this is strictly correct in principle. If a party to a contract wishes to claim relief in respect of a misrepresentation as to a matter which did not constitute a term of the contract, his claim will fail unless he is able to show that he relied on this representation in entering into the contract; in general, however, if a party wishes to claim relief in respect of a breach of a term of a contract (whether it be a condition or warranty) he need prove no actual reliance. Nevertheless, where a question arises as to whether a sale of goods was one by description, the presence or absence of reliance on the description may be very relevant in so far as it throws light on the intention of the parties at the time of the contract. If there was no such reliance by the purchaser, this may be powerful evidence that the parties did not contemplate that the authenticity of the description should constitute a term of the contract—in other words, that they contemplated that the purchaser would be buying the goods as they were. If, on the other hand, there was such reliance (as in *Varley v Whipp* [1990] 1 QB 513, where the purchaser had never seen the goods) this may be equally powerful evidence that it was contemplated by both parties that the correctness of the description would be a term of the contract (so as to bring it within section 13(1)) (p 584).

The test applied by Balcombe LJ was that of reliance based upon an objective assessment of what the parties said and did in the circumstances of the case. In this regard the material factors were as follows: (a) both parties were motor dealers; (b) the tractors had been inspected by the plaintiff's managing director before making an offer and indeed the offer made was less than the provisional figure initially negotiated in the light of the defects found at the inspection; (c) the terms of the invoice included the specific phrase 'sold as seen no warranty given or implied'.

In the light of the above factors, it was held that from an objective standpoint the parties could not have intended that the authenticity of the description (ie that this was a FTG 2800) should be a term in the contract. Significantly, both Balcombe and Mann LJJ approved in the Court of Appeal Donaldson LJ's dictum in *Hughes v Hall* [1981] RTR 430 where in relation to the application of the Fair Trading Act 1973 he said:

> I think that, if a clause was included in the contract saying 'sold as seen and inspected', *prima facie* and subject always to what else might be expressly said in the contract, that would negative a sale by description. It would be a sale of a specific object as seen and inspected. (p 437)

It would appear that in this circumstance the description cannot be treated as material in influencing the decision to buy.

Exclusion of description requirement

In the *Harlingdon Ltd* case it was argued, at first instance, that there was an actual usage or custom in the London art market which excluded the application of s 13. Although s 6(2)(*a*) of UCTA 1977 (as amended by Sched 2, para 19 of SGA 1979) provides that 'as against a person dealing as consumer' obligations arising from undertakings as to compliance with description cannot be excluded or restricted, the definition of 'dealing as a consumer' in s 12 of UCTA 1977 excludes a person who makes the contract 'in the course of a business'. In this case the clause is subject to the test of reasonableness which is discussed in greater detail below (see pp 71–90). There is no reason to suppose that in *Harlingdon Ltd* such an exclusion clause would not have been maintained, especially since it would hardly be likely to deter art experts from using their skills in the market place to discover masterpieces. Moreover, it is the present position that art expert buyers, in the absence of fraud or a fiduciary relationship, have no obligation to disclose information relating to the true identity of a painting.

Any clause excluding or limiting contractual description will have to be construed in the light of the common law. Obviously, if the contract goods are unascertained, an attempt to exclude all undertakings as to description would destroy the certainty of subject matter in the contract. It is otherwise where the attempt is made to exclude liability for trivial breaches as in *Arcos Ltd v EA Ronaasen and Son* (1933).

In *Harlingdon* and *Don Commercials*, the decision of the Court of Appeal that s 13(1) of SGA 1979 cannot apply because of the absence of a sale 'by description', avoided the need for the parties to exclude the term under s 6 of UCTA 1977 and thus expose themselves to the 'reasonableness' text. It would appear, therefore, that s6 of UCTA 1977 can be undermined simply by framing the matter of description into the general law of express contractual terms. Furthermore, it is unlikely that the EC Directive on Unfair Terms in Consumer Contracts (implemented by the Unfair Terms in Consumer Contracts Regulations 1994 (SI 1994 No 3159) will be relevant here, because whilst its scope is not limited to exclusion clauses it only regulates terms in consumer contracts (see below pp 83–90).

Undertakings as to quality

The SGA 1979 and the SGSA 1982 imply conditions as to fitness and quality. No other warranties or conditions to such effect may be implied except insofar as they may be annexed to the contract by custom or trade usage (s 14(4) of SGA 1979, ss 4(7), 9(7) of SGSA 1982). The usage must fulfil all the normal tests of a custom and it will become part of the contract so long as it is reconcilable with the terms of the contract (*Peter Darlington Partners Ltd v Gosho Co Ltd* [1964] 1 Lloyd's Rep 149). As such, this subsection is an illustration of the general rule that the intention of the parties with respect to a contract must be gleaned in the light of the surrounding circumstances. However, the normal rule applicable is that of *caveat emptor* which is reflected in s 14(1) of SGA 1979:

> Except as provided by this section and s 15 below and subject to any other enactment, there is no implied condition or warranty about the quality or fitness for any particular purpose of goods supplied under a contract of sale.

This approach is also mirrored in ss 4(1) and 9(1) of SGSA 1982.

The *caveat emptor* doctrine has been mitigated by the implied terms as to quality. The rationale here is colourfully illustrated by Lord Ellenborough's *dictum* in *Gardiner v Gray* (1815) 4 Camp 144 to the effect that a person does not buy goods simply for the pleasure of depositing them on a dunghill. Before considering the implied terms of quality and fitness for purpose, some common themes applicable to both must first be discussed.

The supply must be in the course of business

This requirement is a feature of consumer protection legislation and applies to both sale (s 14) and supply transactions (ss 4, 9 of SGSA 1982). There is also an implied term that the supplier of a service who acts in the course of a business will supply the service with reasonable care and skill (s 13 of SGSA 1982). The phrase also appears in the Trade Descriptions Act 1968 and the Consumer Protection Act 1987. Moreover, under UCTA 1977, a distinction is drawn between the effect of exemption clauses where a person acquiring the goods deals as consumer and those cases where he does not. In this respect, a person acquiring goods deals as consumer only if the supplier makes the contract to supply the goods in the course of a business (s 12 of UCTA). This requirement reflects the policy of risk spreading so that the Law Commission *First Report on Exemption Clauses in Contracts* No 24, para 82 (1969) justifies distinguishing between private and business purchasers on the basis of the:

> ability of the business purchaser to take into account the likelihood of defects, to reduce their incidence by arrangements for re-examination and servicing (which may be allowed for in the price paid) and to make suitable dispositions, by insurance and in his costings, to cover the risks which he has to bear.

The EC Directive on Unfair Terms in Consumer Contracts (93/13/EEC) confines consumers to natural persons. It is possible under the Directive that a small business trading as a natural person or partnership can count as a consumer if the goods purchased, though normally only used in business, are not the kind of goods usually purchased by that particular business. The UCTA 1977 cuts down the definition of consumer by excluding contracts involving the sale of goods not ordinarily supplied for private use or consumption and sales by auction (s 12(1)(c),(2) UCTA).

Little guidance is given in legislation as where precisely to draw the line between business and private sales. The definition of 'business' under the SGA 1979 (s 61(1)) and the SGSA 1982 (s 18) provide that it includes 'a profession and the activities of any government department . . . or local or public authority'. It would appear therefore that the element of profit is not a prerequisite for the finding of a business activity under this legislation. However, there must be some element of regularity of business activity and the leading authority here is the House of Lords' decision in *Davies v Sumner* [1984] 1 WLR 1301. This case was decided under the Trade Descriptions Act 1968, the defendant being acquitted of applying a false trade description because the sale was not in the course of a trade or business due to the absence of regularity.

It could be argued that the requirement of regularity is unduly restrictive and reflects the rationale of the Trade Descriptions Act 1968, namely, the additional duties imposed on suppliers should only fall on those who, because of the regularity of their dealings, could be expected to have some competence in relation to the goods supplied. Such reasoning does not easily apply to finance leasing transactions (see Chapter 12). It is significant that under s 46(2) of the Consumer Protection Act 1987, banks or finance companies who have only acquired goods for the purposes of supplying them on hire, hire purchase or conditional sale, are not treated as suppliers for the purposes of liability for defective products and consumer safety. Such liability is visited upon the dealer who is considered to have introduced the goods in question into the general stream of commerce.

The view of the House of Lords in *Davies v Sumner* [1984] 1 WLR 1301 failed to take sufficient account of the variety of situations in which the phrase 'dealing in the course of a business' appear. In the case where contractual liability is strict, for example the implied conditions under the SGA 1979 and the SGSA 1982, the consumer protection rationale could suggest a wide interpretation of acting in the course of a business. Thus in *Corfield v Sevenways Garage Ltd* [1985] RTR 109, a car repairer sold a car from his garage forecourt and the Divisional Court held this to be in the course of business even though selling was an infrequent sideline. However, the Court of Appeal in *R & B Customs Brokers Co Ltd v United Dominions Trust Ltd* [1988] 1 WLR 321, following the House of Lords' decision in *Davies v Sumner*, considered that the phrase 'in the course of a business' should be given a uniform interpretation in all consumer protection legislation. Unfortunately, such an approach ignores the range of situations in which the phrase appears. Nonetheless, even if it is insisted that some degree of regularity is normally required, there are situations where the first transaction entered into by a supplier can be treated as being made in the course of business, for example, one-off adventures integral to a business activity. As Dillon LJ pointed out in *R & B Custom Brokers*:

> . . . there are some transactions which are clearly integral parts of the businesses concerned, and these should be held to have been carried out in the course of those businesses; this would cover, apart from much else, the instance of a one-off adventure in the nature of trade, where the transaction itself would constitute a trade or business. (pp 330–1)

In some situations the categorisation of a 'business' may be regarded by the court as vital for the application of the reasonableness test under s 11 of UCTA 1977. This may explain the approach of Scott-Baker J in *St Albans City and District Council v International Computers Ltd* (1994) *The Times*, unreported, when he said:

> But for the extended definition of 'business' in the 1977 Act, the |council| would be treated, for the purposes of s 3, as dealing as a consumer. Council officials are not, in the ordinary sense of the word, businessmen, although it is to be hoped that they act in a businesslike way. Their contracts are governed by specific financial constraints, the need for public evaluation and often competitive tendering. They do not operate in the same commercial field as a business and probably find it impracticable to insure against commercial risks. The plaintiff's bargaining position, whilst on the one hand better than, say, an individual buying a car from a motor dealer, was weaker than that of the defendants.

The facts of this case arose out of the community charge fiasco, the defendants having agreed to supply the plaintiff Local Authority with a database to operate the Community Charge Register. The contract limited the defendant's liability for loss to £100K. When the plaintiffs extended the population figures from the data base to be returned to the Secretary of State for the Environment in December 1989, the population was overestimated by 2,966 owing to an error in the software. As a result the community charge rate was set too low which resulted in a loss to the Council of £1,314,846. It was held that the local authority did not deal as a consumer for the purposes of s 12 of UCTA 1977, which provides:

(1) A party to a contract 'deals as consumer' in relation to another party if
    (a) he neither makes the contract in the course of a business nor holds himself out as doing so; and
    (b) the other party does make the contract in the course of a business; and
    (c) in the case of a contract governed by the law of sale of goods or hire purchase, or by section 7 of this Act, the goods passing under or in pursuance of this contract are of a type ordinarily supplied for private use or consumption.

It would appear therefore that s 12 focuses upon a contract in the course of a business, that is, an integral part of the business. This is the point made in *R & B Customs Brokers Ltd*—the purchase of the car was not an integral part of the company's business which was that of freight forwarding. It could be argued in *St Albans* that although levying the community charge could be seen as an integral part of the 'business' of the Council, acquiring the means to do so was not. However, s 12(1)(c) of UCTA 1977 contains an important restriction upon those who 'deal as consumers'—this does not apply to goods which are not of a 'type ordinarily supplied for private use or consumption'. It is unlikely that this type of hardware and software package would pass this test, because in no way could it have been considered a computer with a software package for an entertainment or educational purpose for home consumption.

A significant exception to the supply in the course of a business is where a private supplier chooses to use a business agent to find a client. In this respect, s 14(5) of the SGA provides:

> The preceding provisions of this section apply to a sale by a person who in the course of a business is acting as agent for another as they apply to a sale by a principal in the course of a business, except where that other is not selling in the course of a business and either the buyer knows that fact or reasonable steps are taken to bring it to the notice of the buyer before the contract is made.

A similar provision can also be found in hire and hire purchase transactions (s 10(5) of SOGIT 1973, ss 4(8), 9(8) of SGSA 1982). Liability is anticipated except where the seller is not in fact selling in the course of a business and prior to contracting the transferee knows this fact, or reasonable steps have been taken to bring it to his notice. Where this is not done the ordinary agency rules apply, so that an undisclosed principal may be sued by a buyer, typically where the agent acting in the ordinary course of business employed to dispose of an asset becomes insolvent. Thus in *Boyter v Thomson* [1995] 3 All ER 135, the seller instructed agents to sell on his behalf a cabin cruiser under a brokerage and agency agreement. The buyer bought the boat thinking it was owned by the agents; he was not told that the agents were acting as such nor did he know the name of the owner nor that the owner was not selling in the course of a business. The boat proved to be unseaworthy and was unfit for the purpose for which it was purchased, and in the House of Lords the seller contended that he could not be sued under s 14(5) because that subsection rendered an agent liable if he was acting for an undisclosed principal, with the result that it was the agents and not the seller who were liable for breach of contract to the buyer. This was rejected and Lord Jauncey, who gave the judgment on behalf of the House of Lords, held:

> In my view subs (5) is applicable to any sale by an agent on behalf of a principal whether disclosed or undisclosed, where circumstances giving rise to the exception do not exist. When the subsection applies the normal common law rules of principal and agent also apply. There having been in this case no attempt to bring to the notice of the respondent the fact that the appellant was not selling in the course of business it follows that the respondent was entitled to claim damages from the appellant in reliance on the provisions of s 14(2), (3) and (5). (p 138)

There may be important public policy issues which dictate that the implied terms as to quality should extend even to private sellers. This would essentially reverse the ordinary presumption to *caveat venditor*. Indeed in Ireland, questions of safety for road users explains the incorporation of s 13(2) of the Irish Sale and Supply of Goods Act 1980 which provides that, except where the buyer is a dealer in motor vehicles, 'there is an implied condition that, at the time of the delivery of the vehicle under the contract, it is free from any defect which would render it a danger to the public, including persons travelling in the vehicle'. This does not apply if the parties agree that the vehicle is not to be used in the condition in which it is when sold, and a document to this effect is signed by them and given to the buyer at the time of delivery. An important *caveat* to this is that the agreement must be fair and reasonable. It is probable that this exception would apply only where there is a state of affairs which would make it unsafe to use the vehicle immediately. If the document is provided merely to cover the seller, it could scarcely be regarded as fair and reasonable in most cases. The Irish contractual approach is an important adjunct to action by enforcement officers. In England, the public interest is solely protected by the criminal law, where s 75 of the Road Traffic Act 1988 makes it a strict liability offence to sell an unroadworthy vehicle, irrespective of the nature of the sales transaction. This remains the position notwithstanding the new amendments made to the SGA.

The implied terms as to quality extend to the goods supplied

The undertakings as to quality extend not only to the contract goods but also to other goods supplied under the contract, for example, a defective bottle in the case of a supply of ginger beer (*Morelli v Fitch and Gibbons* [1928] 2 KB 638), or mineral water (*Geddling v March* [1920] 1 KB 668). The reference in these cases is to s 61 of SGA 1979 (s 18 of SGSA 1982) where the definition of 'quality of goods' covers 'their state or condition'. In the celebrated case *Wilson v Rickett Cockerell and Co Ltd* [1954] 1 QB 598, the Court of Appeal held the seller liable for damage to property caused by a detonator which was included in a consignment of Coalite. From this case, it would appear that all the goods supplied under the contract have to be of merchantable quality which is of significance with regard to 'free gifts' and promotions supplied with goods.

The protection conferred by the implied terms as to quality also extend to labels and instructions accompanying the product. Perhaps the most important case in this context is *Niblett Ltd v Confectioners' Materials Co Ltd* [1921] 3 KB 387. In this case, a sale of tins of condensed milk bearing labels which infringed a registered trade mark, was held to be in breach of the implied condition of merchantibility (*per* Bankes LJ at p 395):

> Quality includes the state or condition of the goods. The state of this condensed milk was that it is packed in tins bearing labels. The labels were as much part of the state or condition of the goods as the tins were. The state of the packing affected the merchantable quality of the goods.

At first instance in *Wormell v RHM Agriculture (East) Ltd* [1986] 1 WLR 336, it was held that accompanying written instructions were 'goods supplied under the contract'. However, this was not relied on by the Court of Appeal who reversed the decision on the facts (see pp 66–7 below).

The implied obligation of satisfactory quality

The Sale and Supply of Goods (Amendment) Act 1994 implemented the recommendations of the Law Commissions set out in their Report, *the Sale and Supply of Goods* (1987) LC No 160, Scot LC No 164, and introduced an implied obligation of satisfactory quality. In fact the Law Commissions Report recommended an 'acceptable quality' standard, but this was changed to satisfactory quality in the amending Act on the basis (a) that it was a higher standard; and (b), equally significantly, there would have been the possibility of confusion between the concept of acceptance for the purposes of cutting off rejection, and the idea of acceptable quality as a standard. It would appear that there is considerable scope for a new body of case law to emerge if the courts treat this new terminology as a legislative signal to adopt a more purposive application of the quality test. Moreover, the introduction of the 'satisfactory quality' standard applies not only to contracts of sale but also to other contracts under which goods are supplied, namely, s 10 SOGIT 1973 (hire purchase); ss 4, 9 SGSA 1982 (supply contracts and hire).

The original merchantability test reflected 19th Century retail practice which was more wholesale in nature as distinct from retail; it was originally designed to provide a broad meaning of commercial saleability for the business community in the case of unascertained goods. The definition was mechanistic in the sense that it focused unduly on fitness for purpose while at the same time failing to accommodate a reasonable durability concept. It is true that whilst the word 'merchantable' was economical in terms of language, it nevertheless did require further elaboration by case law which itself vacillated between an acceptability and a usability test. In addition, considerable confusion was seen in the previous case law concerning the effect of the 1973 amendment to the 1893 Act, where an attempt was made to define the concept of merchantability. In *Rogers v Parish (Scarborough) Ltd* [1987] QB 933 Mustill LJ took the view that the 1973 Act was an amending Act which should be construed free from technicality and which could be referred to without resort to the old case law. By way of contrast, Lloyd LJ in *M/S Aswan Engineering Establishment Co v Lupdine Ltd* [1987] 1 WLR 1 considered that the 1973 amendment was a reproduction of Lord Reid's speech on the *ratio* in *Henry Kendall and Sons v William Lillico and Sons Ltd* [1969] 2 AC 31 and that it was therefore appropriate to refer to old case law.

One standard of quality

A new standard has been set in s 14 SGA (as amended) which is not centred upon a vague concept of fitness for purpose but rather upon what a reasonable person would regard as 'unsatisfactory'. Essentially it could be argued that this reflected the modern approach adopted by Mustill LJ in *Rogers v Parish (Scarborough) Ltd* when in referring to the purposive approach seen under the old legislation he adopted a broad approach so as to include 'the purpose for which "goods of the kind" are commonly bought . . .' (p 944). The adoption of 'satisfactory' does have the advantage of communicating to consumers the standard required in a more meaningful way than does merchantability. Of course it could be argued that there is a bifurcation between consumer and commercial transactions and that satisfactory quality is not an appropriate standard for commercial transactions in the sense that the goods may still be commercially useful. In many respects, this is the logic of s 15A which provides that non-consumer buyers cannot reject for breach of ss 13–15 SGA where the breach is so slight that it would be unreasonable to reject them.

There is no differentiation in the standard expected for different types of goods or different transactions. The creation of different categories of transaction or different types of buyer and seller would give rise to disputes based upon delineation. As the Law Commission put it at para 3.8:

> [Al]though it might (for example) seem obvious that 'new' goods should be of a different standard from 'second-hand' goods, is this really always so? A 'second-hand' Rolls-Royce motor car sold after only 300 miles driving, should probably have all the qualities of a brand new car of that marque. On the other hand, 'new' goods may be sold as 'seconds' or their substandard quality otherwise indicated.

Differentiating transactions would also be difficult and distort the sale structure. For example, if there were different standards of quality (as distinct from remedies) between retailers then a shopkeeper who had bought from his wholesaler might find that there had been no breach of contract by the wholesaler but that he himself might be in breach as against the consumer.

The satisfactory quality test

This creates an objective standard of quality and moves away from a fitness for purpose and usability approach towards that formulated by Dixon J in the Australian High Court in *Grant v Australian Knitting Mills* [1933] 30 CLR 387 (affirmed [1936] AC 85):

> [The goods] should be in such an actual state that a buyer fully acquainted with the facts and, therefore, knowing what hidden defects exist and not being limited to their apparent condition would buy them without abatement of the price attainable for such goods if in reasonably sound order and condition and without special terms. (p 418)

The inclusion of a purposive adjective 'satisfactory' means that the goods must meet a standard that a reasonable person would consider to be satisfactory. It is not this buyer's expectations that are relevant, which could allow the standard to decline perhaps because of inertia by the buyer and could furthermore allow the seller to establish that goods of a particular type could reasonably be expected to have a number of defects on delivery (see *Millars of Falkirk Ltd v Turpie* [1976] SLT 66).

The issue of satisfactory quality is still tempered by defects or other matters which have been drawn to the buyer's attention before the contract is made, or (if the buyer examined the goods before the contract was made) which that examination of the goods ought to have revealed (s 14(2C)). In addition the issue of quality is determined by description and price because clearly goods of a different description may well be expected to have a different quality whilst price also must be a guide to quality (s 14(2A)). This was recognised by Slade LJ in *Harlingdon Ltd v Hull Fine Art Ltd* (1991):

> The complaint, and only complaint as to the quality of the picture, relates to the identity of the artist. There is no other complaint of any kind as to its condition or quality. If the verdict of the experts had been that the artist was in truth Gabriele Munter, the claim would not have arisen. Having concluded that this was not a contract for the sale of goods by description . . . I see no room for the application of s 14. If the plaintiffs fail to establish a breach of contract through the front door of s 13(1), they cannot succeed through the back door of s 14. (p 572).

This explains the approach in *Bartlett v Sidney Marcus* [1965] 1 WLR 1013 which was a pre-1973 definition case. In this case, a plaintiff bought a used car which he was told had something wrong with the clutch and oil pressure gauge but that neither would be serious. After a few weeks other problems appeared and the plaintiff sued for the cost of repairing them. At first instance, the judge held that the car was not of merchantable quality. This was overturned on appeal where Lord Denning held: '. . . a buyer should realise that, when he buys a secondhand car, defects may appear sooner or later and in the absence of an express warranty, he has no redress . . .' (p 755). Even if a car is sold as new this does not necessarily mean that it should be perfect. Thus in *Bernstein v Pamsons Motors (Golders Green) Ltd* [1987] 2 All ER 220, Rougier J held that although a purchaser of a new car was entitled to expect a better quality vehicle than the buyer of a secondhand car, nevertheless, teething problems had to be expected. The defect in this case though (a drop of sealant had got into the lubrication system) went beyond mere teething trouble. A buyer was entitled to a car, not a running fight with a defective machine.

The issue of price was also relevant in the determination of merchantability. In the pre-1973 definition case of *BS Brown and Son Ltd v Craik Ltd* [1970] 1 WLR 752, which was accepted as authority in *Aswan Engineering* (1987), the House of Lords held that goods will be unmerchantable if they can only be resold at a substantially reduced price. Such an approach was also mirrored in *Shine v General Guarantee Corp Ltd (Reeds Motor Co (a firm), third party)* [1988] 1 All ER 911. In this case, the Court of Appeal held that there had been a breach of s 14(2) as the plaintiff had thought he was buying a secondhand enthusiast's car in good condition at a fair price when in fact he was buying, at the same price, a car which no one, knowing its history (a car insurance write-off because it had been submerged in water for over 24 hours), would have bought at other than at a substantially reduced price. At the same time it has to be admitted that pecuniary considerations are only a guide and there is authority that defective goods can be unmerchantable *per se*, for example as in the case of underpants impregnated with sulphate (*Grant v Australian Knitting*

Mills Ltd [1936] AC 85). Similarly in *Lee v York Coach and Marine* [1977] RTR 35, a secondhand Morris car that was unsafe to drive was held unmerchantable even though the cost of repair was small.

The list of aspects of quality

This is a wide list in which no element has priority, the implication being that not all the elements will always be relevant. Further, it is clear from s 14 (2B) that unlisted other matters may be taken into account.

1. Fitness for purpose

That is, all purposes for which goods of the kind in question are commonly supplied. This is a reversal of the old law as represented by *Aswan Engineering* [1987] 1 WLR 1 where it was held that it was not necessary for the purposes of merchantability that the goods be suitable for all purposes. Even so, under the new provisions a seller supplying goods only for one common purpose can narrow the description of the goods so as to exclude other common purposes. As such, this would appear to be statutory recognition of the broad judicial approach in *Harlingdon* (1991) and *Don Commercials* (1994). At the same time if the buyer has a particular uncommon purpose in mind he can always make this purpose known to the seller and rely upon s 14(3) SGA.

Undoubtedly there is inherent flexibility in the concept of 'common' purpose and indeed there is a danger that future judicial discussion will waft into metaphysical dimensions. What is common? At what point does a purpose split into (different) purposes of both parties?

2. Appearance and finish

This is separated from the 'freedom from minor defects' category in order to avoid any possible confusion arising that a minor defect must include a defect in appearance or finish. Again the description will be relevant as to whether the goods are 'new' or 'secondhand', and so will the price.

3. Freedom from minor defects

The *de minimis* principle still applies and the description of the goods will be highly relevant, for example, some goods have inherent blemishes, notably, earthenware products. The new Act does not define 'minor defect' nor 'appearance and finish', quite simply because much will depend upon the facts in each particular case. The Act does not guarantee against minor defects, that is, setting down an absolute standard. In this respect, it is for example hard to categorise goods described as 'seconds' as having 'defects', and many of the jurisprudential puzzles which feature in wrongful birth actions in tort are applicable here.

The practical effect of the appearance and finish aspect and minor defects is that it will be easier to resist *Millars of Falkirk* (1976) type of cases. In that case the buyer was left with no remedy at all for a leak in the power-assisted steering system of his new car. Such a minor defect, albeit curable, is not something which a consumer should now have to face without the remedy of repudiation unless, of course, he was aware of this at the time of sale or it had been brought specifically to his attention.

4. Safety

There is overlap with Parts I and II of the CPA 1987 and also with the General Product Safety Regulations 1994. However, the Law Commission did not think that a reference to safety should be omitted (see para 3.46) in that the SGA performs a different function. Thus the new legislation confirms that sellers have quite onerous obligations towards buyers about safety. Even so, the strict English application of the contract doctrine of privity, by which third party beneficiaries to contracts have no legal claim, means that only the immediate buyer benefits from the strictness of the seller's SGA duties. Subsequent purchasers in a contractual chain or donees of gifts from the buyer have, by definition, no contractual claim although subsequent purchasers may have such a claim against the intermediate buyer where the latter acts in the course of a business.

Where the complaint has to do with quality rather than safety, the law has resolutely resisted imposing liability. There is nothing under the 1994 Act amendment akin to the French concept of *action directe* circumventing privity rules which protect manufacturers from contractual claims. Moreover, horizontal privity rules would protect the original seller from a donee and also successors in title, for example, where goods are brought from the first buyer. It is likely that there will be developments on this front as the European Commission's *Green Paper on Guarantees for Consumer Goods and After-Sales Services* (Com (93) 509) makes proposals to circumvent vertical and horizontal priority barriers to contract claims based on legal minimum quality provisions.

5. Durability

There is no definite indication of how long goods should last under the Act for the simple reason that this will depend upon the treatment they get. Moreover, different types of goods have different life expectancies so it is difficult to be prescriptive here. In addition, the way in which goods are made up is relevant, for example, a failure of a component may or may not give rise to a right to reject the finished product; for example, a battery in a watch which fails would not normally give rise to a right to reject the watch. The requirement of durability in the Act relates to a reasonable period of time and this bites at the time of supply. This allows for the same limitations of actions period to run with the other implied terms. At the same time it should be noted that the requirement of durability does not mean that the goods should remain for a reasonable time at the same level of quality as they were supplied because this would not take into account natural deterioration: the requirement of durability relates to the goods lasting for a reasonable time. The length of time for which goods may reasonably be expected to endure depends upon their description and price as well as use, and also the nature of the treatment they receive. In this respect the requirement of durability is an aspect of quality. The case of *Business Application Specialists Ltd v Nationwide Credit Corp Ltd* [1988] RTR 332 is instructive here in the sense that it represents a borderline decision which would be decided differently under the new law. The facts involved the sale of a secondhand Mercedes car which developed faults requiring repair which was unusual for a Mercedes of that age and mileage. It was held that the car was merchantable because some defects and some ordinary wear and tear should be expected with a secondhand motor car. Surely this must now be a matter of degree, especially with an expensive secondhand car.

Durability and contracts of supply

The requirement of durability applies to contracts of supply including hire and hire purchase and it bears in this context the same meaning as for contracts of sale; as the Law Commission pointed out in para 3.70:

> It does not mean that throughout the period of the hiring the goods must necessarily remain in the same condition as when they were supplied. Exactly how durable the goods must be will depend on all the circumstances. However, the length of the period hire and type of hiring involved may well be relevant.

Clearly, hiring a car for three years and a suit for one evening will sound in different levels of durability: it is natural to expect signs of wear and tear after several months in the case of a motor vehicle, which will require servicing and perhaps replacing parts. Even so, in the case of contract hire of motor vehicles the requirement of durability for the whole contract period is often expressly incorporated in the contract, where, of course, the hirer pays extra rental for facilities such as servicing and the provision for a replacement vehicle.

Durability and limitation periods

Where goods are not durable, the mischief lies not in the fact that they ceased to perform adequately, but rather that, at the date of supply, they did not have the capacity to endure. This is important for limitation purposes and the case of *Parasram v Witter Towbars Ltd* (1993) unreported, is instructive in this regard. Here the plaintiff bought a towing bracket from the defendants at a caravan exhibition in London in November 1985 and then put it away without unpacking it, only fitting it to his car in June 1986. In July 1986, while driving the car in Norway towing a caravan, an alleged defect in the coupling of the caravan meant that the car went out of control and was dragged off the road. A writ was issued in June 1991 for breach of contract. The issue related to the relevant limitation period, because whereas six years had not quite passed since the accident, more than six years had passed since the sale and delivery.

The limitation period rule is that the cause of action accrues not when the damage is suffered, but when the breach actually takes place (*Battley and Another v Faulkner and Another* (1820) 3 B & Ald 288.) It was argued by the plaintiff that at the time of the delivery the coupling was of merchantable quality but that it ceased to be so very shortly before the accident and that therefore the cause of action was complete and the limitation period began to run not in November 1985 but in July 1986. This argument was rejected by Sir Godfray le Quesne QC (sitting as a deputy judge of the High Court) on the basis that the merchantable quality warranty 'relates to the goods at the time of delivery and it is a warranty in this case that at the time of delivery they are such that they will continue to be of merchantable quality for a reasonable time. If within a reasonable time the goods break down what that shows is that there was a breach of warranty at the time of the sale. The breach was latent then but has become patent'. This approach is consistent with authorities (see notably *AB Kemp Ltd v Tolland* [1956] 2 Lloyd's Rep 681). Indeed in *Crowther v Shannon Motor Co* [1975] 1 WLR 30 Lord Denning, with whose judgment the other members of the Court of Appeal agreed, said in relation to the sale of a second-hand Jaguar car:

> On the dealers' own evidence, a buyer could reasonably expect to get 100,000 miles life out of a Jaguar engine. Here the Jaguar had only done 80,000 miles. Yet it was in such a bad condition that it was 'clapped out' and after some 2,300 miles it failed altogether. That is very different from a minor repair. The dealers themselves said that if they had known that the engine would blow up after 2,000 miles, they would not have sold it. The reason obviously was because it would not have been reasonably fit for the purpose. Some criticism was made of a phrase used by the judge. He said 'What does "fit for the purpose" mean?' He answered 'To go as a car for a reasonable time'. I am not quite sure that that is entirely accurate. The relevant time is the time of sale. But there is no doubt what the judge meant. If the car does not go for a reasonable time but the engine breaks up within a short time, that is evidence which goes to show that it was not reasonably fit for the purpose at the time it was sold. It was 'nearing the point of failure', said the expert, Mr Wise. The time interval was merely 'staving off the inevitable.' That shows that at the time of the sale it was not reasonably fit for the purpose of being driven on the road. (p 33)

It was held in the *Parasram* case that the coupling must have been unsafe and defective at the time of delivery and therefore the claim against the defendant was struck out.

It should be noted that there is no requirement under the amended legislation that the supplier should carry a minimum amount of spare parts for products it introduces into the stream of commerce. The rationale for this approach is that this would put the retailer at the mercy of manufacturers' solvency or production ability. Nonetheless there may be cases where the supplier would be liable under s 14(2) for failing to carry spare parts, for example, following the supply of a discontinued model where the absence of common spare parts in the sense of normal wear and tear will go to the issue of durability of the product in question.

The determination of satisfactory quality is at the point of delivery, which is the bench-mark for the durability criterion as an aspect of quality. However, there are difficulties with latent defects, for example, characteristics not known to be harmful at the time of delivery, or immunities to harmful substances being subsequently discovered. These issues were considered by the House of Lords in *Henry Kendall and Sons v William Lillico and Sons Ltd* [1969] 2 AC 31 where the majority held that subsequent knowledge should be taken into account as otherwise, Lord Guest argued, it would be tantamount 'to approach the true situation with blinkers' (p 108). With respect, there is much to be said for the minority view expressed by Lord Pearce which is based upon certainty in transactions and would not expose the parties to shifts in scientific knowledge right up to the time of trial. It is surely reasonable to maintain that the parties assumed to contract in the light of the scientific knowledge prevailing at the time of delivery. In the light of the emphasis in the new legislation the majority approach would appear to be the existing position. Of course, this poses the question that in the light of these changes, how much longer can consumer and commercial law coexist in the same statute?

The *Henry Kendall* case demonstrates that liability for merchantability and now satisfactory quality is strict, and it is no defence that the seller took all reasonable care that the goods were merchantable. As such, the issue of fault is irrelevant, which is beneficial to a buyer especially since s 4(1)(*e*) of the Consumer Protection Act 1987 restricts recovery in tort with its development risks or state of the art defence (see Chapter 6).

Excepted defects

There is no condition as to satisfactory quality where defects have been drawn to the buyer's attention before the contract is made, or if the defects should have been obvious from examination. Thus s 14(2C) of the SGA (as amended) (replicated in s 10(2) of SOGIT 1973 as substituted by the CCA 1974 and ss 4(3), 9(3) of SGSA 1982) provides:

> The term implied by subsection (2) above does not extend to any matter making the quality of goods unsatisfactory—
> (a) which is specifically drawn to the buyer's attention before the contract is made,
> (b) where the buyer examines the goods before the contract is made, which that examination ought to reveal, or
> (c) in the case of a contract for sale by sample, which would have been apparent on a reasonable examination of the sample.

Proviso (a)

It is difficult to understand this defence because it is already included within the statutory definition of satisfactory quality as it will affect the description under which the goods are sold. The requirement that the defects be disclosed to the buyer is one of degree and it is probable that some positive act of drawing attention seems to be required.

Proviso (b)

There is no requirement that the buyer examines the goods. At common law, the merchantability undertaking was excluded by the mere opportunity for pre-contract examination, which is retained in the case of sales by sample. Under the amended s 14(2C)(*b*), the crucial issue is what defects the examination actually carried out ought to have revealed. The standard applied here is objective, based upon the reasonable man in the seller's position ignoring any peculiar idiosyncrasies of the buyer. In *R & B Customs Brokers Co Ltd v United Dominions Trust* [1988] 1 WLR 321, a car bought on conditional sale was delivered to the customer before the relevant documentation was completed. The customer discovered during this period that the car had a leaking roof and it was argued that, as a result of the customer's examination of the car before the contract was made, he had knowledge of the defect so as to exclude liability. Undoubtedly, such an approach will prejudice any buyer who takes delivery before concluding the contract of supply.

Proviso (c)

The purpose of a sample is to give the potential buyer an opportunity of examining it so that he can decide whether or not it is suitable. Under the previous law there appeared to be nothing to prevent the buyer still relying upon the implied term that goods had to be merchantable. This new provision ensures that a sale by sample will now prevail over s 14(2) (as amended).

The implied obligation of fitness for purpose

The implied condition of satisfactory quality is supplemented by the fitness for purpose provision found in s 14(3) of SGA 1979 which provides:

> Where the seller sells goods in the course of a business and the buyer, expressly or by implication, makes known—
> (a) to the seller, or
> (b) where the purchase price or part of it is payable by instalments and the goods were previously sold by a credit-broker to the seller, to that credit-broker,
> any particular purpose for which the goods are being bought, there is an implied condition that the goods supplied under the contract are reasonably fit for that purpose, whether or not that is a purpose for which such goods are commonly supplied, except where the circumstances show that the buyer does not rely, or that it is unreasonable for him to rely, on the skill or judgment of the seller and credit-broker.

Similar obligations can be found in relation to other supply contracts (see s 10(3) of SOGIT 1973 as substituted by the CCA 1974 and ss 4(4)–(6), 9(4)–(6) of SGSA 1982). It would seem that two factors are especially relevant. First, knowledge on the part of the seller, bailor, transferor or their agent of the purpose for which the goods are sought. Secondly, reliance upon the skill or judgment of the seller, bailor or transferor.

The statutory undertaking requires that the goods be 'reasonably fit' for the normal purpose or special purpose as communicated to the supplier (see below). This is the case irrespective of whether the supplier himself has exercised all reasonable care and skill and has not been careless, so liability is strict. Thus in *Frost v Aylesbury Dairy Co* [1905] 1 KB 608, the supplier was held liable under this section for the supply of milk for household purposes contaminated with typhoid. This should be contrasted with the decision of the Court of Appeal in *Griffiths v Peter Conway Ltd* [1939] 1 All ER 685 where it was held that a buyer could not rely on this section when she contracted dermatitis (from a Harris Tweed coat supplied) because of her unusually sensitive skin. Similarly, in *Ingham v Emes* [1955] 2 QB 366, a woman contracted dermatitis when her hairdresser applied a particular dye to her hair, but she failed to recover damages since she had not informed the hairdresser of her allergy. Moreover, the hairdresser had performed the recommended test for the allergy with favourable results and had no reason to suspect that she was unusually sensitive. It would seem that the criterion of reasonableness therefore relates to 'normal' situations. Consequently, had the dye in *Ingham* provoked a reaction even to a 'normal' customer, but the effect was exacerbated because of the particular customer's sensitive skin, the hairdresser could not avoid or limit liability on this ground (see *Parsons (Livestock) Ltd v Uttley, Ingham and Co* [1978] QB 791).

Sometimes the question of fitness under s 14(3) relates to issues of remoteness of liability. This can be demonstrated in *Vacwell Engineering Co Ltd v BDH Chemicals* [1971] 1 QB 88 where a chemical supplied by the defendants, although fit for the plaintiffs' purposes, exploded on contact with water, though this was unknown to the plaintiffs. It was held that the defendants were liable because they ought to have foreseen the possibility of the chemical coming into contact with water and they had not warned the buyers of this danger. The extent to which instructions and warnings can limit liability will be discussed below (see pp 66–7).

The question of knowledge

The problem of ascribing to the supplier knowledge of the purpose for which goods were intended, is complicated by the fact that the goods may sometimes have more than one purpose. The overlap here with the satisfactory quality provision is obvious and often the two will coincide. However, s 14(3) comes into its own where the purpose in question is not a common one. This was the case in *Ashington Piggeries Ltd v Christopher Hill Ltd* (1972) where cattle food suitable for animals generally was bought for the particular purpose of being fed to mink, and it turned out to be poisonous to mink.

There is no real problem where the supplier expressly notifies the buyer of the purpose he has in mind. When the goods have only one normal purpose, the seller's knowledge of this purpose will normally be assumed. Thus in *Preist v Last* [1903] 2 KB 148, a hot water bottle burst causing injury to the purchaser's wife and it was held that there was a breach of the implied condition even though nothing was said about the purpose. The reason for this is clear in Collins MR's judgment where it was said that, in the case of a purchase of goods capable of a multitude of purposes, in order to invoke the implied condition, it was necessary to show that the goods were sold with reference to a particular purpose:

> ... in order to give rise to the implication of a warranty, it is necessary to show that, though the article sold was capable of general use for many purposes, in the particular case it was sold with reference to a particular purpose. But in a case

> where the discussion begins with the fact that the description of the goods by which they were sold points to one particular purpose only, it seems to me that the first requirement of the subsection is satisfied . . .. The sale is of goods which, by the very description under which they are sold, appear to be sold for a particular purpose. (p 153)

It follows that even though s 14(3) of SGA 1979 provides for extraordinary use (s 10(3) of SOGIT 1973 as substituted by CCA 1974 and ss 4(5), 9(5) of SGSA 1982), in order for the buyer to obtain the benefit of this he must specify that use. Thus in *Cammell Laird and Co Ltd v Manganese Bronze and Brass Co Ltd* [1934] AC 402, the contract was for the provision of two propellers for a specified ship and it was held that the sellers knew the purpose for which the propellers were required, ie that they should be suitable for the ship in question.

The meaning of the requirement of specificity for a particular purpose was considered in *Kendall v Lillico* (1969). This case involved the sale of 'Brazilian groundnut extractions' required for compounding as food for cattle and poultry by the first buyers. They sold to the second buyers for the purpose of compounding into food for pigs and poultry. The second buyers compounded the goods into food for birds and the third buyers bought the compound and fed it to poultry which died because, unknown to anyone at the time of supply, the compound included minute traces of poison rendering it unfit for poultry. It was held that there had been a breach of the implied condition as to fitness for purpose, the court refusing to read the word 'particular' in s 14(3) in the sense of special as opposed to general purpose. Lord Morris said:

> The degree of precision or definition which makes a purpose a particular purpose depends entirely on the facts and circumstances of a purchase and sale transaction. No need arises to define or limit the word 'particular'. (p 93)

It would appear that as long as the buyer communicates the purpose for which the goods are required, he does not have to specify all of the particular applications so long as they fall within the scope of normal purpose. This is clear in the approach taken by the House of Lords in *Ashington Piggeries Ltd v Christopher Hill Ltd* (see above). The majority view was that, the buyers having intimated that the herring meal was required for animal food, it was not necessary to specify the kind of animal(s) to which the food might be given. Moreover, it was accepted by the House of Lords that if the sellers had not known that the herring meal was to be used as food, no condition of fitness for purpose would have been implied.

Communication of knowledge to agent or credit-broker

Section 14(3) of SGA 1979 makes specific provision for the situation where goods are taken on credit terms. This solves the common law problem where a particular purpose is made known by a consumer to a dealer who may not have had ostensible or actual authority to receive such communication on the part of the financing institution. Similar provisions are also found in relation to other supply situations (see s 10(3) of SOGIT 1973 as substituted by the CCA 1974 and ss 4(4), 9(4) of SGSA 1982). This can prove particularly problematic in the financing leasing context (see Chapter 12).

The statutory agency anticipated under s 14(3)(b) is in line with the trend towards consumer protection. It reflects the business reality of the situation, in that for the consumer there is no distinction between vendor credit and lender credit. The logic here is carried a stage further in s 75 of CCA 1974 which applies in three-party debtor–creditor–supplier agreements as it allows the debtor a 'like claim' against the creditor as he has against the transferor. In *Porter v General Guarantee Corporation Ltd* [1982] RTR 384, s 75(2) of CCA 1974 was clearly misapplied. This case involved an unroadworthy car sold by a dealer to the finance company which was then supplied to the debtor on hire purchase. A hire purchase agreement is a two-party debtor–creditor–supplier agreement to which s 75 does not apply. In this situation, the dealer's liability to the finance company should have been founded on the sale contract between them. Connected lender liability is discussed at greater length in Chapter 2.

Section 56 of CCA 1974 provides that in antecedent negotiations the supplier is deemed to act as agent for the creditor. In particular, the effect of s 56(4) is very wide since it defines antecedent negotiations to include:

> For the purposes of this Act, antecedent negotiations shall be taken to begin when the negotiator and the debtor or hirer first enter into communication (including communication by advertisement), and to include any representations made by the negotiator to the debtor or hirer and any other dealings between them.

Thus, negotiations will include representations and 'other dealings' which extend back in time to when the debtor or hirer reads an advertisement inserted by the negotiator. Antecedent negotiations terminate on the formation of a regulated agreement. It should be noted that the definition of credit broker under the SGA 1979, SOGIT 1973 and the SGSA 1982 refers to a person acting in the course of a business of credit brokerage and effecting introductions of 'individuals', which would appear to exclude a registered company as a single consumer (see s 189(1) of CCA 1974). It follows also that it is not credit-broking merely to advertise credit facilities or even carry application forms. The key issue is the forwarding of a completed proposal form to the creditor or owner (see *Brookes v Retail Credit Cards Ltd* [1986] CLY 370). At the same time, the CCA 1974 exempts certain categories from liability here: first, lawyers involved in contentious business (s 146(1)–(4)); second, where introductions are not effected by someone acting in the capacity of an employee canvassing off trade premises (s 146(3)). The sense of this second exception is to apply (especially) to women who solicit business for friends from mail order catalogues.

The question of reliance

It is not enough that the seller knows of the particular purpose of the goods sold, the buyer must also have relied upon the credit-broker or seller's skill and judgment at the date of the contract. It is not necessary to show exclusive reliance so that in the *Cammell Laird* case (1934), notwithstanding that the buyers laid down detailed specifications as to the propellers made by the sellers, there was still, in Lord Macmillan's words, 'an important margin within which the [seller's] skill and judgment had scope for exercise' (p 419). This approach was confirmed in the *Ashington Piggeries* case where it was recognised that both the seller and buyer had their own areas of expertise and the issue was whether the defect fell within the respective area of expertise of the buyer. The onus of showing reliance has now shifted away from the buyer and it is for the seller to prove that there was no reasonable reliance.

There is no doubt that the shift in the burden of proof means that reliance will now be assumed. If the supplier is on an equal footing with the buyer there will be no implied undertaking. In *Teheran-Europe Co Ltd v Belton (ST) Ltd* [1968] 2 QB 545, the facts involved the sale of machinery to a Persian company and it was held that there was no reliance on the seller's skill or judgment since the seller was ignorant of the foreign market where the goods were destined for resale. At the same time, the fact that both buyers and sellers are members of the same commodity market does not of itself show that the buyer does not rely on the seller. Indeed, it was pointed out in *Henry Kendall* (1969) that if the seller is himself the manufacturer of the goods the implied condition will normally apply.

Even if the buyer relies on the seller's skill or judgment, the implied condition cannot be invoked where this reliance is unreasonable. Thus, a sale of 'Coalite' in *Wilson v Rickett Cockerell and Co Ltd* (1934) was a sale under a trade or patent name which the Court of Appeal considered to preclude reliance. Nonetheless, the mere fact that the buyer has inspected the goods does not necessarily preclude reliance. Certainly undertakings in the contract that the buyer has not relied upon the seller's skill and judgment will not be conclusive, especially in consumer sales where s 6 of UCTA 1977 precludes contracting out of the implied condition of fitness. Of course, it is still a matter of degree as the contract may be concluded specifically on the basis of non-reliance. Even so, the obligation of satisfactory quality will still remain.

The significance of instructions and warnings

Instructions placed on the goods may indicate unreasonableness of reliance. In principle a careful approach should be adopted here since the seller should not be able to avoid the strictures of UCTA 1977 merely by expressly stating no reliance. The only modern English case concerning instructions is that of *Wormell v RHM Agriculture (East) Ltd* [1987] 1 WLR 1091 (rev [1986] 1 WLR 336). In this case, the plaintiff farmer was prevented from getting onto his land to spray his crops in order to kill wild oats until much later than normal during the wet spring of 1983. He therefore consulted the defendant sellers of agricultural products and asked them to recommend a herbicide that could be used later than usual. Their recommendation was a Shell weedkiller called 'Commando', and, accordingly, the plaintiff purchased some to the value of £6,438. The full technical instructions on the can stated that the contents ought not to be applied beyond a recommended stage of crop growth as damage might result to the crop. The plaintiff understood this to mean that, although damage to the crop might result, the 'Commando' would nevertheless be effective to kill the wild oats; and, as the weed infestation was so serious, he was prepared to run the risk of some loss to his crop of winter wheat. The 'Commando' was thus applied later than normal. However, although there was no damage to the crop, the herbicide was almost totally ineffective in killing the weeds. The plaintiff sought damages from the defendants for breach of the implied terms of s 14(2) and (3). At first instance the judge found as a matter of fact that the instructions were misleading and ambiguous. The defendants argued, *inter alia*, that there was no reliance on the seller's skill and judgment but rather a reliance by the buyer on his own understanding of the manufacturer's instructions. The judge found that the manufacturer's misleading instructions attached to the goods sold by a retailer was a breach of s 14(3), even though the seller himself did not have sufficient technical expertise to know whether the instructions were accurate.

The Court of Appeal reversed this decision, but it was held that instructions were relevant in deciding fitness for purpose. Since, the 'Commando' had a clear warning that the contents should not be used after a certain time, this was deemed to put the plaintiff on notice not to use the herbicide and he could not complain that his own misunderstanding of the consequences of ignoring the warning had rendered the herbicide unfit for the purpose for which it was supplied. It would seem that following this case, the importance of instructions cannot be underestimated. Where they are unduly complicated they themselves may be subject to scrutiny for fitness for purpose, as they could be considered as part of the goods supplied under the contract. Indeed, it could be argued that where instructions are not adequate there may be a breach of the merchantability provision. This is recognised in the Law Commission Working Paper No 85 (1983) in relation to self-assembly furniture where it was said:

> The goods would, of course, have to be in a condition in which they could be assembled, and if they were sold without adequate instructions it is unlikely that they would meet the required standard of quality. (para 4.16)

Implied obligations in supply and services contracts

The general effect of SOGIT 1973 and SGSA 1982 is to equate the implied conditions applied to sale in transactions of supply.

In the case of the supply of services, s 13 of SGSA 1982 states that, where the supplier is acting in the course of a business, 'the supplier will carry out the service with reasonable care and skill'. This is the common law position and s 16(3) provides for the possibility of a court implying stricter terms so that the reasonable care provision may be regarded as the minimum legal requirement. At the same time, the reasonableness provision under ss 14 and 15 of SGSA 1982, extends to time of performance and price where these are not stipulated in the contract. Obviously, these are questions of fact to be decided in each case.

Problems may arise with regard to hybrid contracts containing both a service and supply element. Section 1(3) of SGSA 1982 states that a contract is a contract of transfer notwithstanding that services are also provided, whilst s 12(3) states that a contract is a contract for the supply of services even though goods are also transferred. It follows that the materials element will be governed by s 4 which as amended refers to satisfactory quality and fitness for purpose (see *Young and Marten Ltd v McManus Childs Ltd* [1969] 1 AC 454) whilst the services element will be governed by the reasonableness provision as a minimum standard laid down in s 13. With regard to the end product following a supply of materials and services, it is a question of the intention of the parties as to whether the service or materials element is the most important factor.

Implied obligations in contracts by sample

The most common situation associated with contracts by sample is where the seller abstracts a small quantity from a larger bulk, or where the buyer is sent a small representative quantity in advance. The special conditions contained in s 15(2) of SGA 1979 (as amended), replicated in other supply contracts (s 11 of SOGIT 1973 as substituted by CCA 1974 and ss 5(1), 10(1) of SGSA 1982), do not apply to every case in which a sample is exhibited, for example in a shop, but only to sales by sample. This is defined in s 15 in its amended form which provides as follows:

> 15—(1) A contract of sale is a contract for sale by sample where there is an express or implied term to that effect in the contract.
>   (2) In the case of a contract for sale by sample there is an implied [term]—
>   (*a*) that the bulk will correspond with the sample in quality;
>   (*b*) . . .
>   (*c*) that the goods will be free from any defect, [making their quality unsatisfactory], which would not be apparent on reasonable examination of the sample.

In shop sales it may still be possible to imply as a matter of general contract law that the goods supplied, in the absence of representation to the contrary, correspond to the goods displayed in the shop.

Essentially a sample is a non-verbal description and whether or not a sale is by sample depends upon the intention of the parties. Thus, it may be that the only undertaking being made is that the sample was honestly and properly taken from the bulk, as was the case in *Gardiner v Gray* (1815) 4 Camp 144. However, the vast majority of cases in which samples are exhibited are, in any case, likely to be sales by description. In *Nichol v Godts* (1854) 10 Exch 191, a sale of 'foreign refined rape oil, warranted only equal to samples' was held to be a sale by description so that a seller could not deliver something which, although equal to sample, could not match the contract description. Of course this presupposes that the description is a meaningful one (see *RW Cameron and Co v L Slutzkin Pty Co* (1923) 32 CLR 81).

It is well established that a buyer may reject goods which do not conform to a contractual sample. Strict compliance is needed so that in the case of *E and S*

Ruben Ltd v Faine Bros and Co Ltd [1949] 1 KB 254, the buyers were held entitled to reject rolls of rubber which, unlike the sample shown, were crinkly and hard. It was irrelevant that the rubber would correspond with the contract sample by the simple process of warming the rubber and it would seem that the only relaxation of this strict rule is under the *de minimis* principle (see *Joe Lowe Food Products Ltd v JA and P Holland Ltd* [1954] 2 Lloyd's Rep 71). Nevertheless, conformity with sample depends upon the nature of the investigation carried out. If the normal trade practice is that a sample be subjected only to visual examination, there is no breach of s 15(2)(*a*) if the bulk does not correspond with it in some manner not discoverable by such visual examination (*Hookway & Co v Alfred Isaacs and Sons* [1954] 1 Lloyd's Rep 491).

Under the old law the sample buyer was given an opportunity to inspect the goods by virtue of s 15(2)(b). The Law Commission in their Report No 160 on *Sale and Supply of Goods* (1987), recommended that s 15(2)(*b*) should be deleted and instead a reference to the buyer having a reasonable opportunity to compare the bulk with the sample should be inserted into s 34. This has now been incorporated into the amended SGA and related legislation.

The requirement of satisfactory quality under s 15(2)(*c*) is part of the wider principle applicable to contracts of supply (see also s 11(*c*) of SOGIT 1973 as substituted by CCA 1974 and ss 5(1)(*c*), 10(2)(*c*) of SGSA 1982). Despite this, there are important differences, for example, there is no requirement to supply in the course of a business, and there is no express defence of defects specified. Perhaps the most important difference is that the buyer cannot complain of defects that a reasonable examination ought to reveal. Thus, whereas a buyer by sample can complain only of latent defects, a buyer 'by description' can complain of any defects except those which his *actual* examination (if any) ought to have brought to light. This less generous treatment does not seem unreasonable because it can surely be expected that the sample should be examined. The buyer can no longer rely upon the general satisfactory quality provision in s 14(2) as this has now been made specifically subject to s 15(2)(c) by s 14(2C).

Other implied terms

The statutory undertakings discussed above are perhaps the best known examples of the implied terms recognised in the common law and have been codified as such. Nevertheless, s 14(4) of SGA 1979, which is replicated in other supply contracts (s 10(4) of SOGIT 1973 as substituted by CCA 1974 and ss 4(7), 9(7) of SGSA 1982), provides, 'An implied [term] about quality or fitness for a particular purpose may be annexed to a contract of sale by usage'. The general rules apply that the usage or custom must be reasonable, universally accepted by the particular trade, certain, not unlawful and not inconsistent with the express or implied terms of the contract. An example of terms routinely implied in contracts of sale is that where goods are ordered from a manufacturer who makes such goods, it is implied that the goods are the manufacturer's own make and supplied under his normal label for the brand (see *Johnson v Raylton* (1881) 7 QBD 438; *Scaliaris v E Ofverberg and Co* (1921) 37 TLR 307). It can be argued that a car dealer has an implied obligation to make pre-delivery checks on a new car to ensure that it meets the manufacturer's specification. In this respect, voluntary codes of practice applied in a particular trade are highly relevant.

It is still possible to refer to the common law position. Sometimes this is difficult to state so that, for example, although the common law did refer to the owner being under an obligation to hire out goods of a reasonable fitness, the level of care associated with this obligation was uncertain, being mainly the product of *dictum* rather than decision. Indeed the Law Commission Working Paper No 77, *Implied Terms in Contracts for the Supply of Goods* (1977), recognised three possible approaches: first, the bailor is strictly liable (*Jones v Page* (1867) 15 LT 619 *per* Kelly CB at p 621); second, the goods must be as fit as care and skill can make them (*Hyman v Nye* (1881) 6 QBD 685 *per* Lindley J at p 682); third, the bailor is liable only if he fails to take reasonable care to ensure that the goods are fit which, as the *via media* of the two other approaches, was eventually adopted in s 9 of SGSA 1982.

Other implied terms seen in the context of hire include an obligation to deliver the goods in substantially the same condition as they were inspected by the hirer. In the case of hire purchase contracts, the supply of documentation including a log book or registration document, has been considered necessary (*Bentworth Finance Ltd v Lubert* [1968] 1 QB 680). The bailee's implied duties normally include not to convert the goods nor to deviate in the case of a carrier's obligation to follow his stipulated route. Different standards of care are applicable to the various types of bailment recognised in the seminal case of *Coggs v Barnard* (1703) 2 Ld Raym 909. The extent of the duties will normally be settled by agreement, as seen in the case of retention of title clauses discussed in Chapter 11.

Exclusion of liability and the unfairness doctrine in consumer contracts

Until the third quarter of the 20th Century the legislative control of clauses which sought to exclude liability in the field of sale of goods was rare although, in the supply context, it has existed since the Hire Purchase Act 1938. A major change was effected by s 3 of the Misrepresentation Act 1967, SOGIT 1973 and also UCTA 1977 which re-enacts and amends these earlier provisions controlling exemption clauses. At the same time there is legislation which specifically seeks to protect consumers, notably, the Consumer Protection Act 1987 (see Chapter 6). More recently, the EC Directive on Unfair Terms in Consumer Contracts (93/13/EEC) has been implemented in the Unfair Terms in Consumer Contracts Regulations 1994 (SI 1994 No 3159) and this deals with standard terms in contracts for the sale and supply of goods and services to consumers, the effect being that such terms do not bind the consumer if they are 'unfair'. As such, this is a significant departure and could amount to the development of a substantive good faith doctrine emerging in the sale and supply context. Indeed, the Continental civilian position is to require bargaining in good faith: the key issue is entering into negotiations upon which a relationship of trust and confidence comes into existence. Thus in a case like *Arcos Ltd v EA Ronaasen and Son* [1933] AC 470 the playing of the market would be considered to be an illegitimate election, that is, by entering into the contract the parties had locked themselves into a contractual regime of prices notwithstanding rising or falling markets.

The EC Directive on Unfair Terms in Consumer Contracts reinforces the bifurcation between consumer and commercial contracts and the significance of status. Indeed the pattern of English contract law in the 20th Century and the modern market-place contradicts the shibboleths of 19th Century contract orthodoxy insofar as this has reflected itself in developing canons of contract law, namely, freedom and sanctity of contract. The rise of consumerism has reflected itself in legislative demands for consumer protection, that is notice and pre-contract reliance, adjustment of the contract on the basis of consumer expectations and changing consumer circumstances. We shall now examine these principal legislative interventions as they impact upon sale and supply of goods.

The Unfair Contract Terms Act 1977

Far-reaching controls on attempts to exclude contractual and tortious liability were introduced by the UCTA 1977. Section 6 contains certain special provisions which relate to the statutory implied terms in contracts of sale, and s 7 (as amended by the SGSA 1982) contains analogous provisions with regard to other contracts for the transfer of goods. Section 7 provides:

—(1) Where the possession or ownership of goods passes under or in pursuance of a contract not governed by the law of sale of goods or hire-purchase, subsections (2) to (4) below apply as regards the effect (if any) to be given to contract terms excluding or restricting liability for breach of obligation arising by implication of law from the nature of the contract.

(2) As against a person dealing as consumer, liability in respect of the goods' correspondence with description or sample, or their quality or fitness for any particular purpose, cannot be excluded or restricted by reference to any such term.

(3) As against a person dealing otherwise than as consumer, that liability can be excluded or restricted by reference to such a term, but only in so far as the term satisfies the requirement of reasonableness.

[(3A) Liability for breach of the obligations arising under section 2 of the Supply of Goods and Services Act 1982 (implied terms about title, etc in certain contracts for the transfer of the property in goods) cannot be excluded or restricted by references to any such term.]

(4) Liability in respect of—

    (a)   the right to transfer ownership of the goods, or give possession; or

    (b)   the assurance of quiet possession to a person taking goods in pursuance of the contract;

cannot [(in a case to which subsection (3A) above does not apply)] be excluded or restricted by reference to any term except in so far as the term satisfies the requirement of reasonableness.

There can be no exclusion of the implied title undertaking, but this is somewhat misleading since it is possible under s 12 of the SGA to sell only a limited interest in the goods (see Chapter 7). The effect of s 7(2) and (3) is that the other implied terms cannot be excluded or restricted at all where the buyer deals as a consumer; they can be excluded outside of consumer supply transactions so long as the supplier can show that such an exclusion is fair and reasonable. Even so, product liability and dangerous goods are regulated by consumer protection legislation and cannot be limited or excluded by any contract terms, notice or other provision (see Chapter 6)

Dealing as consumer

Whether a person acts in the course of a business is a key element in establishing whether a person 'deals as consumer'. Section 12(1) of UCTA 1977 provides as follows:

> —(1) A party to a contract 'deals as consumer' in relation to another party if—
> (a) he neither makes the contract in the course of a business nor holds himself out as doing so; and
> (b) the other party does make the contract in the course of a business; and
> (c) in the case of a contract governed by the law of sale of goods or hire-purchase, or by section 7 of this Act, the goods passing under or in pursuance of the contract are of a type ordinarily supplied for private use or consumption.

The Court of Appeal in *R & B Custom Brokers Co Ltd v United Dominions Trust Ltd* [1988] 1 WLR 321, applied the criteria identified in cases under the Trade Descriptions Act 1968 including *Davies v Sumner* (1988) in resolving this question (see pp 49–53 above). It was held that a private company which was buying a car for a director did not acquire the vehicle 'in the course of a business'. The acquisition of a car for the private and business use of a director was not considered by both members of the Court of Appeal (Neill and Dillon LJJ) to be an integral part of the company's business. Furthermore, there was an insufficient degree of regularity to make the purchase of the car by the plaintiffs something which was done in the course of their business (compare *St Albans City and District Council v International Computers Ltd* (1994) *The Times 11 November*, which is discussed on pp 51–2).

The requirement that the goods must be of a type ordinarily supplied for private use or consumption is obviously problematic. This is illustrated by the facts in *R & B Customs Brokers* where a car can be used both for business and private use. It is surely a matter of degree whether the goods are 'ordinarily' supplied for private use, but s 12(3) of UCTA 1977 provides that the onus is upon the supplier to prove that the buyer is not a consumer. The two special cases in s 12(2) should also be noted, namely, a buyer is not to be treated as a consumer where he buys at auction and nor where the sale is by competitive tender. In the case of a commercial agent who sells on behalf of a consumer undisclosed principal, then the sale is made by the agent in the course of a business and will be fully regulated by the UCTA. It is unlikely that s 14(5) SGA affects the liability of an agent in this respect because this relates only to s 14 of *that* Act so the consequence would appear to be that the agent will be liable notwithstanding that he is acting for a private seller (see *Boyter v Thomson* [1995] 3 All ER 135 discussed at p 52)

Exemption clauses affected by the UCTA 1977

The UCTA not only limits clauses which purport expressly to exclude or restrict liability but also deals with clauses which have this effect, such as excluding a particular remedy, for example, set-off (*Stewart Gill Ltd v Horatio Myer and Co Ltd* [1992] QB 600) or alternatively imposing a short time period during which claims must be brought. In addition s 10 states that a term excluding or restricting liability which is contained in a separate contract rather than in the contract giving rise to the liability is ineffective insofar as it attempts to take away a right to enforce a liability which under the Act cannot be excluded or restricted. The Act will therefore apply where a term in a contract between a manufacturer of a product and a purchaser purports to affect the rights of the purchaser against the seller under the SGA 1979.

The ambit of the UCTA 1977 over exclusion clauses includes attempts to disclaim, by notice, liability in tort for negligence. Thus s 2(1) of UCTA 1977 nullifies contractual provisions and notices excluding or restricting liability for negligence resulting in death or injury. Where a party to a contract deals as consumer or on the other's written standard terms of business (*McCrone v Boots Farm Sales Ltd* (1981) SLT 103) that other cannot by reference to a contract term limit, exclude or restrict his liability (ss 3, 13(1) of UCTA 1977), and this applies to terms and notices (s 13(2) of UCTA 1977). In determining what is meant by 'written standard terms' it is not necessary that all the terms be fixed in advance. It is rather a question of the extent to which the original terms may be altered by the other party so that it can be considered a particularised or individual contract. As Scott-Baker J held in *St Albans City and District Council v International Computers Ltd* (1994):

> In the *Flamar Pride* [1990] 1 Lloyd's Rep 434, at p 438, Potter J concluded that where there were negotiations and a number of alterations were made to the defendant's standard terms so as to fit the particular circumstances of the plaintiff, the case fell outside the section. However, I do not take it that all terms have to be fixed in advance by the supplier. In many contracts there may be negotiations as to, for example, quality or price, but none as to the crucial exempting terms.

The UCTA also applies to product guarantees which attempt to exclude or restrict the consumer's rights. Section 5(1) of UCTA 1977 states:

> —(1) In the case of goods of a type ordinarily supplied for private use or consumption, where loss or damage—
>   (a) arises from the goods proving defective while in consumer use; and
>   (b) results from the negligence of a person concerned in the manufacture or distribution of the goods,
> liability for the loss or damage cannot be excluded or restricted by reference to any contract term or notice contained in or operating by reference to a guarantee of the goods.

A wide approach is taken here to 'defective goods' which covers design and production defects whilst 'loss or damage' extends beyond death or personal injury to all types of injury. Anything in writing is a guarantee if it 'contains or purports to contain some promise or assurance' (s 5(2)(*b*)).

The requirement of reasonableness

Part I of UCTA 1977 permits a party to restrict or exclude liability by reference to the requirement of reasonableness in the following cases:
  (a) negligent damage to property (s 2(2));
  (b) standard form contracts (s 3(2));
  (c) indemnity clauses (s 4(1));
  (d) implied terms in supply contracts (ss 6, 7);
  (e) misrepresentation (s 3 of Misrepresentation Act 1967, as amended by the UCTA 1977).
Except for criterion (a), the requirement of reasonableness can only be invoked outside a consumer context.

The reasonableness test is set out in s 11 with further guidelines provided in Sched 2 to UCTA 1977. Section 11(1) of the 1977 Act states:

> In relation to a contract term, the requirement of reasonableness for the purposes of this Part of this Act, section 3 of the Misrepresentation Act 1967 and section 3 of the Misrepresentation Act (Northern Ireland) 1967 is that the term shall have been a fair and reasonable one to be included having regard to the circumstances which were, or ought reasonably to have been, known to or in the contemplation of the parties when the contract was made.

The onus lies on the party relying on the exclusion clause to show that it is reasonable (s 11(5)).

The requirement of reasonableness is determined at the time of contracting, which is an important difference from the 1973 Act. Under the SOGIT 1973, the test of reasonableness was to be applied taking account of all the circumstances including those which occurred after the making of the contract, whereas under the UCTA 1977, the test is to be applied to the terms of the contract at the *time* of contracting. In this respect, s 11(4) provides that where an exclusion clause seeks to restrict liability, regard should be had to the availability of resources and insurance to meet the liability. Of great practical importance is s 11(5) which provides that the onus is upon the party who claims that an exclusion clause is reasonable, to satisfy the court that it was. So in *Walker v Boyle* [1982] 1 WLR 495, for example, a clause was held unreasonable, although Dillon J listed no reasons why this was so.

Some guidance as to the requirement of reasonableness has emerged from the House of Lords in *George Mitchell (Chesterhall) Ltd v Finney Lock Seeds Ltd* (1983) (the facts of which are set out in Chapter 4). Care should be taken here because it was the wording of the SOGIT 1973 which was considered, and although this is substantially similar to the 1977 Act, it differs in some respects. Hence the 1973 Act provides that exclusion clauses are void 'to the extent that' they did not comply with reasonableness, whereas, under the UCTA 1977, a term shall not be effective 'except *in so far* as the term satisfies the requirement of reasonableness'. Although the House of Lords did not give a concluded opinion, the inclination of the judgments was that the court could not use the test to limit a plaintiff to a proportion of his losses. It would seem that the change made under the UCTA 1977 does not affect this point. A second guideline which emerges from this decision is that the application of the reasonableness test is not merely the exercise of a discretion, but is a decision. Accordingly, a first instance decision will only be reversed on appeal if it proceeded on some erroneous principle or was plainly and obviously wrong. Given this approach, it is likely that inconsistency will continue to be a feature of cases decided under the reasonableness test of the UCTA.

The 1977 Act also deals with clauses exempting a party to a contract from liability for misrepresentation. Under s 8 of UCTA 1977, s 3 of the Misrepresentation Act 1967 is replaced by the following:

3—If a contract contains a term which would exclude or restrict—
  (*a*) any liability to which a party to a contract may be subject by reason of any misrepresentation made by him before the contract was made; or
  (*b*) any remedy available to another party to the contract by reason of such a misrepresentation,
that term shall be of no effect except in so far as it satisfies the requirement of reasonableness as stated in s 11(1) of the Unfair Contract Terms Act 1977; and it is for those claiming that the term satisfies that requirement to show that it does.

No guidelines are given for the interpretation of s 8 except that the term to be included must have been a fair and reasonable one having regard to the circumstances which were, or ought reasonably to have been, known to or in the contemplation of, the parties when the contract was made (s 11(1)). In *Howard Marine and Dredging Co Ltd v A Ogden and Sons (Excavations) Ltd* [1978] QB 574, a case decided under s 3 of the 1967 Act, Lord Denning considered the following factors to be relevant: the parties were of equal bargaining position, the representation made was innocent, and in any case the plaintiffs had failed to prove that they had reasonable grounds for believing the truth of the statement.

The question of reasonableness is determined as between the actual parties. Hence in *South Western General Property Company Ltd v Marton* (1982) 263 EG 1090, a clause in an auctioneer's catalogue attempting to avoid the effects of the Misrepresentation Act 1967 was held unreasonable. The other party was a builder who bought a plot of land at auction to build a house for himself and his family. He had obtained the auctioneer's catalogue only a day before the sale and the purported effect of the clause was to relieve the sellers from telling more than a part of the material facts, thereby obliging the buyer to check the remainder for himself. There are suggestions in the judgment that the decision would have been otherwise had the buyer been a property speculator. This allows a court to adjust its decision according to the other party involved. Such a phenomenon may be illustrated further by the facts in *Phillips Products v Hamstead Plant Hire* (1985) 4 TrL 98, which involved the hire of a crane and driver. As a consequence of the driver's negligence, damage was caused to the plaintiff's factory, but the conditions of hire excluded such liability. This exclusion clause was considered to be unreasonable on the basis of the following factors. First, the hire period was short and the plaintiffs therefore had little time to arrange insurance. Second, the plaintiffs were not regular hirers of such equipment. The result might have been otherwise had the hirers received previous notice of their obligation to insure which, of course, invites scrutiny of the issue relating to incorporation of terms (see *Olley v Marlborough Court* [1949] 1 KB 532). The House of Lords in *Smith v Eric S Bush* [1990] 1 AC 831 held that a term purporting to exclude liability for negligent house surveys did not satisfy the test of reasonableness. The principal factors were that the houses were fairly cheap, so that it was not reasonable to expect the buyers to commission their own structural surveys, and that the surveyors could easily have insured against the risk without severely affecting their charging structure. At the same time, however, the House of Lords indicated that a disclaimer might be reasonable if the survey task was a difficult one and that the value of the house was substantial with the result that insurance against professional liability was either unavailable or very expensive.

A clause that is otherwise unreasonable will not necessarily be saved because it is a clause of long standing in a widely-used standard form. Nonetheless, a standard form drafted by both parties or by bodies representing both parties is more likely to be considered reasonable. Thus in *RW Green Ltd v Cade Bros Farms* [1978] 1 Lloyd's Rep 602, a clause in a contract used for many years, with the approval of bodies representing both sides, was held to be reasonable. On the other hand in *Walker v Boyle* [1982] 1 WLR 495, one of the National Conditions of Sale (19th edn) which were not drafted by bodies representative of all parties, was held unreasonable.

Some propositions do emerge from the case law. First, the court will take into consideration the whole of the exclusion clause in determining the question of reasonableness. The rationale here is that s 11(1) states that the time for assessing the reasonableness of the clause is the time at which the contract is made and at this point it will not be known which part of it will be relied upon by the defendant. Second, the courts do not have the power to sever the unreasonable parts of an exclusion clause leaving the reasonable parts in force (see *Stewart Gill Ltd v Horatio Myer and Co Ltd* [1992] QB 600). The significance of this for drafting exclusion clauses is clear—the different elements of the clause should be set out in sub-clauses so that a failure of one part will not invalidate the clause as a whole.

Statutory guidelines

Supplementary guidelines to the reasonableness test are included in Sched 2 to the 1977 Act. These guidelines are similar to those in the original 1973 Act and apply to sale and supply contracts by virtue of s 11(2) of UCTA 1977. Even so, the guidelines have been used in other cases as factors to be considered where the statute applies (see *Woodman v Photo Trade Processing Ltd* reported by

Lawson in (1981) 131 NLJ 933, at p 935). These guidelines, although not exhaustive of the factors to be considered, include the following:

(a) the strength of the bargaining positions of the parties relative to each other, taking into account (among other things) alternative means by which the customer's requirements could have been met;

(b) whether the customer received an inducement to agree to the term, or in accepting it had an opportunity of entering into a similar contract with other persons, but without having to accept a similar term;

(c) whether the customer knew or ought reasonably to have known of the existence and extent of the term (having regard, among other things, to any custom of the trade and any previous course of dealing between the parties);

(d) where the term excludes or restricts any relevant liability if some condition is not complied with, whether it was reasonable at the time of the contract to expect that compliance with that condition would be practicable;

(e) whether the goods were manufactured, processed or adapted to the special order of the customer.

If one party freely consents to a clause, a court is unlikely to hold it unreasonable. Paragraphs (a)–(c) and perhaps (d) of Sched 2 reflect this fact. Clearly a pertinent factor in the determination of the free consent issue, is whether one party has exercised superior bargaining strength to impose terms on the other. The central theme of the House of Lords decision in *Photo Production Ltd v Securicor Transport Ltd* [1980] AC 827, is that the parties' arrangements will stand if there is no inequality. In this respect, alternative courses of action available to the party will be relevant. Thus in *RW Green Ltd v Cade Bros Farms* (1978), farmers bought seed potatoes under a contract which limited the supplier's liability to the cost of the seed. Nonetheless, the farmers could have bought at a slightly higher price certified seed, which, being certified, was less likely to be suffering from the virus affecting the seed actually bought.

Only genuine alternative courses of action available will be relevant to the reasonableness question. This is illustrated in *Woodman v Photo Trade Processing Ltd* (1981) where insurance was said not to be a suitable alternative to cover the loss of a precious film. What was needed was a guarantee that extra care would be taken not to lose the film. Insurance is only mentioned in UCTA 1977 (s 11(4)(b)) with regard to clauses which seek to restrict liability to a specified sum. In this respect the court, in holding a clause unreasonable, has pointed to the facts that a seed merchant, seeking to rely on the clause, could have insured against the risk of crop failure caused by supplying the wrong variety of seed, and that such insurance would not materially have increased the price of the seed (see *George Mitchell (Chesterhall) Ltd v Finney Lock Seeds Ltd* [1983] 2 AC 803).

The criteria identified in Sched 2 operate within the normal principles of incorporation of exclusion clauses under the common law. Under Sched 2, para (c), a clause is more likely to be held reasonable if the party knew or should have known of it when he entered into the contract. A distinction should be drawn here with the reasonableness of a clause which is the main test under UCTA 1977. The wider the purported exclusion, the more likely it is to be held unreasonable. In *Rasbora Ltd v JCL Marine* [1976] 2 Lloyd's Rep 645, which was a case decided under SOGIT 1973, the builders of a power boat purported to exclude liability for breach of s 14 of SGA 1979. The only undertaking made was to repair or replace defective parts as a result of the use of faulty materials or of faulty workmanship. Obviously, this undertaking was of no use when, as happened, the boat caught fire and sank. In such a case, Lawson J held that the sale was a consumer sale so that the exclusion clause was void insofar as it excluded the implied conditions under the SGA 1979. However, he went on to say that even if the sale had not been a consumer sale, the exclusion clause was unreasonable since the buyer would be left with no remedy insofar as it purported to exclude the merchantability provision.

In *St Albans and District Council v International Computers Ltd* (1994) *The Times*, 11 November, (the facts are discussed on pp 51–2), Scott-Baker J considered s 11 and Sched 2 of UCTA as well as the House of Lords authorities in *George Mitchell (Chesterhall) Ltd* (1983) and *Smith v Eric S Bush* (1990) and concluded that the determining factors pointing to the unreasonableness of the clause on the facts were:

(1) The parties were of unequal bargaining power. This was so notwithstanding the fact that the local authority had received independent advice;

(2) The defendants had not justified the limitation figure of £100,000 which was small, both in relation to the potential risk and the absolute loss;

(3) The defendants were insured. Computer software is a product which carries a significant risk in terms of consequences. In considering the issue of reasonableness it is normal to relate the question of insurance cover to the contract price. However, given the risks involved in developing software it is almost inevitable that the defendant would have had to pay more for insurance cover and this would have had to have been passed on to the customer;

(4) The practical consequences: As a matter of principle, Scott-Baker J considered that the loss should fall on ICL since they were best placed to insure: 'I think that he who makes the profit should carry the risk'. An analogy was drawn here with *Smith v Bush* (1990) but there the question was one of the reasonableness of a disclaimer of liability by a surveyor who had negligently valued a 'modest house' and Lord Griffiths held (at p 858):

> Bearing the loss will be unlikely to cause significant hardship if it has to be borne by the surveyor, but it is on the other hand quite possible that it will be a financial catastrophe for the purchaser who may be left with a valueless house and no money to buy another.

This was surely not the case in *St Albans* as the local authority's position was not that of an ordinary consumer. Moreover, the concept of profit maker and risk assumption is not symbiotic as it ignores the idea of a bargain.

Limited contracting-out: Warnings and modifications of description

It may still be possible to contract out of the implied obligations owed under supply contracts. In this respect, s 6 of UCTA 1977 provides that liability for breach of the obligation arising under the implied terms, cannot be excluded or restricted by 'reference to any contract term'. This provision has a narrow ambit and it does not prevent a supplier attempting to shrink the core of the obligations, rather than excluding the implied terms. Thus, for example, the seller may argue that a sale is not by description but is rather a contract for the sale of a specific unique chattel. In *Cavendish-Woodhouse Ltd v Manley* (1984) 82 LGR 376 a clause in an order for furniture specified 'bought as seen', and the Divisional Court held that the words did not purport to exclude liability but merely indicated that the buyer had seen the goods which he had bought (compare *Hughes v Hall* [1981] RTR 430). Even so in the old case of *Shepherd v Kain* (1821) 5 B & Ald 240 which involved the role of a vessel described as 'copper-fastened' and 'with all faults, without allowance for any defect whatsover,' it was held that such a clause did not protect the supplier where the vessel was not in fact copper-fastened because the 'with all faults' provision had to be read consistently with the description of the vessel as copper-fastened. Nevertheless, a seller may state expressly that he is not an expert and no reliance should be placed upon any opinion he expresses (see *Harlingdon and Leinster Enterprises* (1990) discussed earlier). Similarly with regard to misrepresentations made, it was held in *Overbrooke Estates Ltd v Glencombe Properties Ltd* [1974] 1 WLR 1335 (followed by the Court of Appeal in *Collins v Howell-Jones* (1980) 259 EG 331), that a clause limiting the authority of auctioneers and the firm's employees to make or give representations or warranties, fell outside the scope of the original version of s 3 of the Misrepresentation Act 1967, since it was a *limitation on the apparent authority* of the auctioneers rather than an exemption clause.

A fine balance has to be achieved between the definition of obligations and exclusion of liability. In *Smith v Eric S Bush* (1990), the House of Lords held that a clause purporting to exclude responsibility for negligence on the part of the valuer of a house was subject to the reasonableness test. The decision was based on s 13(1) UCTA and the position taken by the court was that but for the term purporting to exclude a duty of care such a duty would have existed. However, it is unlikely that the 'but for' test would apply in the SGA context because in determining the particular purpose for which goods are bought a warning must be taken into account. A seller of goods may expressly warn the buyer not to use the goods for a specified purpose so that any implied term of fitness for purpose would be negatived. There is an increasing trend to restrict liability by reference to labelling and the insertion of instructions for use. The general approach of the UCTA 1977 relating to contractual liability is confined to contractual terms and it is, therefore, desirable that instructions and labels should be regarded as terms if they are to be controlled by UCTA 1977. Nevertheless, s 13 also covers 'notices' which exclude or restrict the relevant duty. 'Notice' is defined in s 14 as including 'an announcement, whether or not in writing, and any other communication or pretended communication'. This is a wide definition which should cover pre-contractual labels or post-contractual instructions included, for example, in sealed goods. Failing this, if a consumer buyer is effectively denied the protection of the implied terms because the instructions or labels have shrunk the central obligations, recourse will have to be made to the common law rules on incorporation and the general controls of reasonableness found in ss 2 and 3 of UCTA 1977. In any case such a term may be *prima facie* an unfair term and would be regulated by the Unfair Terms in Consumer Contracts Regulations 1994 (see pp 83–90).

The application of the UCTA to contracts of supply

The structure of supply contracts, especially finance leasing arrangements, poses specific problems in the application of the UCTA. This phenomenon can be illustrated in *W Photoprint Ltd v Forward Trust Group Ltd* [1993] 12 Tr L 146. In this case, the parties over a period of years had made over 80 hire purchase or leasing agreements with each other in relation to all types of goods and equipment for Photoprint's business. As such, the defendant had provided the plaintiff with a financial facility up to a certain limit. The equipment was never supplied directly by the defendant who would customarily buy them from a supplier and then lease them or make a hire purchase contract with the plaintiff. In 1988, the plaintiff company decided that it needed a new processor. The operations director learnt from the second defendants that they would soon be marketing a new advanced type of processor. In view of the enhanced capabilities of the processor and the satisfactory experience with the processors supplied by the second defendants, he decided that the processor on offer was an obvious choice. He relied solely on a brochure supplied by and telephone conversations with them the second defendants, whose representative informed him that he had not seen the machine either and was relying on American colleagues for his information.

The plaintiff company ordered the processor and entered into a hire purchase agreement with the first defendants. The machine never worked satisfactorily and it was accepted that it was not of merchantable quality and not reasonably fit for the purpose for which it was required. The plaintiff company purported to terminate the agreement on this basis, the processor was removed by the second defendants who returned the price to the first defendants, who in turn subsequently credited the plaintiff company with the same amount. The plaintiff company's claim was for substantial consequential losses. The first defendants sought to rely on a clause in the hire purchase agreement as being reasonable and effectively excluding any such liability.

The plaintiff had signed the relevant agreement with Forward Trust adjacent to a statement to the effect that the terms and conditions had been read, and that attention had been drawn to the exclusion clause. This provided as follows:

> 5(a) Where the customer deals as a consumer as defined by s 12 of the Unfair Contract Terms Act 1977 or in Scotland this agreement is a consumer contract as defined in s 25 of that Act then:

(i) Forward does not let the goods subject to any undertaking express or implied statutory or otherwise (subject always where applicable to the requirement of reasonableness imposed by the 1977 Act) save those implied by ss 5 to 11 of the Supply of Goods (Implied Terms) Act 1973 (as to the title to quality and fitness of the goods and their conformity with description and sample).

(ii) It is hereby declared that nothing in this agreement and in particular the preceding paragraphs of this subclause shall affect the statutory rights of the customers under the said ss 5 to 11 of the 1977 Act.

(b) Where the customer does not deal as a consumer within the definition in the said s 12 of the 1977 Act or in Scotland the agreement is not a consumer contract within the definition in the said s 25 of the 1977 Act:

(i) The customer declares that he has examined the goods and that they are in every respect satisfactory and suitable for the purpose for which they are required and that he had relied on his own skill and judgment in choosing the goods.

(ii) That subject to ss 3, 5 and 11 in England and ss 17, 21 and 24 in Scotland of the 1977 Act relating to the requirement of reasonableness Forward does not let the goods subject to any undertaking express or implied whether statutory or otherwise save the condition as to title to the goods implied by s 5 of the said Act.

The agreement was subject to s 10(2) of the SOGIT 1973 implying a condition of merchantable quality. In addition it was on written standard terms and therefore fell within the provision of s 3(1) UCTA. Nevertheless the defendant argued, relying on the exclusion clause, that the goods were not let 'subject to any undertaking express or implied whether statutory or otherwise' and that s 10 never became any part of its contractual obligations because the exclusion clause defined the extent of the liability that it was assuming.

This argument was not specifically addressed by the plaintiffs and as a matter of principle it is difficult to maintain, since the obligation is already imposed by the 1973 Act and it is inconsistent with this statutory obligation that it should be excluded. More recently in *Lease Management Services Ltd v Purnell Secretarial Services* (1994) Tr LR 337, CA, a clause purporting to exclude liability of a finance house 'in respect of any condition, warranty or representation relating to the suitability or fitness of the equipment for any purpose for which it may be required' was rejected. The purpose of the defendant acquiring the goods (a photocopier) was to produce paper plates. This was a fundamental term in the contract and the exclusion clause would have enabled the plaintiff to disregard any express warranty made. The Court of Appeal rejected the general proposition that an exclusion clause will be reasonable in a hire or hire purchase contract where the finance company does not inspect the goods or participate in antecedent negotiations.

Examination of the goods and estoppel

It was acknowledged in the *Photoprint* case that the plaintiff had not examined the goods even though they had signed an undertaking to this effect. In *Lowe v Lombank* [1960] 1 WLR 196 a similar clause was held not to have raised an estoppel but even if it did, Forward Trust would have been precluded from relying upon this by virtue of the rule that estoppel cannot be invoked to deprive a party of his statutory rights (*Campbell Discount Ltd v Gall* [1961] 2 All ER 104).

The reasonableness provision

It was held in this case that the clause which was made expressly subject to the requirement of reasonableness was not uncertain on the basis that, as a matter of law, it either applied or it did not. DB Johnson, QC, sitting as a Deputy High Court Judge, distinguished with *Davies v Davies* [1887] 36 Ch D 359 in the following terms:

> In my judgment, the clause is not uncertain. *Davies v Davies* does not assist the plaintiff and is plainly distinguishable. The plaintiff in that case was in a dilemma. If the covenant concerned was construed as an absolute restriction then it was undoubtedly void because it amounted to an absolute restraint of trade. If on the other hand, and in order to avoid that consequence, it was argued that the covenant was not absolute but only 'so far as the law allows', then it was too uncertain . . . By contrast the second and third lines of the clause (commencing 'Forward does not let') constitute an exclusion which is not itself void. The provision subject to which it is stated to operate is simply a statement of the law which would in any case be applied in order to decide whether the exclusion stands or fails. I do not regard the exclusion in the clause as ambiguous. . . .

In addition there was no question that the clause had been incorporated into the contract because the plaintiff had signed the agreement alongside the clause drawing attention to the disputed clause.

The application of the reasonable test

In applying the reasonableness test in respect of the guidelines in Sched 2, the following factors emerged in this case:

1. The plaintiff would have been able to enter a similar contract with another party without the disputed term. But if the plaintiff had asked for the exclusion clause to be removed it was probable that Forward Trust would have acceded provided that the plaintiff paid for the insurance needed to cover Forward Trust's exposure to risk.
2. The plaintiff had chosen the machine.
3. The plaintiff was very familiar with hire purchase and leasing arrangements; this was not a case of the plaintiff being sent by the supplier to a captive finance company.
4. The plaintiff could have financed the acquisition of the machine in other ways.
5. Whilst as a matter of fact the machine required a two-weeks' settling in period for it to be assessed, the argument of the plaintiff that it was unfair to allow Forward Trust to exclude liability when the plaintiff itself could not assess the machine was dismissed on the basis that this problem was not in the contemplation of the parties when the contract was made. Further, there was the declaration in the contract that the plaintiffs had examined the machine and found it satisfactory and they

had relied on their own skill and judgment. It was held that Forward Trust had satisfied the burden of proof placed on them and had shown that the exclusion clause was a fair and reasonable one.

Criminal use of ineffective exemption clauses

Under the Consumer Transactions (Restrictions on Statements) Order 1976 (SI 1976 No 1813) enacted under the Fair Trading Act 1973, it is a criminal offence for anyone, in the course of a business, to display or publish or include in a written document, an exemption clause which is void by virtue of s 6 of UCTA 1977. However, it should be noted that s 6 itself does not render an exemption clause void as against a consumer unless the clause, as a matter of interpretation, purports to exclude or limit liability under ss 13–15 of SGA 1979 (see *Hughes v Hall* [1981] RTR 430).

The Unfair Terms in Consumer Contracts Regulations 1994

The Unfair Terms in Consumer Contracts Directive was adopted by the European Union on 5 April 1993 (OJ 1993 L95/29). The implementation of the Directive in the UK was accompanied by two consultation papers (see *Implementation of the EC Directive on Unfair Terms in Consumer Contracts (93/13/EEC): A Consultative Document* (DTI, October 1993) and *Implementation of the EC Directive on Unfair Terms in Consumer Contracts (93/13/EC): A Further Consultation Document* (DTI, September 1994). The mischief of the new legislation is to protect consumers within the European Union and is viewed as a necessary element in the creation of the internal market. The theory is that such legislation stimulates inter-Member State consumer transaction by increasing consumer confidence, and also assists suppliers in their task of selling goods and supplying services through the harmonisation of the law.

The Directive has been introduced by statutory instrument (SI 1994 No 3159) leaving the UCTA untouched. This saved on parliamentary time and also the risk of failing to integrate the new measure fully with the preceding law. It was argued that the UCTA and the Directive should be aligned by introducing a common test of fairness but this was not pursued, because the two tests are not the same and nor is the nature of the contractual terms which they cover. In particular, the Directive regulates only terms in consumer contracts and is not limited to exclusion contracts, whilst the UCTA deals mainly with exclusion clauses and does extend to contracts other than non-negotiated consumer contracts.

Scope of the Regulations

They are limited to contracts between a consumer and a seller or supplier of goods or services. The preamble of the Directive explains that its scope does not include *inter alia* contracts of employment, contracts relating to succession rights, contracts relating to rights under family law and contracts relating to the incorporation and organisation of companies or partnership agreements. Contracts regulated by international conventions are also excluded, by virtue of Article 1(2). Notwithstanding these exclusions, the Directive is still broader in scope than the UCTA with respect to contracts which create or transfer an interest in land, contracts involving the transfer of securities and also contracts of insurance.

Seller and supplier

Regulation 2(1) defines a 'seller' as a 'person who sells goods' and 'supplier' as a 'person who supplies goods or services' and 'in making a contract to which these Regulations apply, is acting for purposes relating to his business.'

Consumer

This is defined in reg 2(1) to mean a 'natural person who, in making a contract to which these Regulations apply, is acting for purposes which are outside his business'. This is a more expansive definition than that seen under the UCTA since it extends protection to small business persons for activities which are incidental to their business. It would follow from this that a farmer buying a fire extinguisher for his business would be covered. Furthermore, the fact that the consumer is a buyer by auction or by competitive tender is irrelevant for the purposes of the Regulations, unlike the UCTA definitions.

Terms not individually negotiated

The Regulations apply only to terms which have not been individually negotiated, the rationale for this as set out in reg 3(3) being that the consumer is unable to influence the substance of such a term. In theory it may be possible to differentiate sharply between terms which have and terms which have not been individually negotiated but in practice the delineation may not be so easy. However, a substance test is included, notably, where part of a term or an entire term had been individually negotiated the application of the Directive to the rest of the contract shall not be excluded, if, on an overall assessment of the contract, it appears that it is a pre-formulated standard contract. But what happens if the supplier offers alternatives from a pool of standard terms? It could be argued that although these terms have been pre-drafted as a mechanism for cutting down transactional costs, nonetheless they have been individually negotiated in the sense that they have been selected by the consumer. In this context the burden of proof is crucial, and by virtue of reg 3(5) the seller/supplier who relies upon the argument that a standard term has been individually negotiated has to prove that this is the case.

Unfairness and good faith

In determining what is an 'unfair term' the requirement of 'good faith' is crucial and is expressly provided for in reg 4. It is important to distinguish carefully between the common law position and that provided for in the Regulations.

Good faith and the common law

The House of Lords has recently rejected any concept of good faith as a specific requirement in negotiating a contract. As Lord Ackner put it in *Walford v Miles* [1992] 1 All ER 453 at 460–1:

> The concept of a duty to carry on negotiations in good faith is inherently repugnant to the adversarial position of the parties when involved in negotiations. Each party to the negotiations is entitled to pursue his (or her) own interest, so long as he avoids making misrepresentations . . .

The approach of English law has been to resort to technicalities such as the doctrine of consideration in dealing with bad faith, for example the opportunistic re-negotiation taking an unfair advantage of a hard-pressed builder seen in *D and C Builders Ltd v Rees* [1966] 2 QB 617. On other occasions the courts have ignored the doctrine such as in the famous Court of Appeal decision in *Williams v Roffey and Nicholls (Contractors) Ltd* [1991] 1 QB 1; although economic duress was not formally argued in this case there is no doubt that this was a factor in the overall judgments, given that the subcontractor had got into financial difficulty principally because the contract was underpriced.

English law has developed principles in relation to deceit and misrepresentation but the conventional rule is that disclosure is unnecessary because it goes to the issue of protecting commercial self interest (see *Bank of Nova Scotia v Hellenic Mutual War Risks Association (Bermuda) Ltd: The Good Luck* [1991] 3 All ER 1). At the same time the courts will have reference to established principles, particularly the rules of incorporation to deal with bad faith silence, so that in *Interfoto Picture Library Ltd v Stiletto Visual Programmes Ltd* [1989] QB 433, Bingham MR referred colloquially to the need for 'putting one's cards face upwards on the table' where the issue related to the disclosure of extortionate standard form provisions as they related to the late return of photographs.

Good faith and the Regulations:

In determining this the preamble of the Directive, which is reproduced in Sched 2 to the Regulations, states:

> [I]n making an assessment of good faith, particular regard should be had to the strength of the bargaining positions of the parties, whether the consumer had an inducement to agree to the term and whether goods or services were sold or supplied to the special order of the consumer. . . . the requirement of good faith may be satisfied by the seller or supplier where he deals fairly and equitably with the other party whose legitimate interests he has to take into account.

There are some familiar concepts here—the strength of the bargaining positions of the parties (Sched 2, para (a), UCTA), the issue of inducement offered to the consumer (Sched 2, para (b), UCTA) and whether the goods are made to the special order of the consumer (Sched 2, para (c), UCTA). Whilst there is no specific reference to reasonableness as part of the general concept of good faith, nevertheless the preamble does refer to good faith as involving an overall evaluation of the different interests involved.

The balancing issue is at the heart of the unfairness concept so that reg 4(1) refers to 'significant imbalance in the parties' rights and obligations under the contract to the detriment of the consumer'. This phrase lacks precision as it assumes that there is parity between contracts and that this is the norm. The difficulty is that whilst there may be significant imbalance this does not necessarily make the contract unreasonable. However, there is no concept of a duty to trade fairly, as the Regulations are not concerned with unfairness arising out of the mere difference in bargaining strength—it is the abuse of this power which has been targeted. In determining what is meant by 'significant imbalance', reg 4(2) refers to 'the nature of the goods or service for which the contract was concluded' (typically new or secondhand goods) and also the surrounding circumstances. The broad context of bargain is maintained and a result not far distant from that arrived at using the more familiar English concept of reasonableness is achieved.

Price and subject matter

Regulation 3(2) provides that whilst terms which directly describe the main subject matter of the contract or the price/ratio quality are not subject to the test of fairness, they are subject to the requirement of intelligibility and therefore will be relevant in making an overall assessment of the fairness of the terms (see worked example (L) in Sched 3).

The plain language provision

Regulation 6 provides that terms offered to consumers in writing must always be expressed in 'plain, intelligible language' and that clauses will be read *contra proferentem*. The burden of proof rests upon sellers and suppliers as to the issue of intelligibility and the interpretation most favourable to the consumer will prevail. This provision will impact upon the development of the fundamental breach doctrine in the wake of *Photo Production v Securicor Transport* [1980] AC 827 by resurrecting the *contra proferentem* approach to exclusion clauses (see *Hollier v Rambler Motors AMC Ltd* [1972] 2 QB 71). In addition the use of plain intelligible language goes to the issue of notice. Under UCTA obscure clauses are, in any case, policed by the concept of reasonableness, whilst in contracts of sale of goods Sched 2 expressly instructs the courts to take into account whether the customer knew or ought to have known of the existence and the extent of the exclusion clause.

Unfair Terms; the indicative list

As we have seen, Sched 2 of the Regulations lists four indicia in making an assessment of good faith. Schedule 3, which implements the Annex in the Directive, contains a list of 17 types of terms which are held to be unfair if they have certain objects or effects. What we have here is an attempt at compromise between the *method* of civil and common law—the latter tends to use a broad test applied in each case whereas the former tends to more finite rules. Even so from a common law perspective the structure is not alien, because ss 6 and 7 of the UCTA list types of contracts where obligations cannot be excluded, whereas in other types of contract the criterion of reasonableness applies. In any case the Annex is not prescriptive, it is merely indicative, a 'list of the terms which may be regarded as unfair' (reg 4(4)). It is a grey list and is by definition non-exhaustive. The preamble to the Directive states:

> . . . for the purposes of this Directive, the annexed list of terms can be of indicative value only and, because of the cause of the minimal character of the Directive, the scope of these terms may be the subject of amplification or more restrictive editing by the Member States in their national laws.

The Annex is a valuable guide to practitioners as to the types of contractual terms that are likely to be deemed to be unfair. Many are in any case included in the UCTA, for example, excluding or limiting liability for death or personal injury, inappropriately relying upon limitation clauses which purport to restrict or exclude the consumer's legal rights if the supplier fails to satisfy their contractual obligation. A worked Example in Annex (b) has already been recognised in the UCTA, where a right of set-off was considered to be an exclusion of liability so that under the Directive the seller or supplier should not, in appropriate cases, be able to contract out of the consumer's right to set off debts owed by the seller or supplier against any claim that the consumer may have against that party. Other examples include permitting retention of deposits in the event of default or penalty clauses, that is, requiring any consumer who defaults to pay 'a disproportionately high sum in compensation'. This should be read in the context of Example (f) in the Annex which refers to unilateral dissolution and retention of sums provisions, typically where in a contract of hire the supplier can dissolve the contract at any time but the consumer must guarantee a fixed term. It would appear therefore that a seller or supplier will only be allowed to rely upon such terms where the contract provides the consumer with an identical right to dissolve the contract on a discretionary basis. Somewhat curiously, while provision is made for clauses which permit the seller to retain sums paid for services not yet supplied by him, no provision is made for the return of sums paid for associated goods that have not been supplied to the consumer.

Other examples in the Annex refer to the need for reasonable notice periods for termination in contracts of indeterminate duration unless there are serious grounds for termination, but no examples of this are provided. One significant innovation relates to unilateral extension of fixed duration contracts, typically, hire contracts. It would appear from this that the supplier must remind the consumer of his right to non-renewal of the hire contract, and the Directive introduces a test of fairness into the renewal period and also into the time given under the contract for the customer to make up his mind whether to renew.

The most important indicative term of unfairness in the Directive relates to unseen terms, so that Example (i) provides that the consumer must have a 'real opportunity of becoming acquainted' with the terms of the contract. It may be inferred, therefore, that the consumer must be afforded a realistic chance of understanding the implications of what he is binding himself to and, of course, this goes to the intelligibility of the terms. As a matter of tactics in complex contractual scenarios, time and date stamping of (typically) the application form and then of the contractual terms should give some protection and act as evidence of the opportunity provided to the consumer to become acquainted with the terms of the contract. A cooling-off period in complex contracts may therefore be advisable even where it is not a statutory requirement.

The Annex also highlights high-handed contractual provisions which attempt to impose terms unilaterally upon consumers. Presumably what is envisaged is that in the drafting of consumer contracts sellers and suppliers will have to identify in advance any reasons for unilateral alteration. Paragraph 2(b) of the Annex allows a seller or supplier contractually to reserve the right unilaterally to alter the conditions of contracts which are of indeterminate duration, so long as the seller or supplier provides reasonable notice to the consumer, but this is not defined.

While the price/ratio is not governed by the test of fairness in the Annex there is a prohibition of unilateral price imposition, which at least initially will be viewed as unfair where the consumer is not given the corresponding right to cancel the contract. The onus is upon the vendor to show that it was fair to pass the price increases on to the consumer. In many cases this will be a difficult burden to discharge, especially when the contracting consumer is of the opinion that he or she had a fixed-price contract. While there is a prohibition on determining the price of goods at the time of delivery in para 1, this does not apply to the provision of services to the consumer. This limitation takes account of the fact that it is difficult to price services adequately prior to the service being provided. Paragraph 1 does not apply to any clause which allows price indexation, provided that the method of indexation is precisely described.

Allowing for exclusive interpretation rights which give the seller or supplier the right to determine whether the goods or services supplied are in conformity with the contract, is deemed to be *prima facie* unfair. Furthermore, where agents are used, whether self-employed agents or employed agents, the principal will be no longer be able to plead lack of capacity or authority by his or her agent. The position of consumers is also strengthened by outlawing clauses which purport to give all the rights under the contract to the seller or supplier with no corresponding obligations, or alternatively those which try to restrict the legal remedies available. There is also an attempt to govern assignment clauses but sensibly these are not prohibited except insofar as the assignment to a third party reduces the guarantees enjoyed by the contracting consumer, unless the latter consents to this. Example (q) is concerned with clauses which confine the consumer's remedy to arbitration. This is already substantially regulated by the Consumer Arbitration Agreements Act 1988.

It should be emphasised that the Directive's Annex of unfair terms is of indicative value only. Furthermore, many of the terms specified in the Annex need not be considered unfair in themselves but may be permitted with adequate notice. The effect of the Annex is to control those terms which permit unilateral actions on the part of the seller or supplier and upon those clauses which purport to limit the rights of consumers.

Remedies and enforcement

Regulation 5(1) provides that an unfair term in a contract concluded with a consumer by a seller or supplier shall not be binding on the consumer. Regulation 5(2) states that the contract shall continue to bind the parties provided that is is capable of continuing in existence without the unfair terms. This is an issue of severance and the applicability of the blue pencil test. It is foreseeable that there will be some incongruity here especially where, for example, a standard form has been challenged by an appropriate organisation but an individual opts to continue with the contract.

Regulation 7 is an important safeguard in that it provides that an EC consumer does not lose protection simply because of a choice of law clause making the applicable law that of a non-EC state.

Who enforces?

The Director General of Fair Trading can take action under reg 8 against an allegedly unfair contract term in general use. The logic of confining *locus standi* here is that the Director General is supposed to balance the interests of business against the interests of consumers in exercising his powers—he is less likely to pursue an aggressive attack on business than a consumer organisation, which reduces the risk of inappropriate and expensive litigation for businesses. The general functions of the Director General are preventative and supervisory, whereas reg 4 is designed for *ex casu* challenges, that is, that a particular term in a particular contract between a dealer and a consumer is unfair. In order to institute this procedure there must be a complaint (reg 8(1)); the Director General has a duty to consider any complaint unless it appears to be 'frivolous or vexatious' (reg 8(1)), and he must give reasons for his decision to apply or not to apply for an injunction (reg 8(4)). Proceedings for an injunction, including an interlocutory injunction, can be brought against any person appearing to the Director General to be using or recommending the use of unfair terms (reg 8(2)). The court has a dual discretion under reg 8(5) to decide whether the Director General's application should be granted and, if so, as to the terms of the injunction. The terms of the injunction could apply to an individual or to a whole industry or all contracts of that industry or to a particular type of contract.

The injunction mechanism can also stimulate the single market concept because it would be open to a foreign consumer organisation or protection body to complain to the Director General about the use of unfair terms by UK businesses and, if the Director General agrees, to bring action.

The relationship of the Regulations and UCTA

The Regulations do not merely duplicate control over exclusion clauses with the UCTA, rather, they regulate the balance of obligations with respect to subsidiary terms. Significantly, the Regulations can provide the basis for a challenge to the obligations of the parties (including price) where these are formulated obscurely, because of the requirement of plain and unambiguous language. However in general the Regulations do not provide a means of challenge merely on the grounds of unfair price. The differences between the provisions of the Regulations and the UCTA are as follows:

1. The UCTA envisages the possibility of a company being a 'consumer' when it enters into a contract outside its line of business (s 12(1)(a)), whereas the Regulations confine 'consumers' to natural persons. Even so, the UCTA cuts down the definition of consumer by excluding contracts involving the sale of goods not ordinarily supplied for private use or consumption and sales by auction (s 12(1)(c)(2)). It is possible under the Regulations that a small business trading as a natural person or partnership can count as a consumer if the goods purchased, though normally only used in business, are not the kind of goods usually purchased by that particular business.

2. The scope of the UCTA is limited to control over terms which exclude or restrict liability, but the Act gives an extended meaning to exemption clauses so that it covers terms which entitle the party apparently in breach to render a contractual performance substantially different from that expected of him. The courts have been inventive in their approach to exclusion clauses, leading some commentators to call for more clarity in the definition of obligations which come within the scope of the legislation. In particular the inclusion of clauses which define liability as part of the formal definition of an exclusion clause (that is, the approach taken is that if there would be an obligation and liability in the absence of the clause, then the clause is brought within s 13(1): see *Phillips Products Ltd v Hyland* [1987] 2 All ER 620; *Smith v Eric S Bush* [1989] 2 All ER 514; *Johnstone v Bloomsbury Health Authority* [1991] 2 All ER 293). Even the extended meaning of an exemption clause does not detract from the fact that UCTA is narrower in scope than the Directive as it refers to terms in general and not a particular category of terms.

3. Whereas the UCTA can deal with limitation of damages clauses and also related issues which seek to extend defences, for example, elimination of a right of set-off (see *Stewart Gill Ltd v Horatio Myer and Co Ltd* [1992] 2 All ER 257), it does not reach the whole range of remedies, whereas these do fall within the Regulations.

Chapter 6

Consumer Protection

The majority of consumer complaints concern defective goods and centre upon claims for pure economic loss. As we have seen, the approach taken under the SGA 1979, SGSA 1982, and SOGIT 1973 is to make the supplier, in the ordinary course of business, strictly liable with regard to the implied terms as to quality. Such an approach may be justified on the basis of risk allocation since the business supplier is in a good position to assess and bear the risk. The major difficulty with this contract-based approach is the doctrine of privity of contract. The purchaser must be the person suffering loss, unless it can be shown that the purchaser was acting as agent for the injured customer. Even here, unless the purchaser was expressly authorised to contract for the principal, such a contract can only be ratified if the purchaser, at the time of making the contract, professed to contract on the principal's behalf. Nevertheless, the courts have been remarkably inventive in circumventing the privity doctrine through the development of the collateral contract device and negligent misrepresentation. Despite this, the privity doctrine still represents a considerable obstacle, as manifested in quasi-sale devices such as finance leasing (see Chapter 12).

In recent years there have been significant statutory interventions protecting the consumer. The most important of these relate to the quality and fitness of goods under supply contracts. Major new legislation purportedly implementing EC Directives, notably the Consumer Protection Act 1987 (CPA) and the General Product Safety Regulations 1994 (GPSR), have changed the basis on which a victim can sue a producer, introduced new criminal offences and extended the powers of the safety enforcement authorities.

Statutory product liability under the Consumer Protection Act 1987, Part I: the ambit of the Act

Part I of the CPA 1987 is the response of English law to the European Community Directive on the approximation of the laws of the Member States relating to liability for defective products. This is specifically provided for in s 1(1) of CPA 1987 which states:

> This Part shall have effect for the purpose of making such provision as is necessary in order to comply with the product liability Directive and shall be construed accordingly.

The basic principle of the CPA 1987 is stated in art 1 of the Directive, namely, 'The producer shall be liable for damage caused by a defect in his product'. Strict liability has become a basis on which a victim can sue a producer. Although the burden of proof is still on the victim to show the damage, the defect and the causal link between them, it is no longer necessary to establish negligence. Furthermore, liability cannot be limited or excluded by any contract term, notice or otherwise (s 7 of CPA 1987). Given the far-reaching nature of this legislation, the different elements will now be considered.

Liability

The basic liability under s 2(1)(a) of CPA 1987 rests upon 'the producer of the product'. A 'producer', under s 1(2), is defined as:

(a) the person who manufactured it;
(b) in the case of a substance which has not been manufactured but has been won or abstracted, the person who won or abstracted it;
(c) in the case of a product which has not been manufactured, won or abstracted but essential characteristics of which are attributable to an industrial or other process having been carried out (for example, in relation to agricultural produce), the person who carried out that process . . ..

It is unfortunate that the word 'manufactured' is not defined. In order to deal with the problem of an assembler of a finished product, s 1(2) allows the consumer to treat any party in the chain of distribution as the producer, unless the latter can identify his supplier. It should be noted that s 1(2)(c) is particularly relevant in the medico–pharmaceutical area where health care professionals may mix medicinal ingredients and, as such, they could be liable as producers. This liability would only be avoided if careful records of the sources of drugs were kept so as to pass on liability to the manufacturer responsible for any defect. Alternatively, it may be possible to argue that the mixing of the ingredients did not change the 'essential characteristics' of the product.

Although primary liability for breach is laid upon the producer of the product, the principle of joint and several liability is introduced into the CPA 1987 in order to ensure that the person injured can find a defendant within the jurisdiction. Thus, three other categories of persons who are not involved in any manufacturing, are treated as if they were producers under s 2.

Own branders
The liability applies under s 2(2)(b) to:

any person who, by putting his name on the product or using a trade mark or other distinguishing mark in relation to the product, has held himself out to be the producer of the product.

The CPA 1987 is not clear as to what constitutes a holding-out and much will depend upon how the branding is perceived by the reasonable consumer.

Importers

The liability envisaged under s 2(2)(*c*) extends to:

> any person who has imported the product into a Member State from a place outside the Member States in order, in the course of any business of his, to supply it to another.

An importer of a product from *outside* the EEC is treated as a producer. The intention here is that victims do not have to pursue claims against manufacturers in foreign countries which may have less favourable laws.

Suppliers

The general approach is that a supplier is not liable under Pt I of the CPA 1987 for defective goods, but he may be liable in contract or negligence, or perhaps be criminally liable under Pt II (discussed below). However, s 2(3) of CPA 1987 enables the persons injured to hold an effective supplier liable where, for example, the product is anonymous. The reference to an effective supplier means in the case of a directly financed transaction the dealer, rather than the financier (s 46(2) of CPA 1987) (see Chapter 12). Liability of an effective supplier is envisaged under s 2(3) as follows:

> Subject, as aforesaid, where any damage is caused wholly or partly by a defect in a product, any person who supplied the product (whether to the person who suffered the damage, to the producer of any product in which the product in question is comprised or to any other person) shall be liable for the damage if —
> (*a*) the person who suffered the damage requests the supplier to identify one or more of the persons (whether still in existence or not) to whom subsection (2) above applies in relation to the product;
> (*b*) that request is made within a reasonable period after the damage occurs and at a time when it is not reasonably practicable for the person making the request to identify all those persons; and
> (*c*) the supplier fails, within a reasonable period after receiving the request, either to comply with the request or to identify the person who supplied the product to him.

The supplier need not identify the actual manufacturer, only the next person back up the chain of supply. It is clear that ultimate liability is envisaged to lie with the producer, own brander or importer, irrespective of whether they are insolvent, that is, 'whether still in existence or not' (s 2(3)(*a*)).

Product

Under s 1(2) of CPA 1987, 'product' is defined to mean:

> any goods or electricity and . . . includes a product which is comprised in another product, whether by virtue of being a component part or raw material or otherwise.

This is a wider definition than that of goods under the SGA 1979. Even fixtures can be goods for the purposes of the CPA 1987 because s 45(1) defines 'goods' to include, 'substances, growing crops and things comprised in land by virtue of being attached to it and any ship, aircraft or vehicle'. The point here is that materials incorporated into buildings will be covered if they turn out to be defective (s 46(3)). Waste can also be a product, for example where it is sold as a by-product or if it is disposed of in a supply situation, rather than a mere discharge, where it may be covered under the Control of Pollution Act 1974.

Specifically exempted are agricultural produce and game which have not gone through an 'industrial process'. The public policy issue here is that farmers should not be strictly liable for defects beyond their control, such as the long-term effects of fertilisers. The difficulty here is that modern methods of farming are highly intensive and sometimes artificial. It seems anomalous that animals injected during their life with hormones, which later cause damage to consumers, will not sound in liability for the farmer under Pt I of CPA 1987.

Defect

A product is defective under the CPA 1987 when it does not provide the safety which persons generally are entitled to expect, taking into account all the circumstances. It would seem that if the real complaint is about shoddiness or unsuitability of the goods, the course of action is still by reference to the implied terms under the SGA 1979, SGSA 1982 and SOGIT 1973. Section 3(1) of CPA 1987 provides as follows:

> Subject to the following provisions of this section, there is a defect in a product for the purposes of this Part if the safety of the product is not such as persons generally are entitled to expect; and for those purposes 'safety', in relation to a product, shall include safety with respect to products comprised in that product and safety in the context of risks of damage to property, as well as in the context of risks of death or personal injury.

The test adopted here is an objective one so that the issue of a person with particular sensitivities is irrelevant. To assist in the application of criteria, s 3, in requiring the courts to take all the circumstances into account, sets out three non-exclusive factors to be considered.

Marketing circumstances and instructions

Section 3(2)(a) provides that regard should be taken as to:

> the manner in which, and purposes for which, the product has been marketed, its get-up, the use of any mark in relation to the product and any instructions form or warnings with respect to doing or refraining from doing anything with or in relation to the product.

The way in which a product is marketed will obviously have a great impact upon the public's expectation. In considering the liability for such unsafe products, the court must take into account the manner in which it has been marketed, its 'get-up' and any warnings and instructions supplied. An important consequence of this is that it should lead to a great improvement in the quality of instructions and warnings produced by manufacturers attached to their products (see *Vacwell Engineering Co Ltd v BDH Chemicals Ltd* [1971] 1 QB 88). It may be argued by analogy that, given the importance under the CPA 1987 placed upon accurate instructions, this should permeate to cases where the buyer sues for economic loss under, for example, s 14 of SGA 1979. This view calls into doubt the approach taken by the Court of Appeal in *Wormell v RHM Agriculture (East) Ltd* [1987] 1 WLR 1091 (see Chapter 5).

Use

Section 3(2)(*b*) provides that a court should take into account, 'what might reasonably be expected to be done with or in relation to the product . . .'. The producer should reasonably foresee what might be done with the goods, such as predictable misuse by a child. If it is not possible to remove the hazard, adequate warnings or instructions will be relevant here.

Time of supply

Section 3(2)(*c*) states that the precise time to which reference should be made is when 'the product was supplied by its producer to another'. Obviously this will be of significance for producers where there is a long shelf-life. As technology and standards change so do public expectations. Section 3(2) of CPA 1987 expressly provides for this as follows:

> and nothing in this section shall require a defect to be inferred from the fact alone that the safety of a product which is supplied after that time is greater than the safety of the product in question.

Without this provision, producers would constantly have to recall and modify older products every time they introduced a safety improvement.

Damage

Pure financial loss is not covered under the CPA 1987, where 'damage' is defined under s 5(1) to mean 'death or personal injury or any loss of or damage to any property (including land)'. The damages recoverable (including congenital disability) are applied as in any other civil case subject to the following:

Damage to the product itself

Section 5(2) provides:

> A person shall not be liable under section 2 above in respect of any defect in a product for the loss of or any damage to the product itself or for the loss of or any damage to the whole or any part of any product which has been supplied with the product in question comprised in it.

It follows from this that if there is an internal defect then damage to that appliance cannot be recovered under the CPA 1987. In this situation the buyer must pursue a claim under the SGA 1979 for his money back or any other settlement. Of course, recovery is still possible under the general damage heading in s 5(1) against either the manufacturer of the appliance or the manufacturer of the component.

Damage to business property

Producers who supply products solely for business use where the only likely consequence of a defect is damage to business property or financial loss, are unaffected by Pt I of the CPA 1987. Essentially, Pt I of the Act is designed as a *consumer* protection measure. Thus s 5(3) states:

> A person shall not be liable under section 2 above for any loss of or damage to any property which, at the time it is lost or damaged, is not—
> (*a*) of a description of property ordinarily intended for private use, occupation or consumption; and
> (*b*) intended by the person suffering the loss or damage mainly for his own private use, occupation or consumption.

It follows from this that a consumer who uses an appliance which is not 'ordinarily intended for private use', such as a heavy goods vehicle, will not be covered beyond death or personal injury under the CPA 1987.

Damage which is trivial

Under s 5(4), no damages are awarded in respect of trivial property damage which is defined as where the total capital loss does not exceed £275. This lower threshold applies only to property, not personal injury. Claims for property losses under £275 will therefore have to be pursued in contract and negligence. It should be noted that the £275 minimum takes account of any reduction in damages through contributory negligence. Section 6(4) applies the Law Reform (Contributory Negligence) Act 1945 and s 5 of the Fatal Accidents Act 1976 relating to contributory negligence, to claims under Pt I of the CPA 1987.

Defences

The burden of proof of causation under the CPA 1987 is upon the victim. Damages may be reduced by his contributory negligence and, in this respect, it could be argued that disregard of instructions breaks the chain of causation. This was a position taken by the House of Lords in *Lambert v Lewis* [1982] AC 225. Here it was held that the chain of causation was broken where the buyer continued to use the goods with actual knowledge of the breach, as regards subsequent consequential loss (compare *Basildon District Council v JE Lesser (Properties) Ltd* [1985] QB 839).

The CPA 1987 specifically provides in s 4 for defences available with respect to 'the person proceeded against' for defects in a product supplied. These defences are found in s 4(1). Section 4(1)(*a*) provides 'that the defect is attributable to compliance with any requirement imposed by or under any enactment or with any Community obligation . . .'. The essential point here is that the producer must show that the defect was the *inevitable* result of compulsory compliance with domestic or Community law. Where standards followed by manufacturers are voluntary rather than mandatory such as British Standard, this is not within the defence anticipated here.

Section 4(1)(*b*) stipulates, 'that the person proceeded against did not at any time supply the product to another'. 'Supply' is defined in s 46 to include:

(a) selling, hiring out or lending the goods;

(b) entering into a hire-purchase agreement to furnish the goods;

(c) the performance of any contract for work and materials to furnish the goods;

(d) providing the goods in exchange for any consideration (including trading stamps) other than money;

(e) providing the goods in or in connection with the performance of any statutory function; or

(f) giving the goods as a prize or otherwise making a gift of the goods.

It appears from this that there does not have to be a sale for money because free promotional gifts incur the same liabilities. The defence is confined to absence of supply, for example where the goods are stolen from the manufacturer or scrapped by him.

The 'no supply' defence has been used by taxi firms as a means of escaping liability under the Act. The reasoning here is that s 46(9) provides that ships, aircraft and motor vehicles do not count as being 'supplied' for the purposes of the Act if the arrangement with the customer is solely to provide transport services 'for a particular period or for particular voyages, flights or journeys'. An interesting point which may arise out of this is whether a car hire firm which imports vehicles from outside the EC could escape liability on the basis that the car hire firm provided services 'consisting in the carriage of . . . passengers . . . in [a] vehicle'. The purpose of s 46(9) is to deal with supply, that is hiring out of a product, and it does not apply to the provision of services, for example, of a driver. In most of the cases in which it is doubtful whether there has been a technical 'supply', notably allowing shoppers to use trolleys and other containers free of charge, the plaintiff would normally be interested only in suing the manufacturer who at some stage must have supplied the product.

Section 4(1)(c) provides:

(i) that the only supply of the product to another by the person proceeded against was otherwise than in the course of a business of that person's; and

(ii) that section 2(2) above does not apply to that person or applies to him by virtue of things done otherwise than with a view to profit . . . .

The CPA 1987 is similar to the SGA 1979 and the SGSA 1982 with respect to satisfactory quality and fitness for purpose, as it imposes liability only on those acting 'in the course of a business'. A private supplier will not face strict liability under Pt I of the CPA 1987 unless the supply is with a view to a profit in the course of a business. Section 4(1)(d) provides 'that the defect did not exist in the product at the relevant time'. This in practice is the most important defence. The relevant time is when originally supplied (s 4(2)). In the case of electricity this is defined as when generated so that defects caused by failures during distribution, are not covered (s 4(2)). Where there has been malicious tampering with a product, if this occurs before the time of supply by, for example, an employee of the manufacturer, the latter will be strictly liable. If it occurs after the time of supply then he will have a defence, although the retailer will be liable for breach of the implied terms under ss 13–14 of SGA 1979 and analogous provisions in contracts of supply.

Section 4(1)(e) states as follows:

> that the state of scientific and technical knowledge at the relevant time was not such that a producer of products of the same description as the product in question might be expected to have discovered the defect if it had existed in his products while they were under his control . . . .

This defence can be best described as 'development risks'. The Directive made the adoption of this defence optional and, despite strenuous attempts by the consumer lobby to have it rejected, the government included it in the Act. The test adopted is objective, based on the reasonable producer, so that the resources and experience of the particular producer will not be relevant. The determining time, as defined under s 4(2), is when the product was supplied and not when it was manufactured. It follows from this that the producer must keep abreast of developments until the product leaves his control. However, merely because safer products are subsequently produced, this does not necessarily mean that a product was defective when put into circulation (s 4(1)(d)). This defence will be highly relevant in the pharmaceutical industry where much will depend upon how strictly it is construed with regard to new drugs. It may be, following the Directive (art 7(e)), that the test is whether the knowledge existed to discover the defect, and not merely that the standard tests and procedures were undertaken by the drug company concerned.

Section 4(1)(f) provides:

> that the defect—
> (i)   constituted a defect in a product ('the subsequent product') in which the product in question had been comprised; and
> (ii) was wholly attributable to the design of the subsequent product or to compliance by the producer of the product in question with instructions given by the producer of the subsequent product.

To qualify for this defence, the component producer must have no responsibility for the design of the finished product or be simply following specifications which prove to be unsuitable.

The CPA 1987 amends the Limitation Act 1980 with respect to time limits for bringing an action (see s 6(6) and Sched 1). There is an overall cut-off point for any proceedings to be brought, which is ten years after the 'relevant time'. The 'relevant time' is defined in s 4 of CPA 1987. A second limitation on actions contained in s 11A(4) of the Limitation Act 1980 (as inserted by the CPA 1987, Sched 1), is that claims for personal injuries or property damage cannot be brought more than three years after becoming aware of the damage, the defect and the identity of the defendant, subject to the ultimate cut-off of ten years. For latent damage, the three-year period commences on the 'date of knowledge' of the plaintiff (s 14(1)(A) of the Limitation Act 1980, inserted by CPA 1987, Sched 1). The reason for the overall cut-off point of ten years is to prevent the threat of legal action stretching out for an unlimited period. Of course, many products will not have a ten-year life span but in this situation the definition of 'defect' takes into account consumption, perishability, and wear and tear as part of what 'persons generally are entitled to expect'.

Undoubtedly, the CPA 1987 does simplify the plaintiff's task in establishing liability, since a victim no longer has to show that the producer was negligent or be party to a contract. Nevertheless, there are important difficulties which still remain. For example, the level of safety that persons are generally entitled to expect, problems with causation, contributory negligence and the development risks defence. Moreover Pt I has other limitations in that it does not in any case apply to all products, neither does it cover damage to business property or to personal property below £275. Lastly, the CPA 1987 is not retrospective, so that products supplied before 1 March 1988 are not covered.

Criminal liability

Promoting safety: Consumer Protection Act 1987, Part II

Under Pt II of the CPA 1987, 'consumer goods' must comply with a general safety requirement. This is a catch-all provision which contrasts with piecemeal safety legislation covering specific products, for example, food, drugs, motor vehicles, and specific places, including factories and mines. Under the general safety requirement, retailers are criminally liable if they knowingly expose an unsafe product for sale, whereas in civil law, under the product liability regime, retailers are liable to third party victims only if they present themselves as the producer or cannot identify the person who supplied them with the product.

The general safety requirement
Liability is not confined to producers as is the case of civil liability, but extends to any supplier. 'Supply' is defined under s 46 as sale, hire, loan, hire purchase, exchange and providing goods in connection with a statutory function (for example, electricity), giving a prize or gift. The 'person' need not be a trader nor a trader supplying the goods he normally supplies. In direct financing, the ostensible supplier, the financier, is not treated as supplier for liability purposes (s 46(2)). It should be noted that liability is confined to 'consumer goods' intended for private use supplied in the course of a business. Under s 10(7) the following are excluded: growing crops and emblements, water, food, feed or fertiliser, gas, aircraft or motor vehicles, drugs, tobacco. This is a much narrower definition than 'product' in Pt I of the CPA 1987. However, when one takes into account other safety legislation such as the Food Safety Act 1990, Agriculture Act 1970, Medicines Act 1968, Misuse of Drugs Act 1971 and the Road Traffic Acts 1972 and 1988, these limitations are not significant. The exception in relation to tobacco recognises the difficulty of making the supply of tobacco a criminal offence. The limitation that 'consumer goods' must be for private use or consumption, whilst a 'product' can be supplied for any use, does not mean that suppliers of industrial or business products can escape their responsibilities, because the Health and Safety at Work Act 1974 will apply.
The general safety requirement is encapsulated in s 10(2) which provides:

For the purposes of this section consumer goods fail to comply with the general safety requirement if they are not reasonably safe having regard to all the circumstances, including—

(a) the manner in which, and purposes for which, the goods are being or would be marketed, the get-up of the goods, the use of any mark in relation to the goods and any instructions or warnings which are given or would be given with respect to the keeping, use or consumption of the goods;

(b) any standards of safety published by any person either for goods of a description which applies to the goods in question or for matters relating to goods of that description; and

(c) the existence of any means by which it would have been reasonable (taking into account the cost, likelihood and extent of any improvement) for the goods to have been made safer.

'Safe' is defined in s 19(1) in terms of risk of causing death or personal injury only, whereas under Pt I liability also arises for damage to personal property exceeding £275. The ambit of s 10(2) is reduced by s 10(3)(a) which provides that compliance with a Community obligation is a defence. This is identical to the defence seen in Pt I but the risk must be directly attributable to compliance. Section 10(3)(b) goes further:

any failure to do more in relation to any matter than is required by—

(i) any safety regulations imposing requirements with respect to that matter;

(ii) any standards of safety approved for the purposes of this subsection by or under any such regulations and imposing requirements with respect to that matter;

(iii) any provision of any enactment or subordinate legislation imposing such requirements with respect to that matter as are designated for the purposes of this subsection by any such regulations.

Meeting the minimum requirements of safety legislation or standards is a complete defence to criminal liability. Contrastingly, it is not a defence to a civil claim where legislative standards are regarded as the minimum which should, in some circumstances, be exceeded by the reasonably prudent producer.

There is a recognition that export goods outside the Community may be made to different standards so that, by virtue of s 10(4), this will provide a defence. More significant for domestic purposes is s 10(4)(b) and (c) which give the retailer a defence provided:

(b) (i) that he supplied the goods, offered or agreed to supply them or, as the case may be, exposed or possessed them for supply in the course of carrying on a retail business; and

(ii) that, at the time he supplied the goods or offered or agreed to supply them or exposed or possessed them for supply, he neither knew nor had reasonable grounds for believing that the goods failed to comply with the general safety requirement; or

(c) that the terms on which he supplied the goods or agreed or offered to supply them or, in the case of goods which he exposed or possessed for supply, the terms on which he intended to supply them—

(i) indicated that the goods were not supplied or to be supplied as new goods; and

(ii) provided for, or contemplated, the acquisition of an interest in the goods by the persons supplied or to be supplied.

This is important because it recognises that retailers may not have the knowledge or the resources to check whether the goods he sells meet the general safety requirement, especially in the case of second-hand goods. The defence applies only to retailers and not to others in the distribution chain who can rely upon another defence of general application under s 39, namely, 'due diligence'.

The 'due diligence' defence

The 'due diligence' defence represents a crucial difference between the idea of strict civil liability under Pt I, and criminal liability under Pt II of the CPA 1987. There is a natural reluctance to make criminals of suppliers who have taken reasonable steps to ensure that their goods accord with modern standards. In this respect s 39 states:

(1) Subject to the following provisions of this section, in proceedings against any person for an offence to which this section applies it shall be a defence for that person to show that he took all reasonable steps and exercised all due diligence to avoid committing the offence.

(2) Where in any proceedings against any person for such an offence the defence provided by subsection (1) above involves an allegation that the commission of the offence was due—
(a) to the act or default of another; or
(b) to reliance on information given by another,
that person shall not, without the leave of the court, be entitled to rely on the defence unless, not less than seven clear days before the hearing of the proceedings, he has served a notice under subsection (3) below on the person bringing the proceedings.

(3) A notice under this subsection shall give such information identifying or assisting in the identification of the person who committed the act or default or gave the information as is in the possession of the person serving the notice at the time he serves it.

(4) It is hereby declared that a person shall not be entitled to rely on the defence provided by subsection (1) above by reason of his reliance on information supplied by another, unless he shows that it was reasonable in all the circumstances for him to have relied on the information, having regard in particular—
(a) to the steps which he took, and those which might reasonably have been taken, for the purpose of verifying the information; and
(b) to whether he had any reason to disbelieve the information.

The emphasis is upon reasonableness of his procedures. Buying goods from a reputable source is not enough as the supplier will be required to entertain elementary precautions, for example, sampling or checking the weight of the goods supplied (s 28(1) of the Weights and Measures Act 1985) and ensuring that the system can cope with mistakes.

The defence of 'due diligence' is an ameliorating feature of most consumer protection strict liability statutes (see for example, s 24(1) of the Trade Descriptions Act 1968). As Lord Reid put it in *Tesco Supermarkets Ltd v Nattrass* [1972] AC 153 at p 174, if a defendant has done all that can reasonably be expected of him, how can he do more? Thus in *Barker v Hargreaves*

[1981] RTR 197, it was held that excusable ignorance could be a defence in the case of latent defects under the Trade Descriptions Act 1968 (TDA). Where a 'due diligence' defence is relied upon, the burden of proof is on the accused. The latter must show that the transgression was due to the act of another, and the general rule for criminal liability is that an employer will not be vicariously liable for his employee's crimes. In *Tesco Supermarkets Ltd v Nattrass*, a shop manager of a large supermarket chain with considerable managerial powers, was held to be 'another person', thereby allowing the company to escape liability for a breach of the TDA 1968 when a misleading price offer was displayed due to his failure to check it. It is otherwise where the employee can be considered to be part of the 'brains' of the company, ie sufficiently senior for his acts to be regarded as those of the company. Moreover under most consumer protection legislation, senior corporate officers will be vicariously liable where a corporation has been found criminally liable under such legislation (see s 20 of TDA 1968, s 132 of the Fair Trading Act 1973, s 169 of CCA 1974 and s 40(2) of CPA 1987).

Safety regulations

Under s 11 of CPA 1987, the Secretary of State has comprehensive powers to issue regulations covering all aspects of product safety but subsuming the regulations already made under the CPA 1961 and Consumer Safety Act 1978. Given the catch-all general safety requirement under the CPA 1987, it is in the interest of retailers that these regulations be made since they will provide a shelter from liability.

The regulations anticipated under s 11(1) will have the purpose of securing:

    (*a*)   that goods to which this section applies are safe;

    (*b*)   that goods to which this section applies which are unsafe, or would be unsafe in the hands of persons of a particular description, are not made available to persons generally or, as the case may be, to persons of that description; and

    (*c*)   that appropriate information is, and inappropriate information is not, provided in relation to goods to which this section applies.

The Minister has a statutory duty to consult organisations he considers are representative of interests which will be affected by a proposed regulation and other appropriate persons. In some cases of urgency he can introduce regulations with a shelf-life of up to 12 months without consultation (s 11(5)). The scope of the power to issue regulations is laid out in s 11(2) and (4) which include such matters as packaging, testing, marks, warnings, instructions and requiring information to be given to enforcement authorities.

The action for breach of statutory duty

A person who buys goods not complying with the regulations will have an action for breach of a statutory duty. However, the defendant may be able to escape liability if he can prove that he exercised all due diligence to avoid the commission of an offence (s 12 of CPA 1987). By virtue of s 41 of CPA 1987, breach of a safety regulation, as distinct from the general safety requirement, is also grounds for a civil action by any person affected which cannot be excluded or limited by any contract term or notice. In effect, safety regulations become part of the definition of 'defective' in respect of personal injuries and have the great advantage of being self-enforcing. This approach contrasts with s 35 of the TDA 1968, which expressly provides that failure to comply with that Act does not render any contract void or unenforceable.

The criminal courts do possess a discretionary power to make compensation orders where a supplier is prosecuted to conviction in the case of personal injury loss or damage (s 35 of the Powers of Criminal Courts Act 1973 as amended by s 67 of the Criminal Justice Act 1982). There is a restriction on the maximum amount of compensation which a magistrates' court may order (currently £5,000) which has serious implications where there are other offences to be taken into account. It may be that s 104(1) of the Criminal Justice Act 1988, which requires the criminal court to give reasons if refusing compensation, will ensure that the power be exercised on a regular basis.

Further CPA 1987 provisions

In addition to the general power under s 11 to make regulations, the Secretary of State and enforcement authorities have further powers to restrict the circulation of unsafe goods:

Prohibition notice   The Minister can issue a prohibition notice (s 13 of CPA 1987) on a named person to prevent that person from supplying a product which the Minister considers unsafe. If goods already supplied by that stockist may endanger consumers, the Minister may serve 'a notice to warn' requiring that person, at his own expense, to publish in the prescribed manner, a warning about any goods supplied that the Minister considers unsafe. The trader has the right to make representations that the goods are safe and to have the notice revoked.

Suspension notice   Under s 14 of CPA 1987, an enforcement authority which has reasonable grounds for suspecting that any safety provision relating to any goods has been contravened, is empowered to serve a notice prohibiting the person responsible for up to six months from supplying, offering or exposing for supply those goods. The trader can appeal to a magistrates' court against the notice and obtain compensation if there has been no contravention.

Forfeiture   This is a drastic power as it gives an enforcement authority power, under s 16 of CPA 1987, to obtain possession of unsafe goods and, if necessary, destroy them. Such an order can be sought from a magistrates' court on evidence that a representative sample is unsafe, and the authority does not need to secure a conviction in this respect. A person affected by a forfeiture order may appeal to the Crown Court to have it withdrawn or delayed.

Promoting Safety: General Product Safety Regulations 1994

As part of the measures to promote an internal single market the General Product Safety Directive (June 1992 92/59/EEC) was passed and this has now been implemented by the General Product Safety Regulations 1994 (SI 1994 No 2328) which came into force on 3 October 1994. In common with the Unfair

Terms in Consumer Contracts Directive (see Chapter 5) no attempt was made at consolidation with existing English law. At one level the Directive does not pose any serious challenge to the existing structures under Part II of the CPA, particularly the emergency procedures for the notification and exchange of information relating to dangerous products and also the extensive powers granted to enforcement agencies, which mirror the CPA. However, in part there is overlap, particularly the general safety requirement with s 10 of the CPA, but in other respects there is divergence. The main difficulty relates to the inelegance of there being two separate systems and thus having to determine the issue which is most appropriate to apply in each circumstance. It is especially unfortunate that the custodial penalties under the Regulations permit imprisonment for only three months (reg 17) whereas the 1987 Act permits six months (s 10(6)).

Scope of the law

The Regulations apply to a 'product', and this is defined in reg 2(1) as:

> any product intended for consumers or likely to be used by consumers, supplied whether for consideration or not in the course of a commercial activity and whether new, used or reconditioned: provided, however, a product which is used exclusively in the context of a commercial activity even if it is used for or by a consumer shall not be regarded as a product for the purposes of these Regulations provided always and for the avoidance of doubt this exception shall not extend to the supply of such a product to a consumer.

As can be seen the scope is wider than the CPA, since unlike in s 10 of that Act there are no specific restrictions such as food and tobacco. The product is limited to items intended for or 'likely' to be used by consumers and this is an enabling definition, since any foreseeable use of even contract hire equipment for DIY. work would be included. However an important *caveat* here relates to products supplied for a commercial activity which are not covered, for example, supermarket trolleys, or shampoo used in a hair salon.

The supply must be 'in the course of a commercial activity' which is not therefore confined to sale, so any exchange or even 'free gift' as part of a commercial activity will qualify as a product. New, used and reconditioned products are also covered and this is significant since secondhand goods are not generally covered by the CPA (see s 10 (4)(c)). Even so, antiques are not covered by the Regulations and whilst there is no definition of 'antique', an accepted meaning is that it includes an item made 100 years previously (see s 9, Customs and Excise Duties (General Reliefs) Act 1979). The Regulations do cover reconditioning before use, provided the supplier makes this clear to the other party (reg 3(b)).

The general safety requirement

The Regulations introduce a general safety requirement (reg 7) and make it an offence for any producer or distributor to offer or agree to place on the market any dangerous product, or to expose or possess such product for placing on the market, or to offer or agree to supply any dangerous product, or expose or process any such product for supply (reg 13). In addition the Regulations provide that producers commit an offence by placing unsafe products on the market and that distributors are guilty of an offence if they supply products which they know or should have presumed to be dangerous. These offences are subject to the due diligence defence (reg 14).

It is essential to make a clear distinction between producers and distributors because the Regulations impose different requirements upon each. A wide definition of producer is given in reg 2 to include.

(a) the manufacturer of a product, if established in the Community, or anyone who presents themselves as manufacturers by affixing their name, trade mark or other distinctive mark to the product and persons who recondition products;

(b) in the case of a manufacturer outside the Community, then either his representative if established within the Community or the importer of the product into the Community;

(c) 'other professionals in the supply chain, insofar as their activities may affect the safety properties of a product'.

It would follow from this that any distributor can be a producer unless the activities involved do not affect the safety properties of the product. Typically, therefore, shop keepers who do not maintain refrigerated products at the right temperature would be producing for this purpose. Nevertheless the definition does not include finance lessors, presumably because it is unlikely that they can formally affect the safety of the product.

The General Product Safety Regulations apply unless there are specific rules of Community law governing all aspects of the safety of the product and insofar as Community law other than the General Product Safety Directive does not make specific provision governing an aspect of the safety of the product (regs 3(c) and 4). In a sense this approach represents a departure from the practice in the earlier years of the Community which sought detailed product regulation, and the new approach represents an attempt to fill the lacunae which exist in the coverage of the vertical specific product safety legislation which exists.

The key concept is the definition of a safe product and this is provided in reg 2 as follows:

'safe product' means any product which, under normal or reasonably foreseeable conditions of use, including duration, does not present any risk or only the minimum risks compatible with the product's use, considered as acceptable and consistent with a high level of protection for the safety or health of persons, taking into account in particular—

(a) the characteristics of the product, including its composition, packaging, instructions for assembly and maintenance;

(b) the effect on other products, where it is reasonably foreseeable that it will be used with other products;

(c) the presentation of the product, the labelling, any instructions for its use and disposal and any other indication or information provided by the producer; and

(d) the categories of consumers at serious risk when using the product, in particular children, and the fact that higher levels of safety may be obtained or other

products presenting a lesser degree of risk may be available shall not of itself
cause the product to be considered other than a safe product.

In large measure these factors reflect the existing UK civil and criminal provisions relating to defective products but lay down a more objective standard than that provided by the CPA 1987 (see s 3). At the same time its scope is relatively wider because it does not link product safety to the circumstances for which the product was being marketed as in s 10 of the CPA 1987, but rather requires that a product must be safe under both normal *and* reasonably foreseeable conditions in (mis)use. The issue of acceptable risk must also be read in the context of the special categories of parties at risk, especially children.

In considering the safety of a product reg 10(1) states that a product is safe if it conforms to the specific rules of UK law concerning health and safety requirements. Where there are no specific rules reg 10(2) lists the standards to be used in order of priority:

(a) voluntary national standards giving effect to a European standard;
(b) Community technical specifications;
(c) in the absence of the above, UK standards such as the BSI codes of practice in respect of health and safety in the product sector concerned or the state of the art and technology, and also 'the safety which consumers may reasonably expect'. General factors such as price may be relevant in determining the reasonableness issue.

Obligations of producers and distributors

Because of the flexible concept of the distributor's obligation to exercise due care and because the obligations of producers are subject to what is appropriate within the limits of their activities, it appears incorrect to state that there is a dual standard operating. Thus, manufacturers would be under a more onerous obligation than someone who by some minor involvement becomes a producer for the purpose of the Regulations. Consequently producers are obliged only within the limits of their activities to provide consumers with the relevant information to enable them to assess the risks in a product throughout the normal or reasonably foreseeable period of its use, where such risks are not obvious without adequate warnings, and to take precautions against those risks (reg 8). A further requirement of reg 8 is for producers (within the limits of their activities) to adopt measures to enable them to be informed of the risks a product might present and to take appropriate action including product recalls. Where appropriate this will involve marking the products or product batches so that monitoring can take place. Such obligations would apply in different measure ('within the limits of his activity') to all who technically fall within the definition of producer.

The essential provision concerned with the distributors' liability is reg 9. A distributor must act with 'due care' to ensure compliance with the general safety requirement and in particular must not supply products to any person which 'he knows or should have presumed, on the basis of information in his possession and as a professional, are dangerous products'. Breach of this provision is an offence (reg 12). A distributor also has within the limits of his activities a subsidiary obligation to that owed by producers, viz monitoring the safety of products placed on the market and passing on information about risks (reg 9(b)). However, whilst producers must actively inform themselves of the risks, distributors merely act as a posting facility by passing on information. At the same time distributors are under a duty to act with due care to ensure compliance with the general safety requirement. This can be assessed by reference to the degree of danger typically presented by the product in question and to the exact role played by him. British lawyers may have been more comfortable with the term 'reasonable care' since the term 'due care' is more associated with motoring offences. There is also the importation of a *mens rea* element in the offence in the sense that it requires either actual knowledge or a fault-based imputed knowledge. The reference to presumed knowledge 'as a professional' emphasises that the test is the objective assessment that is to be made in the circumstances by a distributor.

A simplified aspect of a distributor's liability arises from reg 13 in that he can be liable for preparatory acts involving products which do not meet safety requirements. It is a strict liability offence under reg 13(b) to 'offer or agree to supply any dangerous product or expose or possess any such product for supply'. In the light of this it is difficult to see what recourse will be made to the *mens rea* offence created by reg 12.

Enforcement

As far as enforcement duties are concerned, many of the enforcement provisions of the 1987 Act are applicable to the Regulations also (see reg 11(a) and (b)) in that s 13 of the 1987 Act (prohibition notices and notices to warn) applies under the 1994 Regulations, and the Regulations constitute safety provisions for the purposes of suspension notices (s 14), appeals procedures for suspension notices (s 15), forfeiture provisions (ss 16 and 17) and powers to obtain information (s 18). It is to be noted, however, that where offences arise under ss 13(4) and 14(6) of the 1987 Act, in conjunction with the 1994 Regulations, the penalty is reduced to a maximum of three months' imprisonment, instead of the six months available under the 1987 Act (reg 11(d)). One way in which the 1994 Regulations improve upon the situation under s 10 of the 1987 Act is that proceedings may commence within 12 months of the offence, rather than the usual six months (reg 16).

False statements as to goods and services

The TDA 1968 creates two main strict liability criminal offences under s 1(1), namely, that of applying a false trade description to goods (s 1(1)(*a*)), and supplying goods to which a false trade description has been applied (s 1(1)(*b*)). These offences are confined to the course of a trade or business (as to the meaning of this see Chapter 5) so that private transactions are excluded. It appears that this includes a club having private membership (see *John v Matthews* [1970] 2 QB 443). The key issue is the question of supply of goods and there is separate provision under s 14 of TDA 1968 for services. It should be noted that in no way does the TDA 1968 enhance the consumer's contractual rights (s 35), its aim simply being to ensure, by criminal sanctions, that the consumer is not misled.

Applying a false trade description to goods

Proof of dishonesty is unnecessary for this offence. Section 4 provides:

(1) A person applies a trade description to goods if he—
    (a) affixes or annexes it to or in any manner marks it on or incorporates it with—
      (i) the goods themselves or
      (ii) anything in, on or with which the goods are supplied; or
    (b) places the goods in, on or with anything which the trade description has been affixed or annexed to, marked on or incorporated with, or places any such thing with the goods; or
    (c) uses the trade description in any manner likely to be taken as referring to the goods.
(2) An oral statement may amount to the use of a trade description.
(3) Where goods are supplied in pursuance of a request in which a trade description is used and the circumstances are such as to make it reasonable to infer that the goods are supplied as goods corresponding to that trade description, the person supplying the goods shall be deemed to have applied that trade description to the goods.

The offence extends to oral misdescription and is not necessarily confined to a contractual relationship with the customer (*Fletcher v Sledmore* [1973] RTR 371).

The definition of 'false trade description' is contained in ss 2 and 3. Section 3 provides that a false trade description is one of material degree and this includes statements which, although literally true, are nevertheless misleading (s 3(2)). The term 'trade description' is defined comprehensively in s 2(1) as follows:

A trade description is an indication, direct or indirect, and by whatever means given, of any of the following matters with regard to any goods or part of goods, that is to say,
(a) quantity, size of gauge;
(b) method of manufacture, production, processing or reconditioning;
(c) composition;
(d) fitness of purpose, strength, performance, behaviour or accuracy;
(e) any physical characteristics not included in the preceding paragraphs;
(f) testing by any person and results thereof;
(g) approval by any person or conformity with a type approved by any person;
(h) place or date of manufacture, production, processing or reconditioning;
(i) person by whom manufactured, produced, processed or reconditioned;
(j) other history, including previous ownership or use.

In *Cadbury Ltd v Halliday* [1975] 1 WLR 649, it was decided that the words 'Extra value' written on the wrapper of a bar of chocolate, did not relate to any of the items listed in s 2 so that no offence was committed. All the items listed in s 2 are matters of which the truth or falsity can be established as a matter of fact. That could not be said of 'value' in this case which is essentially a matter of opinion. There is also a further power to exempt goods sold for export (s 32) and trade descriptions which are covered under other statutes such as food and drugs legislation.

Section 1 of TDA 1968 is a powerful deterrent and can apply to an honest trader who misdescribes his goods. In *R v Ford Motor Company* [1974] 1 WLR 1200, the Court of Appeal had to determine whether the trade description 'new' was a false one where a car, damaged in the care of forwarding agents, was repaired and supplied by the dealer as a 'new car'. The court held that a new car which is damaged and then repaired so as to be 'as good as new' can still be regarded as 'new'. Much depends upon the type of damage and the quality of the repairs so that, for example, where an engine is damaged, a car may be restored to newness through a new engine being installed. It should be noted that the criterion 'new' applies not just to the condition of the car but also with regard to whether the car has been registered. Thus in *R v Anderson* (1987) *The Times*, 31 December, the defendant had sold, as new, a Nissan car which, though in mint unused condition, had been registered in the retailer's name. The Court of Appeal upheld the defendant's conviction on the basis that a purchaser would understand the description 'new' to indicate that the vehicle had had no previous registered keeper.

A mileometer reading on a motor vehicle is a trade description within the Act. A person who sells a vehicle in the course of his trade or business is supplying the vehicle with the description attached (*Holloway v Cross* [1981] 1 All ER 1112). If, however, the motor trader defendant is not responsible for turning back the mileometer and covers up the reading, the motor trader should be able to escape from liability on the basis that no false description was in fact applied to the goods (s 1(1)(*b*)). Any notice of disclaimer provided that it is 'bold, precise and compelling' (see *Zawadski v Sleigh* [1975] RTR 113) should establish the defence. In the case where the disclaimer itself is misleading, this will amount to a false trade description (*Corfield v Starr* [1981] RTR 380). The significance of the TDA 1968 is that it applies, in auction situations, strict liability to a false trade description which cannot be excluded by a disclaimer even though, as a matter of civil law, such an exclusion clause could satisfy the reasonableness test under UCTA 1977 (see *Derbyshire County Council v Vincent* (1990) *The Times*, 19 June).

Supplying or offering to supply goods

The expression 'offering to supply' was given a wide meaning by s 6 in order to avoid the difficulty found in *Fisher v Bell* [1961] 1 QB 394. In this case flick knives displayed in a window were categorised by the court as an 'invitation to treat' rather than an offer for sale. Section 6 avoids this problem by extending to 'exposing goods for supply'. The main issue here is 'possession for supply' and it is sufficient if the goods are in a stock room so that, in effect, they do not have to be exposed for supply at the business premises of the supplier (*Stainthorpe v Bailey* [1980] RTR 7). The word 'supply' is a wide one and covers free gifts in the course of a business as well as extending to hire and hire purchase transactions.

Where the false trade description has not been applied by the retailer, the special defence of 'reasonable diligence' in s 24(3) of TDA 1968 may be relied upon. This is different from the general defence of 'due diligence' which looks for proof of mistaken belief. Under the special defence, the issue is whether the defendant did not know and could not with reasonable diligence have discovered, the false trade description. However, if the retailer knows of the trade description even though he is not aware of its falsity, the offence is committed (*Tarleton Engineering Co v Nattrass* [1973] 1 WLR 1261).

Trade descriptions used in advertisements

The TDA 1968 makes special provision for advertisements. 'Advertisement' is widely defined under s 39(1) to include a catalogue, a circular and a price list. The trade description must be made in the course of a trade or business and be part of the advertisement so that genuine news items are excluded. Section 5(2) states that the trade description shall be taken as referring to all goods of the class, whether or not in existence at the time the advertisement is published. In determining whether goods are of a class to which an advertised trade description relates, s 5(3) provides that regard shall be had not only to the form and content of the advertisement but also to the time, place, manner and frequency of its publication and all other matters making it likely or unlikely that a person to whom the goods are supplied would think of the goods as belonging to the class in question.

Misleading price indications

This is now regulated by Pt III of CPA 1987. A new general offence of giving a misleading price indication is provided in s 20. The question of what is misleading is determined under s 21 on the basis of an objective test and extends to both the price itself and any method of determining the price. It should be noted that the offences only apply where a misleading price indication is given to a consumer by a person in the course of his business. The new provisions apply not only to goods but also to services, accommodation or facilities. Section 20(6) defines consumer as follows:

(a) in relation to any goods, it means any person who might wish to be supplied with the goods for his own private use or consumption;

(b) in relation to any services or facilities, it means any person who might wish to be provided with the services or facilities otherwise than for the purposes of any business of his; and

(c) in relation to any accommodation, it means any person who might wish to occupy the accommodation otherwise than for the purposes of any business of his.

In laying down the offences, s 20 distinguishes according to whether or not the price indication was misleading when it was given. If this is the case, two defences are available to the defendant. First, the due diligence defence in ss 24 and 39; second, that he was a prior party in the chain of distribution recommending a price which, under s 24(4), he reasonably believed was being followed. Where an advertisement becomes subsequently misleading, an offence is committed under s 20(2) if, in the course of a business, the supplier reasonably expected reliance on the advertisement and he has not taken steps which are reasonable to prevent reliance on this indication.It is not necessary in a s 20 CPA prosecution for indicating misleading prices to produce an individual customer to whom the misleading price was indicated (*MFI Furniture Centres Ltd v Hibbert* (1995) *The Times*, 21 July).

There is no doubt that in determining compliance with ss 20–21 of CPA 1987, the initiatives of the Office of Fair Trading in encouraging business self-regulation through codes of practice, will be highly relevant. This is anticipated under s 25(1) which gives the Secretary of State, after consulting the Director General of Fair Trading, the power to issue such codes of practice containing detailed guidance as to legitimate and illegitimate price comparisons and price related matters. Compliance by the defendant with the Code may be relied upon by him for the purpose of showing that the commission of an offence under ss 20 and 21 has not been established. By containing such provisions in a Code, the Secretary of State has power to alter it or withdraw approval. Such an approach ensures flexibility in an ever-changing market situation.

Persons contravening s 20 are liable on conviction on indictment to a fine not exceeding the statutory maximum under s 20(4). Prosecutions under s 20, in common with other consumer protection legislation (for example s 19(1) of TDA 1968), must be brought either by the end of the period of three years from the day that the offence was committed, or within one year of its discovery by the prosecutor, whichever is the earlier (s 20(5)).

Licensing under the Consumer Credit Act 1974

At the heart of the CCA 1974 is the licensing system. Any person who by way of business provides credit under regulated agreements (see Chapter 2), must have a licence (s 21 of CCA 1974). Unlicensed trading activies are *prima facie* unenforceable and both criminal and civil sanctions may apply (ss 39–40 of CCA 1974). An elaborate machinery is provided for the making by the Director General of Fair Trading of an enforcement order following unlicensed activity (s 40 of CCA 1974). In addition, Pt III of the Fair Trading Act 1973 (FTA) gives the Director General powers to seek the cessation of business activities detrimental to consumers (s 34(1) of FTA 1973). In identifying such conduct, reliance is placed on information forthcoming from local authority consumer protection departments. Moreover, a central registry of convictions is kept to enable the Office of Fair Trading to identify businesses for possible action. A recent example of the Director General threatening to use his licensing powers can be seen when he did so in relation to finance houses using eponymous names in the context of the supply of photocopiers, unless a clear signal has been given by the finance company that it is not part of the same group as the manufacturer or supplier (compare *Lease Management Services Ltd v Purnell Secretarial Services* (1994) Tr LR 337, CA).

When the Director is satisfied that a trader is indulging in conduct detrimental to consumers, the FTA 1973 provides for a three-fold procedure. First, s 34(1) instructs the Director to seek a written assurance from the trader or his 'accessory' (for example, where a new company has been formed) that he will refrain from continuing that course of conduct. Second, where he is unable to obtain satisfactory written assurances, the Director may bring proceedings before the Restrictive Practices Court (s 35). In respect of 'small traders' there is an alternative power to bring proceedings in the county courts (s 41). The appropriate court may order the respondent to refrain from such conduct, or alternatively, accept an undertaking from the respondent in this respect. Lastly, breach of such an undertaking or court order will amount to a contempt of court. It should be noted that there are wide powers to prevent avoidance of the process by transferring business between companies in a group (s 40). A list of assurances, court orders, and contempt orders given each year can be found in the Office of Fair Trading Annual Report.

The effect of illegality

Unless otherwise expressly or implicitly provided by statute, illegality does not render a contract totally void, only unenforceable. Much depends upon the statute creating the offence. Thus under s 170(1) of CCA 1974, the intention is to deprive breaches of the CCA 1974 of any legal consequences other than those provided by the Act, but this will not apply to separate civil or criminal wrongs. In contrast, under the CPA 1987 it has already been seen that there are different rules relating to each part of the statute. Part I, dealing with statutory product liability, imposes only civil sanctions, whilst breach of any safety regulation made under Pt II or code of practice relating to price indications under Pt III, does not, in the absence of any provision to the contrary, render the agreement void or unenforceable (s 41(3)).

Part II

Contract and Conveyance

Chapter 7

The Passing of Property under the Sale of Goods Act 1979

In any system of property law a complete specification of rights and duties raises at least two questions. The first issue concerns the allocation of rights and duties between the parties to the transaction, whilst the second focuses upon the rights and duties of the parties as against the rest of the world. However, it is important to guard against an over-functionalist and simplistic account of property. It may be that commercial law, in the context of supply contracts, is too unknown, except to lawyers, to have much effect on the working of the market.

The traditional common law analysis where a third party wishes to acquire an indefeasible interest in a chattel, is to direct the latter to the 'owner'. The difficulty is that 'ownership' is an elusive concept and indeed Blackstone, in his *Commentaries on the Laws of England* (1765), not only fails to define ownership but does not even mention it as a juridical concept. Similarly, the SGA 1979 fails to define 'ownership' as only the term 'property' is defined in the Act, which equates it with 'general property' (s 61(1)). It may be that 'general property' and ownership are treated as being coterminous. This is borne out by Chalmers in his 1890 commentary on *The Sale of Goods Including the Factors Act 1889*:

> The essence of sale is the transfer of the ownership or general property in goods from seller to buyer for a price . . . . The general property in certain goods may be in one person while a special property in them is in another person, as in the case of a pledge where the pledgee has only a special property, the general property remaining in the pledgor . . . . (p 93)

A distinction is drawn between the content of the right of property (general or special), the definition, creation and extinguishing of which involve questions of law from property as the *res* or thing itself. It is obvious that the word 'property' is not used in the latter sense under the SGA 1979 since the word 'goods' is adopted for that purpose. Despite this, the close connection between the idea of ownership and the idea of things owned demonstrated by the use of the word 'property' to designate both, has caused confusion. Thus, when the legislature thinks that an interest should be alienable and transmissible it will be reified and capable therefore of ownership. This point is illustrated by the SGSA 1982, the general effect of which equates contracts of hire, work and materials and services with sale.

115

Relativity of title

English land law can be categorised as an example of a multititular system, ie a ranking of claims, the efficacy of which depends upon the nature of the legal interest underlying it, in whom it is vested and against whom it is championed. It was not until the Law of Property Act 1925, which anticipates that title can now be registered, that much of the technicality and obscurity of English land law was finally obviated. In similar fashion to the case of land, relativity of title is the key concept for the understanding of the property provisions in the SGA 1979, though the transient value of chattels, together with the difficulty of proving title, makes the chain of title short. Herein lies the rationale for the conditions and warranties found in s 12. If s 2 of the Act anticipates the sale transaction as requiring a perfect title to be transferred, this would in effect make s 12 redundant. Such is not the case as s 12 elaborates upon the possibility of a sale of a limited interest, whilst s 5(1) contemplates in its definition of 'goods' the transfer of a possessory interest to goods (but compare *Mitsui and Co Ltd and another v Flota Mercante Grancolombiana SA, The Ciudad de Pasto, The Ciudad de Neiva* [1989] 1 All ER 951).

Although one can define ownership as roughly entailing exclusive possession, use, and the right to transfer it voluntarily to another, a wider and perhaps more insistent question is what principles decide *which* individuals have ownership rights and over *what* things. In some respects, the weakness of the common law method of approach to this question has confused the issue. Consequently, although property rights are defined as against the entire world, the legal dispute is usually fashioned as a contest between two parties. This form of adjudication tends to postpone the interests of third persons who may have an entitlement to the property in question (compare *Thomas v Heelas* 27 November, 1986 (CAT No 1065)). To meet this problem we find the emergence of a title undertaking, a development which is intertwined with accelerating commercial activity in society. As the volume of sales increased, taking them outside the scope of fairs and markets and the doctrine of market overt (which has now been repealed by the Sale of Goods Amendment Act 1994), the need for the seller to guarantee title became very pressing. However, the precise ambit of such an implied undertaking was a matter of doubt especially since it conflicted with the *caveat emptor* doctrine.

The implied title undertaking

The quiet possession guarantee

It would seem that the common law was in a confused state when Chalmers came to codify the implied undertaking regarding title. Consequently, it is little wonder that he looked to Benjamin's seminal 19th century *Treatise on Sale* for clarification. Indeed, in the fifth edition of Benjamin the editors claim that the SGA 1893 'is largely based upon and follows the lines of the Treatise'. In the fourth edition treatment of implied warranty of title, Benjamin cites the relevant American law, the civil law and the French Code so that the warranty of quiet possession appears prominently in the discussion. In the civil law this is the main title undertaking and Benjamin uses this only to *support the argument that there existed a general common law warranty of title*. However Chalmers, influenced by real property concepts, made quiet possession supplementary to the general ownership guarantee, namely, the right to sell together with freedom from encumbrances. Thus s 12(2) provides that:

(a) the goods are free, and will remain free until the time when the property is to pass, from any charge or encumbrance not disclosed or known to the buyer before the contract is made, and

(b) the buyer will enjoy quiet possession of the goods except so far as it may be disturbed by the owner or other person entitled to the benefit of any charge or encumbrance so disclosed or known.

This division of title did not have a common law basis. On the other hand, the condition of right to sell in s 12(1) did have an apparent meaning and it is little wonder that it was this concept which was used and developed.

There is no doubt that Chalmers was influenced by the real property covenant of quiet possession. His 1894 *Commentary on The Sale of Goods Act 1893* (1894) cites, 'the Conveyancing and Law of Property Act 1881 (44 and 45 Vict C41), which it is to be noted applied to "conveyances" of personalty, a covenant for title and quiet possession is always imported unless expressly negatived' (p 26). In *Niblett v Confectioners' Materials Co* [1921] 3 KB 387, Atkin LJ considered the warranty to resemble 'the covenant of quiet enjoyment of real property' (p 403). Furthermore, the warranty, it was said, could include the tortious acts of the vendor himself, but no authority was cited in support of this proposition. Such a conclusion is anomalous since s 12(1) already gives the buyer a right to sue the seller for failure to transfer the property in the goods irrespective of which prior seller first failed to transfer the required property rights. On the basis of the *Niblett* case, it would seem that tortious acts *within* the scope of the warranty of quiet possession are confined to those of the immediate seller, and any extension to include tortious acts of third parties would destroy the legal predictability of the warranty. An important aspect of this issue in terms of practical effect can be seen in the conflict between a finance company as owner and an innocent third party purchaser seeking the protection of Part III of the Hire Purchase Act 1964 (as amended). This conflict is discussed in detail in Chapter 10.

The above approach applies to other contracts of supply so that, eg, ss 2(2) and 7(2) of SGSA 1982 provide that there is an implied warranty that the goods will be free from charges and encumbrances and that the transferee will have quiet possession. In the case of a contract of hire, s 7 of SGSA 1982 does not provide an implied term that the goods are free from incumbrances and charges. The only issue here relates to quiet possession. Thus in the case of a finance lease (see Chapter 12), the lessor impliedly warrants that the hirer will enjoy uninterrupted use and enjoyment of the goods for the period of the hire. This may prove problematical for a sub-lessee where the intermediary lessor (the finance lessee) had no right to sub-lease the goods. Use of the goods by the sub-lessee might amount to conversion, but if the action is brought by the finance lessor after the subsidiary hiring term expired, it will be difficult to establish that such action creates an incursion upon the subsidiary hirer's quiet possession. Of particular interest in this context is the 'wraparound' lease. The structure here normally includes an initial lease from a lessor to a user of the equipment (this lease although first in time is destined to become a sub-lease), followed by a sale of the equipment by the lessor to a third party owner (the wrap lessor) and its leaseback to the lessor (the wrap lessee) for a longer term. The leaseback or wraparound lease is for a longer period than the sub-lease. The equipment is ordinarily subject to an existing debt incurred by the wrap lessee to a financial institution (the lessor under the wrap lease) to purchase the equipment. Such debt is secured by the equipment and by an assignment of the rents to be paid by the user. Following the expiration of the lease to the user, the lessor (the wrap lessee) can sub-let the goods for the period up to the time of the expiration of the main contract. Clearly, with such complex commercial arrangements, the implied obligation that the supplier has the right to hire out the goods and that they are free, and will remain free, from any charge or encumbrance not disclosed to the sub-lessee before the agreement is made, is very important.

The general property guarantee

The precise ambit of the general property concept introduced into the SGA 1893 remains ambiguous. When Chalmers drafted the implied obligation to pass good title under s 12, influenced by real property concepts, he used 'right to sell' terminology instead of, for example, 'right to pass property or title'. In this respect, s 12(1) provides:

> (1) In a contract of sale, there is an implied condition on the part of the seller that in the case of a sale he has a right to sell the goods, and in the case of an agreement to sell he will have such a right at the time when the property is to pass.

Initially in *Monforts v Marsden* (1895) 12 RPC 266, the implied condition as to title was restrictively construed. As Lord Russell held:

> I think that all that the first implied condition as to title meant was that the man had a right to sell the thing as it was in the sense of being able to pass the property in the thing to the vendee . . . In other words, it is a warranty of good title to the thing; it is not a covenant as to the quality of the thing, as to the workability of the thing, or that the machine shall be delivered under such circumstances in which the vendee shall be entitled to work it. (p 269)

It was unlikely that Chalmers was going to depart from the previous common law and give protection to peripheral title rights. In so far as the common law recognised any implied title obligations, these did not exceed beyond 'core' property rights, and this approach was confirmed at first instance in *Niblett Ltd v Confectioners' Materials Co Ltd* (1921) unreported, Bailhache J presiding). The Court of Appeal ([1921] 3 KB 387) unanimously reversed this decision and resolved to read s 12 literally and not in the light of previous authorities. As

Bankes LJ said in that case, 'I think section 12 has a much wider effect and that the language does not warrant the limitation imposed by Lord Russell' (p 395). The judgments of both Bankes and Scruton LJJ equate the right to sell with freedom from legal restrictions so that, for example, Scrutton LJ said:

> The respondents impliedly warranted that they had a right to sell them. In fact they could have been restrained by injunction from selling them, because they were infringing the rights of third persons. If a vendor can be stopped by process of law from selling he has not the right to sell. (p 398)

The consequence of this approach is that whenever a seller can by legal process be restrained from selling the goods, he will not have a right to sell. However, the relationship between right to sell and quiet possession was not discussed by the majority in *Niblett*. This is unfortunate because the structure of the section with its division of title between right to sell, warranties of quiet possession and freedom from encumbrances, suggests that title interferences are divided between these undertakings, and that a distinction should be drawn between title defects of a serious and less serious nature. As Roskill LJ said in *Microbeads AG v Vinhurst Road Markings Ltd* [1975] 1 WLR 218, 'It follows that in my view these two subsections create and were intended to create independent rights and remedies for an aggrieved buyer according to whether it is the implied condition or the implied warranty which is broken' (p 226). When title encompasses lesser property rights such as trademarks, patents as well as government legislation affecting goods, the court may more readily find breaches of the warranty envisaged under s 12(2).

In the case of contracts for bailment, s 7 of SGSA 1982 provides that there is an implied condition that the bailor has a right to bail the goods and not necessarily that he is the owner of the goods. With regard to hire purchase, s 8(1) of SOGIT 1973 (as substituted by Sched 4 to CCA 1974) provides that there is an implied condition that the creditor-owner will have the right to sell the goods *when* the property is to pass. An important distinction may be drawn here with the contract of sale where, following *Rowland v Divall* [1923] 2 KB 500, a buyer can reject the goods notwithstanding long use if his seller had no right to sell at the time of delivery. Nevertheless, the reasoning adopted in *Rowland v Divall* is that the *purpose* of a sale transaction is to transfer a perfect title which is not the case with a hire contract, nor with hire purchase at least until the time when the property is to pass. From the perspective of consumer protection, this position is unsatisfactory because the hirer under a hire purchase contract must wait to be dispossessed before he can reject the goods. This is discussed in Chapter 10. Moreover, this approach is contrary to the trend in commercial law to equate hire purchase with sale transactions.

The difficulties involved in quantifying damages often lead the draftsman of the finance lease to include a right to sub-lease in the main leasing contract (see generally p 292). This right to sub-lease will *prima facie* be limited to the duration of the main leasing agreement, unless the sub-hirer can establish that the finance lessor held out the lessee as being the owner or as being authorised to sublet for a period not limited to the main hiring agreement. Such a conclusion is unlikely in the light of the fact that the courts, at least in hire purchase cases, have consistently held that the owner is not estopped from denying the hirer's authority to sell by mere delivery of possession unless there is some representation which can be spelled out from the owner's conduct. It normally follows that the termination of the main leasing agreement will automatically terminate the sublease. Indeed, if the sub-hirer refuses to deliver up possession, he may be sued for 'wrongful interference' by virtue of s 3 of the Torts (Interference with Goods) Act 1977.

The problems posed above demonstrate the difficulty of developing a clear theory of ownership or property in English law. The analytical jurist would see property in terms of *dominium* or ownership, which is often categorised as the attribution to the owner of all conceivable powers relating to the object of ownership, in so far as those powers are recognised by the legal order. In this respect, property is seen as a real right, a right *in rem*, which can be transferred only by handing over possession. Terminological problems arise with this approach by virtue of the fact that ss 16–20 of SGA 1979 envisage a transfer of property as between seller and buyer by agreement. It may be, therefore, that title and property terminology used in the SGA 1979 mean different things. Under the Act, the passing of property is said to affect only the relations of the parties *inter se* whereas title passage binds third parties. The argument here is that the section headings 'Transfer of property as between seller and buyer' (ss 16–20) and 'Transfer of title' (ss 21–26) which contain the exceptions to the *nemo dat* doctrine in close juxtaposition, support this conclusion. Such an approach fails to take into account the practical consequences of property passing. Indeed whether the property in the goods has passed to the buyer is a matter of central importance. The answer is crucial for the resolution of those issues to which property rights are normally relevant.

Effects of property passing

Risk and frustration

The principle of *res perit domino* is enshrined in s 20(1) of SGA 1979 which provides that risk is transferred when property passes. This is of relevance also with regard to the doctrine of frustration. By virtue of s 7(1), if there is an agreement to sell specific goods and subsequently the goods, without any fault on the part of the seller or buyer, perish before the risk passes to the buyer, the agreement is avoided (see Chapter 9).

Insolvency of a party

The courts are often called upon to determine whether property has passed when one party has become insolvent and it is necessary to decide whether the goods are assets which can be used to discharge his debts. Where property has passed, the relationship between seller and buyer is simply one of creditor and debtor. Nonetheless, ss 41–48 of SGA 1979 will give the unpaid seller certain real remedies. such as the unpaid seller's lien and the right of stoppage in transit (see Chapter 13).

Third party claims

The House of Lords' decision in *Leigh and Sillavan Ltd v Aliakmon Shipping Co Ltd* [1986] AC 785 emphasised that if the goods are damaged in transit between the seller and buyer, the latter will only be able to sue the carrier, in the absence of a bailment relationship between them, if property has passed before the harm occurs. In a similar fashion, if the seller makes an unauthorised resale of the goods, the question of property location will determine the issue of whether his liability is merely for breach of contract or whether the resale amounts to conversion.

The security of property principle

The general principle is that of *nemo dat quod non habet* (see Chapter 10). However, a party who has merely a possessory title to the goods will have, in some circumstances, the power to dispose of them by virtue of statutory intervention to protect innocent third parties who are misled by appearances.

Tracing rights

The infiltration of the trust doctrine into the contract of sale is highly significant, especially in the light of the line of cases dealing with retention of title clauses (see Chapter 11).

The transfer of property

It is a prerequisite of the passing of property that there should be identification. This has a long historical lineage in the common law where great importance was accorded to specificity as seen in the *Year Books* (18 edn 4, 14). Here the Justices all agreed that a grant to kill and take a deer in the grantor's part conferred no property in any deer. Similarly in *Heyward's Case* (2 Coke 36), Coke said:

> If I have three horses and I give you one of them, in this case the election ought to be made in the lifetime of the parties, for inasmuch as none of the horses is given in certain, the certainty, and thereby the property, begins by election.

Inevitably, this requirement of identification will pose problems in English law since the passage of property is linked to agreement rather than conveyance.

The requirement of identifiability is linked in no small measure with the concept of 'goods' as the subject matter of the contract. The categorisation here of the nature of the goods will resolve such questions as:

    (a) whether the contract is a sale or an agreement to sell;
    (b) when property in the goods passes from the seller to the buyer;
    (c) whether specific performance of the contract may be decreed;

(d) whether there is a valid contract of sale;

(e) whether the doctrine of frustration applies to the contract in question.

The categorisation of goods

Existing and future goods

The goods which form the subject matter of a contract of sale may be either existing goods which are owned and possessed by the seller, or they may be future goods in the sense that they are to be manufactured or acquired by the seller. It is clear from s 12 of SGA 1979 that it is not necessary for the seller to be the absolute owner of such goods subject to the implied statutory condition as to right to sell the goods. The mere possession of the goods will be enough for them to be categorised as 'existing' goods.

A contract for the sale of future goods can only be an agreement to sell, even though the seller anticipates in the contract of sale to effect a present sale of the goods. This must be the case as a matter of logic since the statutory definition of future goods encapsulated in s 61(1) provides that such goods are 'to be manufactured or acquired by the seller after the making of the contract of sale'. There is nothing unusual, in the absence of a misrepresentation on the part of the seller, in his offering for sale of goods which he expects or hopes to acquire. Thus in *Varley v Whipp* [1900] 1 QB 513, all parties proceeded upon the assumption that there was a contract for the sale of 'specific goods' notwithstanding that at the time of the contract the reaper which was the subject matter of the sale was owned by a third party.

Specific and unascertained goods

Specific goods are defined by s 61(1) as being, subject to contrary intention, 'goods identified and agreed on at the time a contract of sale is made'. The meaning of specific goods under the SGA 1979 may vary depending upon the context in which it is used in the Act. In *Howell v Coupland* (1874) LR 9 QB 462, a contract of sale of 200 tons of potatoes to be grown on a specified field was held to be a sale of specific goods, whereas, in *HR & S Sainsbury Ltd v Street* [1972] 1 WLR 834, a contract of sale of 275 tons of barley, which was believed by both parties would be the yield of the seller's farm in the summer, was held to constitute a sale of unascertained goods.

One major difficulty is that the expression unascertained goods is nowhere defined in the Act although it does use the expression by way of contrast to specific goods. It would appear that unascertained goods must mean such goods which are not identified and agreed upon at the time the contract is made but which will become ascertained at some later stage. The distinction between 'specific' and 'unascertained' goods may therefore only be one of degree. From this, it is consistent to categorise unascertained goods into the following types:

(a) goods to be manufactured or grown by the seller;

(b) goods of a designated type;

(c) an unidentified part of a specific whole which, for convenience, may be categorised as quasi-specific goods.

The need to distinguish between specific and unascertained goods is particularly acute for the passing of property in part of a bulk (see Chapter 7).

Future specific goods

The uncritical approach to future goods would be to categorise them as being unascertained. However, the definition of future goods anticipated in the SGA 1979 does allow for the categorisation of the goods being specific, for example, property which in the course of nature may grow from the existing property of the seller including progeny in the case of animals, or crops as seen in *Howell v Coupland* (1876). In any case, the common law recognised this by allowing the legal title to after-acquired potential property to vest in the purchaser automatically upon its coming into existence, without any new act or transfer of the kind that would be mandatory. The 17th Century case of *Grantham v Hawley* (1615) Hob 182 introduced into the common law the concept of potential existence so that, if the process of creation had already begun, it was possible to own something which in the normal course would lead to fruition: 'A parson may grant all the tithewool that he shall have in . . . a year; yet perhaps he shall have none but that shall grow upon his sheep that he shall buy hereafter; for there he hath it neither actually nor potentially' (p 132a). This doctrine was never applied to the fruits of manufacture where the courts relied instead on the vague 'new act doctrine' the scope of which is notoriously uncertain (*Lunn v Thornton* (1845) 1 CB 379).

Ascertained goods

The importance of ascertainment of goods goes to the heart of identifiability. Section 16 of SGA 1979 provides for the case where the contract goods are not identified at the time when the contract is made:

> Where there is a contract for the sale of unascertained goods no property in the goods is transferred to the buyer unless and until the goods are ascertained.

It is envisaged, under s 61(1), that specific goods are those identified at the time of the contract whilst ascertained goods are those which were unidentified when the contract was made but become identified subsequently as the contract goods. For the most part, ascertained goods are treated as an aspect of specific goods which is a recognition of the fact of identification. Two important distinctions do remain: first, the seller cannot substitute goods for the specific goods which have lawfully been rejected by the buyer since, by definition, the contract is concerned with these goods only; secondly, the frustration of a contract for the purposes of ss 6 and 7 of SGA 1979 refers only to specific goods.

The ascertainment of the goods is a condition precedent to the passing of property. The SGA 1979 has the appearance of being somewhat disjointed here. It is hard to justify the inclusion of s 16 under Pt III of the Act, the heading of which is 'Transfer of property as between *seller* and *buyer*', especially since no reason is given for restricting the parties' freedom of contract in this respect. This is not to say that the property will pass when the goods are ascertained because this depends upon the intention of the parties.

Ascertainment

The issue of what constitutes ascertainment of goods is crucial to the issue of property passage. The Law Commission Working Paper, *Rights to Goods in Bulk* No 112 (1989) made no proposal for reform permitting property in goods to pass when the parties intended it to pass. The prevailing argument was that such a solution could lead to uncertainty, not least because the parties themselves might have unclear intentions. To a large extent this approach reflects the continued materialism of the common law in that, as the Working Paper put it (at para 4.5), how can a buyer be said to own something where there is an agreement to supply goods which are only described in general terms?

Even after the 1995 reform, property cannot pass in goods where there is merely a generic description without reference to a specific bulk. In adopting this approach an important legislative opportunity was lost to protect prepaying consumers. Potentially a significant distinction can be drawn between the position of a commercial creditor and consumer creditors in relation to prepayments. The commercial creditor, faced with imperfect information and characterised by risk aversion, will contract on terms which reflect the risk perceived and potential borrowers will seek to convey information of reassurance especially as to the assumption of risk. On the other hand, consumer prepayment creditors will very often fail to see themselves as creditors who risk losses in the case of default, and even if there is an understanding of this the consumer will rarely have ease of access to the requisite information concerning the nature and size of the trader's business and the latter's exposure to insolvency. Such lack of symmetry between commercial and consumer creditors could invite a difference in treatment in terms of legal response. The new amendments to the SGA confine relief to a property claim in identifiable goods and this cannot by definition extend to those who have contracted for a service nor to non-identifiable goods. It is necessary therefore to examine whether there is a solution in equity protecting prepaying buyers in unidentified goods.

The present law and unidentified goods: A solution in equity?

Equitable infiltration and sale

In *Re Wait* [1927] 1 Ch 606, Atkin LJ pointed out that if the parties do intend to create equitable rights these can only operate outside of the sale context. More recently such an approach was echoed by Lord Mustill in *Liggett v Kensington*, reported *sub nom Re Goldcorp Exchange Ltd* [1994] 3 WLR 199 when he stated (at p 206) that 'under a simple contract for the sale of unascertained goods no equitable title can pass merely by virtue of the sale'. It is important to deal with the facts of this case because they provide an illustration of the current legal issues as they relate to non-ascertainment of goods, notably the parameters of equitable tracing and the constructive trust doctrine.

The ascertainment of goods issue can be set out within short compass in relation to the general facts, which involved a gold trading house, Goldcorp Exchange Ltd, which was hopelessly insolvent and in the hands of receivers (including Mr Kensington) appointed to the company by the Bank of New Zealand. Such was the extent of the insolvency that if the claim of the Bank under the floating charge was to be satisfied then there would be nothing left for the unsecured creditors. There were many disappointed customers as Goldcorp had invited members of the public to invest in gold coins and bullion and they (including Mr Liggett) had done so on the basis that Goldcorp would sell them the precious metal and store and insure it free of charge until they asked for delivery or alternatively sold their investments. The gold was stored on a 'non-allocated' basis, which meant that it was stored as a mass and not separated out into portions for each customer. Goldcorp gave a 'certificate of ownership' to these investors and represented that they would 'own' the metal, and further represented that its stacks of metal were audited monthly to ensure that it had sufficient stocks to meet all its commitments. In reality there were insufficient gold stocks. There was no doubt that Goldcorp was in breach of contract and were guilty of misrepresentation but rescission had not occurred before the Bank's floating charge had crystallised. The difficulty for the plaintiffs was in establishing a proprietary claim and this they failed to do. Perhaps the most obvious way for the claimants to establish a proprietary claim was to show that property in the bullion had passed to them upon conclusion of the contract of sale. The problem was that this claim related to the sale of unascertained generic goods and as Lord Mustill, who gave the opinion of the Privy Council pointed out, from 'the very nature of things' no legal title could pass until specific bullion for a specific customer had been ascertained: 'It makes no difference what the parties intended if what they intended is impossible: as in the case with an immediate transfer of title to goods whose identity is not yet known' (p 208).

The Privy Council strongly endorsed the approach in *Re Wait* and *Re London Wine Co (Shippers) Ltd* [1986] PCC 121. In the latter case the London Wine Company were dealers in wine and operated a scheme whereby customers could buy wine as an investment. The wine was sold either lying in bond (to which charges for duty, delivery and documentation together with VAT were added to the price quoted), or alternatively as where duty had been paid and delivered. People interested in buying wine filled in an application form. When an order was received, the company prepared an invoice subject to its usual terms and conditions which included the following term:

> All goods and documents relating thereto shall be subject to a particular lien for all monies owing in respect of the goods and also to a general lien for all sums owing to the company either by customers or any person who has been the owner of the goods whilst in possession of the company . . .

The contemplation was, therefore, that the wine would belong to the purchasers who were described as 'sole and beneficial owners'. There was also a provision for the wine to be stored subject to a storage charge and an insurance payment. When the customer paid for the wine, he received a certificate of title from the company, the purpose of which was to enable the customer to establish title to the wine sold. Since the wine at issue before the judge was bought as an investment, it was clearly to the advantage of the customers to keep the wine in storage. In this respect, the warehousing policy of the company was crucial as to whether the wine bought had not only been ascertained, but also unconditionally appropriated for the purpose of passing of property. In fact, with a completed sale the company stock book would allocate the wine sold to a particular consignment reference number at a particular warehouse, but there was no notification of the sale to the warehouse concerned. It was held by Oliver J that no act of appropriation had taken place at the date of the receivership, that is, there was no link between the wine sold with any given consignment or warehouse.

The *Goldcorp* case does emphasise the limits of passing property in bulk under existing law, namely:

(1) The goods must be segregated from those of the vendor's trading stock;

(2) The vendor's records must be kept in order recording 'transfer of ownership';

(3) The vendor must not act as if the goods were his own.

If these conditions are not met, a court will conclude that the purchaser is a tenant in common for the entire bulk. Each customer will have a proportionate share as an equitable tenant in common exactly corresponding to the amount of, for example, bullion purchased for each customer. Once specific bullion has been purchased with customers' monies, then 'equity looks on done as what ought to be done', so that these customers have traceable equitable proprietary rights in the bullion which are protected by a proprietary remedy.

This was indeed the position in *Re Stapylton Fletcher Ltd* and *Re Ellis Son and Vidler Ltd in administrative receivership*) [1995] 1 All ER 192 in relation to bulk purchase of wine. The facts of *Re Stapylton Fletcher Ltd* are similar to *London Wine* and many of the claims failed, including an argument that there was a resulting trust of the purchase-money where the company held none of the wine in question. In *Stapylton Fletcher Ltd* where wine which fulfilled particular customers' purchases had been physically segregated from the sellers' common stock, it was held that there had been sufficient appropriation to pass title notwithstanding that what was set aside represented the aggregate of a particular wine bought by several customers in separate transactions and was not allocated to them individually. As Judge Paul Baker QC said at p 210:

> It is the segregation of the stock from the company's trading assets, whether done physically or by giving instructions to a bonded warehouse keeper, which causes the goods to be ascertained for the purposes of section 16 [of the Sale of Goods Act 1979]. The goods are then identified as those to be handed over for storage in performance of the contract of sale.

As between the buyers, they became tenants in common of the entire stock proportionate to the ratio of their own wine to the entire mass. Therefore, although the company remained in possession at all material times, after the appropriation, the character of its possession changed from that of a seller to that of a bailee. It would have been pointless to insist that the buyers take delivery for a short time and then redeliver the wine to the company for storage. The case is therefore no authority for the proposition that in sale of goods, allocation in the books of the seller is sufficient appropriation to the buyer.

Clearly, what is sufficient appropriation will depend upon the circumstances. In the *London Wine* case (1975) the issue of warehouse receipts acknowledging to a category of claimants that the warehouse held wine to their account did claim the attention of the court. On the facts, it was held that since the goods were unascertained, no property could pass by virtue of the attornment, although there was little doubt that both the warehouseman and the vendor were estopped from denying their acknowledgement. Nevertheless, since the wine had not been appropriated to the contract, no interest had in fact been created which could affect a good faith purchaser who was not 'privy' to the estoppel (see *Simm v Anglo American Telegraph Co* (1879) 5 QBD 188).

An equitable lien and sale of goods?

A pre-paying purchaser may wish to claim a purchaser's lien on any goods satisfying the contract description in the seller's possession. In *Re Goldcorp* (1994) the Court refused to apply the remedial equitable lien concept presumably being influenced by the approach of Judge Paul Baker QC in *Stapylton Fletcher Ltd* where he said at (pp 213-14):

> [The] court must be very cautious in devising equitable interests and remedies which erode the statutory scheme for distribution on insolvency. It cannot do it because of some perceived injustice arising as a consequence only of the insolvency'.

In *Re Wait* (1927), Atkin LJ ruled out the possibility of a purchaser's lien for the recovery of the purchase money paid over because in his view the Code, in defining the remedies of the buyer, provides a complete and exhaustive statement (pp 636ff). Nevertheless, the nature of buyer's remedies listed in the Act only reflect the seller's *contractual* obligations, for example, damages and specific performance. The Act does not deal with rescission for innocent misrepresentation, ie the restoration of the *status quo ante*. This is exactly what the purchaser is seeking to do in asserting his purchaser's lien. Is there, thus, any inconsistency in holding that no lien exists over a mass of personalty by virtue of an equitable assignment and, at the same time, allowing a purchaser a lien over the mass for the recovery of money paid for the relevant part? In fact, no conflict need arise. Whereas the first proposition rests on sufficiency of identity of the relevant property so that equity can acknowledge the purchaser's ownership, the latter depends upon whether there is sufficient identity of property such that the vendor would be acting unconscientiously if he were to dispose of the property without either accounting to the purchaser, such as through discharge of indebtedness, or through seeking his consent.

The point here is that the equitable lien is not the specific equitable right that is related to trust or specific performance, but rather it expresses an equitable idea which is that of unjust enrichment. As such, the equitable lien, being a right against property, is different from a common law lien, in that the latter is founded on possession and gives, except as modified in statute, a right to detain the property until payment, whereas an equitable lien exists quite irrespective of possession. Such liens are well known in the context of realty. A vendor of land, who has parted with the legal title before payment, has an equitable lien over the land to the extent of the purchase money unpaid, subject to a good faith purchaser of the legal estate without notice. In addition, a purchaser of land who has paid his purchase money before conveyance has a lien in equity to the extent of the purchase money paid. Significantly, the Australian High Court decision in *Hewett v Court* (1983) 57 ALJR 211, suggests that the list of equitable liens may not be a closed one.

The facts of the Australian case involved a contract for work and materials with respect to the construction of a mobile home for the purchaser. It was agreed that title to the home would not pass until payment had been made in full, and there was provision in the contract that payment was to be made in stages. When the appellants had paid 60 per cent of the total contract price, the construction company became insolvent. It was held that the appellants had an equitable lien upon the house to secure payment of the amount of money which they had paid under the contract. The mobile home had been sufficiently identified for the purpose of equitable intervention since, prior to the insolvency of the construction company, the appellants had inspected the mobile home and had chosen tiles for the roof.

The construction contract in *Hewett* may not have been specifically enforceable because of the provision incorporated that title was not to pass until the mobile home had been completed. However, the majority of the court held that the remedy of specific performance was not a prerequisite for the purchaser's lien. (There are contrary *dicta* in relation to vendors' liens: *Capital Finance Co Ltd v Stokes* [1969] 1 Ch 269 (at p 278); *London and Cheshire Insurance Co Ltd v Laplagrene Property Co Ltd* [1971] Ch 499 (at p 514); *Re Bond Worth* [1980] Ch 228 (at p 251)). Deane J considered the matter in the greatest detail, and summarised his reasoning in the following terms (at p 221–2):

> Nor, in my view, is there any valid reason in principle why the mere existence of any one of the recognised grounds for refusing specific performance of, for example, a contract for the sale of land should automatically preclude a lien over that land to secure the purchaser's right to be paid instalments of the purchase price of that property. The basis of specific performance lies in the equitable doctrine that personal obligations under a contract should be enforced where damages would be an inadequate remedy. The basis of equitable lien between parties to a contract lies in an equitable doctrine that the circumstances are such that the subject property is bound by the contract so that a sale may be ordered not in performance of the contract, but to secure the payment or repayment of money. In the ordinary case of a purchaser who desires the actual performance of this contract with a defaulting vendor, an equitable lien to secure repayment of instalments of purchase price is only of real value if specific performance of the contract would not be decreed.

The clear inference here is that the equitable lien doctrine derives from the principle that 'equity regards as done what ought to be done', that is, the championing of an 'interest' which the law cannot enforce but which ought to be enforced. A major difficulty with the approach is that it contradicts the 'equality is equity' principle in that, if equity gives a lien, some creditors will be paid in full while others will receive hardly anything. Undoubtedly, the force of this argument influenced the dissenting judgments of Wilson and Dawson JJ who said (at pp 218–19).

> The insolvency of the company is no reason of itself for placing the appellants in a secured position so as to achieve an advantage over other creditors. The other creditors may have included persons who paid moneys by way of deposit or otherwise for transportable houses but who were unable to identify, or sufficiently identify, a particular house as the one which was being constructed pursuant to the contract between them and the company. No equity dictates that those whose houses had reached a particular point of construction, such as the pitching of the roof, should be preferred in the realisation and distribution of the company's assets to those whose contracts with the company had been performed to a lesser extent.

The policy issue confirmed above goes to the heart of the distribution problem among creditors on insolvency.

Even the objection based on unfair preferences expressed by Wilson and Dawson JJ in the *Hewett* case can be overcome in equity. In Canada, for example, there have been some significant developments through the work of the British Columbia Law Reform Commission in Working Paper No 52 (1987), which has championed the buyer's lien on a seller's account as a means of protecting a prepaying consumer in a sale of consumer goods made in the usual course of the seller's business. In contrast, the Cork Committee on insolvency Law and Practice, Cmnd 8558 (1982) was unimpressed by arguments based on consumer preference:

> The customer who pays in advance for goods or services to be supplied later, extends credit just as surely as the trader who supplied in advance goods or services to be paid for later. There is no essential difference. Each gives credit; and if the credit is misplaced, each should bear the loss rateably. (para 1,052)

Some Canadian courts in addition to using the equitable lien device on the purchase price paid, have also held that unfinished prefabricated houses were impressed with a constructive trust (*Pettkus v Becker* (1981) 117 DLR (3d) 257). By means of this device, the financing buyer is entitled to priority on the builder's insolvency with respect to advances made against earlier debenture-holders and the trustee in bankruptcy of the manufacturer of the prefabricated houses (compare *Re Blyth Shipbuilding Co* (1927) discussed below, pp 135–6).

There is no doubt that to the extent that an equitable lien arises by express written agreement in respect of goods, it will constitute a charge which will require registration. Despite this, a failure to register the charge may not be fatal since the property will be impressed by the lien antecedent to its acquisition. In the case of a company, the charge will be registrable under s 400 of the Companies Act 1985 and non-registration will not invalidate the security against the liquidator (*Re Connolly Bros Ltd (No 2)* [1912] 2 Ch 25). To the extent that the lien operates by law, it will not need registration as a charge under the Companies Act 1985 (*Capital Finance Co Ltd v Stokes* [1969] 1 Ch 261). In addition, since the policy of the Bills of Sale Acts is to strike at documents rather than transactions, it is probable that an equitable lien arising by operation of law will not be struck down, since the essence of an equitable lien is a restitutionary remedy imposed to prevent another's unjust enrichment. The concomitant of this approach is that if other arrangements for security have been made, for example the insertion of a retention of title clause in the supply contract, an equitable lien will be excluded as being contrary to the parties' intention. As Slade J (as he then was) held in *Re Bond Worth* [1980] Ch 228:

> On the present facts there is in my judgment no room for implying any vendor's lien arising by operation of law, after completion of the purchase, bearing in mind the express agreement of the parties in the terms embodied in the retention of title clause, which was designed to secure payment of the full purchase price . . . (p 251)

The main dilemma regarding the application of the equitable lien concept is whether the saving provisions of the common law in s 62(2) of SGA include rules of equity and if this is the case, whether particular provisions in the Act are inconsistent with the existence of equitable liens. The first assumption has been accepted as authoritative and is unlikely to be seriously challenged. More problematical is whether the seller's lien in s 39 which depends upon possession of goods is antithetical to the existence of the equitable lien. It was argued by Atkin LJ in *Re Wait* that equitable infiltration into commercial law would be inconvenient yet it is hard to justify this restrictive approach, not least because in other contexts the existence of equitable liens has not stifled commerce.

Property passing as an aspect of intention

The emphasis on the protection of possession in the early common law, together with the close link between possession and ownership, make it difficult to explain how English law came to recognise the transfer of ownership by agreement. This contradicts possibly the most famous maxim of Roman law which is ascribed to Diocletian in the Code (C 2.3.20), namely, in *inter vivos* transactions there must be transfer or delivery of possession in order to pass ownership. Certainly, the position of Glanvill (X 14) and Bracton (ff 61b–62) was that no property passed in sale until there had been delivery.

It has been argued that the 19th Century position of property passing by agreement was a mistaken application of 15th Century jurisprudence. It is significant that when Lord Blackburn introduced the idea of property passing by agreement, at the same time, the Massachusetts court was taking the opposite view in *Lanfear v Sumner* (1821) 17 Mass 110. The English position was firmly established in the 19th century so that Lord Watson said in *McEntire v Crossley Bros Ltd* [1895] AC 457:

> [I]t does not in the least follow that, because there is an agreement of sale and purchase, the property in the thing which is the subject matter of the contract has passed to the purchaser. That is a question which entirely depends upon the intention of the parties. The law permits them to settle the point for themselves by any intelligible expression of their intention. (p 467)

By 1883, as Benjamin notes in his third edition, the US approach mirrored that adopted in England.

Section 17 of the Act lays down the basic rule that property in specific goods only passes when the parties intend:

(1) Where there is a contract for the sale of specific or ascertained goods the property in them is transferred to the buyer at such time as the parties to the contract intend it to be transferred.

(2) For the purpose of ascertaining the intention of the parties regard shall be had to the terms of the contract, the conduct of the parties and the circumstances of the case.

The question of finding a common intention (express or implied) as to the passing of property, has proven problematic because the parties themselves will often be more concerned with the practical side of the transaction, such as arranging delivery and payment, rather than satisfying esoteric legal criteria of property passing. Moreover, because the common law rejected an objective test as to the passing of property, the courts had to lay down a series of more or less arbitrary rules for the attribution of intention which have been encapsulated in s 18. This contains five rules dealing with the transfer of property under the contract of sale. The fourth rule in s 18 is somewhat of an oddity since it is concerned with the delivery of goods on approval or on a sale or return basis and is not, therefore, made pursuant to a contract of sale (see Chapter 10).

Rules for ascertaining intention

The first three rules of s 18 are concerned with contracts for the sale of specific goods.

Rule 1—Where there is an unconditional contract for the sale of specific goods in a deliverable state, the property in the goods passes to the buyer when the contract is made, and it is immaterial whether the time of payment or the time of delivery, or both, be postponed.

Rule 2—Where there is a contract for the sale of specific goods and the seller is bound to do something to the goods for the purpose of putting them into a deliverable state, the property does not pass until the thing is done and the buyer has notice that it has been done.

Rule 3—Where there is a contract for the sale of specific goods in a deliverable state but the seller is bound to weigh, measure, test, or do some other act or thing with reference to the goods for the purpose of ascertaining the price, the property does not pass until the act or thing is done and the buyer has notice that it has been done.

The meaning of the term 'specific goods' in relation to property passing was considered by the Court of Appeal in *Kursell v Timber Operators Ltd* [1927] 1 KB 298. In this case the plaintiff sold to the defendants all the trees in a Latvian forest which conformed to certain minimum specifications within a 15-year period. The buyer paid a first instalment of the price but before he could cut much timber the forest was nationalised. The Court of Appeal held that the timber had not passed to the buyer and that the risk remained with the seller because there was not a sale of specific goods. First, it was really a contract for the sale of a right of severance and the trees did not become 'specific or ascertained' for the purposes of s 17 until they were put in a deliverable state.

Second, the trees were held not to be specific goods until cut. This approach is overly harsh and it is submitted that contract goods need only to be described by the contract in such a way that they are identifiable at the time the contract is made for them to be specific.

It should be emphasised that the s 18 rules are merely presumptive of intention and can be displaced by contrary intention as a matter of construction of the contract, or by rule of law such as that encapsulated in s 16. To discover the intention of the parties as required under the Act, regard must be paid to the terms of the contract, the conduct of the parties and the circumstances of the case. This vague and general statutory language seen in s 17(2) allows considerable latitude. Thus in *Re Anchor Line Ltd* [1937] 1 Ch 1, the Court of Appeal inferred that a provision in the contract placing the risk on the buyer was an indication that property had *not* passed because, under the normal rule encapsulated in s 20(1), risk passes with property (see p 148). It follows from this that an obligation to insure will be an important indication of who bears the risk which, in turn, is presumptive of the fact of property passage.

Rule 1

The presumption in rule 1 is weak because it assumes that 'where there is an unconditional contract for the sale of specific goods' property passes *irrespective* of the question of delivery or payment. Such a presumption in a consumer context is likely to be displaced as it would visit upon the consumer the risk of the contract goods being damaged or destroyed in the interim period between the conclusion of the contract and the delivery of the goods. The presumption makes little practical sense because the business seller is in a better position to insure the goods. It is little wonder, therefore, that Diplock LJ was so insistent in *RV Ward Ltd v Bignall* [1967] 1 QB 534: 'The governing rule . . . is in s 17 and in modern times very little is needed to give rise to the inference that the property in specific goods is to pass only on delivery or payment'.

Two questions are posed by r 1:

    (1)   What is an 'unconditional contract'?
    (2)   When are goods 'in a deliverable state'?

'Unconditional contract'
These words have given rise to particular problems because the expression 'condition' is used in two different senses under the SGA 1979. The first sense is as a major term in the contract (condition as opposed to warranty), but this cannot be the meaning here because this interpretation would almost entirely obliterate the operation of the rule. It is probable that the second interpretation is the correct one in that 'unconditional contract for the sale of specific goods' means no more than a contract of sale under which the passing of property is not made subject to a condition precedent. The courts have in a few instances, no doubt influenced by a desire to protect innocent buyers, construed this also to include a condition subsequent, which is odd since by its nature this does not suspend the operation of a contractual provision. Thus in *Varley v Whipp* [1900]

1 QB 513, it was held that the sale of a secondhand reaping machine which had been little used, a description which was completely inaccurate, was not an unconditional sale. Such a strained interpretation is now no longer necessary with the repeal of the original s 11(1)(c) of the 1893 Act, which provided that the buyer lost his right to reject specific goods as soon as property passed. It was understandable that the judges should give an unnatural interpretation to the words 'unconditional contract' in s 18, rule 1 simply in order to avoid depriving a buyer of his right to reject goods.

'Deliverable state'

In addition to the requirement of specificity, the goods must be in a deliverable state. Under s 61(5) of SGA 1979, goods are in a deliverable state when they are in such a condition that the buyer would under the contract be bound to take delivery of them. It follows that if something still has to be done to the goods they will not be in a deliverable state and the property will not pass. A leading decision here is *Underwood Ltd v Burgh Castle Brick and Cement Syndicate* [1922] 1 KB 343. The facts involved the sale of a condensing engine, weighing over 30 tons, cemented to the floor of the seller's premises which had to be detached and dismantled before it could be delivered by rail, as the contract specified. The seller subsequently detached the engine; but it was severely damaged whilst being loaded without any fault on the part of the seller, and, apparently, before the buyer had notice that it had been detached. The risk issue raised in this case was decided in favour of the buyers on the ground that s 18, rule 1 did not apply because the sellers had to do something which they had not done to put the engine into a deliverable state. In coming to his conclusion, Bankes LJ remarked:

> A 'deliverable state' does not depend upon the mere completeness of the subject matter in all its parts. It depends on the actual state of the goods at the date of the contract, and the state in which they are to be delivered by the terms of the contract. (p 345)

The key issue as to whether or not the goods are in a deliverable state depends upon whether the contract imposes an obligation to do something in relation to the goods. In this respect, the goods are not prevented from being in a deliverable state if, for example, there has been a serious breach of a condition entitling the buyer to reject the goods. Thus in *Lord Eldon v Hedley Bros* [1935] 2 KB 1, it was agreed that property had not passed under a contract by which the buyer could refuse to take delivery of or pay for mouldy or unmerchantable hay. It was held that the contract was in such terms as to show that the parties intended that property should pass to the buyer when the contract was made (compare *Vigers Bros v Sanderson* [1901] 1 KB 608).

If the goods are to be repaired then the obligation to repair may be a condition precedent to the passing of property. Of course, this is a matter of construction of each particular contract, as is illustrated in *Phillip Head and Sons Ltd v Showfronts Ltd* [1970] 1 Lloyd's Rep 140, a case under s 18, rule 5(1) which also contains the phrase 'deliverable state'. In this case it was held that a carpet which the sellers were to lay was not in a deliverable state, mainly because it was a heavy bundle and difficult to use so that it was of little use to the buyer. It appears that if the contract anticipates a supply and installation, then as a matter of construction, property will not pass until the work of installation has been completed. The question of intention is of overriding importance, so that the issue of whether or not a contract is for the sale of goods or for work and materials is itself not decisive.

Rule 2

Rules 2 and 3 of s 18 deal with the passing of property in conditional contracts for the sale of specific goods. Under rule 2, the property in goods is not to pass until the seller puts the goods in a 'deliverable state'. This contrasts with rules 1, 3 and 5 as these deal with situations where the goods are already in a deliverable state. As a matter of consistency, the phrase 'deliverable state' must have the same meaning as rule 1.

Rule 3

This rule applies only where the seller is bound to weigh, test, measure or do something with reference to the goods for the purpose of working out the price. The civilian view, as adopted in art 1585 of the French Civil Code, is that so long as the goods sold must be weighed, counted or measured, the sale is not perfect. The incorporation of this principle into English law is rather odd especially in view of the fact that ascertainment and payment of the price under s 8 of SGA 1979 are not generally prerequisites for the passing of property. Moreover, its inclusion from civilian law is further disjointed because, instead of being defended on Pothier's grounds as flowing logically from an objective requirement of a perfect sale, it has rather assumed the form of a rule of interpretation for ascertaining the intention of the parties. Little wonder, therefore, that the rule is of slight practical importance (see *Nanka-Bruce v Commonwealth Trust* [1926] AC 77 PC).

Rule 5

The basic rule of law in relation to unascertained goods is contained in s 16 which requires that goods be identified or appropriated as the subject matter of the contract of sale. Where there is a contract for the sale of unascertained goods, no property in the goods is transferred to the buyer unless and until the goods are ascertained. Unascertained goods may be goods identified by description only, for example generic goods, or they may be a portion of a specific whole not yet identified, or they may be future goods. It should be noted that the 1995 amendment to the SGA has not removed s 16 which still remains although subject to the new s 20A relating to sale of goods forming part of a bulk (see below pp 142–6). This explains the additions inserted into s 18 r 5 by the 1995 Act, namely, subss (3) and (4). Indeed, the structure of the amended rule 5 provides both for appropriation of goods in a deliverable state and for ascertainment by process of exhaustion. The presumed intention of the parties as to the passing of property is as follows:

Rule 5—(1) Where there is a contract for the sale of unascertained or future goods by description, and goods of that description and in a deliverable state are unconditionally appropriated to the contract, either by the seller with the assent of the buyer or by the buyer with the assent of the seller, the property in the goods then passes to the buyer; and the assent may be express or implied, and may be given either before or after the appropriation is made.

(2) Where, in pursuance of the contract, the seller delivers the goods to the buyer or to a carrier or other bailee or custodier (whether named by the buyer or not) for the purpose of transmission to the buyer, and does not reserve the right of disposal, he is to be taken to have unconditionally appropriated the goods to the contract.

(3) Where there is a contract for the sale of a specified quantity of unascertained goods in a deliverable state forming part of a bulk which is identified either in the contract or by subsequent agreement between the parties and the bulk is reduced to (or to less than) that quantity, then, if the buyer under that contract is the only buyer to whom goods are then due out of the bulk—
   (a) the remaining goods are to be taken as appropriated to that contract at the time when the bulk is so reduced; and
   (b) the property in those goods then passes to that buyer.

(4) Paragraph (3) above applies also (with the necessary modifications) where a bulk is reduced to (or less than) the aggregate of the quantities due to a single buyer under separate contracts relating to the bulk and he is the only buyer to whom goods are then due out of that bulk.

Appropriation

By virtue of r 5(1), in the case of a contract for the sale of unascertained or future goods by description, property in the goods will pass to the buyer when goods of that description, in a deliverable state, are unconditionally appropriated to the contract, either by the seller with the assent of the buyer, or by the buyer with the assent of the seller. Such an assent may be express or implied. Suffice it to say that, as long as the goods correspond with description, the important issue is that of appropriation. If the goods do not correspond with description, as is the case where there has been a breach of s 13, property will not pass simply because there can be no appropriation of the goods on the basis that they did not form part of the agreed subject matter of the contract.

In *Re Blyth Shipbuilding and Dry Dock Co Ltd* [1926] Ch 494, the difficulties associated with the expression 'appropriation' were considered. The facts of the case were concerned with the construction and sale of a ship; the contract provided that 'materials and things appropriated' to the vessel would belong to the purchaser following the payment of this first instalment. Following the insolvency of the ship construction company, one of the issues was whether the worked and unworked material lying around the shipyard at the relevant time had been appropriated to the contract. Although the expression 'appropriation' was being used in a contract as distinct from being given

its statutory use, nevertheless the Court of Appeal read it in its proper technical sense. The word 'appropriated' was described by Sargant LJ as a 'term of
legal art' with a definite meaning (p 518). In this respect it was held that for
appropriation to take place, there had to be some definite act which, in the
instant case, amounted to the affixing of the property to the vessel itself.

The issue of appropriation is often determined by an express provision in the
contract. This is highly relevant with the burgeoning of retention of title clauses
over the last 15 years. One example is the case of *Hanson (W) (Harrow) v Rapid
Civil Engineering And Usborne Developments* (1987) 38 Build LR 106, where
the terms of a supply contract of timber expressly reserved title in the lumber
until payment and could not, therefore, in the absence of sale to the main contractors of a building site, be claimed by them under s 25(1) of SGA 1979. Here
the passing of property was governed by express contractual provision and not
the SGA 1979 since delivery of the materials was not considered to be a 'disposition' for the purposes of the Act (see Chapter 10).

Appropriation by the buyer

Rule 5(1) indicates that the act of appropriation may be made by the buyer.
When the buyer selects the goods, he will often have appropriated them before
the contract is concluded so the goods will then be specific. In certain circumstances, for example, in a mail-order business, the buyer may impliedly confer
on the seller a power of selection from stock which he has not seen. This is of
significance with regard to risk, which would appear to be on the buyer where
the article is put in the post. Nonetheless, it does offer some protection against
the insolvency of mail-order traders (compare *Badische Anilin und Soda Fabrik
v Basle Chemical Works* [1898] AC 200). The position of the prepaying financing buyer in relation to sale of goods forming part of a bulk is considered in
greater detail below (see pp 142–6).

Appropriation by the seller

One of the clearest indications of appropriation is where the seller expressly
informs the buyer that he is setting aside specific goods, as in the case where a
notice of appropriation is sent. As soon as this has been concluded, appropriation cannot be unilaterally withdrawn by the seller. There is some weak authority which suggests that if the buyer has not yet acted on the notice of
appropriation then it can be withdrawn (see *Borrowman, Phillips and Co v Free
and Hollis* (1878) 4 QBD 500). This will only be the case if the notice is
regarded as being provisional and, in this sense, cannot therefore be truly
categorised as a notice of appropriation.

In general the question of appropriation has to be determined by reference
to conduct on the part of the seller. Here, rule 5(2) operates as a presumption
that delivery to a carrier or other bailee is treated as though they were agents
of the buyer, irrespective of the fact that they may have been engaged by the
seller. Delivery is defined in such a way as to include actual and constructive
possession as well as encompassing issues of attornment. Sale and delivery
are distinct acts, though sometimes the delivery of goods may amount to

appropriation of them within rule 5. Of course, actual delivery is the last opportunity for appropriation which may often occur before then, as in the case where the seller acknowledges that he holds the goods on behalf of the buyer (*Wardar's (Import and Export) Co Ltd v W Norwood and Sons Ltd* [1968] 2 QB 663).

For appropriation to be effective it must be unconditional, and if there is any equivocality about the appropriation it will be ineffective to pass property. Two contrasting cases may be cited to illustrate the difficulty of determining whether there has been sufficient appropriation. In *Aldridge v Johnson* (1857) 7 E & B 885, the plaintiff agreed to buy 100 quarters of barley out of a particular parcel of 200 quarters which he had inspected. It was agreed that the buyer was to send his own sacks which the seller was to fill. The seller filled most of the sacks, but emptied the barley back into his granary just before he became bankrupt. The court held that as soon as the seller filled some of the sacks with the barley, property passed in that quantity of barley filled. On the other hand in *Carlos Federspiel and Co SA v Charles Twigg and Co Ltd* [1957] 1 Lloyd's Rep 240, the court came to the opposite conclusion. In this case the sellers agreed to sell a number of cycles and tricycles fob a British port. They made preparations for shipping them, for example, they had arranged boxes in which the goods were packed and marked with the port of destination. The goods were never shipped and the sellers went into liquidation. The buyers claimed the goods from the liquidator on the ground that the property had passed by virtue of rule 5(1) since they had been unconditionally appropriated to the contract. The Queen's Bench Division of the Commercial Court, Pearson J presiding, rejected this contention on the basis that it was the intention of the parties that no property in the goods should pass until shipment and that, although preparations for shipment had been made, this did not amount to an unconditional appropriation so as to pass the property. Pearson J summed up the law relating to appropriation in the following way:

First, r 5 of s 18 of the Act is one of the rules for ascertaining the intention of the parties as to the time at which the property in the goods is to pass to the buyer, unless a different intention appears. Therefore the element of common intention has always to be borne in mind. A mere setting apart or selection by the seller of the goods which he expects to use in performance of the contract is not enough. If that is all, he can change his mind and use those goods in performance of some other contract and use some other goods in performance of this contract. To constitute an appropriation of the goods to the contract the parties must have had, or be reasonably supposed to have had, an intention to attach the contract irrevocably to those goods, so that those goods and no others are the subject of the sale and become the property of the buyer.

Secondly, it is by agreement of the parties that the appropriation, involving a change of ownership, is made, although in some cases the buyer's assent to an appropriation is conferred in advance by the contract itself or otherwise.

Thirdly, an appropriation by the seller with the assent of the buyer may be said always to involve an actual or constructive delivery. If the seller retains possession, he does so as bailee for the buyer. There is a passage in Chalmers' *Sale of Goods Act*, 12th edn at p 75 where it is said—

'In the second place, if the decisions be carefully examined, it will be found that in every case where the property has been held to pass, there has been an actual or constructive delivery of the goods to the buyer.'

I think that is right, subject only to this possible qualification, that there may be after such constructive delivery an actual delivery still to be made by the seller under the contract. Of course, that is quite possible, because delivery is the transfer of possession, whereas appropriation transfers ownership. So there may be first an appropriation, constructive delivery, whereby the seller becomes bailee for the buyer, and then a subsequent actual delivery involving actual possession, and when I say that I have in mind in particular the cases cited, namely, *Aldridge v Johnson* and *Langton v Higgins*.

Fourthly, one has to remember s 20 of the Sale of Goods Act, whereby the ownership and the risk are normally associated. Therefore, as it appears that there is reason for thinking, on the construction of the relevant documents, that the goods were, at all material times, still at the seller's risk, that is *prima facie* an indication that the property had not passed to the buyer.

Fifthly, usually, but not necessarily, the appropriating act is the last act to be performed by the seller. For instance, if delivery is to be taken at the seller's premises and the seller has appropriated the goods when he has made the goods ready and identified them and placed them in position to be taken by the buyer and has so informed the buyer, and if the buyer agrees to come and take them, that is the assent to the appropriation. But if there is a further act, an important and decisive act, to be done by the seller, then there is *prima facie* evidence that probably the property does not pass until the final act is done. (pp 255–6 footnotes omitted)

Undoubtedly one factor that influenced the Court in *Federspiel* was the reluctance to interfere in the internal warehousing arrangements of business and to get involved in a grand stocktaking exercise. This point may be demonstrated historically in Heath J's dictum in *Mucklow v Mangles* (1808) 1 Taunt 318: 'A tradesman often finishes goods, which he is making in pursuance of an order given by one person, and sells them to another'(p 319). Compare *Hendy Lennox Ltd v Grahame Puttick Ltd* [1984] 1 WLR 485 discussed on pp 244–5).

Sometimes the circumstances will demonstrate an intention towards unconditional appropriation. In this respect, the facts in *Healy v Howlett and Sons* [1917] 1 KB 337 are instructive. Here the seller contracted to sell to the buyers 20 boxes of mackerel in Valentia, County Kerry. The boxes were placed on rail, but were not marked with the buyer's name and they were sent to Holyhead along with 170 other boxes for delivery to other customers. When the fish arrived at Holyhead, the railway company allotted 20 boxes out of 190 boxes to the buyers who found that they were not in a merchantable condition. The seller sued for the price of the goods on the ground that the property had passed under s 18, r 5(1) since the goods had been appropriated to the contract when they were placed on rail at Valentia. It was held that there was no appropriation because none of the 190 boxes had been marked with the buyer's name so as to distinguish them from the remainder. As Ridley J said:

The essence of the authorities which decide that the appropriation of goods to the contract by delivery to the carrier at the beginning of the transit may be sufficient to pass the property is that it should be known to whom the goods are appropriated, and not that the question as to who is to bear any loss that may happen should be open to any discussion or be determined by accident. (p 345)

In *Re Stapylton Fletcher Ltd* [1995] 1 All ER 192, Judge Paul Baker QC distinguished *Healy v Howlett* on the basis that the seller still retained control over the appropriation of goods, whereas in *Carlos Federspiel* the seller had not completed the arrangements for shipping the goods and could still withdraw them if he wished. This was not a case of segregation for a specific purpose so that constructive delivery to the buyer had been achieved. Even so, in *Carlos Federspiel* whilst the issue was ascertainment, nonetheless, there had been in effect a subjective appropriation so the distinction drawn is a very fine one.

Assent to appropriation

Whoever performs the act of appropriation, rule 5(1) indicates that assent must be given either before or after appropriation. This demonstrates that the act of appropriation by itself does no more than ascertain goods earmarked to the contract of sale. However, the courts will readily infer assent as is seen in *Pignataro v Gilroy and Son* [1919] 1 KB 459. The material facts were that the sellers sold 140 bags of rice to the buyer and on 28 February 1918, the sellers gave the buyer a delivery order for a quantity at Chambers Wharf and said that the remaining 15 were available for collection at the sellers' warehouse in Long Acre. The sellers requested the buyer to take the bags away but the buyer did nothing until 25 March. When the buyer sent someone to collect the 15 bags from the warehouse, he discovered that they had been stolen a little while before. The buyer then brought an action for non-delivery, but this was denied by the King's Bench Division where it was held that the sellers had appropriated the goods to the contract with the implied assent of the buyer so that property passed by virtue of s 18, rule 5(1). It would seem, following this case, that a refusal to give the necessary assent for appropriation would amount to a repudiatory breach unless the buyer could show good cause such as where the goods are not of merchantable quality.

It may be that the parties wish to reach the point of identifying goods without intending that property should pass immediately. This is especially important in international transactions involving c i f contracts where the buyer will want to know details of shipping, even though property will not pass until the shipping documents are in his possession and the price paid.

Ascertainment by process of exhaustion

Section 18 r 5(3) gives statutory expression to the rules on ascertainment by exhaustion which have already been recognised by the courts (see *Karlshamns Oljefabriker v East Port Navigation Corp (The Elafi)* [1982] 1 All ER 208). The new rule 5(3) applies where there is one contract and one buyer. This is extended in rule 5(4) where there are two or more contracts in which the buyer is the same person and where the bulk is later reduced to, or to less than, the total of the goods covered by the contract. The 'necessary modifications' referred to in rule 5(4) is that 'that contract' must be read as 'those contracts'. It should be emphasised that the new rules are confined to the goods being in a deliverable state so as to retain the internal consistency of s 18, and also they will only apply if no different intention appears.

Conditional appropriation

The s 18 presumptions do not apply to cases of conditional appropriation, although s 19 does provide for the specific situation where the seller has retained his ownership of the goods until conditions stipulated by him are met. Section 19 of the Act deals with reservation of a right of disposal in specific or appropriated goods in the following terms:

(1) Where there is a contract for the sale of specific goods or where goods are subsequently appropriated to the contract, the seller may, by the terms of the contract or appropriation, reserve the right of disposal of the goods until certain conditions are fulfilled; and in such a case, notwithstanding the delivery of the goods to the buyer, or to a carrier or in other bailee or custodier for the purpose of transmission to the buyer, the property in the goods does not pass to the buyer until the conditions imposed by the seller are fulfilled.

(2) Where goods are shipped, and by the bill of lading the goods are deliverable to the order of the seller or his agent, the seller is *prima facie* to be taken to reserve the right of disposal.

(3) Where the seller of goods draws on the buyer for the price, and transmits the bill of exchange and bill of lading to the buyer together to secure acceptance or payment of the bill of exchange, the buyer is bound to return the bill of lading if he does not honour the bill of exchange, and if he wrongfully retains the bill of lading the property in the goods does not pass to him.

It could be argued that because s 17 already provides that property passing is an aspect of intention, then s 19 is superfluous. Moreover, even if property does not pass by virtue of s 19, this does not prevent a buyer, who has obtained possession of the goods or documents of title, passing a good title to a third party under s 25(1) (see Chapter 10). A particular instance of the general principle laid down in s 19(1) is the provision in s 19(2), where the seller is *prima facie* deemed to reserve the right of disposal where goods are shipped and, by virtue of the bill of lading, the goods are deliverable to the order of the seller or his agent (see *The Ciudad de Pasto* (1989)). Property in the goods sold passes unconditionally where the bill of lading for the goods is made out in favour of the purchaser or his agent or representative as consignee. It is common in international sales for the seller to take the bill of lading to his own order and only indorse it to the buyer against payment, as is the case in cif contracts. The normal method of payment before the advent of the documentary credit was the bill of exchange, and s 19(3) provides that property does not pass to the buyer where he has not honoured the bill of exchange. However, this should not be confused with the power of disposal. In *Cahn v Pockett's Bristol Channel Steam Packet Co Ltd* [1899] 1 QB 643, it was held that where the buyer negotiates the bill of lading to an innocent third party who takes without notice of the buyer's failure to pay or honour the bill of exchange, such third party will acquire property in the goods as against the unpaid seller by virtue of s 47(2) of SGA 1979 and s 10 of FA 1889.

Under s 47(2) of SGA 1979, the unpaid seller loses his lien if a document of title has been transferred to a buyer where the buyer has transferred this to a person who takes in good faith and for valuable consideration (see Chapter 13). Section 47(2) provides:

Where a document of title to goods has been lawfully transferred to any person as buyer or owner of the goods, and that person transfers the document to a person who takes it in good faith and for valuable consideration, then—
(a) if the last-mentioned transfer was by way of sale the unpaid seller's right of lien or retention or stoppage in transit is defeated; and
(b) if the last-mentioned transfer was made by way of pledge or other disposition for value, the unpaid seller's right of lien or retention or stoppage in transit can only be exercised subject to the rights of the transferee.

Despite this, the unpaid seller's lien or stoppage *in transitu* is not affected by any sub-sale or other disposition, unless the seller assented thereto, which may, for example, take the form of attornment or estoppel. It would seem, following *DF Mount v Jay & Jay* [1960] 1 QB 159, that s 47 is limited to the case where the buyer transfers to the sub-buyer the same delivery order as that issued by the original seller, although the Court held that there was no limitation with respect to s 25(2) of SGA 1893 (now s 25(1) of SGA 1979). Significantly, it was held that s 25(2) was not confined to specific goods and that the sub-buyer (the holder of the delivery note) effectively overrode the rights of the unpaid seller. It should be noted that a delivery order is an undertaking to deliver possession and, as such, is not a document of title. Even so, s 1(4) of FA 1889, for the purpose of that Act, defines a document of title as including *inter alia*: '. . . any bill of lading, dock warrant, warehouse-keeper's certificate and warrant or order for the delivery of goods . . .' This is also the position under s 61(1) of SGA 1979. For examples of documents which were held not even to come under the extended definition see *Gunn v Bolckow, Vaughan and Co* (1875) 10 Ch App 491 and *Dublin City Distillery Ltd v Doherty* [1914] AC 823. The delivery order has no precise definition in English law, having at various times been referred to as a 'delivery note', 'overside order', 'ship's release' and 'warrants' (see *Colin and Sheilds v W Weddell and Co Ltd* [1952] All ER 337; *Inglis v Robertson and Baxter* [1898] AC 616; *Wardar's (Import and Export) Co Ltd v W Norwood and Sons Ltd* (1968) 2 QB 663).

The question of ascertainment of goods and the effect of a delivery order was examined in the pre-World War I decision of *Ant Jurgens v Louis Dreyfus and Co* [1914] 3 KB 40. In this case, an English broker entered into a contract with a merchant who did business in England and Germany, to purchase 2,640 bags of mowra seed on behalf of his principal. The merchant, who had received a shipment of 6,400 bags of this seed in Germany, issued its negotiable delivery order on its German branch in favour of the broker in return for his cheque. The broker's cheque was dishonoured, but he sold the delivery order to a buyer who demanded delivery of the seed. The merchant refused delivery because of the dishonoured cheque. The court held that under s 10 of the Factors Act 1889 and s 47 of SGA 1893, the transfer of a document of title to the buyer who took in good faith and for value had the effect of defeating the seller's lien in the same way as a negotiable bill of lading would have done. In addition, the Court held that the fact that the delivery order was given for unspecified goods would not have prevented this result, following *Capital and Counties Bank Ltd v Warriner-Bretherton Ford and Co* (1896) 1 Comm Cas 314. Here a warehouse, in response to a delivery order given by the seller-bailor of goods, issued its negotiable warrant to the buyers of 1,500 quarters of wheat which had not been separated from 2,918 quarters of wheat from the warehouse. The buyer endorsed the warrant to the bank to cover an overdraft. The buyers failed to pay for the wheat, and the seller called upon the warehouse to stop delivery. Matthews J held that the wording of s 9 of FA 1889 (substantially reproduced in s 25(1) of SGA 1979) which states that where a person 'having bought or agreed to buy goods' means that, where the buyer obtains a document of title to the goods, this is legally equivalent to having possession of the goods with the consent of the owner, even though the goods have not been ascertained.

The approach taken by Matthew J in the *Capital Counties* case has been criticised on the basis that s 25(1) of SGA 1979 must be read consistently with s 16. Moreover following the *Aliakmon* case [1986] AC 785, the sub-buyer will not be able to sue the warehouseman or carrier in negligence. It was to confront this problem that the Law Commission Working Paper No 112 proposed as one solution the reform of the Bills of Lading Act 1855, s 1, namely, to transfer the rights and liabilities under the contract of carriage to the recipient, regardless of whether title had also been transferred. The initial consultation was to consider rights to goods in bulk which dealt with s 16 as well as s 1, Bills of Lading Act 1855. In view of the urgency for reform in the latter case the Commission dealt with it first, with resulting legislative expression in the Carriage of Goods by Sea Act 1992. This still left the problem of s 16 and passing of property in part of a bulk. It is this commercial context which is addressed by the Sale of Goods (Amendment) Act 1995.

Passing of property in part of a bulk

Prior to the 1995 Act the buyer's ability to claim goods upon the insolvent winding-up of the seller could depend upon whether ascertainment and appropriation had occurred. This level of fortuity was often based on warehousing practice, and it was considered to compromise commodity trading in the UK especially the futures market, which is based upon warrants for quantities of goods in store. The Law Commission therefore recommended that the law should be changed in relation to the purchase of goods from an identified bulk to enable a prepaying buyer to acquire an undivided proprietary share in the bulk before the portion was ascertained. This has now been implemented in ss 20A and B of the SGA.

The definition of bulk
   Section 61(1) of the SGA (as amended) provides that this extends to 'goods of the same kind', 'in defined space' and 'interchangeable with other goods of the same number or quantity'. The purpose of this definition is to exclude a seller's general stock—the bulk must be identified by the parties as containing goods which are the subject of the contract. It could be argued from this definition of 'bulk' that it would therefore not apply on the facts of *Re Goldcorp* (1994) (see above pp 124–6) to the non-allocated claimants.

The basic rule

Property in an undivided share in the bulk is presumed to have been intended to pass to the buyer only when two conditions have been satisfied: First, the bulk must have been identified; second, at least part of the price must have been paid. The presumption would give way to evidence of a contrary intention that property was intended to pass at a later date. In this respect s 20A provides:

> *Undivided share in goods forming part of a bulk*
> (1) This section applies to a contract for the sale of a specified quantity of unascertained goods if the following conditions are met—
>   (a) the goods or some of them form part of a bulk which is identified either in the contract or by subsequent agreement between the parties; and
>   (b) the buyer has paid the price for some or all of the goods which are the subject of the contract and which form part of the bulk.
> (2) Where this section applies, then (unless the parties agree otherwise), as soon as the conditions specified in paragraphs (a) and (b) of subsection (1) above are met or at such later time as the parties may agree—
>   (a) property in an undivided share in the bulk is transferred to the buyer; and
>   (b) the buyer becomes an owner in common of the bulk.

It is clear from the above that the new section is concerned with sales of quantities and not shares as expressed as fractions or percentages of an identified bulk. As a result it is vital to distinguish between agreements to sell a share of an entity and the new provision which caters for specified quantities of a bulk, since there are special rules governing the latter case which cater for shortfalls in the bulk perhaps due to evaporation or leakage. It was always the common law position as expressed in s 2(2) of the SGA that there could be a sale between one part-owner and another of a specified entity such as a house or ship or painting. What the new law has done is extend this principle to a part share in a bulk by removing the need for actual division of the goods before property could pass.

Co-ownership and the identified bulk

The special regime relates to a sale of a quantity of an identified bulk. The Law Commission Working Party Paper No 112 considered a uniform legal response by converting the buyer's claim to a quantity into a claim to a share. However, this was considered to give the buyer a potential windfall benefit if the bulk was larger than was assumed, at the expense of other creditors. The rules are set out in s 20A(3)–(6) as follows:

> (3) Subject to subsection (4) below, for the purpose of this section, the undivided share of a buyer in a bulk at any time shall be such as the quantity of goods paid for and due to the buyer out of the bulk bears to the quantity of goods in the bulk at that time.
> (4) Where the aggregate of the undivided shares of buyers in a bulk determined under subsection (3) above would at any time exceed the whole of the bulk at that time, the undivided share in the bulk of each buyer shall be reduced proportionately so that the aggregate of the undivided shares is equal to the whole bulk.
> (5) Where a buyer has paid the price for only some of the goods due to him out

of a bulk, any delivery to the buyer out of the bulk shall, for the purposes of this section, be ascribed in the first place to the goods in respect of which payment has been made.

(6) For the purpose of this section payment of part of the price for any goods shall be treated as payment for a corresponding part of the goods.

Discrepancies in the identified bulk

Where there is a shortfall in the bulk quantity s 20A(3) provides that the seller is still contractually obliged to deliver the quantity agreed upon. However, if the seller has sold all of the bulk which is then discovered to be less than assumed, the prepaying co-buyer's undivided share would by virtue of s 20A(4) be reduced equally proportionately, although this will not prejudice the buyer's contractual claim against the seller. This is important because the new provisions are silent about allocation of risk in relation to these shortfalls.

Co-ownership—a sui generis *concept*

The Law Commission considered this to be an interim state which posed logical difficulties in relation to shortfalls, while at the same time identifying the need to ensure that trade is not impeded as would be the case if the normal common law rule applied, entailing a duty to account to the other co-owning buyers who received short deliveries. This is still the rule applied in relation to sales of shares in a bulk. The established position is that co-ownership is not a defence to an action based on conversion or trespass to the goods (Torts (Interference with Goods) Act 1977, s 10(1)) and as far as demanding delivery all of the co-owners must act in concert (*Harper v Godsell* (1870) LR 5 QB 422 at p 428). There is also a system of remedies for co-owners who wish to bring about a division in goods (Law of Property Act 1925, s 188). The dilemma in drafting the new law was to ensure that trading procedures were championed, as distinct from judicial procedures.

The rules are set out in s 20B as follows:

Deemed consent by co-owner to dealings in bulk goods

(1) A person who has become an owner in common of a bulk by virtue of section 20A above shall be deemed to have consented to—
   (a) any delivery of goods out of the bulk to any other owner in common of the bulk, being goods which are due to him under his contract;
   (b) any dealing with or removal, delivery or disposal of goods in the bulk by any other person who is an owner in common of the bulk in so far as the goods fall within that co-owner's undivided share in the bulk at the time of the dealing, removal, delivery or disposal.

(2) No cause of action shall accrue to anyone against a person by reason of that person having acted in accordance with paragraph (a) or (b) of subsection (1) above in reliance on any consent deemed to have been given under that subsection.

(3) Nothing in this section or section 20A above shall—
   (a) impose an obligation on a buyer of goods out of a bulk to compensate any other buyer of goods out of that bulk for any shortfall in the goods received by that other buyer;

(b)   affect any contractual arrangement between buyers of goods out of a bulk for adjustments between themselves; or

(c)   affect the rights of any buyer under his contract.

In summary the following principles emerge from the new law:

1.   There is deemed consent by any co-owning buyers to a buyer taking delivery of his quantity on a 'first come, first served' basis (s 20B(1)).

2.   Distribution is based upon a 'first come, first served' basis in order to avoid imposing any fiduciary duties on the seller or insolvency practitioners or any co-buyer (s 20B(1) and (2)). The practical effect of this is that a carrier or an insolvency practitioner is not expected to check the whole bulk before releasing it, and neither is there an obligation on buyers who have taken delivery of their quantity to compensate co-buyers who received a short delivery as a consequence (s 20B(3)). However, this does not affect any contractual arrangements between buyers for adjustments between themselves; for example, it is common in the grain trade to have adjustment procedures between the buyer and the seller, and the new legislation does not affect this commercial practice in any way.

The new remedy and insolvency proceedings

A statutory adjustment scheme was considered by the Law Commission in the case of shortfalls in the bulk which would be triggered by the seller's insolvency. This was rejected on the basis of practicality, since it would have imposed upon buyers who took more than their legitimate proportionate share a duty to disgorge the surplus. In turn this would have placed the risk of their solvency on other buyers, and the problems would have increased where there was a fluctuating bulk. Furthermore, there were theoretical objections to placing a duty of apportionment on an insolvency practitioner, especially a receiver who is a representative of the debenture-holders. The quasi-proprietary nature of the new remedy means that it is effectively abandoned in the collectivity of proceedings which is the characteristic of insolvency.

The dilemma of the fluctuating mass

The new regime does not apply to the case where the bulk in question is fluctuating in the sense that the seller continues to add similar goods and to withdraw them to fulfil particular orders as was the case, for example, in *Re Goldcorp* (1994) see above pp 124–6). In particular the problems relate to additions of the identified bulk and whether preparing buyers can claim these goods and also the situation where there have been depletions and whether a prepaying buyer has a proprietary claim in what is left of the original bulk. It would seem therefore that the resolution of these problems lies in established tracing principles and also proprietary claims at common law.

The equitable tracing rules are set out in Chapter 11 as they apply to tracing money. It should however be noted that the intermediate balance rule which is at the heart of any form of tracing (see *James Roscoe (Bolton) Ltd v Winder* [1915] 1 Ch 62; *Bishopsgate Investment Management Ltd v Homan* [1944]

3 WLR 1270) was extended by the Privy Council in *Re Goldcorp* (1994) to cover goods as well as money. In that case, Thorp J held at first instance that property in the bullion passed to the category of claimants known as the Walker & Hall claimants because there had been both ascertainment and appropriation. However, when Walker & Hall was acquired by Goldcorp Exchange, the latter intermingled the Walker & Hall claimants' bullion with its own trading stock of bullion, withdrew bullion from the mixture and then added more bullion without any specific intention to make restitution to the Walker & Hall claimants. The Privy Council held that the Walker & Hall claimants could not claim more than the intermediate balance of bullion left in the mixture before the subsequent additions. That intermediate balance was very small, so that although they were the only class of claimants that acquired title, their victory turned out to be a pyrrhic one.

Proprietary claims at common law

In England, there has been a reluctance to admit that parties to a sale can have a proprietary interest in a certain mass as tenants according to their respective proportions. Indeed, sometimes it is considered a misnomer to apply tenancy in common principles to sale, since the purpose of a sale transaction is to transfer property in goods which have been specifically identified, in the sense of being unconditionally appropriated, to the contract of sale. Unfortunately, such an argument fails to take into account the fact that English law rarely finds chattels to be unique for the purposes of the remedy of specific performance, where the courts tend to start with the assumption that damages are usually adequate. Despite this, a more fundamental objection is that focusing attention on whether property had passed is itself based upon the often fictitious intention of the parties.

The cases which are said to establish tenancy in common were concerned not so much with the transfer of property but rather the transfer of risk (*Inglis v Stock* (1884–1885) 10 App Cas 263; *Sterns Ltd v Vickers Ltd* [1923] 1 KB 78; *Inglis v James Richardson and Sons* (1913) 29 OLR 229 (Cit)). The issue of the transfer of risk must have figured largely in the approach taken in *The South Australian Insurance Co v Randell* (1869) LR 3 PC 101. This case concerned an action on a policy of insurance against fire (involving the stock of wheat and other grains in a mill) which contained an exemption clause concerning 'goods held in trust'. It was held that the clause was inapplicable to grain (which had not been insured separately) since it was never intended by the parties that the identical wheat delivered should be returned by the millers to the depositors. The transaction was thereby characterised as a sale to the millers. This conclusion contrasts with the approach taken in the USA in the so-called 'grain elevator' cases, where, if the parties can show an intention to sell an unseparated fraction of a whole mass, they are granted a joint interest amounting to such a proportion of the whole as the indicated number, weight or measure bears to the entire amount. The grain bin may have been emptied and refilled several times before the holder demanded delivery, but it has been held that this practice does not militate against the finding of a tenancy in common. The essential issue is whether the bailee can extract for himself at will without accounting to the others; if so, no tenancy in common is presumed (see now UCC art 2: 105(4)).

An approach in line with that in the US had recently been upheld by the House of Lords in *Mercer v Craven Grain Storage Ltd* (1994) unreported, where the court purported to give effect to the terms of the contract and the claimants were treated as still retaining proprietary rights to what remained of the original bulk even though it had become a fluctuating mass.

The common law authorities revolve around three situations:

(a) the mixture of materials belonging to different owners (*confusio* or *commixtio*);

(b) the accession of one thing belonging to one owner on to another's property (*accessio* or *adjunctio*);

(c) the creation of a new thing made wholly or partly from materials belonging to another (*specificatio*).

Each of these scenarios will now be considered in turn.

Mixture of materials belonging to different owners

The common law has approached the mixture of fungibles in an identifiable mass from the point of view of the law of property (see Blackstone, *Commentaries on the Laws of England*, Book II (1765) at p 405). The outcome depends upon whether or not the act of confusion has taken place with the consent of the owners; where there has been an accidental or inadvertent admixture, the several claimants become owners in common according to their contribution to the resultant mass. Thus in *Sandeman & Sons v Tyzack and Branfoot* [1913] AC 680, bales of jute were shipped to various consignees. Following the discharge of the ship, some bales were missing and some others were not marked and could not be identified as belonging to any particular consignment. Lord Moulton stated the principles of law which govern the confusion of chattels when he said:

> My lords, if we proceed upon the principles of English Law, I do not think it a matter of difficulty to define the legal consequences of the goods of A becoming indistinguishably and inseparably mixed with the goods of B . . . if the mixing has taken place by accident or other cause, for which neither of the owners is responsible, a different state of things arises. Neither owner has done anything to forfeit his right to the possession of his own property, and if neither party is willing to abandon that right the only equitable solution of the difficulty, and the one accepted by law, is that A and B become owners in common of the mixed property. (pp 694–95).

This principle has been applied in many cases (see for example *Buckley v Gross* (1863) 3 B & S 566, 575 per Blackburn J; *Spence v Union Marine Insurance Co* (1868) LR 3 CP 427; *Gill & Duffus (Liverpool) Ltd v Scruttons Ltd* [1953] 1 WLR 1407. See also *Jones v Moore* (1841) 4 Y & C 351, where the price of the salvaged oils was distributed amongst the parties concerned as owners in common). In this respect it is worth noting that s 188 of the Law of Property

Act 1925 empowers the court to order a division of chattels based upon a valuation or otherwise following an application by a person(s) interested in a moiety or upwards. Furthermore, a co-owner excluded from possession has the right to rent from the other (see *Jones (AE) v Jones (FW)* [1977] 1 WLR 438).

Mixture with consent

In *Indian Oil Corporation Ltd v Greenstone Shipping SA (The Ypatianna)* [1988] 1 QB 345 it was held by Staughton J that if there is an accidental mixing or mixing with consent of liquids (oil in this case) so that they are irreversibly confused together, then the application of the *confusio* doctrine here would mean that the owners are tenants in common of the whole mass in the proportions in which they have contributed to it. It is also probable that this rule applies to dry mixtures, not least because the Sale of Goods (Amendment) Act 1995 which inserted the new sections 20A and B into the SGA provides for interim co-ownership of goods before they are ascertained, which would tend to indicate that co-ownership should be the general solution.

Mixture with consent is at the heart of commodity processing bailments, typically where a party performs the processing, converting or finishing of material supplied by shippers and then returns the finished or semi-finished material or an agreed quantity of equivalent material in exchange for a fee. This phenomenon was upheld by the New Zealand Court of Appeal in *Coleman v Harvey* [1984] 1 NZLR 723 and the facts are worth dwelling upon. The defendant owned a company which refined silver from 'silver scrap' found in coins, X-ray film, torpedo batteries, and jewellery. In 1978, a contract was concluded between the defendant on behalf of his company and the plaintiff, relating to the refining of silver coins supplied by the plaintiff, which was calculated to produce 166 kg of fine silver. In addition to the coins, the company agreed to refine materials from its own sources, and, out of ingots so produced, hold in store the 166 kg for the plaintiff who, in return, agreed to supply the company with other material containing silver for a period of twelve months. The ingots were disposed of in the ordinary course of business. When the plaintiff demanded the ingots, 49 kg of silver were delivered, leaving an outstanding balance of 117 kg. The defendant's company went into receivership and the question before the court was whether the plaintiff had a proprietary interest in the unrefined metal in the possession of the insolvent company capable of being converted by the defendant as a joint tortfeasor with his company.

The defendant claimed that the original delivery of the coins constituted a sale and that the coins lost their identity by chemical process, the property then passing to the company. It was held by the New Zealand Court of Appeal that since the plaintiff's coins were intended to be embodied in the ingots to be set aside for him, this was not a case of sale; rather, the transaction constituted a loan of something not to be returned in its original state but to be replaced by something similar or equivalent, that is, commodity processing. The case was distinguished from the Privy Council decision in *The South Australian Insurance Co v Randell* (1869) LR 3 PC 101 which involved the mixing of farmers' corn by a miller. In that case it was held that there was a sale by each farmer to the miller, great importance being attached to the fact that the farmers had no more than a right to claim at any time an equal quantity of corn of like quality without reference to any specific bulk from which it was to be taken. This was not the position in *Coleman*, where the New Zealand Court of Appeal held that until the company performed its contract to appropriate to the plaintiff specific ingots, the plaintiff should be treated as having a proprietary interest as a tenant in common in any silver to which his coins contributed. Accordingly, he could recover in conversion against the defendant. It is worth noting that in England, s 10 of the Torts (Interference with Goods) Act specifically provides that co-ownership is no defence to an action founded on conversion or trespass to goods where the defendant, without the authority of the other co-owner, either:

(a) destroys the goods, or disposes of the goods in a way giving a good title to the entire property in the goods, or otherwise does anything equivalent to the destruction of the other's interest in the goods; or

(b) purports to dispose of the goods in a way which would give a good title to the entire property in the goods if he was acting with the authority of all co-owners.

Mixture without consent

Where the confusion has taken place without the consent of the party with whose property the substance has been mixed, English law appears to give the property in the resultant mass to the innocent party. In this respect, as early as 1615, Coke CJ in *Warde v Aeyre* (2 Bulst 323) as follows:

> ... if I S have a heap of corn and I D will intermingle his corn with the corn of I S he shall have all the corn, because this was so done by I D of his wrong ... and if this should be otherwise, a man should be made a trespasser, *volens nolens*, by the taking of his goods again, and for the avoiding of this inconvenience, the Law in such a case is, that he shall now retain all. (pp 323–24).

Nevertheless, there may be important exceptions, notably, if the amount of the goods wrongfully mixed is small in comparison with the wrongdoer's goods (see *Sandeman v Tyzack* (1913)). Such an approach is correct in principle because there is no compelling reason why the supplier should enjoy a windfall which may be at the expense of the debtor's other creditors.

This approach is confirmed in *Indian Oil Corp Ltd v Greenstone Shipping Co SA* [1988] QB 345 where it was known with reasonable precision how much was contributed by the innocent party. Here the owners of a vessel on which the receivers' cargo of Soviet crude oil was shipped had mixed that cargo with other oil belonging to the owners already on the vessel. It was possible to work out with considerable precision the amounts of oil belonging to the two parties. Any doubt about the quantity would have been resolved in favour of the innocent party. Indeed, Staughton J approved a general statement of Lord Eldon in *Lupton v White* (1808) 15 Ves 432 that in some cases, a decision has to be made 'not upon the notions that strict justice was done, but upon this: that it was the only justice that could be done'. Presumably, had there been a diversity in quality in the intermixed substances, the whole would be divided and greater allowance made to the owner whose substance was better or finer than the other. The significance of this case cannot be underestimated because the practice of commingling consignments by different shippers is accepted in many areas of commerce, for example, most of the Grain and Feed Trade Association standard contracts contain a *pro rata* clause.

The issue of identification

Where the property can be identified, different principles will apply. Although the wrongdoer may have been liable in conversion, this should not deprive a defendant of his own identifiable property, as in *Spence v Union Marine Insurance Co* (1868) LR CP 427. In this case, the plaintiffs claimed from their insurers the value of 41 bales of cotton as a total loss from a ship that was wrecked. There were 2,493 bales specifically marked; 2,262 bales were saved and of those bales only 617 could be identified. The plaintiffs, who held a bill of lading for 43 bales received two as indubitably theirs. They sought compensation for the other 41 because the insurance value of the total loss was worth more than any proportionate share granted of the recovered cotton, because the price of cotton had fallen. The Court held that the exact size of the plaintiff's interest as co-owners could be determined, and this consisted of 43/2,493 of the 231 bales entirely lost, which amounted to the value of four bales. Thus, they were offered 39 bales minus two (the two bales actually delivered) which made 37.

Accession

The distinction between the creation of a new thing, and the accession of one thing belonging to one owner on to another's property, is particularly elusive. In the former, labour competes with material, but in the second, material competes with material. Of course, in practice, labour also enters into accession through the act of bringing the two materials together. There must be cases where both the materials as well as labour are equally essential, especially in the case of an artistic creation using precious materials such as diamonds. Nevertheless, the distinction remains, although in principle it is inappropriate to take into account the relative economic value of the elements involved, particularly where one of those elements is skill.

Affixation as an accession to personal property

This problem is particularly acute in the context of hire purchase contracts. Much has been written about what constitutes attachment, and certain tests have been identified (see generally Goode, *Hire Purchase Law and Practice* 2nd edn (1970), Chap 33). At one extreme is the test whether the annexation is so complete as to destroy the utility of the principal chattel. Such a test may be objected to on the basis that it is too harsh on the owner of the accessory, as it involves another exception to the *nemo dat quod non habet* rule, that is, that a transferor cannot transfer a better title than he himself has (see for example *Regina Chevrolet Sales Ltd v Riddell* [1942] 3 DLR 159). At the other extreme is the test whether the accessory is so affixed that it cannot be removed without material damage to the principal goods. Thus, in *Rendell v Associated Finance Pty Ltd* [1957] VR 604, a financier supplied a Chevrolet truck on hire purchase to Pell subject to a provision for the ownership of any new accession. Pell obtained a secondhand engine for the truck from Rendell on hire purchase. Following Pell's default under the main hire purchase agreement, the defendants recovered the truck. The plaintiff's successfully sued in concession for the engine and the court held that since there was no accession there was no conversion. The fact that the attached engine was obviously essential to the operation of the goods was considered irrelevant since the goods were identifiable and severable without much damage to the property (see also *Firestone Tyre and Rubber Co v Industrial Acceptance Corpn* (1975) 75 WWR 621).

None the less, where the buyer of goods subject to a retention of title clause attaches his own property to the goods, the legal position may be regulated by an express term in the contract of supply. This could very well provide that title to the accessory should pass to the supplier notwithstanding the fact that the degree of annexation is not such as to satisfy the common law test for an accession (see *Akron Tyre Co Pty Ltd v Kittson* (1951) 82 CLR 477). The question whether the agreement constitutes a bill of sale does not arise here, since the passing of property in the accessory takes place following the occurrence of an external act.

Where the goods are identifiable but not separable

If a manufacturer wrongfully joins the supplier's property with his own in such a way that they are identifiable but cannot be separated without substantially damaging the supplier's property, this should not necessarily deprive the manufacturer of his property because the case is one of identifiable items and not one of confusion. As Matthews has put it ((1981) 34 CLP 159):

> ... just because A takes possession, not only of his own property, but also B's property joined to it, that does not mean he can deal with it as he pleases. If A thereafter purports to sell or dispose of the whole there is nothing to prevent B suing A in conversion, or money had and received (by waiving the tort). For, as we have said, this is not the Roman law of 'accession'. B may through his wrongdoing be deprived of *de facto* possession vis-à-vis A, but since his property remains identifiable then *de jure* it is still his. For A to avoid a conversion on disposing of the goods A must make quite clear that he is disposing only of his own property, and not of B's and any successor in title of A will have the same duty ... (p 176).

It is well settled that chattels affixed to realty become part of the realty, but this is not so as far as the common law relating to movables is concerned. That there is much confusion is illustrated by the judgment of Blackburn J in *Appleby v Myers* (1867) 2 LR CP 651:

> It is quite true that materials worked by one into the property of another became part of that property. This is equally true, whether it be fixed or movable property. Bricks built into a wall become part of the house; thread stitched into a coat which is under repair, or planks and nails and pitch worked into a ship under repair, become part of that coat or ship ... (pp 659–60).

The examples given (other than bricks in a wall) involve contracts of repair where it is intended that property in the new materials, as well as the labour expended, is being sold; that is, they are contracts for work and materials. Here there is a consensual element to the whole arrangement and it does not support the Roman law approach that the accessory becomes part of the dominant chattel.

The creation of a new thing

There is very little English authority on the commingling of two or more products in such a way as to perpetrate a loss of separate identity. It seems probable that the maker of the new thing becomes its owner irrespective of whether he had contributed to an action in conversion or wrongful interference. This approach was confirmed by Goff LJ in the Court of Appeal in *Clough Mill Ltd v Martin* [1985] 1 WLR 111 where Blackstone's *Commentaries* (1830, 17th ed) was cited as authority for the proposition that if A's material is lawfully used by B to create new goods, whether or not B incorporates other material of his own, the property in the new goods will generally vest in B, at least where the goods are not reducible to the original materials. Certainly this appears to be the position in Scotland. A dramatic example is *International Banking Corp v Ferguson Shaw and Sons* [1910] Sess Cass 182) when A turned B's oil into lard; it was held that B was entitled only to compensation and not to the lard.

The Scottish Law Commission (Memorandum 28, *Corporeal Movables: Mixing, Union and Creation* (1976)) has considered the problems regarding the ownership of a new product where another's materials have been used in the process of manufacture and there is neither a contract nor any question of good faith purchase between the parties. Two alternatives are suggested. The first provides that where materials cannot be conveniently separated, *pro rata* common ownership shall be enjoyed. This alternative involves a tenancy in common and may lead to problems where the value and character of the different contributions vary considerably. The second approach attributes specific ownership to the party who has economically contributed most to the new thing. However, it is questionable whether it is possible to measure relative economic worth of labour and materials, especially in a manufacturing environment requiring a large initial outlay in machinery and energy. Under both alternatives, it is envisaged that the court would be given a discretion where the producer is in bad faith. It is understandable that the improver should not receive any legal protection if he makes an improvement with full knowledge of the ownership rights of another. With such knowledge, the improver's conduct is little more than an effort to exact payment for work performed without the owner's consent.

Although it was not really at issue in the *Clough Mill* case (1985), both Robert Goff and Oliver LJJ in the Court of Appeal said that, at common law, property in new goods made from material supplied could vest in the supplier so long as there was an agreement to this effect:

> There is no reason in principle why the original legal title in a newly manufactured article composed of materials belonging to A and B should not lie where A and B have agreed . . . (p 171).

This approach was also alluded to by Rubin J at first instance in *Borden v Scottish Timber Products* [1979] 2 Lloyd's Rep 169:

> . . . unless the terms of the contract of supply contained some special terms I find it difficult to discover any adequate reason why a court in the exercise of a discretion should order the manufacturer of the article to deliver that article to a supplier of a raw material particularly in a case where the raw material forms only a part and not an outstandingly large part of the elements required for the manufacturing process. (p 171).

The theory here is that if the parties' agreement is put into effect, the buyer does not confer on the seller an interest in the property which could then be analysed in terms of mortgage or charge: when the new goods come into existence the ownership of them automatically vests in the seller. It is in the context of retention of title clauses, discussed in Chapter 11, that the general law on co-ownership of personalty has emerged in the case law.

Chapter 8

Delivery and Payment Obligations

Under the SGA 1979, property passage is linked to contract rather than conveyance (ss 17(1) and 19(1)). It follows from this that property passage and delivery may not necessarily coincide. Nevertheless, s 27 of SGA 1979 provides that it is the duty of the seller to deliver the goods and there is also a reciprocal duty on the buyer to accept them and pay for them in accordance with the terms of the contract. In much the same way delivery of possession is the essence of contracts of hire and hire purchase.

The nature and content of delivery

Delivery is defined in s 61(1) of SGA 1979 as a 'voluntary transfer of possession from one person to another'. The SGA 1979 does not define 'possession', but s 1(2) of FA 1889 provides:

> A person shall be deemed to be in possession of goods or of the documents of title to goods, where the goods or documents are in his actual custody or are held by any other person subject to his control or for him or on his behalf.

It is clear from this that actual custody is very important and this is confirmed in *Beverley Acceptances Ltd v Oakley* [1982] RTR 417.

Possession as a common law concept is notoriously difficult to define (see *Four Point Garage Ltd v Carter* [1985] 3 All ER 12 set out on p 212). This is because the question of actual custody often gives way to 'constructive delivery' which sometimes involves an attornment. There may be symbolic delivery, as in the case of handing over control of an asset, or alternatively the transfer of a document of title. Delivery to the buyer's agent may amount to a transfer of possession and this is specifically provided for in s 32(1) of SGA 1979 as follows:

> Where, in pursuance of a contract of sale, the seller is authorised or required to send the goods to the buyer, delivery of the goods to a carrier (whether named by the buyer or not) for the purpose of transmission to the buyer is prima facie deemed to be a delivery of the goods to the buyer.

It is important to determine what constitutes delivery for two reasons: first, failure to perform this act renders the supplier liable for non-delivery and allows the buyer or hirer to sue in conversion under the Torts (Interference with Goods) Act 1977; second, there is a presumption under s 28 of SGA 1979 that delivery and payment are concurrent conditions. It is for the parties to determine the method of delivery, but certain rules of delivery are set out in s 29 of SGA 1979 which are also applicable to hire purchase transactions. According to s 29(1), the presumption is that the buyer is to collect from the seller's place of business, or if the specific goods are situated elsewhere, at that place. Section 29(4) adds that where goods are held by a third party such as a warehouseman, unless there is an attornment or the transfer of a document of title there is no delivery.

The time of delivery and acceptance

Where the seller by the terms of the contract has a duty to send the goods, delivery to the carrier is by virtue of s 32 *prima facie* delivery to the buyer. This will not be the case where the carrier is an employee or bailee of the supplier, and neither will it apply in c i f contracts since the essence of this transaction is the delivery of documentation, such as a bill of lading. Where no time is fixed, the time of delivery, in the case where the seller has a duty to send the goods, is within a reasonable time (s 29(3)) and at a reasonable hour (s 29(5)). Failure to deliver within a reasonable time may amount to a breach of condition by the seller. Thus, any deviation from a time stipulated in the contract of supply may justify the other party in treating the whole contract as at an end. Moreover, the decision of the House of Lords in *Bowes v Shand* (1877) 2 App Cas 455, demonstrates that early shipment is as much a breach as late shipment. In this case the sellers agreed to ship rice during the months of March and/or April, but the bulk of the rice was in fact shipped in February. Even though it made no difference to the quality of the rice shipped, it was held that the buyers were entitled to reject the goods.

The seller's authority to fix the terms of the contract of transportation will be determined by the contract of supply. If the seller exceeds this authority by concluding a transit contract on terms unduly prejudicial to the buyer, he can refuse to accept delivery (s 32(2)). Obviously this has significance if the goods are lost or damaged in transit (see *Thomas Young and Sons Ltd v Hobson and Partners* (1949) 65 TLR 365). It may be that the parties agree that delivery is to be made as required by the buyer. In this instance, the buyer must require delivery within a reasonable hour and within a reasonable period. If the buyer, through prevarication about delivery, tries to extend the period of the contract of supply then, following some appropriate notice given to the buyer, this will justify the seller as treating the contract as being repudiated (see *Allied Marine Transport Ltd v Vale do Rio Doce Navegacao SA (The Leonidas D)* [1985] 1 WLR 925).

Where the presumption in s 28 of SGA 1979 applies, delivery must be made in exchange for the price. Of course, time of delivery can be made the essence of the contract as seen in *Bunge Corporation v Tradax Export SA* [1981] 1 WLR 711 (see Chapter 4). In the case of hire and hire purchase contracts, the tender of delivery is essential and, insofar as the agreement does not cover delay in delivery, the rules of sale will apply by analogy. In fact, s 10(2) of SGA 1979 refrains from laying down a rule that delivery is of the essence of the contract. This is also the position regarding acceptance of delivery except where the goods are perishable, or where there is a 'spot' contract where immediate delivery is envisaged. Section 48(3) enables the seller to resell perishable goods without notice to the buyer if the price is not paid when due. It is worth noting that the Law Commission No 160 Proposals on *Sale and Supply of Goods* (1987), implemented by the Sale and Supply of Goods Act 1994, do not apply to a breach of a stipulation as to time, or any other *express* term of the contract which is classifiable as a condition.

Delivery of wrong quantity

There are no provisions under the SGSA 1982 and SOGIT 1973 with respect to delivery of wrong quantity. The analogy provided with the approach taken under the SGA 1979 is an obvious one. Thus under s 30 of SGA 1979, if the seller supplies a quantity of goods different from that contracted for, the buyer can reject what is tendered, subject to the *de minimis* rule, and any trade usage or course of dealing between the parties (s 30(5)). Such a strict rule is open to abuse where there is a minor discrepancy and it is for this reason that the amended s 30(2A) provides that a non-consumer may not reject the whole delivery when the shortfall or excess is so slight that rejection of the whole would be unreasonable. The buyer has no right to terminate the contract for delivery of the wrong quantity—he has a right to reject, presumably subject to a right to cure. Of course, this has introduced an element of uncertainty into the law, but this may be justified insofar as it would, in future, avoid technical breaches justifying rejection of the contract allowing the party to escape from an improvidential bargain where, for example, the market price has fallen.

In the case where the seller delivers too little, s 30(1) provides that the buyer can either reject the goods, or, if he accepts them, he must pay for them at the contract rate. Interestingly, there is no express provision for damages even though the buyer may have suffered loss, presumably on the basis that the latter has waived the breach of contract (see Chapter 4). The exercise of the option to accept or reject assumes that the buyer knew the true facts. Moreover, the seller cannot excuse a short delivery on the ground that he will deliver the remainder in due course because s 31(1) provides that, 'Unless otherwise agreed, the buyer of goods is not bound to accept delivery thereof by instalments'. The rules as to rejection for instalment delivery are more flexible and will be discussed later.

The counterpart to the delivery of too little is the delivery of too much. Under s 30(2) the buyer has the alternative of accepting the contract quantity and rejecting the surplus, or he can accept or reject the whole quantity. If the buyer accepts all the goods delivered he must pay for them at the contract rate (s 30(3)). There is nothing anomalous about the rule which allows the consumer buyer to reject the whole delivery in this circumstance because the consumer buyer cannot be expected to go to the expense of separating the surplus goods.

The old law was that unless a contract of sale was severable, unless the goods were of a different description the rule was that a buyer who had accepted some of the contract goods would be treated as if he had accepted them all. The main difficulty with this approach was that the difference between description and quality was often very slight, so that it was impossible to justify the distinction in terms of legal response. The current reformed position is that unless the parties otherwise agree there is a right of partial rejection not just for failure to correspond with description. In the case of excess delivery the buyer is given a right of partial rejection in that he may accept the contract quantity and reject the rest. The rationale for this is that where the seller delivers more than the contract quantity he is considered to make an offer to supply the buyer with the excess at the contract rate and the buyer may accept this offer by accepting the extra goods. On the other hand, where the seller delivers less than the contract quantity he is considered to be offering a new contract which the buyer accepts by accepting the short delivery.

Delivery by instalments

Unless otherwise agreed, s 31(1) of SGA 1979 provides that the buyer of goods is not bound to accept delivery of the goods by instalments. The question of whether the contract is one by instalments is a matter of construction (s 31(2)), but it would seem that this issue is not necessarily determinative of the matter as to whether the contract is severable. If the contract is not severable, even though the goods are delivered by instalments, a partial breach gives rise to a right to reject all the goods. Section 31(2) of SGA 1979 provides:

> Where there is a contract for the sale of goods to be delivered by stated instalments, which are to be separately paid for, and the seller makes defective deliveries in respect of one or more instalments, or the buyer neglects or refuses to take delivery of or pay for one or more instalments, it is a question in each case depending on the terms of the contract and the circumstances of the case whether the breach of contract is a repudiation of the whole contract or whether it is a severable breach giving rise to a claim for compensation but not to a right to treat the whole contract as repudiated.

It is a question in each case depending on the terms of the contract and circumstances whether the breach of contract is a repudiation of the whole contract, or whether it is a severable breach giving rise to a claim for damages. An attempt to lay down some principles to apply to s 31(2) was made in *Maple Flock Co Ltd v Universal Furniture Products (Wembley) Ltd* [1934] 1 KB 148. In this case the seller had delivered too great a quantity of rag flock in one instalment and it was held that this was not a breach which amounted to a repudiation because it was unlikely to recur. Two factors weighed heavily with the Court of Appeal. First, the quantitative ratio of the breach to the contract as a whole, and second, the degree of probability that the breach would be repeated.

An important distinction should be drawn between a single severable contract and a number of distinct and separate contracts. In the case of the latter, breach of one separate contract is unlikely to justify repudiation of the others. Even though s 31(2) appears only to contemplate two remedies for the buyer, repudiation of the whole contract or damages, there is in fact a third possible course of action available to him. There is nothing objectionable about the buyer retaining the goods and rejecting the defective instalment subject to the rules governing partial acceptance under s 11(4) of SGA 1979 (see Chapter 14). This appears to be correct as a matter of legal logic since termination of a contract is not equivalent to a rescission *ab initio* (see *Johnson v Agnew* [1980] AC 367). Such an analysis is significant in the context of retention of title clauses where there has been part payment (see Chapter 11). The position may be summarised as follows:

(1) The buyer is not prevented from rejecting the defective delivery by reason of the fact that he has accepted previous deliveries.

(2) The buyer may reject the whole defective delivery.

(3) Significant factors are the seriousness of the breach and also the ratio of the breach to the contract as a whole (see *Robb A Munro v Meyer* [1930] 2 KB 312).

A difficulty which has not yet been resolved in the case law concerns the effect of repudiation in a severable contract (compare the position with non-severable contracts discussed in Chapter 14) on the delivery of prior instalments. A literal reading of s 31(2) does contemplate that the buyer has the right to reject these prior instalments even though they may be in conformity with the contractual obligation. This will be of significance as a mechanism for perhaps retrospectively validating the buyer's previous wrongful rejection.

Delivery and the consequences of repudiation

The seller's duty to tender delivery and the buyer's duty to accept it are reciprocal obligations. If the buyer indicates that he will not take the delivery, the seller is entitled to accept this anticipatory breach and need not tender delivery. However, if the seller is unwilling or cannot in any case make delivery the contract should be discharged on the basis of mutual abandonment.

Where the buyer wrongfully neglects or refuses to take delivery then this may amount to repudiation where it is not a sale by instalments (s 31(2)). What constitutes repudiation is a question of fact which is gleaned from the buyer's own conduct, notably, whether he demonstrates unequivocally his intention not to accept delivery or he disables himself in some way from taking delivery. A repudiation or breach of condition by the buyer entitles the seller to elect to treat himself as discharged from his further obligations under the contract. There is a fine line, however, between the so-called 'right' to cure (see below) and the buyer's non-acceptance of goods which are alleged to be defective: the seller may treat the buyer's persistence here as an anticipatory repudiation and bring an action for damages for the breach.

Where the seller cannot perform

A contentious problem arises where the buyer counter-claims, in an action brought by the seller for damages for non-acceptance of the goods, that the seller was or would have been incapable of performing the contract in accordance with its terms. The controversial Court of Appeal decision in *Braithwaite v Foreign Hardwood Co Ltd* [1905] 2 KB 543 has exercised courts in subsequent cases. In that case the plaintiffs sold to the defendants 100 tons of rosewood logs on cif terms (this is gleaned from other reports of the case) which were to be delivered in instalments. The buyers repudiated the contract on the grounds that the sellers had allegedly broken a term in their contract that it would not ship rosewood to the buyer's competitors. In fact there was no such term. The sellers had already shipped some of the rosewood and they did not initially accept the buyer's repudiation. Indeed when the bill of lading for shipment reached London through their agents they informed the defendants that they were prepared to exchange it for cash. The buyers refused. Some three weeks later the ship carrying the first instalment arrived in England and a short time later the sellers' agents sold the instalment of rosewood (63 tons) on the market for less than the contract price. The legal issue in this case was whether the buyers' rejection of the rosewood on an invalid ground was retrospectively justified by the fact that 17 out of the 63 tons were not of the contract description. It was held at first instance and by the Court of Appeal that the buyers were liable in damages for failing to accept the first and also subsequent deliveries. On one level this decision is hard to reconcile with the conventional position that a buyer who gives a bad ground for rejecting can still justify his rejection by demonstrating that a good ground did in fact exist. However, on a careful reading of *Braithwaite* it is possible to reconcile the decision with the conventional rule for the following reasons:

1. The buyer's repudiation came before the seller's breach, so the contract had already terminated (see *Continental Contractors Ltd v Medway Oil and Storage Co Ltd* [1925] 23 Ll LR 124 at p 132).

2. In any case the buyers would have been wrong to reject the whole tender of 63 tons (including 17 tons which did not conform to description), since the contract did not exactly specify the instalment details regarding the size of consignments and exact dates for delivery.

One of the difficulties which emerges from *Braithwaite* is, when did the seller accept the buyer's repudiation? In *Fercometal SARL v Mediterranean Shipping Co SA (The Simona)* [1984] AC 788, the House of Lords in a charterparty case concluded that in *Braithwaite* the buyer's repudiation had been accepted by the sellers and that the decision itself was in line with the well-established principle in *Heyman v Darwins Ltd* [1942] AC 356 to the effect that a wrongful repudiation by one party has no legal effect until is is accepted by the other party. Lord Ackner in *The Simona* (with whom all the other Law Lords agreed) went on to say that if there been no such acceptance then *Braithwaite* was wrongly decided. This still leaves the problem of when the act of acceptance took place. In *The Simona* the House of Lords said that the buyer's repudiation was accepted by the sellers' act of selling the disputed consignment on the market shortly after its arrival in England, ie by the sale of the goods in the market. The difficulty here is that by this time the sellers themselves were in breach in relation to the 17 tons of consignment which did not conform to the contract description. Nevertheless this breach only related to the goods and not to the documents, and it is now settled that a buyer cannot reject documents by reference merely to a defect in the goods which would justify rejection of the goods. This was confirmed by the House of Lords in *Gill and Duffus SA v Berger and Co Inc* [1984] AC 382. The facts involved a sale by sample to the buyers on cif terms 500 tonnes of Argentine 'bolita' beans. The contract stipulated that payment should be made against shipping documents on first presentation and that a certificate of quality at the port of discharge given by General Superintendence Co Ltd should be final. The buyers wrongly rejected the goods on the invalid ground that the shipping documents did not include a certificate of quality. The sellers did not treat the rejection as repudiation and re-tendered the shipping documents, having also procured a certificate of quality. This tender was refused and the sellers then chose to treat this refusal as a wrongful repudiation. In arbitration it was found that a commercially significant percentage of the consignment (1.8 per cent) contained coloured beans (bolita beans are white) and that these goods did not conform with description. The House of Lords held that it was not open to a buyer under a cif contract to justify the rejection of conforming documents if it subsequently turned out that goods shipped under the documents did not in fact conform with the contract. The sellers were released from further performance of their obligations under the contract by reason of the buyer's rejection. A cif buyer who had accepted the shipping documents could subsequently reject the goods if they were defective or alternatively sue for damages, but this was because the cif contract remained on foot. The significance of this analysis to the *Braithwaite* case is that had the facts involved a domestic sale, the seller's acceptance of the buyer's repudiation would have been too late, as the facts involved a sale on cif terms the seller's breach related only to the goods and could not justify the buyer's refusal to pay against the documents — by so doing they released forthwith the seller from further performance of his obligation. As Lord Ackner put in in *The Simona* at p 805:

> When A wrongfully repudiates his contractual obligations in anticipation of the time for their performance, he presents the innocent party B with two choices. He may either affirm the contract by treating it as still in force or he may treat it as finally and conclusively discharged. There is no third choice, as a sort of *via media*, to affirm the contract and yet to be absolved from tendering further performance unless and until A gives reasonable notice that he is once again able and willing to perform. Such a choice would negate the contract being kept alive for the benefit of *both* parties and deny to the party who unsuccessfully sought to rescind, the right to take advantage of any supervening circumstance which would justify him in declining to complete.

It is therefore clear from the authorities that following acceptance of repudiation the seller will be absolved from delivering the goods (see *Braithwaite v Foreign Hardwood Co Ltd* [1905] 2 KB 543, 552; *Cohen & Co v Ockerby & Co Ltd* [1917] 24 CLR 288; *Cooper Ewing & Co v Hamel and Horley Ltd*

[1922] 13 Ll LR 446, 590, 592; *British and Beningtons Ltd v North Western Cachar Tea Co Ltd* [1923] AC 48, 63–6; *YP Barley Producers Ltd v EC Robertson Pty Ltd* [1927] VLR 194, 209; *Gill & Duffus SA v Berger & Co Inc* [1984] AC 382, 395–396).

Where at the time of repudiation the seller has committed a repudiatory breach, the buyer can resist an action for non-acceptance even though that at that time he did not know of the breach or that at that time the seller could not have performed.

Where the seller does not accept the repudiation

There may be circumstances where the issue of acceptance of the repudiatory conduct represents to the seller that he will no longer require performance and the seller relies upon this. This is an aspect of estoppel and it will be necessary to demonstrate a clear and unequivocal representation followed by reliance (see *The Simona* (above), but compare the extravagant approach of Brennan J in the High Court of Australia in *Foran v Wright* [1989] 168 CLR 385 (Mason J dissenting)). Applying this analysis to *Braithwaite*, even if the sellers had been in breach at the time of acceptance of the repudiation this did not mean that they were irrecovably in breach—they might have been able to make a subsequent conforming tender in time. The buyer's conduct prevented them doing so and, in this sense, the buyers were stopped from relying on the sellers' non-conforming delivery. It was unreasonable to expect the sellers to make a further effort to ship conforming goods within the appropriate period. It follows therefore that the buyer cannot rely on the non-performance as a defence to liability for non-acceptance, nor can the buyer reduce the seller's damages by relying on defects in the tender if those defects could have been cured by a subsequent good tender. Such a cure was possible in *Braithwaite* but not in *Gill and Duffus SA*, where Lord Diplock said that the basic measure of damages (which in that case was the difference between the contract price and the price obtainable in the market for the documents representing the goods at the relevant date) might:

> fall to be reduced by any sum which the buyers could establish they would have been entitled to set up in diminution of the contract price by reason of a breach of warranty as to description or quality of the goods represented by the shipping documents that had actually been shipped by the sellers if those goods had in fact been delivered to them. (p 392).

Where the seller having anticipated a repudiatory breach accepts this, it will be on the buyer to show that the seller would have been unable to perform the contract in any case and this will have to be taken into account by the court in assessing damages which may, therefore, be nominal in the case of the seller's total inability to perform (see *Bunge Corp v Vegetable Vitamin Foods (Private) Ltd* [1985] 1 Lloyd's Rep 613).

The effect of non-rejection clauses

Sometimes clauses are inserted into supply contracts which purport to deprive the buyer of his right to reject and also set out the damages computation. A non-rejection clause in domestic sales will be governed by the UCTA and the Unfair Terms in Consumer Contracts Regulations 1994 (SI 1994 No 3159), but none of the limits imposed by this legislation on the efficacy of such contract terms apply to international sale of goods (in the case of UCTA) or commerical sales (as far as the Regulations are concerned). Even in the case of international sales, the common law approach has been hostile to such clauses which purport to exclude the right to reject for a breach of description, and the case law in this context has tended to reflect the fundamental breach doctrine (see for example *J Aron and Co (Inc) v Comptoir Wegimant* [1921] 3 KB 435). The fundamental breach doctrine is now a rule of construction which is less rigorously applied to limitation clauses than to exclusion clauses (see *Ailsa Craig Fishing Co Ltd v Malvern Fishing Co* [1983] 1 WLR 164). A non-rejection clause effectively excludes liability and will be treated *contra proferentem*, and it is quite clear that the courts in construing a non-rejection clause will not tolerate a delivery of goods which do not in any way conform to the contract description; rather the interpretation will take account of the commercial sense of the contract (see *Vigers Bros v Sanderson Bros* [1901] 1 QB 609; *Montague L Meyer Ltd v Osakeyhtio Carelia Timber Co Ltd* [1930] 36 Com Cas 17).

The duty to accept delivery

It is anticipated under s 27 of SGA 1979 that the buyer is under a duty to accept goods tendered in conformity with the contract. If the buyer wrongfully refuses to accept delivery, s 37(1) provides as follows:

> When the seller is ready and willing to deliver the goods, and requests the buyer to take delivery, and the buyer does not within a reasonable time after such request take delivery of the goods, he is liable to the seller for any loss occasioned by his neglect or refusal to take delivery, and also for a reasonable charge for the care and custody of the goods.

This does not affect the rights of the seller where the neglect or refusal of the buyer to take delivery amounts to a repudiation of the contract (s 37(2)).

In the case where the non-conforming goods have been delivered to the buyer, s 36 of SGA 1979 provides that, in the absence of any contrary agreement, the buyer is not bound to return the goods to the seller. It is sufficient if he intimates to the seller that he refuses to accept them. Even though he is not obliged to return them, the buyer must make the goods available to the seller. Meanwhile, as an involuntary bailee of the goods, he must exercise reasonable care in respect of them, but otherwise any risk of damage is on the seller. Where the buyer has had to keep the goods for some length of time before the seller recovered the goods, although the buyer has no lien on the rejected goods for repayment of the price, he may nevertheless recover in restitution for a reasonable charge for the care and custody of the goods.

Curing a defective delivery in non-consumer sales

Defective performance does not necessarily mean that the contract is terminated for breach. Indeed the common law rule is that the defaulting party enjoys the right to cure a defective performance, (see the House of Lords' decision in *Motor Oil Hellas (Corinth) Refineries SA v Shipping Corp of India (The Kanchenjunga)* [1990] 1 Lloyd's Rep 391). However the right to cure is circumscribed by the time permitted for performance in the contract which, of course, presupposes what is the appropriate time period. In addition, there are some subsidiary issues, namely, whether damages are available to the aggrieved party in respect of any consequential loss due to the original tender and also whether a right to cure subsists in the absence of a rejection by the aggrieved party of the original tender. It should be noted that the right to cure does not mean substitution unless this conforms with contractual stipulations relating to the description of the goods ordered.

In this respect a distinction should be drawn between contractual terms which are conditions as distinct from warranties, as there is authority that a substitute tender must be accepted where there is a breach of warranty, the aggrieved party's appropriate remedy being damages for breach of warranty (see *ERG Petroli SpA v Vitol SA (The Ballenita)* [1992] 2 Lloyd's Rep 355). In a sense this coheres with an important public policy issue, which is that of promoting performance of contracts. The point of s 15A of the SGA (as amended) is that it provides a check on the right to withdraw from a commercial contract by reference to the concept of reasonableness.

Classification of terms and the right to reject

The right to reject depends upon the classification of terms and the distinction between 'condition' and 'warranty'. The latter is defined in s 61 but 'condition' is not defined although it can be inferred from the definition of warranty that a condition is a central term going to the main purpose of the contract. It should be noted that s 11(3) does not say that there is a right to reject for breach of condition, but this may be because it is concerned with conditions and warranties in general. However, the buyer's right to reject for breach of condition is confirmed obliquely by s 11(4), which provides that where the contract is not severable and the buyer has accepted the goods or part of them:

> the breach of a condition to be fulfilled by the seller can only be treated as a breach of warranty and not as a ground for rejecting the goods and treating the contract as repudiated unless there is an express or implied term to that effect.

A careful distinction should be drawn here between rejection of the goods and termination of the contract, that is, suspension of an obligation and termination. There are two separate rights—the word 'and' between 'goods' and 'treating' should be read disjunctively in the sense that there are two separate rights here. Significantly, ss 11 (3) and 61 also refer to 'a right to reject the goods and treat the contract as repudiated'.

Part of the confusion in this context centres around the concept of a 'condition' which is used in two senses in the SGA, that is, as an event upon which an obligation depends (s 18, rr 1 and 5) and also as a promise (ss 12–15). Obviously a correct classification of 'condition' is essential because where condition is used in its suspensive sense the other party's obligation to perform has not yet arisen. On the other hand, a promissory condition where there has been a breach will require the aggrieved party to take positive steps to reject and terminate the contract and if he fails to do so he may be taken to have affirmed it.

The relationship between termination and the right to cure

The aggrieved party's obligations (for example, payment) are suspended until the seller performs, while the aggrieved party's right to terminate arises when the primary obligations under the contract (including delivery) can no longer be performed in accordance with the contract. The buyer's obligation to accept the goods is co-terminous with the delivery period set down in the contract—it is not, therefore, an indefinite obligation (see *Agricultores Federados Argentinos Sociedad Cooperativa Lda v Ampro SA Commerciale, Industrielle et Financiere* [1965] 2 Lloyd's Rep 157). It follows that if the time for performance has expired, a rejection of the seller's performance will amount to a termination of the contract.

The issue of the aggrieved party's right to rely upon a defence of failure to perform depends upon whether delivery and payment are concurrent conditions. Of course this is the case under the SGA. As a matter of general law whether the parties' obligations are concurrent or independent, or perhaps where there is a condition precedent to the other party's performance, depends upon the 'intention and meaning of the parties as it appears on the instrument itself, and by the application of common sense to each particular case' (*Stavers v Curling* [1836] 3 Bing NC 355, 368; 132 ER 447, 452). A distinction should be drawn between the remedy of refusal to perform and the remedy of termination, not least because the former is a less drastic remedy than the latter in that it only suspends the obligation. It must be the case that the aggrieved party is entitled to refuse to perform where there has been a failure by the other contracting party due to a breach of a condition or the breach of an intermediate term which robs him of substantially the whole benefit which it was intended that he should obtain from the contract, so long as the time for performance has expired.

Intermediate terms

It is elementary to state that whether a breach of an intermediate term gives rise to a right to terminate or not, depends upon the nature and consequences of the breach. This test is, however, especially difficult to apply in the context of the right of cure, quite simply because where there is a defect the innocent party may not know what the full consequences of the breach are likely to be and, of course, one unknown factor is whether the seller will effectively cure the breach. The consequence of this conundrum is that the courts may be tempted to assess the matter with judicial hindsight where perhaps the prejudice will be more precisely determinable in the light of subsequent events. In this context the preferred approach which coheres with the commercial sense of the transaction could be that seen in *Embiricos v Sydney Reid Co* [1914] 3 KB 45, where the issue was whether the defendants were justified in treating a charterparty as being frustrated on the basis of war having broken out between Turkey and Greece. Unexpectedly the Turkish authorities did allow Greek ships to pass through the Dardanelles and they were not seized at that point. However, the defendants had by then cancelled the contract on the basis of subsequent impossibility. Scrutton J held that if there was a reasonable likelihood of initial restraint this amounted to frustration notwithstanding that this restraint could be lifted from time to time—the true test adopted was 'reasonable commercial probabilities' at the relevant time. Applying this test therefore to the issue of breach and cure the issue translates itself into a simple proposition namely, is it reasonable at the time of the defective tender to regard its effects, if left uncured, as likely to be serious?

Warranties

Where the seller performs defectively and the breach is of a warranty, then the buyer can insist upon the seller curing the defect. If the seller refuses to do so then this could constitute repudiation and thereby justify the buyer in terminating the contract. The basis of this action is not the original breach of warranty but rather the refusal to perform. However, it is important not to be dogmatic here, as not every refusal to perform can amount to repudiation, for example, a minor breach which is persistently ignored does not necessarily constitute a repudiation because there has been no absolute refusal to perform. In this context the test laid down in *Maple Flock Co Ltd v Universal Furniture Products (Wembley) Ltd* [1934] 2 KB 148 at 157 would appear to be appropriate. As discussed above the issue of repudiation by the seller was considered in terms of (a), the ratio quantitatively which the breach bears to the contract as a whole; and (b) the degree of probability or improbability that such a breach will be repeated.

The loss of the so-called right to cure

In the absence of repudiation, the defaulting party has until the expiration of the period of time permitted for performance under the contract to cure the defective performance or in the absence of a time period being stipulated in the contract, within a reasonable time. It follows that where time is of the essence then defective performance means that no right to cure can emerge, simply because the condition precedent of the buyer's liability (payment) cannot be triggered since a subsequent tender or delivery will be out of time. Where time is not of the essence, whilst the buyer will have the right to damages for delay, the fact of delay will not entitle the aggrieved party to terminate the contract (*Raineri v Miles* [1981] AC 1050). In this situation the issue revolves around the time period for curing the defect—is it a reasonable time or a time after which the delay amounts to a substantial failure in performance or a delay which can be considered to go to the root of the contract? These tests can lead to different results, for example, a delay may be unreasonable in the context of how hard the aggrieved party has pressed for performance but it may not rob him of substantially the whole benefit of the contract. There appear to be two lines of authority.

In *McDougall v Aeromarine of Emsworth Ltd* [1958] 1 WLR 1126 there was a clause in a contract to build a yacht which provided that the seller would use his 'best endeavours' to build it by a certain time but this could not be guaranteed. It was held by Diplock J that this clause placed on the sellers a duty to deliver within a reasonable time. However, it should be noted that whilst ultimately in this case the time was not fixed, nevertheless the seller did give an undertaking to use his 'best endeavours' to get the yacht ready by a certain date and the reasonableness test used would appear therefore to be appropriate. It is significant that the issue of reasonableness was measured in terms of the purpose of the contract which was to use the yacht during the yachting season and the buyer terminated at a time when he could be described as having substantially lost this benefit.

There are other cases where it has been held that the aggrieved party can only terminate where the delay is so long that it goes to the root of the contract. The *locus classicus* here is *Hong Kong Fir Shipping Co Ltd v Kawasaki Kisen Kaisha Ltd* [1962] 2 QB 26, where it was held that the obligation to provide a seaworthy vessel by a specified date was of an intermediate kind, and that the delays were such as not to entitle the charterer to rescind the contract because they did not frustrate the commercial purpose of the charterparty. In many of these time cases the test for delay is equated with frustration of the contract (see *Universal Cargo Carriers Corp v Citati* [1957] 2 QB 401; *Stanton v Richardson* [1872] LR 7 CP 421). In a sale of goods case with a term as to quality, breach of which is not a breach of condition, it would appear that the buyer will only be entitled to terminate if the delay in remedying the defect would deprive the buyer of substantially the whole benefit which it was intended he or she would receive from the contract.

Where no term is specified in the contract, the court will imply a term that performance must be within a reasonable time (s 29(3) SGA). The issue then is whether failure to cure within a reasonable time amounts to repudiatory breach as distinct from merely entitling the buyer to damages. As a matter of consistency, where time is stipulated in the contract the seller is only entitled to cure the defect until such time as the buyer is deprived of substantially the whole benefit under the contract. It follows therefore that this should also be the position where a reasonable time is implied, that is, the issue is whether the fact of delay deprives the buyer of substantially the whole benefit under the contract (compare *Thomas Borthwick (Glasgow) Ltd v Bunge & Co Ltd* [1969] 1 Lloyd's Rep 17).

Curing defective tender beyond the contract period

Waiver

Where the buyer waives the time for performance then he is bound to accept substitute performance and the aggrieved party cannot terminate on the expiration of the original contract date. Of course, the aggrieved party may revert to the strict position and make time of the essence either by extending the time for performance by fixed periods (see *Nichimen Corp v Gatoil Overseas Inc* [1987]

2 Lloyd's Rep 46, 53) or, alternatively, by fixing time by reference to the concept of reasonableness.

Equitable relief against forfeiture

There is an inherent jurisdiction in equity to grant relief against forfeiture of a lessee's interests where the lease entitles the landlord to terminate for breach of a covenant under a lease (*Shiloh Spinners Ltd v Harding* [1973] AC 691, 723). While the jurisdiction is not confined to leases or to interests in land (see for example CCA 1974, ss 88–9 which require formal notice of termination and give the hirer at least seven days to make good his default) there are policy issues which restrict its operation in sale of goods contracts. Forfeiture is invoked where it is apparent upon the face of the document (for example, a right to terminate for a minor breach) that there is a disparity in the bargaining power—it is not immediately apparent that such relief will be granted where a right to termination is invoked upon the expiration of the time for performance. Moreover, there is authority that such relief is restricted to cases where specific performance would otherwise be available (*Steedman v Drinkle* [1916] 1 AC 275) and this will not normally be granted in sale of goods contracts. Furthermore it has been held that it does not extend to a loss of purely contractual interests (see *Scandinavian Trading Tanker Co AB v Flota Petrolera Ecuatorina (The Scaptrade)* [1933] QB 529) as distinct from proprietary and possessory interests in personalty (*BICC plc v Bundy Corp* [1985] Ch 232). The overriding policy issue is to prevent uncertainty in commercial transactions. To extend forfeiture to the right to cure which itself is uncertain would doubly impact upon the policy of promoting certainty in commercial transactions. As Goff LJ put it in *The Scaptrade*, it 'is of the utmost importance [that the parties] should know where they stand'.

Consequential loss from original defective tender

When a seller tenders a defective performance which is rejected the seller is treated as if he has not tendered at all. It follows therefore that the seller does not commit a breach of contract in making an initial defective tender which is then subsequently cured. As Cockburn CJ said in *Frost v Knight* [1872] LR 7 Ex 111 at 114:

> The promisee has an inchoate right to the performance of the bargain, which becomes complete when the time for performance has arrived. In the meantime he has a right to have the contract kept open as a subsisting and effective contract.

It follows from this that since there has been no breach of contract there can then be no action for damages in contract, for example, for consequential losses that may have been incurred as a result of the abortive first delivery. Typically such losses could be storage expenses incurred in anticipation of a satisfactory first delivery. It appears from *EE and Brian Smith (1928) Ltd v Wheatsheaf Mills Ltd* [1939] 2 KB 302 that where the seller tenders delivery (in this case Chinese white peas) which the buyer rejects, it does not prevent the seller so long as he is within the contractual stipulated date for performance from delivering another shipment which, if it accords with the contract, the buyer must accept and pay for. As Branson J held (at p 314):

> In my view, the position of the parties to such a contract is such that when the seller tenders documents which he says are a fulfilment of the contract, the seller does not become in breach. All that the buyer has said is: 'You have not fulfilled your contract'. That is all he can say, because it cannot be predicated in the particular case that if the first tender is not a proper tender, there may not yet be another tender which is a proper tender.

On the facts of this case there was no substituted tender so that the sellers were in breach.

The issue of consequential losses incurred from an initial defective delivery could at first sight be dealt with by a simple rule, merely, the right to cure being excluded where an aggrieved party suffers loss in the sense that the buyer has acted in reliance on the original tender. The main problem with this approach is that it fails to address the *de minimis* argument, and in *The Ballenita and BP Energy* [1992] 2 Lloyd's Rep 455 it was held that minimal reliance would not deprive the seller of the right to cure. The test was whether the nature of the reliance made it inequitable for the sellers to exercise a right to cure and that merely making alternative arrangements to purchase gasoil on the assumption that the original sellers would be unable to deliver was not sufficient. Moreover, there was not sufficient reliance to overturn the right to cure where there had been merely preliminary acts of preparation to receive the delivery of gasoil such as 'designating the tanks into which the cargo was to be put, reserving a berth and completing customs formalities. (p 460).

The dilemma is to identify a judicial rationale for compensating for consequential losses. One approach could be to do so on the basis of implying a collateral term not to make an invalid tender and that a breach of this duty sounds in damages. The main problem with this approach is that it fails to take into account the significance of the buyer's election, that is, to accept or reject the defective performance. As Devlin J pointed out in *Compania Naviera Maropan SA v Bowaters Lloyd Pulp and Paper Mills Ltd (The Stork)* [1955] 2 QB 68, in the case of imperfect performance 'the contract gives the other party the right to elect to treat the imperfect performance as it if were a fulfilment of the contract (even if he knows that in fact it is not) and to claim damages if any result from the imperfection' (p 75). A better approach is to treat the first tender as a non-repudiatory breach. Indeed s 11(3) states that a breach of condition does not automatically give the right to treat the contract as repudiated but rather that it may do so, that is, by giving rise to a right to correct a misperformance by making a fresh tender of conforming goods (see generally Apps [1994] *LMCLQ* 525).

Non-conforming goods and rejection

The opportunity of curing a defective tender is lost where the buyer has accepted the goods or is deemed to have accepted them, because there is no concept of revocation of acceptance in English law. Of course, if the seller offers to substitute performance and the buyer rejects this conduct will go to the issue of mitigation of loss. Furthermore, if the seller proceeds to repair the goods or agrees to do so then the parties may be held to this on the basis of either a collateral agreement or estoppel.

Loss of a right to cure defective performance

The situations where this occurs may be summarised as follows:
  (a) where the breach goes to the issue of competence of the contract-breaker, for example where the breach is such that the innocent party has lost faith in the contract-breaker's ability to perform, typically, where negligence has been demonstrated. In this respect it is important to recall that the function of contract is to promote performance and not compensation in lieu of performance;
  (b) where the breach renders a radically different performance to that originally envisaged under the contract. An obvious analogy may be drawn here with frustration, so that in broad terms there is a correlation between a breach of condition and an excused frustrating event on the one hand, and a breach of warranty with a non-excused non-frustrating event on the other;
  (c) the consequences of the breach are difficult to assess. This is particularly the case in a commercial contract where there may be a string of sellers, sub-sellers and sub-buyers. The point of withdrawal here is that it frees the innocent party to pursue its claim for damages but at the same time without prejudicing the sub-stratum of the under-contractual relationships. The breach is such that it affects the innocent party's ability to perform either the contract in question or the associated parasitic contracts. Typically, the ability of the innocent party to perform a sub-contract may feed upon (as a condition precedent) the contract-breaker's performance. Thus in *Re Moore and Landauer and Co* [1921] 2 KB 519 the court focused upon the possibility that the buyers might have sub-contracted on the basis of the 30 tins packaged together as requested rather than the 24 tins which were packaged and were actually delivered.

Consumer sales and curing defective performance

The Law Commission No. 160 (1987) rejected the idea of introducing a statutory right for buyers to demand cure because such a right could ultimately weaken the protection of consumers, as this would eventually have entailed that sellers could insist upon cure. The right of termination in this context is a blunt instrument in that it provides an all-or-nothing type of solution but at least it does have the benefit of certainty. However, in practice, as the Law Commission pointed out at para 4.14, this solution is not problematical because of the way in which consumers behave:

The primary task of the law in this situation (and the law is hardly ever directly involved) is to provide a regime against which potential disputes can be most satisfactorily resolved. And in this resolution the generally weak bargaining position of the buyer is an essential consideration: this is the very basis of modern consumer law. We have reached the conclusion, therefore, that for the consumer transaction, the regime which applies must be a simple one. Such is the present law. In legal theory the consumer has the absolute right to reject for any defect. True he may seldom exercise that right, almost always being prepared to accept repair or replacement. However, if the seller is unreasonable it is against that legal background that the discussion takes place.

As a matter of principle the dilemma of the law providing for a right to cure defective performance is more apparent than real, quite simply because it is accepted that such a 'right' will in any case lapse where the time for delivery has expired or where the initial defective delivery has destroyed the buyer's confidence in the seller. In consumer cases the time for delivery is most often fixed and is not as in commercial cases extended over a period of time. In any case it is possible to argue that where a commercial seller delivers goods to a consumer buyer such a breach will destroy his confidence and will therefore amount to repudiation.

Policy considerations

A so-called 'right to cure' promotes the performance of contract and minimises waste in the sense that if the wrongdoer can cure the defective performance the buyer is adequately compensated, and any expenditure incurred will not therefore be thrown away. A significant consideration is that such a right prevents parties from escaping improvident bargains, for example, by giving one party the excuse of terminating for a technical breach in order to avoid a fall in market prices. Moreover, it can be argued that a right to cure coheres with commercial reality in that the buyer will normally seek a fresh tender of the goods and that a right to cure coheres with what the parties would agree to in any case. At the same time the right to cure is a valuable self-help remedy in that it throws the risk of the contract performance back on the party in breach, that is, he must cure his performance or be left with termination of the contract and damages for breach.

Examination of the goods

Unless otherwise agreed, when the seller tenders delivery of goods to the buyer he is bound, on request, to afford the buyer a reasonable opportunity of examining the goods for the purpose of ascertaining whether they are in conformity with the contract. Section 34 of SGA (as amended) provides:

> (2) Unless otherwise agreed, when the seller tenders delivery of goods to the buyer, he is bound on request to afford the buyer a reasonable opportunity of examining the goods for the purpose of ascertaining whether they are in conformity with the contract, and, in the case of a contract for sale by sample, of comparing the bulk with the sample.

In a similar fashion it would seem that, before accepting delivery and rendering himself liable to pay instalments of rent, the hirer has a right of examination equivalent to that of the buyer (*Farnworth Finance Facilities Ltd v Attryde* [1970] 1 WLR 1053) (see Chapter 14).

The question of what constitutes a reasonable opportunity for examination is often linked with the place of examination. In *Perkins v Bell* [1893] 1 QB 193, it was held that there was a presumption that the place of delivery was the place of inspection, although this presumption may be rebutted if it is impracticable to inspect goods at the delivery point. Thus, inspection at a sub-buyer's premises may be considered reasonable if the goods are packed in such a way that they can only be examined when they reach the place where they are to be used, and where the original vendor knows, or it is a necessary inference of the contract of supply, that the goods are going further (*Molling and Co v Dean and Son Ltd* (1901) 18 TLR 217). A problem that could arise here concerns the nature of the buyer's duty, if any, to re-collect the goods from the sub-buyer. It would seem, following s 37 of SGA 1979, that the buyer is under no such duty and in this situation it would appear to be the seller's responsibility to recover the goods. This can be an onerous task where there has been a sub-sale to an overseas buyer. In *Molling and Co v Dean and Son Ltd*, the sub-sale of a consignment of books was anticipated by the original seller and because of the method of package, it was considered by the court reasonable to examine the goods at the sub-buyer's premises. It was held that the responsibility for retransporting the goods fell on the original seller, notwithstanding that they had been sub-sold to an American buyer.

Difficulties arise where the goods are suffering from a latent defect. However, it is clear that the issue is whether the buyer has had an opportunity for reasonable examination and not whether he has had the time to discover the defect. Of course, the nature of the goods will be relevant in determining a reasonable time for the examination of goods. Indeed this point was specifically recognised in *Bernstein v Pamsons Motors (Golders Green) Ltd* [1987] 2 All ER 220 where Rougier J held that the more complicated the nature of the goods, the longer the time that is allowed. Unless the contract provides otherwise, the buyer is not allowed the time to make an exhaustive evaluation of the goods. This issue goes hand in hand with the criteria for acceptance of goods in contracts of supply (see Chapter 14).

Acceptance notes and reasonable time

Section 34 of the SGA (as amended) gives the buyer a reasonable opportunity to examine the goods. The mechanism of reasonable opportunity to examine the goods is also used to deal with acceptance notes. If there is a term in the contract of sale which deprives the buyer of a reasonable opportunity to examine the goods, such a term would not be effective by virtue of s 13(1)(b) of UCTA 1977 which provides that exclusion or restriction of liability extends to 'excluding or restricting any right or remedy in respect of the liability'. In the case of non-consumer sales, such an exclusion would be subject to the criterion of reasonableness.

The duty to pay

The right of the seller to sue for the price is limited to the case where property has passed to the buyer. Where the buyer refuses delivery, the seller can sue in damages for non-acceptance only (see Chapter 13). If the buyer has the right to repudiate the contract then he can decline to pay the price, or if he has paid it, it can be recovered on the basis of total failure of consideration.

It is the duty of the buyer not only to accept the goods, but to pay for them in accordance with the terms of the contract of sale (s 27 of SGA 1979). A similar undertaking is usually found in contracts of hire and hire purchase transactions. A claim for payment of the price should be distinguished from a claim for breach of contract. In the case of the former, the creditor must show the occurrence of an event such as property passing, but with regard to the latter, the rules of remoteness, mitigation and penalty apply.

The basic rule laid down in s 28 of SGA 1979 is that delivery and payment of the price or rent are concurrent conditions. This is a natural concomitant of the right envisaged in s 34 to examine the goods. It is curious that s 10(1) of SGA 1979 provides that, in the absence of a different intention, stipulations as to time of payment are not deemed to be of the essence of a contract of sale. Everything depends upon the circumstances of the contract, including the importance to the parties of timely payment and the seriousness of the consequences of payment that is untimely. If time is of the essence of delivery, since under the SGA 1979 payment and delivery are presumed to be contemporaneous, time will also be of the essence of payment. The SGA 1979 provides specifically for this in s 48(3) which states:

> Where the goods are of a perishable nature, or where the unpaid seller gives notice to the buyer of his intention to resell, and the buyer does not within a reasonable time pay or tender the price, the unpaid seller may resell the goods and recover from the original buyer damages for any loss occasioned by his breach of contract.

It follows from this that in the case of perishable goods, time of payment is of the essence. As regards non-perishable goods, the presumption of s 10(1) can be overturned by the simple expedient of the seller giving notice to the buyer of his intention to resell. Even where time is not of the essence of the original contract, the delay in payment may be so great as to show an intention to repudiate (*Pearl Mill Co Ltd v Ivy Tannery Co Ltd* [1919] 1 KB 78).

Part payment and termination

There is no provision in the SGA 1979 as to payment by instalments, but it may be implied from s 31(1) that payment is *prima facie* to be made by lump sum. Of course, the parties themselves in the contract may anticipate payment by instalments. The effect of any part payment made will depend upon whether it is a genuine advance instalment of the purchase price, or whether it is a deposit intended to operate as security for the due performance of the buyer's obligations. In the case of the former, if the supply contract is not concluded then part payment may be recovered on the basis of total failure of consideration. Under the common law the deposit in this circumstance is forfeited. Nevertheless, in the case of prospective regulated consumer credit agreements, s 59 of CCA 1974 provides that the intended deposit becomes recoverable on the grounds of total failure of consideration.

In *Dies v British and International Mining etc Corpn* [1939] 1 KB 724, the buyers paid 37 per cent of the price of the goods in advance and then defaulted in the payment of the balance, so the sellers refused to deliver the goods. The buyers admitted their liability for damages but recovered the advance payment on the basis of total failure of consideration. The distinction between a part payment which is recoverable and a forfeitable deposit which is not, is a matter of construction of the contract. In this respect, the *Dies* case may be construed as the buyer's obligation to pay the whole price being replaced by their liability to pay damages (see Chapter 13). Significant problems arise where a buyer is required by the contract to pay a deposit in advance which has not been paid and where this would have been forfeited on breach. In principle, the time of payment should not be relevant. This is confirmed in *Damon Cia Naviera v Hapag-Lloyd (The Blankenstein)* [1985] 1 WLR 435, where a buyer contracted to buy a ship for $2.36 million and to pay a deposit of 10 per cent of the price. The contract expressly provided that, if the buyer failed to complete, the deposit would be irrecoverable. It was held that this deposit was forfeitable even though the seller had resold the ship at a small loss which was far less than the amount of the deposit. The plaintiff, as seller who was suing for the recovery of the deposit, succeeded in upholding what was, in essence, a penal claim. As such, the case demonstrates the court's disinclination to extend equitable relief to forfeiture in commercial contracts (see *Goker v NWS Bank* (1990) *The Times*, 23 May).

The House of Lords in *Johnson v Agnew* (1980) drew a distinction between rescission of the contract *ab initio* which has retrospective effect, and a mere subsequent termination of the contract. This has repercussions if a buyer is under an obligation to pay in advance but does not do so, and the contract is subsequently terminated. Thus in *Hyundai Heavy Industries Co Ltd v Papadopoulos* [1980] 1 WLR 1129, a shipbuilding case in which the price was payable by instalments as the work proceeded, the House of Lords held that the buyer could be sued for an instalment which fell due on 15 July despite the fact that the seller exercised a cancellation right on 6 September. This approach is over-formalistic and overlooks that the buyer's duty to pay is surely conditional on subsequent performance by the other party. Even if the contract involves an element of manufacture and sale, it cannot be appropriate that the seller can sue for the recovery of an advance substantial payment where he has incurred only minimal advance expenditure prior to cancellation.

The method of payment

The method of payment traditionally anticipated in contracts of supply, is cash. However, a buyer may pay by negotiable instrument, credit card, charge card, gift voucher or trading stamps, dependent upon which of these methods of payment has been agreed in advance or accepted by the seller as payment of the price. The seller in a sale transaction can agree to any form of payment he wishes, and this includes the acceptance of other goods as a trade-in for part of the price, so long as this does not turn the contract into one of exchange rather than sale (see Chapter 2).

Where the seller accepts payment by negotiable instrument, it is normally deemed to be a conditional payment. It is possible for such a negotiable instrument to be accepted as absolute payment but an intention must be strictly shown (*Maillard v The Duke of Argyle* (1843) 6 M & G 40). In the case of a credit card transaction, following *Re Charge Card Services Ltd* [1988] 3 WLR 764 it is clear that there is no general principle of law that, whenever a method of payment is adopted which involves a risk of non-payment by a third party, there is a presumption that the acceptance of payment through a third party is conditional on the third party making the payment. The Court of Appeal in this case analysed the credit card transaction in terms of quasi-novation, namely, by the underlying credit card scheme, the credit card company had bound the supplier to accept the card and had authorised the cardholder to pledge the company's credit.

Chapter 9

Risk of Loss and Damage to the Goods

The concept of risk is not defined in any of the statutes dealing with contracts of supply. To a large extent, the treatment of risk under the SGA 1979 focuses upon its parasitical qualities, ie feeding off the primary obligations of delivery and payment of the price under s 27 of the Act. Risk has a narrowly defined ambit, otherwise the maxim of *caveat emptor* has little or no content. The buyer takes upon himself all risks as to the quality and the fitness of the goods, subject to the statutory implied terms discussed in Chapter 5. At the same time it is well established that any gains made will *prima facie* accrue. This is also the position with bailment and hire purchase contracts where it is justified on the basis that the bailor should not be allowed the double benefit of rent and gains (see *Tucker v Farm and General Investments Trust Ltd* [1966] 2 QB 421).

Where the goods are at the supplier's risk, it may not be possible for the supplier to perform, following a mishap. It does not necessarily follow, however, that he incurs liability to the transferee for non-delivery. This question is bound up with the issue of impossibility and will be considered separately from the doctrine of risk in this chapter.

The general principle of risk

The passing of risk with regard to loss or damage occurring after the contract is made, is governed by s 20 of SGA 1979:

(1) Unless otherwise agreed, the goods remain at the seller's risk until the property in them is transferred to the buyer, but when the property in them is transferred to the buyer the goods are at the buyer's risk whether delivery has been made or not.

(2) But where delivery has been delayed through the fault of either buyer or seller, the goods are at the risk of the party at fault as regards any loss which might not have occurred but for such fault.

(3) Nothing in this section affects the duties or liabilities of either seller or buyer as a bailee or custodier of the goods of the other party.

The basic presumption in s 20(1) is *res perit domino*, ie the passing of risk is linked with the passing of property. In a modern consumer retailing situation, linking risk to property passage does appear to be anomalous. The buyer must bear the risk of loss of accidental destruction where property has passed, in the absence of a contrary agreement, even though payment and delivery under s 28 of SGA 1979 are concurrent conditions. A simpler rule would focus upon who should bear the insurance cost. Certainly, where goods form part of the seller's stock-in-trade, the party in possession should insure and should therefore bear the loss. In practice, if the seller is insured and has recovered the loss under the insurance contract, the insurance company may be subrogated to the seller's right to collect the price from the buyer to whom the risk had passed with the property.

The operation of the risk doctrine goes hand in hand with the s 18 'rules' (discussed above, pp 131–9). Thus in *Underwood Ltd v Burgh Castle Brick and Cement Syndicate* [1922] 1 KB 343, which involved the sale of a bulky condensing machine, it was held that the goods were not in a deliverable state at the time of damage inflicted to it, so that neither property nor risk had passed to the buyers. Similarly, in contracts of sale or return under s 18, r 4, the seller *prima facie* retains the property and the risk in the goods (see pp 205–6). Moreover, it may be that until the buyer accepts the goods, the risk will remain with the seller and it would seem that there is nothing to prevent the buyer rejecting the goods merely because they have been accidentally damaged. This seems to be borne out by the decision in *Head v Tattersall* (1871) LR 7 Ex 7, the facts of which concerned the sale of a horse, warranted to have been hunted by the Bicester hounds; the plaintiff being given a week in which to return the horse if it did not answer the description. The horse was accidentally injured before the week was up. On close analysis of this case, what seems to be at issue was the buyer's title, ie the property in the horse passed to the buyer immediately but defeasibly, so that when he rejected the horse, he divested himself of the title and revested it in the seller. If a risk analysis had been adopted, the conclusion would be that the horse was at the seller's risk during the period allowed for its return. Nonetheless, what would have happened if the horse had died? Rescission would not have been possible because the goods could not be returned. In *Chapman v Withers* (1888) 20 QBD 824, it was held with little discussion that the buyer, who had presumably paid the price, might maintain an action for breach of a warranty that the horse was 'quiet to ride'. Damages for breach of this warranty were assessed at £42, but it is not clear whether or not this represented the price paid by the buyer.

As noted above, the s 20(1) rule is only a presumption which is subject to a contrary intention. This may be implied from the circumstances of the case and is intimately connected with the obligation to insure. It is for this reason that in fob and cif contracts, risk normally passes on shipment, irrespective of when property passes, because the buyer will be able to rely on a marine insurance policy with respect to the goods.

Risk and unascertained goods

In certain circumstances it is possible for the parties to contract for the passage of risk before appropriation of goods to a supply contract. This can be seen in *Sterns v Vickers* [1923] 1 KB 78 which concerned a contract for a quantity of white spirit out of a larger bulk held by a storage company. The seller gave the buyer a delivery order for the contract quantity and, when this was presented to the storage company, they attorned to the buyer. The buyer decided to leave the spirit in the tank for their own convenience. In the meantime, the spirit deteriorated and the Court of Appeal held that the risk had passed. The exceptional nature of this decision has been emphasised in subsequent cases, the material factor here being the acceptance of the delivery warrant which gave the buyer an immediate right to possession and, therefore, an insurance interest (see *Healey v Howlett and Sons* [1917] 1 KB 337). It may be that in the light of the new rules relating to co-ownership of an identified bulk, which are silent as to risk, this decision will no longer be regarded as exceptional as risk will be assumed to have passed in the circumstances covered by ss 20A and B (see pp 142–6).

Risk and the relevance of fault

Deterioration due to the inherent make-up of the goods is something which the buyer must accept. It is otherwise where deterioration has resulted from delay due to the fault of one party (s 20(2)). This is particularly significant where there has been a wrongful failure to take delivery of the contract goods on time (see *Demby Hamilton and Co Ltd v Barden* [1949] 1 All ER 435).

The fact that the buyer is late in taking delivery does not mean that the seller is not bound to take all reasonable care of the goods. Section 29(3) of SGA 1979 provides that allocation of risk does not relieve the seller of his duty as bailee. Where property passes before delivery and the buyer fails to take delivery, the seller becomes either an involuntary or gratuitous bailee. Even so, he is under a duty to take reasonable care of the goods and will be entitled to claim a reasonable charge for the care and custody of the goods (s 37(1)). The seller cannot be accused of non-delivery and his obligations relating to satisfactory quality, under s 14, do not extend beyond the appointed time of delivery, so that any subsequent harm to the goods can only entitle the buyer to damages. On the other hand, where risk has passed to the buyer and delivery is delayed due to the seller's fault, who, when acting as bailee, carelessly allows the goods to be damaged, this will go to the definition of unsatisfactory quality and the buyer may be able to reject on this basis. It cannot be the case that the innocent party has agreed to bear the consequences of the other's fault.

The party at fault only bears the risk of loss or damage *caused* by the fault. It is for the party at fault to show that the harm would have happened anyway, whereas under s 20(2) of SGA 1979 the innocent party's burden is only to show that the harm '*might* not have occurred but for such fault'. More difficult problems arise where both parties are at fault, to which there are two possible solutions. The first approach is to apportion the damage between the parties by the application of the Law Reform (Contributory Negligence) Act 1945; the second approach is to focus upon the chain of causation, ie the opportunity for the goods to be damaged would not have arisen but for the delay, but the seller's negligence may be treated as breaking the chain of causation so that he will bear the risk.

Risk and goods in transit

If the seller, without authority, makes an unreasonable contract with the carrier, s 32(2) entitles the buyer to refuse to treat the delivery to the carrier as delivery to him, so that neither property nor risk will pass. Similarly, the goods may be carried at the seller's risk if he fails to give the buyer sufficient insurance cover. Under s 32(3) of SGA 1979, if the goods are being sent by sea (as distinct from by land or air) under circumstances where it is usual to insure, it is presumed that the seller is to give the buyer sufficient notice of the shipment so that, if he fails to do so, the goods are carried at his risk. This rule has been applied to fob contracts where the normal position is (following *Inglis v Stock* (1885) 10 App Cas 263) that risk passes on shipment since the buyer is responsible for arranging shipping space even where property has not passed, for example, where an unascertained part of a specific whole is sold or there is a right of disposal (see *Wimble, Sons and Co v Rosenberg and Sons* [1913] 3 KB 743). It should be noted that the goods will only be at the seller's risk if his failure to give notice disabled the buyer from insuring (compare *Produce Brokers Co Ltd v Olympia Oil and Cake Co Ltd* [1917] 1 KB 320).

As regards the period of transit, the seller's risk is modified by s 33 which states:

> Where the seller of goods agrees to deliver them at his own risk at a place other than that where they are when sold, the buyer must nevertheless (unless otherwise agreed) take any risk of deterioration in the goods necessarily incident to the course of transit.

The issue of 'any risk of deterioration in the goods necessarily incident to the course of transit' is qualified by s 14 which requires not merely that the goods shall be sound when delivered to the carrier, but that they shall be capable of withstanding the conditions of normal transit. Of course, the buyer is not at risk as regards abnormal incidents, such as delay in transit as in *Healey v Howlett* (1917). Sometimes the issues involve very fine questions of interpretation so that in *Mash and Murrell Ltd v Joseph I Emanuel Ltd* [1962] 1 WLR 16, supply of potatoes which became rotten during the course of a sea voyage, were held at first instance by Diplock J, to constitute a breach of s 14, but the Court of Appeal reversed the decision on the basis that the conditions met on the voyage had been unusual. Obviously the more hazardous the method of transportation, the greater the scope there is for the category of risks 'necessarily incident to the course of transit'.

Impossibility of performance

The contract of supply may be set aside due to impossibility of performance. The contractual terms will be highly relevant here and it may be that, as a matter of construction, the contract will stipulate for alternative performance. In certain circumstances the supply of particular goods may be prohibited and if this prohibition is in force when the contract is made, the contract affected will be void for illegality. However, if the parties foresee that subsequent events may mean that performance is not legally possible, the loss may be determined according to the contractual allocation of risk.

Initial impossibility

The question of damage occurring in contracts of supply goes hand-in-hand with assumption of risk and the implied terms applicable to such contracts. Nevertheless, where the loss or damage changes the *nature* of the goods, it would appear that the matter is dealt with by s 6 of SGA 1979 which states:

> Where there is a contract for the sale of specific goods, and the goods without the knowledge of the seller have perished at the time when the contract is made, the contract is void.

This section is understood to confirm the ratio in the difficult case of *Couturier v Hastie* (1856) 5 HLC 673. Here the defendant, acting as *del credere* agent for the plaintiffs, sold a cargo of wheat thought to be on a particular ship sailing from Salonika. In fact, before the contract was made, the cargo had been lawfully sold by the master of the ship since, owing to inclement weather (overheating), the cargo was unfit for further transit. The buyer refused to pay for the goods and the plaintiffs sued the defendants who, as *del credere* agent, had guaranteed the buyer's performance. The House of Lords held that, as the buyer was not obliged to pay, neither were the defendants.

The exact basis of the decision in this case is very difficult to state. It was possible to justify the decision on the basis of one of four hypotheses:

(1) The contract was void for mistake.

(2) The contract was void for lack of subject matter, ie *res extincta*.

(3) The contract was void on the basis that there was an implied condition precedent that the goods were in existence.

(4) If one party cannot perform, for example deliver the goods, he cannot make the other party perform, ie pay the price.

The draftsman of the 1893 SGA adopted the analysis based upon *res extincta* and this has been re-enacted in s 6 of SGA 1979 .

A careful analysis of the House of Lords' decision in *Couturier* would show that the buyer, as a matter of construction of the contract, had not assumed the risk of the non-existence of the subject matter of the contract. This is a more appropriate basis for determining liability. With this in mind, it may be possible to argue that s 6 is capable of being displaced by contrary agreement because s 55(1) allows the parties to contract out of or vary 'any right, duty, or liability' which would arise by implication of law. The difficulty with this argument is that precisely s 6 does not impose 'any right, duty, or liability' but rather avoids them. As an alternative, it may be possible to construe any statements made as to the existence of goods as either a collateral warranty or else as a misrepresentation. If one adopts the first approach, there is the problem of finding good consideration because the main contract is treated as being void; the second approach presupposes that an express statement to the effect that the goods exist has been made, which will not always be the case.

There is authority which suggests that in appropriate circumstances a seller of non-existent goods may be held liable through a strict interpretation of s 6. Thus in *McRae v Commonwealth Disposals Commission* (1951) 84 CLR 377, the defendants contracted to sell to the plaintiffs a shipwrecked tanker on a certain reef. It was held that s 6 did not apply since the goods were not *in esse*, that is, not only was there not, and had never been any tanker, but even the reef was non-existent. Similarly on the facts in *Associated Japanese Bank v Crédit du Nord SA* [1989] 1 WLR 255 which involved a sale and leaseback of non-existent machinery, it is unlikely that this contract would have been caught by s 6 of SGA 1979. In adopting this approach, the Act is in danger of appearing disjointed because parallel cases falling just within it will be void, whereas those falling just outside it will centre upon the construction of the contract. This straitjacket approach may be inevitable as s 6 is one of the few provisions in the SGA 1979 which is not expressed to give way to a contrary intention. Such an approach is unfortunate and, as a matter of principle, there is considerable appeal in Lord Diplock's *dictum* in *Christopher Hill Ltd v Ashington Piggeries* [1972] AC 441 that the SGA 1979 should not 'be construed so narrowly as to force on parties to contracts for the sale of goods, promises and consequences different from what they must reasonably have intended' (p 501).

The scope of s 6 is comparatively narrow. The operation of this section as well as s 7 (which deals with frustration) are expressed to be applicable where 'specific goods' have 'perished'. It seems appropriate, therefore, to focus upon the meaning of both of these concepts.

Specific goods

Section 61 defines 'specific goods' as 'goods identified and agreed upon at the time a contract of sale is made' (see Chapter 7). It is sufficient at this stage merely to note that the modern tendency in the case law is to confine the scope of 'specific goods' to mean *existing* goods which have actually been identified or agreed upon (compare *Howell v Coupland* (1876) 1 QBD 258).

Perish

The SGA 1979 does not define 'perish'. Clearly, it applies to cases of physical destruction and, presumably, where goods have ceased to exist in a commercial sense. In *Barrow, Lane and Ballard Ltd v Phillip Phillips and Co Ltd* [1929] 1 KB 574, goods which were stolen were held to have perished. Care must be taken with this decision since it cannot be the case that all stolen goods are *per se* considered 'perished', at least until all hope has been abandoned for their recovery. The case is authority for the proposition that where a contract for the sale of specific parcels of goods (nuts in this instance) is indivisible, the perishing of part of the goods will render the contract void under s 6. There are difficulties here because the sellers did deliver bags which had not been stolen when delivery was required under the contract, whilst the buyers paid the price without question. On the assumption that the contract was void, the buyer should only have been liable to pay a reasonable price which would not necessarily reflect the contract price. In addition, the seller should not have been under an obligation to deliver. To consider the contract void in these circumstances does involve a legal fiction, especially in the light of the fact that the sellers delivered and the buyers paid for a substantial part of the goods (150 bags of nuts out of a parcel of 700). Moreover, at common law it is evident, following *HR and S Sainsbury v Street* [1972] 1 WLR 834 (discussed at p 122), that the buyer may always, if he wishes, waive his right to full and complete delivery and insist on having the remainder, so long as he is willing to pay the full contract price or the appropriate part of a divisible price. It is difficult to see how this can be reconciled with the statutory provision that the contract is void.

It is not possible to reconcile the case law dealing with perishability. Much depends upon the facts and the commercial sense of the transaction. Thus in *Asfar and Co Ltd v Blundell* [1896] 1 QB 123, dates saturated in sewerage were held to have perished, whereas in *Horn v Minister of Food* [1948] 2 All ER 1036, potatoes which had so rotted as to be worthless were held not to have perished because they were still 'potatoes'. As a matter of principle, this latter approach can be supported because, taken to its logical conclusion, a seller who had sold goods in breach of their contract description under s 13 of SGA 1979 could avoid this through recourse to s 6. In the light of advancements in technology, especially irradiation techniques, the issue of whether goods have perished will be one of degree and it may be that the question will be more intimately linked with the contract date for delivery.

Subsequent impossibility

If the risk is not on the buyer, s 20(1) of SGA 1979 presumes the risk to be on the seller. Although the rules of risk allocation determine who bears the loss of goods, they will not determine the case of subsequent impossibility, ie from contingencies not expressly or impliedly dealt with by the allocation of risk. In this circumstance, the contract may be set aside because of the doctrine of frustration.

The only provision in the SGA 1979 dealing with frustration is s 7 which states:

> Where there is an agreement to sell specific goods and subsequently the goods, without any fault on the part of the seller or buyer, perish before the risk passes to the buyer, the agreement is avoided.

The scope of this section is comparatively narrow. We have already considered the meaning of 'specific goods' and of 'perish'. It should be noted that the presumption in s 18, rule 1 is that a contract for the sale of specific goods passes both the property and risk at once (see pp 132–4) so that it cannot be said that the subsequent destruction of the goods can frustrate the contract. In any case, s 7 is only a rule of construction which can be avoided by contrary agreement.

Even where s 7 does not apply, the contract may be frustrated at common law. In the case of unascertained goods, it is unlikely that the contract will be set aside for frustration as the seller should be able to find alternative goods on the basis of *genus numquam perit* (but compare *Re Badische Co Ltd* [1921]

2 Ch 331). Of course, where goods have been appropriated to a contract then it is possible for frustration to apply, for example, damage or destruction to the contract goods as in *Appleby v Myers* (1867) LR 2 CP 651. Moreover there may be frustration where the goods are partially ascertained where part of a bulk is sold (compare *Re Wait* [1927] 1 Ch 606). In *Howell v Coupland* (1876) it was held that an agreement to sell a crop to be grown on a particular field could be frustrated by the failure of the entire crop.

Effects of frustration

This will depend upon whether the goods are specific or not. In England, contracts for specific goods are governed by the common law because s 2(5)(c) of the Law Reform (Frustrated Contracts) Act 1943 expressly excludes from its operation:

> ... any contract to which [s 7 of the Sale of Goods Act 1979, which avoids contracts for the sale of specific goods which perish before the risk has passed to the buyer] applies, or to any other contract for the sale, or for the sale and delivery, of specific goods, where the contract is frustrated by reason of the fact that the goods have perished.

Under the common law, following *Chandler v Webster* [1904] 1 KB 493, if the seller had been paid in advance he could keep the money irrespective of delivery, and if the price had fallen due before the frustrating event, the seller could actually sue for it. This approach was tempered by the House of Lords in *Fibrosa Spolka Akcyjna v Fairbairn Lawson Combe Barbour Ltd* [1943] AC 32 where it was held that a buyer could recover his prepayment on the basis that there had been a total failure of consideration. The difficulty is that the seller has no claim for expenses necessarily incurred before the frustrating event, and there is no provision for the apportionment of loss. The doctrine of risk will be highly pertinent here because if the risk is on the seller, the buyer will not have to pay for goods which are not delivered to him under a contract which is subsequently frustrated. Even so, the expanding ambit of the law of unjust enrichment may ensure that benefits received by the buyer which survive the frustrating event cannot be kept without payment.

The narrow scope of s 7 of SGA 1979 should be noted. It only applies to sale contracts and has no application in analogous supply contracts, for example, a contract for work and materials. Moreover the frustrating event anticipated under s 7 is confined to the perishing of specific goods so that other frustrating events including war, supervening illegality, requisitioning or destruction of goods other than by perishing are not covered. In these situations the principles of unjust enrichment will apply insofar as they have been encapsulated in the Law Reform (Frustrated Contracts) Act 1943. Under this statute the main drawbacks of the law resulting from the *Fibrosa* case are remedied.

The general common law rule is that frustration does not retrospectively annul the contract: it only brings the contract to an end as from the occurrence of the frustrating event. The 1943 Act provides significant rules for readjustment in the light of prepayments made or part delivery.

Prepayment of money

Section 1(2) of the 1943 Act provides that money due but not paid before frustration occurs ceases to be payable, and that if the money has actually been paid it must be paid back. Frustration is thus given some retrospective effect, but an allowance is made at the court's discretion to provide that a person to whom a prepayment was made (or due) may be allowed to keep (or recover) a reasonable sum not exceeding the amount of the prepayment to cover his expenses. What is a reasonable sum depends upon the circumstances of the case.

There is provision in the case of an instalment contract to sever the executed part from the frustrated part of the contract. Section 2(4) of the 1943 Act states:

> Where it appears to the court that a part of any contract to which this Act applies can properly be severed from the remainder of the contract, being a part wholly performed before the time of discharge, or so performed except for the payment in respect of that part of the contract of sums which are or can be ascertained under the contract, the court shall treat that part of the contract as if it were a separate contract and had not been frustrated and shall treat the foregoing section of this Act as only applicable to the remainder of that contract.

This enables the court to turn a partial failure of consideration in respect of the whole contract into a total failure of the frustrated part, allowing the payer to recover his payment made.

Part delivery

Where the seller has delivered part of the goods but has been paid nothing, s 1(3) of the 1943 Act provides that if one party has 'obtained a valuable benefit' before the time of discharge as a result of anything done by the other party in or for the purpose of performance of the contract, the court, in the exercise of its discretion, can order the recovery of a just sum not exceeding the value of the benefit. Section 1(3) provides:

> Where any party to the contract has, by reason of anything done by any other party thereto in, or for the purpose of, the performance of the contract, obtained a valuable benefit (other than a payment of money to which the last foregoing subsection applies) before the time of discharge, there shall be recoverable from him by the said other party such sum (if any), not exceeding the value of the said benefit to the party obtaining it, as the court considers just, having regard to all the circumstances of the case and, in particular—
> (a) the amount of any expenses incurred before the time of discharge by the benefited party in, or for the purpose of, the performance of the contract, including any sums paid or payable by him to any other party in pursuance of the contract and retained or recoverable by that party under the last foregoing subsection, and
> (b) the effect, in relation to the said benefit, of the circumstances giving rise to the frustration of the contract.

Difficult questions have arisen regarding the valuation of the benefit received. In *BP Exploration Co (Libya) Ltd v Hunt* [1979] 1 WLR 783 (affirmed on one point only by the House of Lords [1982] 2 AC 352), Robert Goff J (as he then was) held that the main issue was the identification and measurement of the benefit before the frustrating event. The value of the benefit is the upper limit that may be awarded subject to the amount which the court considers just, taking into account all the circumstances of the case. The valuation for the purposes of the Act must be made at the date of the frustrating event, which of course may render any benefit derived by the buyer nugatory where the frustrating event destroys the benefit, as in *Appleby v Myers* (1867). Nonetheless, the approach adopted here is *obiter*. It may be that the destruction of the subject matter does not affect the power of the court to award something under s 1(3), though it will be a factor which will have to be accommodated in the determination of the 'just sum'. Where goods have been disposed of many years before the frustrating event, the learned judge held that they must be valued at the date of disposal, no allowance being made for the benefits which the defendant may have had from the proceeds of sale during this time.

Although the 1943 Act has mitigated some of the harshness of the common law rules, it has introduced an element of haphazardness into the law. We have already noted the exception relating to the sale of specific goods where the cause of frustration is the perishing of the goods. This will inevitably give rise to strange and narrow distinctions. In addition, even under the 1943 Act the seller's right is limited: he cannot recover more than the total of the sums paid and due before the frustrating event, which means that he can recover nothing if payment was due only upon delivery of the goods (s 1(2)). Moreover, the Act can be excluded by contrary agreement (s 2(3)), for example by a provision that the obligations of one or both parties are to remain binding despite the impossibility of performing the primary obligations under the contract of supply.

Part III

Security in Transactions

Chapter 10

The Transfer of Title

The concept of *nemo dat quod (qui) non habet*, or security of property, was firmly rooted in classical Roman law, which provided for absolute ownership limited only by the very narrow exception of the *bona fide* possessor with a *titulus*. The *nemo dat* doctrine has a long history in the common law. It appeared in Perkins' *Profitable Book* which was published in 1532 in Law French citing the Yearbooks as authority. Although Noy's Maxims first published in 1641 also has the rule, no authority is cited. It appears to have become fashionable to quote the rule in one of its Latin versions only in the 19th Century which may have been due to the use of the Latin as being more respectable and impressive, and possibly more comprehensible, than Perkins' Law French.

There is a certain logic in the proposition that one cannot transfer what one does not have. This was eloquently expressed in the Californian Appeal case of *Bathelmess v Cavalier* (1934) 2 Cal App 2d 477: 'Title like a stream cannot rise higher than its source' (p 487). It was not until the 18th Century that the judges began questioning the previously unquestioned assumptions of property law, in the context of negotiable instruments with the introduction of the 'good faith purchaser' principle. By the 18th Century, the law merchant had been absorbed into the common law and the attention of the King's courts began to be concentrated upon the development of a body of doctrines to encourage the free circulation of goods and commercial paper. The emphasis was now on 'good faith purchase' and not 'good faith performance'.

It is significant that the SGA 1979 retains the primacy of the *nemo dat* principle whilst the exceptions are contained in ss 21–25 of the Act. There must, therefore, be compelling reasons for an owner to lose his interest in his goods. In this respect the late Professor Gilmore, one of the architects of the American Uniform Commercial Code (UCC), which is generally regarded as facilitating the transferability of goods by making buying more attractive through not requiring an elaborate investigation of property rights, said: 'In a society that recognises property as something more than theft, you do not go around lightly destroying property rights; you must have a compelling reason for awarding A's property to C . . .' ((1981) 15 *Georgia LR* 603). This explains the requirement in art 9:203(1)(c) of the UCC that the debtor should have 'rights in the collateral' as this is simply an embodiment of the common law precept that one cannot convey what one does not have. It is also important to bear in mind that, since title under English law is relative, even the exceptions to *nemo dat*, which must be treated as curing the seller's defective title, do not necessarily mean the granting of an absolute indefeasible title. This phenomenon can be illustrated in *Lloyds Bank Ltd v Bank of America* [1938] 2 KB 147, where Lord Greene MR explained that:

> Where the right of ownership has become divided among two or more persons in such a way that the acts . . . |contemplated – see s 2(1) Factors Act 1889| can never be authorised save by both or all of them, these persons together constitute the owner.

Several policy factors emerge: estoppel of the true owner; ostensible ownership and possession; the significance of negotiability in order to stimulate trade.

Exceptions to the security of property principle

Estoppel

Section 21(1) of SGA 1979 provides:

> Subject to this Act, where goods are sold by a person who is not their owner and who does not sell them under the authority or with the consent of the owner, the buyer acquires no better title to the goods than the seller had, unless the owner of the goods is by his conduct precluded from denying the seller's authority to sell.

Although the SGA adopts the term 'precluded' rather than 'estoppel', s 21(1) is usually classed as an example of the doctrine of estoppel, the rationale of which according to Coke is that 'a man's own act or acceptance stoppeth or closeth up his mouth to allege or pleade the truth' (Co. Litt 352a). Inasmuch as it is true to say that a rule which prevents the owner from asserting his rights in effect takes them away from him, it cannot be the case that the estoppel of such a person can bind another (who is not privy to the estoppel) with a title paramount. Thus, Battersby and Preston have suggested ((1972) 35 *MLR* 268) that the word 'owner' in s 21(1) must mean 'the owner of the title that is being transferred', since otherwise it would have an extremely limiting effect on the section because the doctrine of estoppel would not apply against a possessor with a defeasible title.

Limitations of the estoppel doctrine

The position of the third party successor to the vendor is pertinent. It has sometimes been maintained, drawing upon the approach taken by Devlin LJ in the Court of Appeal in *Eastern Distributors Ltd v Goldring* [1957] 2 QB 600, that the effect of s 21 is to transfer to the buyer a real title and not a metaphorical title by estoppel. In this case a van owner signed hire purchase proposals which made a dealer appear to be the owner. This was part of a scheme to enable the customer to obtain another vehicle on credit, without having to pay the deposit required by the then current credit regulations. The scheme failed but the dealer used the documents which the owner had given him; he was able to sell the van to a hire purchase company although having no right to do so. The hire purchase company acquired a good title because although the dealer had no right to sell, the owner's conduct in completing false forms estopped him from asserting this. It was held:

> ... that apparent authority to sell is an exception to the maxim *nemo dat quod non habet*; and it is plain from the wording that if the owner of the goods is precluded from denying authority, the buyer will in fact acquire a better title than the seller. (*per* Devlin LJ at p 611)

Subsequent case law has experienced difficulty in determining the exact basis of the decision. In *Stoneleigh Finance Ltd v Phillips* [1965] 2 QB 537, Davies LJ referred to an 'ostensible title to sell' in connection with *Eastern Distributors*, while in *Snook v London and West Riding Investments Ltd* [1967] 2 QB 786, Russell LJ stated that the plaintiff in that case was estopped by his own conduct (pp 803–4). Other decisions have referred to the *Eastern Distributors* case as being based on ostensible ownership and not ostensible agency. It appears that the position is very confused especially since, on the facts, the decision in *Eastern Distributors* could have been justified on more conventional agency principles, because the owner had consented to give the van to a mercantile agent for the purpose of sale as well as relevant documentation relating to the van. This scenario seems to be on all fours with the mischief contained in s 2(1) of FA 1889 (see pp 198–201).

There are real difficulties in reconciling the proprietary estoppel doctrine with statutory interpretation since the SGA 1979 adopts the rule that property passes by agreement and not by conduct. Moreover, the proprietary estoppel approach fails to take into account the dynamic nature of the sale transaction as it concentrates on the assumption that there are three parties, viz, an owner, a rogue and a good faith purchaser. In fact, the goods may have passed through several hands and the innocent purchaser may have been persuaded to enter into the sale transaction by a rogue who knew the extent of an agent's authority. If title is a rule of evidence or impressed with an equity and not of absolute conveyance, the rogue, as sub-purchaser, will not prevail against the owner. The essential issue is whether goods are freely negotiable: the development of the doctrine of estoppel in the context of chattels has stressed the need for a representation either by words or by conduct.

The limited extent of the doctrine of estoppel is illustrated by *Shaw v Commissioner of Police of the Metropolis* [1987] 1 WLR 1332, where the owner of a Porsche motor car entrusted it to a rogue to find a buyer. Unfortunately, the owner signed a letter stating that he had sold the car to the rogue. Relying on that letter, a good faith purchaser agreed to buy the car under a conditional contract which did not pass property until the rogue vendor was paid. The Court of Appeal held that the owner of goods was precluded by s 21 of the 1979 Act from denying an intermediate seller's authority to sell goods of which the seller was not the owner, only if the goods were 'sold' by the intermediate seller. Statutory estoppel did not apply where there was merely an agreement to sell since, under s 2(5) of SGA 1979, an agreement to sell does not involve a transfer of property.

When the owner has enabled the representation to be made, the question of whether he owed a duty of care and, if so, whether he has broken that duty, must be material. The *locus classicus* here is *Henderson and Co v Williams* [1895] 1 QB 521, the facts of which are as follows. Bags of sugar belonging to O (the original owner) were stored in Williams's warehouse. O was defrauded by a rogue into 'selling' the goods to the rogue and in this respect, O instructed Williams to hold the goods on behalf of the rogue. This enabled the rogue to sell the goods to Henderson. Before buying, Henderson enquired from Williams who assured him that the rogue did have a right to the goods. The fraud was then discovered. The first contract, between O and the rogue, was held void for mistake. The warehouseman therefore refused to deliver up the goods to Henderson, the innocent buyer. It was held that both the warehousemen and O were estopped from denying the rogue's title because they had held him out as having a right to the goods. This case may be contrasted with *Farquharson Bros and Co v C King and Co Ltd* [1902] AC 325, which involved a clerk employed by the plaintiffs, who had authority to send delivery orders to the dock company with whom timber belonging to the plaintiffs was lodged. The clerk fraudulently transferred the timber to himself through the dock company under a fictitious name, and using that name he purported to sell the timber to the defendants. The House of Lords held that the plaintiffs were not estopped from denying the title of the defendants on the grounds that the plaintiffs had made no representation of any kind to them. Their Lordships were clearly of the opinion here that the plaintiffs owed no duty of care to the defendants in this situation.

It is necessary not only to establish a duty of care but also to demonstrate that there has been a breach of such a duty. This is a difficult burden to discharge, as is evident in the case law. Perhaps the most celebrated instance of a duty of care being established in recent times is *Mercantile Credit Co Ltd v Hamblin* [1965] 2 QB 242. In *Hamblin* the defendant signed hire purchase forms in blank which she entrusted to an apparently respectable dealer to complete so that she could obtain a loan on the security of a car. She kept possession of her car throughout but by her actions she enabled the dealer to offer to sell the car as his own to the plaintiff finance company and offer the defendant to take the car on hire purchase terms from the plaintiffs. The defendant, however, thought that she was signing some sort of mortgage instrument. The Court of Appeal held that there was a sufficient relationship of proximity between the finance company and the defendant to give rise to the duty of care, because had she read the document she would have seen that the finance company was a specified recipient of the form and would have relied upon the form for the purpose specified in the form. However it was held that although a duty of care was established, she had not failed to take care in that it was not unreasonable for her to have trusted the dealer, so that her negligence was not the proximate cause of the finance company being induced to buy the car.

The *Hamblin* case was applied by the Court of Appeal in *Beverley Acceptances Ltd v Oakley* [1982] RTR 417 where the pledgee of two Rolls-Royce cars was held to owe a duty of care to the plaintiff financiers where the pledgor had been given temporary possession of the two cars and the registration books. The pledgee gave up the keys of the compound (where the cars were kept) for a specific purpose, namely, because the pledgor had represented to him that temporary possession was necessary for assessment of insurance. It was held that although a duty of care was owed to the persons who accompanied the pledgor, since this was the purpose of giving up possession, there had, nevertheless been no breach of this duty. As Donaldson LJ put it (at pp 424–5):

> These were elderly and valuable cars, and [the pledgee] would no doubt have been wise to have insured his own interest in them. But, whether he did so or not [the pledgor] had a very clear insurable interest in the motor cars, because he would remain liable to [the pledgee] to repay the loan even if the cars were stolen or destroyed. As the cars were both elderly and valuable, it was not an improbable story which [the pledgor] told, namely, that he had representatives of the insurers with him and they wanted to inspect the cars. Such representatives might well want to verify the age . . . they might want to see the registration documents.

The scope of the estoppel doctrine is extremely limited and it is well to recall the approach of Lord Wright in *Mercantile Bank of India Ltd v Central Bank of India Ltd* [1938] AC 287: 'There are very few cases of actions for conversion in which a plea of estoppel by representation has succeeded' (p 302). The emphasis on wilful conduct means that common law doctrine does not go very far in entrustment cases, since it is settled that mere possession of property does not convey a title to dispose of it (*Central Newbury Car Auctions Ltd v Unity Finance Ltd* [1957] 1 QB 371). At the same time it should not be forgotten that possession is at the root of title, ie *beati possidentes*. It is still the case that the purchaser in good faith can acquire ownership through adverse possession in England by being in possession for six years. The Limitation Act 1980 purports to bar the owner's right to bring suit to recover his property or its value after the prescribed period (Limitation Act 1980, ss 2, 3). Nevertheless, a possession-based rule for transferring property does create difficulties since it impedes the temporal division of ownership and, in a sense, it can be said to encourage theft since it makes the tracing of claims for more than one generation difficult.

Estoppel and failure to supply relevant information

An issue which has exercised the courts is whether there are any legal effects of a failure by a finance company to register a hire purchase or related agreement such as a lease or contract hire arrangement with a motor file information register operated by either HPI plc or more recently CCN Systems. The failure by a finance company 'owner' of a car to register with HPI was fully considered by the House of Lords in *Moorgate Mercantile Co Ltd v Twitchings* [1977] AC 890. In that case, the plaintiff finance company brought an action in conversion against a dealer, which turned on the issue of estoppel as a source for protecting the defendant motor dealer/purchaser of the vehicle. The minority approach in the House of Lords and the Court of Appeal judgments referred to the possibility of finance companies registering with HPI as a mechanism for protecting property and failure here formed the basis of a duty of care, that is, common membership by the major financiers of motor vehicles of the HPI scheme created a relationship of propinquity between them. By contrast, the majority were reluctant to substitute a desirable practice into a requirement. It is clear from the majority judgments that the mere fact that the true owner could reasonably foresee that his carelessness would lead the buyer to believe that the seller was the owner of the goods, or, that the true owner had no interest in the goods, did not give rise to a duty. The decision would appear to be squarely in line with the current case law which restricts liability in negligence for economic loss (see *Caparo Industries plc v Dickman* [1990] 2 AC 605).

The extent of the duty of care in negligence also arose in *Debs v Sibec* [1990] RTR 91, illustrating a failure by a private individual to report the condition of a car to the police, a report which could ultimately have resulted in registration of this information with HPI. In August 1987, the plaintiff bought for £57,000 a Mercedes Benz car equipped with many extras. He was robbed of this car and, during the robbery, his life was threatened unless he signed a document containing his name and address, together with an acknowledgement that he had received a sum of money in full and final settlement for it. The robbers, in taking the ignition key and registration document, maintained the threat (through subsequent phone calls) against going to the police and reporting the incident, by promising to kill his children on the occurrence of this eventuality. A month passed by before the plaintiff was persuaded to go to the police. In the meantime, the car was sold to a dealer merely on the production of the 'receipt' and the top half of the registration document. The dealer checked with HPI that the car was not stolen or on hire purchase and agreed to buy it for £46,950. This was done without either securing the address of the immediate seller or through making contact with the plaintiff. The car was then sold to a second dealer and then, at the defendant's request, to Forward Trust Ltd for £51,000 who also had checked with HPI. Soon afterwards, the police traced the car to the defendants. The plaintiffs succeeded in their claim for damages for conversion against the defendants. One argument put forward was that there had been an estoppel by representation by virtue of the written receipt. This was rejected quite properly on the basis that the representation was not a voluntary one in that it had been induced by force. The case neatly illustrates the narrowness of the estoppel by negligence doctrine. In this respect, Simon Brown J adopted a suppositive argument: even if the plaintiff had been negligent in failing to report the theft, supposing he had reported it, this would not have been included on the HPI register when the first dealer checked the records. It followed that if the defendant was to succeed, the scope of the duty of care would have to extend to each purchaser in a chain of purchasers with the result that protection would or would not be gained, according to when an inquiry of HPI would reveal the theft. This was rejected by the court on the basis of *Twitchings*. From this it would appear that in the absence of a legislative initiative, the common law environment which champions security of property is unaffected by the failure to register credit or other information.

Estoppel and a 'right' to cure?

One further aspect of the doctrine of estoppel will be considered: the possibility of estoppel on the part of the seller 'curing' an initial defective title. There appears to be nothing wrong in legal logic with the idea that a seller can cure a defective title. As the number of encumbered goods in the economy increases, it may be unfair to shift to the seller all of the credit and crime risks with regard to the title to chattels. One way of doing this is through adopting a limited notion of 'cure'. Just as the vendor selling goods to which he has no title is estopped from denying the validity of the transfer, so also, where the seller subsequently acquired a good title, the buyer is protected by the estoppel, ie the estoppel is 'fed'. The basic problem here is determining at what stage the estoppel arises in the absence of waiver by the buyer. This is especially problematic in view of the fact that s 12(1) of SGA 1979 envisages that a seller who does not have a right to sell at the time of the sale commits a breach of condition. This point arose and was considered in *Barber v NWS Bank plc* (Unreported) 17 November 1995 (CA) the facts of which are set out below (see p 223). It may be that a way of avoiding this dilemma is through s 11(4) which relegates a breach of condition to that of a warranty in a non-severable contract where the buyer has accepted the goods. The main difficulty here is that Atkin LJ's judgment in *Rowland v Divall* [1923] 2 KB 500 would seem to preclude this possibility:

> The whole object of a sale is to transfer property from one person to another, and I think that in every contract of sale of goods there is an implied term to that effect that a breach of the condition that the seller has a right to sell the goods may be treated as a ground for rejecting the goods and repudiating the contract notwithstanding the acceptance within the meaning of the concluding words of [the subsection] . . . . (pp 506–7)

In fact, there is no warrant for this view in the Act itself, and it is doubtful whether Atkin LJ contemplated that his proposition would apply in cases where the seller had been able to remedy the breach before the repudiation by the buyer. It is noteworthy that in *Rowland v Divall* the seller never acquired the right to sell the car which was recovered from the buyer after four months' use and it follows, therefore, that the buyer could not be regarded as having accepted the goods (see Chapter 14).

It does seem harsh that if the seller can and does cure his defective title before the buyer's repudiation, the latter can nevertheless repudiate the contract, despite prolonged use and perhaps depreciation of the asset. The Law Reform Committee, 12th Report, *Transfer of Title to Chattels*, Cmnd 2958 (1966) at para 36, recommended that the buyer should not be able to recover the price in full in the situation where he had use of the goods. This approach has been echoed in subsequent Law Commission Reports, but interestingly in the most recent Law Commission Report, *Sale and Supply of Goods* No 160 (1987), the problems of quantifying the buyer's unjust enrichment have precluded any recommendation for reform in this area (para 6:4).

Although it may be the case, as the Law Commission Report on *Sale and Supply of Goods* No 160 (1987) points out (para 6.5), that the valuation of the buyer's unjust enrichment on termination through his prolonged use of the goods will be uncertain, nonetheless if there has been a subsequent acquisition of title there can be no objection in principle to this feeding the title of the buyer if the latter had not, by that time, elected to treat the contract as repudiated. Under English law, the buyer would be subject to a claim in conversion by the true owner. In this circumstance, an allowance must be made against the tortfeasor's liability in damage to the extent of the value of the improvements made to the chattel in good faith (see s 6 of Torts (Interference with Goods) Act 1977).

The abolition of market overt

Under English law, recovery is based not on ownership in the sense of absolute title, but rather on the better right to possess, and the *jus tertii* cannot be pleaded against a possessor. Consequently, there is no theoretical reason why a thief should not sue a second thief although, in practice, the first thief will probably not want to draw attention to himself. It was only in the case of market overt that an indefeasible absolute title to chattels was known to the common law. The 12th Report of the Law Reform Committee (1966) recommended (para 11) that the rule should be extended to the sale of goods in all retail establishments. The effect of this recommendation would have been to shift the right of action available to the *bona fide* purchaser of goods under s 12 of SGA 1979 to the owner. Significantly, the abolition of the market overt doctrine, by the Sale and Supply of Goods Act 1994, represents a swing away from such an approach which would champion transactions as distinct from ownership.

Voidable title

Since English law fails to distinguish between contract and conveyance, no property can pass if the contract of sale is void. The emergence in England of voidable title theory in the 19th Century may indicate a judicial propensity towards sophisticated allocation of risk, since it enabled the courts to protect some good faith purchasers without overturning the security of property principle. This is reproduced in s 23 of SGA 1979 which provides:

> When the seller of goods has a voidable title to them, but his title has not been avoided at the time of sale, the buyer acquires a good title to the goods, provided he buys them in good faith and without notice of the seller's defect of title.

The formalistic position adopted depends upon the intention of the parties; whether the owner intends to transfer possession only or whether he intends to transfer title to the wrongdoer. However, the fundamental flaw with the voidable title approach is, how can the owner's subjective intent supply the innocent purchaser with realistic criteria for judging the legitimacy of the transaction? In addition, the owner–intent cases can be seen as an example of inductive judicial reasoning (see for example *Ingram v Little* [1961] 1 QB 31; *Lewis v Averay* [1972] 1 QB 198).

One of the most celebrated cases in this context is *Cundy v Lindsay* (1878) 23 App Cas 459. A rogue persuaded Lindsay to 'sell' linen to him on credit by pretending to be Blenkiron and Co, a known and reputable customer. The rogue then resold to Cundy whilst Lindsay, unpaid by the rogue, sued Cundy for conversion. In this case, a risk analysis based on fault may have stressed that in the supply of cotton there was a rapid turnover, unlike the slower legal mechanism for the transfer of realty which often involves noting a property interest on a register, and that the owners having been tricked acted quickly and tried to reduce the risk to third parties. On the other hand, it is possible to argue that the owners were negligent in not spotting the discrepancy on the letter heading, which they should have done, given the fact that the degree of commercial pressure was less than in an *inter praesentes* shopping situation. The House of Lords rejected any analysis based on fault, preferring a formalistic approach.

Interestingly, in *Cundy v Lindsay* the unsuccessful third party was represented by Benjamin, the Louisiana lawyer who had fled to England after the US Civil War. It was Benjamin who sharpened the 'title' concept both in Louisiana and in England where, on at least two occasions, he unsuccessfully presented the point of view of security of transactions. Thus in *Russell v Favier* (1841) 18 La 585, Benjamin, a young man of 30, unsuccessfully represented a purchaser of a slave from a lessee who had improperly sold it. He argued:

> A purchaser of movable effects at public auction who buys bona fide from an individual to whom the real owner has intrusted the possession, acquires a good title even though the owner had given the possession without authority to sell—or in other words, possession is such proof of title to movables as to enable the possessor to convey a good title to bona fide purchasers in the ordinary course of business, unless the possession has been feloniously obtained [citing New York cases]. The distinction is this: if possession be obtained feloniously as by theft, the possessor can pass no title; but if obtained fraudulently, it suffices to enable him to pass title to third persons . . . . (p 587)

But this position failed because the court held that 'title' had not passed to the wrongdoer. Thirty-seven years later in *Cundy v Lindsay*, Benjamin argued that 'title' had gone to the impersonator and so could be passed on free of the 'equity'.

The issue of the 'equity' of the original owner envisaged by Benjamin in *Cundy v Lindsay*, is very important. For example, if a wrongdoer transferred a chattel to an innocent purchaser who subsequently transferred to a purchaser with notice of the initial wrongdoing, the second purchaser's right or duties would depend on the definition of voidable title used by the courts. If voidable title is defined as an inferior title then it would include no power to cut off the rights of the original owner (security of property). This was the approach of Cresswell J in *Billiter v Young* (1856) 6 E & B 1, in holding that the voidable title rule was based not upon the fact: '. . . that the second vendee had a good title, and therefore the first sale was not void, but that the first sale was not void . . . and therefore the second vendee had a good title' (p 25). Such an approach militates against Atkin LJ's *dictum* in *Re Wait* (1927) that an equitable interest can only arise *dehors* the contract of sale since the first vendee will be deemed to have a legal estate subject to a trust.

Another interpretation which is traditionally adopted in England is that the title transferred is a perfect one subject to a condition subsequent based on rescission. This approach coheres with security in transactions. Sometimes *Buckley v Gross* (1862) 3 B & S 566, is cited as authority for this proposition, but on the facts this seems unlikely. In that case various quantities of tallow, the property of different persons, were deposited in a warehouse on one of the banks of the Thames. During a warehouse fire the tallow melted and flowed down the Thames. Several portions of this molten tallow were picked up by A who sold it to B. The latter was charged with being in possession of tallow supposed to have been stolen or unlawfully obtained. This charge was dismissed before the magistrate, although the tallow was ordered to be detained under the Metropolitan Police Act (1839) 2 and 3 Vict c 71. The tallow was sold before the time prescribed by the Act had elapsed and the question arose whether a good faith purchaser from the police could prevail against B who had been the previous possessor. It was held by Blackburn J:

> Their possession [ie the police] was the possession of the true owner and not the wrongdoer whose possession was terminated by their taking possession. It is therefore not necessary to consider whether the sale of the tallow to the defendant by the police was right or wrong . . . . (p 575)

This case was concerned with the interpretation of the Metropolitan Police Act, but more fundamentally, there was no question of the original owner of the tallow complaining here. This contrasts with *Peirce v London Horse and Carriage Repository Ltd* (1922) WN 170, where the original owner attempted to recover his car from the defendants. Insofar as this case is cited as authority for the proposition that the title transferred is a perfect one subject to a condition subsequent based on rescission, close examination of this case does reveal considerable difficulties.

The facts of the case are as follows. The plaintiff exchanged an Excelsior car with King in return for a lorry. King deposited the Excelsior with the defendant and instructed him to sell it on his behalf taking, at the same time, a Ford car from the defendant as part payment of the price he expected to receive. The defendant sub-sold the car to B who sold it further to J. In the meantime, King was convicted of theft of the lorry and it was returned by the plaintiffs to the original owner. The plaintiff demanded the car from the defendant who mistakenly thought that the car had been stolen. The defendant informed all of the sub-buyers who returned the car to their immediate sellers having fully reimbursed the price each had paid. When the defendant discovered that the car had not been stolen but that King had a voidable title to it, they refused to surrender the car except on the terms that the plaintiff pay them the price of the Ford and certain storage charges. The plaintiffs sued in detinue, and the Court of Appeal held that the defendant acquired an indefeasible title from B since the latter was a good faith purchaser irrespective of the fact that, at the date of the resale to them, the defendant had notice of King's fraud. The decision does seem anomalous since it was hardly the case that the sub-buyers were giving up the car and payment respectively (without appreciation or depreciation in price) in a freely negotiated contract as the case suggests. The different transactions were unravelled because the sub-sellers (the defendant and B) laboured under the mistake that they were in breach of the implied title under- taking in s 12 of SGA 1893. If this is so, the relevant time for notice was that of the original sub-sale when the defendant had no notice of the fraud since the subsequent sale could have been avoided on the grounds of mistake. Moreover, it is odd that neither s 23 nor s 25(2) of SGA 1893 nor s 9 of FA 1889 are men- tioned in the report. Essentially, the issues which are in focus here involve policy questions including the extent to which chattels are negotiable, as well as the nature of the notice requirement for rescission.

It is interesting how the courts have ensured the primacy of the security of property principle, not by reference to the 'equity' of the original owner, but rather by taking a wide approach to the question of notice of rescission. Thus in *Car and Universal Finance Ltd v Caldwell* [1965] 1 QB 525, the owner of a car sold it to a plausible rogue and allowed the rogue to take it away in return for a cheque. The cheque was dishonoured and the seller immediately informed the police requesting them to try to get his car back. After this, the rogue resold the car to X who took it in bad faith knowing of the fraud. X then re-sold it to the plaintiffs who bought in good faith. It was held that since the rogue could not have been contacted, the original seller had rescinded the contract by informing the police and doing everything practicable to make public his inten- tion to rescind, for example, by informing the AA. Subsequently in *Newtons of Wembley Ltd v Williams* [1965] 1 QB 560, it was held that informing the police and a motorists' organisation like the AA or RAC was sufficient to rescind the contract when the rogue could not be found. Of course, this is of little comfort to the innocent buyer and it is for this reason that the Law Revision Committee's 12th Report Cmnd 2958 (1966) recommended (paras 16, 40(4)) that the rule as to avoidance laid down in *Caldwell's* case should be reversed and actual communication required. Nevertheless, the approach taken in *Caldwell* (1965) has been endorsed in *Thomas v Heelas* 27 November, 1986 (CAT No 1065). In this case the court held that, when an owner sought to recover goods in the possession of somebody who was not a party to the void- able transaction, the onus was on the possessor to show that he had good title. Clearly this is an onerous task especially where the chain of title is long. Indeed, over six months had elapsed between the owner's original rescission by inform- ing the police and the eventual discovery of the car.

The fundamental issue being addressed here is whether goods may be con- sidered to be negotiable. It is considered, often without examination, that the protection of the good faith purchaser assists the free flow of commerce and is more suited to a society which assumes exchange or contract rather than prop- erty. The basic thrust of this approach is to draw a distinction between com- mercial and non-commercial transactions, it being argued that outside the commercial setting there is no compelling reason to depart from the common law which protected ownership. This may explain the common law's restric- tive attitude to the assignment of choses in action, but its championing of negotiable instruments. Nevertheless, this clear-cut approach is not entirely sat- isfactory for at least two reasons. In the first place, it is an over-simplification to draw an analogy between goods and negotiable instruments. The latter must circulate widely and rapidly as a medium of exchange, and it is inherent in the attribute of negotiability that the purchasers' needs for costly information concerning prior claims of defence should be minimised. Goods do not circulate in this way. Moreover, owner-risk prevention (against theft or fraud) is quite different in the case of a negotiable instrument where, for example, the risk that a note may be stolen and payment rightfully obtained by a transferee from the thief, can be minimised by putting the note in order form. This is not possible in the case of goods. Secondly, there are other policy factors which have to be taken into account which may restrict transferability. Inalienability can take many forms as where ownership is legal but sales are not permitted, or where sales are forbidden but gifts are permitted, or alternatively where sales are permitted at a 'fair' price but not gifts. The justifications for restraint on alienation range from protection for third parties through over-exploitation in the common pool, or protection of quality or disadvantaged persons which can include ordinary consumers. With regard to the latter, even negotiable instruments have been curtailed. Thus, s 123 of CCA 1974 makes it difficult to attain the status of a holder in due course by the taking and negotiation of negotiable instruments in connection with a regulated agreement (see Chapter 2). It would appear from this that the primacy of the *nemo dat* doctrine may be defended on the basis of both principle and policy.

Mercantile agency and the Factors Act 1889

During the 19th Century there were a series of statutory interventions in England through the Factors Acts 1823–89, the purpose of which was to accommodate the perceived requirements of trade. The factors legislation grew up in the wake of increasing trade in the 19th Century, particularly in the practice of the English consignee/factor in making advances on goods to a foreign consignor. The Select Committee of the House of Commons in 1823, *On the Law Relating to Merchants, Agents or Factors*, upon whose report the various Factors Acts were based, contended that the practice of the consignee himself treating the goods of all his consignors as his own and borrowing upon them *en bloc*, was a practice which was beneficial to commerce, and that the lender should be given good title against the consignor. One suggestion of the Committee was to introduce into English law the civilian concept of *possession vaut titre*, ie primacy being accorded to the fact of possession. In a similar vein in 1873, the Indian Law Commissioners, under the draft cl 81 of the Indian Contract Bill, proposed:

> The ownership of goods may be acquired by buying them from any person who is in possession of them provided that the buyer acts in good faith and under circumstances which are not such as to raise a reasonable presumption that the person in possession has no right to sell them.

As in 1823, this approach was rejected on the basis that it would make British India an asylum for cattle stealers from Indian States.

The factors legislation incorporates the principle of apparent ownership. The key to the FA 1889 is s 2(1) which provides:

> Where a mercantile agent is, with the consent of the owner in possession of goods or of the documents of title to goods, any sale, pledge or other disposition of the goods, made by him when acting in the ordinary course of business of a mercantile agent, shall, subject to the provisions of this Act, be as valid as if he were expressly authorised by the owner of the goods to make the same; provided that the person taking under the disposition acts in good faith, and has not at the time of the disposition noticed that the person making the disposition has not authority to make the same.

Who is a mercantile agent?

In a sense the FA 1889 is curiously named since it deals with classes of agent other than the factor. The broad definition of mercantile agent makes it no longer necessary to distinguish between factors and brokers so, according to s 1(1) of the 1889 Act, mercantile agent means: '. . . a mercantile agent having in the customary course of his business as such agent authority either to sell goods, or to consign goods for the purpose of sale, or to buy goods, or to raise money on the security of goods' The essential issue is that a 'mercantile agent' is one who, by way of business, is customarily entrusted with goods as agent. In this respect, a person who induces another to let him have goods on the representation that he can sell them to another is not, without more, a mercantile agent. Quite often the presence of a commission will help to assert his status. Thus in *Budberg v Jerwood and Ward* (1935) 51 TLR 99 it was held that the Act did not apply to defeat the title of an owner who entrusted her jewellery to a friend for the purposes of sale, because of the absence of a commission which negatived any suggestion of a business relationship. There is an apparent conflict between s 1(1) which refers to 'customary course' and s 2(1) which alludes to 'the ordinary course of business of a mercantile agent'. In *Oppenheimer v Attenborough* [1908] 1 KB 221, the question arose whether the agent for sale is authorised to pledge. The court expressed the opinion that the 1889 Act made no difference to the pre-existing law. With respect, this approach cannot be sustained especially in view of the inclusion of 'ordinary course of business'. Moreover, the definition of mercantile agent stipulates four kinds of activity and it is obvious that the ordinary kind of business of each will be different. Indeed, it appears from Hansard that the clause as originally drafted contained the words 'such a mercantile agent' which shows what the intention of the draftsman was (see *Hansard*, 3rd series, col 339, p 230).

Disposition in the ordinary course of business

The 1889 Act is a compromise reached by the instigators of the legislation, namely, the Institute of Bankers and the London Chamber of Commerce, bodies which represented the rival interests of the bankers and the merchants. The entrusting concept found in previous factors legislation is incorporated in the 1889 Act through the provision in s 2 that the sale or pledge must be 'in the ordinary course of business of a mercantile agent'. A degree of illogicality has entered into English law because although the courts recognise, for example, that a car log book and registration certificates are not documents of title, nevertheless, have given them some special status in relation to 'ordinary course of business of a mercantile agent'. Thus in *Pearson v Rose and Young Ltd* [1951] 1 KB 275, the Court of Appeal unanimously held that a disposition of a car with its log book was not in the ordinary course of business because the mercantile agent was in the possession of the log book without the consent of the owner. The fact of physical possession was ignored for the purpose of the disposition.

This was taken a stage further in *Stadium Finance Co Ltd v Robbins* [1962] 2 QB 664. In this case a dealer had been given possession of the owner's Jaguar car in order that he should find a buyer. The owner kept the ignition key, clearly intending to control the sale himself. Inadvertently he left the registration book in the locked glove compartment. It was held by the Court of Appeal that as the dealer had not been given possession of the registration book and ignition key, a subsequent sale could not be in the ordinary course of business, even though he obtained a duplicate key and was able to hand a key and the registration book to the hirer. However, it is difficult to accept such reasoning and perhaps the best approach is to draw a distinction between the possession of the car itself, which must require the subjective consent of the owner, and the subsequent disposition which objectively requires a log book or registration document for the sale to be within the ordinary course of business. Significantly in *Astley Industrial Trust Ltd v Miller* [1968] 2 All ER 36, Chapman J considered that the Court of Appeal decisions were wrong on this latter point. He did distinguish the two cases on the ground that with brand new cars the registration book is by no means so important regarding title, and that the sale of a new car without the book or registration document can apparently be in the ordinary course of business.

Consent of the owner

The English courts have adopted a wide approach with regard to the question of the consent of the owner. Thus in cases involving jewellers, the courts would point to evidence of a contrary intention which overrode s 18, r 4 of SGA 1979 (*Weiner v Gill* [1906] 2 KB 574). While there must be actual consent to the agent's possession by the owner, it is irrelevant that this consent was obtained by a trick. In *Folkes v King* [1923] 1 KB 282, a motor agent was given possession of the owner's car and authorised to sell it for him for not less than £575, but in fact he sold it for £340. The buyer knew nothing of the cash restriction which the owner had placed upon the agent's actual authority and bought it in good faith. The agent was a mercantile agent and the buyer, therefore, obtained a good title. Moreover, so long as possession was originally given by the owner, withdrawal of that consent is immaterial (s 2(2) of the 1889 Act) unless the buyer knew that it had been withdrawn, in which event he might no longer take in good faith in any case. The burden of proof is upon the buyer that he took in good faith and without notice that the sale was made without the owner's authority (*Heap v Motorists Advisory Agency Ltd* [1923] 1 KB 377).

In contrast under s 23 of SGA 1979, lack of good faith must be proved by the original owner (*Whitehorn Bros v Davison* [1911] 1 KB 463).

Sellers in possession

Section 8 of FA 1889 deals with the case of a seller under a sale or agreement to sell, in possession of goods or of the documents of title to the goods. This was virtually duplicated in s 25(1) of SGA 1893 (now s 24 of SGA 1979) which provides as follows:

> Where a person having sold goods continues or is in possession of the goods, or of the documents of title to the goods, the delivery or transfer by that person, or by a mercantile agent acting for him, of the goods or documents of title under any sale, pledge or other disposition thereof, [or under any agreement for sale, pledge or other disposition thereof], to any person receiving the same in good faith and without notice of the previous sale, has the same effect as if the person making the delivery or transfer was expressly authorised by the owner of the goods to make the same.

The words in brackets are additional words included in the FA 1889.

A literal construction of s 24 of SGA 1979 would suggest that, although the owner is deemed to authorise the delivery of the goods or the transfer of the documents of title, he is not deemed to have given his authority to the sale, pledge or other disposition. This contrasts with the 'notional mercantile agency' device adopted in s 9 of FA 1889 where the buyer in possession is treated as if he were such a mercantile agent. The significance of this is that s 2(1) of FA 1889, the main mercantile agency provision, allows the mercantile agent, within certain constraints, to pass title by delivery of goods unaccompanied by documents. As a result of this notional mercantile agency, the effect of s 9 is wider than s 8. The differences between the two sections were noted by Pearson LJ in *Newtons of Wembley Ltd v Williams* [1965] 1 QB 560:

> Under section 8, the effect of the disposition by the seller is that it shall have 'the same effect as if the person making the delivery or transfer were expressly authorised by the owner of the goods to make the same'. On the other hand, in section 9 there is a different provision as to the effect of the transaction, because it is to have 'the same effect as if the person making the delivery or transfer were a mercantile agent in possession of the goods, or documents of title with the consent of the owner'. It is also to be observed that almost identical provisions were inserted in section 25 of the Sale of Goods Act 1893. Section 25(1) of the Act of 1893 is almost exactly the same as section 8 of the Act of 1889; section 25(2) of the Act of 1893 is almost identical to section 9 of the Act of 1889; and the same difference in the effect of the transaction is preserved in those two subsections. Thus there cannot be any suggestion that the difference in language is merely *per incuriam*. (pp 577–8)

The approach taken in s 8 of FA 1889 is consistent with the multititular characteristic of English law. Prior to the amendment made in s 8, any purchaser of goods from a seller in possession who did not transfer documents of title, would have been liable to the true owner in conversion. There is now a statutory defence to such an action because, by virtue of s 25(1) of SGA 1893, the true owner is deemed to have authorised the delivery of the goods to the buyer and must, therefore, have waived his right to immediate possession. The catalyst for the passing of title under s 25(1) of 1893 SGA is the transfer of documents of title. It is odd that s 8 does not include a notional mercantile agency, as seen in s 9 of FA 1889. The difficulty is to determine the precise intention of Chalmers in his failure to reproduce s 3 of FA 1877 which provided for such a concept. In his *Commentary on the Sale of Goods Bill and the Factors Act* 1889, published in 1890, Chalmers merely notes that the effect of s 8 was to extend s 3 of the 1877 Act to goods as well as documents of title, while the editors of Blackburn, writing in 1910, refer to s 8 as re-enacting s 3 in more precise language. The real reason for the difference in treatment may be due to the legacy of the historical function of the factor who was a buying and selling agent. Up to the mid-19th Century, the factor enjoyed a dominant financial role in domestic and international trade and would sell in his own name while the foreign merchant trusted him with actual possession of the goods. The new classes of agent as well as buyers and sellers may have been grafted on to the same mischief which covered earlier factors legislation. Consequently, since the factor was never a seller *qua* owner in possession, there was no need to incorporate the notional mercantile agency provision since the factor's possession would be as a mercantile agent in any case.

The good faith notice requirement

The question of the notice requirement for good faith purchase is particularly pertinent under a literal interpretation of s 24 of SGA 1979. This section provides that goods may be delivered 'under any sale, to any person'. Thus, delivery need not be to the first purchaser from the seller but to a sub-purchaser direct from the original seller. The problem revolves around the question concerning the obligation to act in 'good faith and without notice of the previous sale' which is required in s 24. The material words read as follows: '. . . the delivery . . . of the goods . . . under any sale . . . to any persons receiving the same in good faith and without notice of the previous sale . . .'. This suggests that only the sub-purchaser needs to be in good faith, and even if the latter is in bad faith, he will acquire title by virtue of the buyer's good faith. The approach taken under s 25(1) of the 1893 Act, which substantially reproduced s 8 of FA 1889, differed from its forerunner, s 3 of FA 1877. This provided that title passed to 'any other person who . . . purchases such goods' so that title is linked to any person who purchased the goods without notice of the previous sale. The present rule, however, requires not only sale but also a delivery. So long as the delivery is to a person (not necessarily a purchaser) who is acting in good faith, the buyer in bad faith may acquire title by virtue of a delivery to a person who takes delivery in good faith. In contrast, under the doctrine of estoppel or s 2 of FA 1889, the second buyer is protected as from the moment of sale which does not necessarily coincide with delivery.

The capacity of the seller

The capacity in which the seller retains possession has engaged the attention of the courts. Some of the cases have suggested that if the seller retains possession but acts in relation to the goods as a hirer, the sub-purchaser will not be protected (see *Staffs Motor Guarantee Ltd v British Wagon Co Ltd* [1934] 2 KB 305; *Eastern Distributors Ltd v Goldring* [1957] 2 QB 600). The modern position is that the capacity in which the seller remains in continuous possession is immaterial. Thus in *Pacific Motor Auctions Ltd v Motor Credits Ltd* [1965] AC 867, a dealer unsuccessfully attempted to achieve a stocking plan by way of a sale and rehiring, and the Privy Council held that the words 'continues . . . in possession' referred to the continuity of physical possession, notwithstanding any private transaction between the seller and the first buyer which might have altered the legal capacity under which the possession was held. Of course, where physical possession has been given up, as in *Mitchell v Jones* (1905) 24 NZLR 932, the second buyer is not protected because of the break in the continuity of possession.

Sub-sale and other dispositions

Section 24 of SGA 1979 does not only apply to resale but extends to any 'sale, pledge or other disposition'. The words 'other disposition' have been held to cover any transaction which, like sale or pledge, transfers some proprietary interest in the goods. This can be illustrated by the facts in *Worcester Works Finance Ltd v Cooden Engineering Co Ltd* [1972] 1 QB 210 where X bought a car from the defendants but paid with a cheque which was dishonoured. He then sold the car to the plaintiffs, although he retained possession for the time being. Meanwhile the defendant, the original owner, sought to rescind the contract because X's cheque had failed. X agreed to this and allowed the defendants to retake the vehicle. When the plaintiffs pointed out that the car now belonged to them and claimed the vehicle or its value from the defendants, the action failed. As against the plaintiffs, X was still a seller in possession, and when X accepted the defendant's rescission of the original contract and returned the car, this was held to be a 'disposition' within s 24 so that title had passed. The effect of this decision was that the plaintiffs had recourse only to X, if this was indeed a worthwhile remedy. In *Hanson (W) Harrow v Rapid Civil Engineering and Usborne Developments* (1987) 38 Build LR 106, it was held that the words 'sale or disposition', included also in s 25(1) of SGA 1979, did not cover the case where there was a term in the contract between the buyer in possession of timber supplied and a main contractor on a building site whereby the latter could use the materials in construction. This did not defeat the seller where there was included in the contract of sale a simple retention of title clause relating to the timber (see Chapter 11).

Buyers in possession

Section 9 of FA 1889 and s 25(1) of SGA 1979 provide for property passing by virtue of the buyer's possession:

> Where a person having bought or agreed to buy goods, obtains, with the consent of the seller, possession of the goods or the documents of title to the goods, the delivery or transfer by that person or by a mercantile agent acting for him, of the goods

or documents of title under any sale, pledge or other disposition thereof [or under any agreement for sale, pledge or other disposition thereof] to any person receiving the same in good faith and without notice of any lien or other right of the original seller in respect of the goods, shall have the same effect as if the person making the delivery or transfer were a mercantile agent in possession of the goods or documents of title with the consent of the owner.

The words in brackets are omitted in s 25(1) of SGA 1979.

If good title has passed to the buyer then s 25(1) will rarely apply. The section refers to a contract of sale where the buyer has 'bought' the goods, which appears to be surprising for the simple reason that in any case the *nemo dat quod non habet* principle will apply. However, the subsection may be important in regard to where the buyer has obtained both property and possession of the goods but title has subsequently been avoided by the seller. In this respect, s 25(1) renders the decision in *Car and Universal Finance v Caldwell* (1965) redundant. Thus s 2(2) of FA 1889 specifically states that the subsequent withdrawal of the consent by the seller does not prevent the application of the Act. It is clear from *Cahn v Pockett's Bristol Channel Steam Packet Co Ltd* [1899] 1 QB 643 and *Newtons of Wembley Ltd v Williams* [1965] 1 QB 560, that the issue of consent in s 9 of FA 1889 and s 25(1) of SGA 1979 is subject to s 2 of the FA 1889's treatment of the seller's consent.

The importance of legal form

The limitation imposed by the words 'agreed to buy' should not be underestimated. This is the distinction between hire purchase (*Helby v Matthews* [1895] AC 471) and conditional sale (*Lee v Butler* [1893] 2 QB 318) which is excessively technical, concentrating on legal form rather than economic substance. It is significant that in accordance with the general assimilation of conditional sale agreements to hire purchase agreements, it is now provided that for the purposes of s 9 of FA 1889 and s 25(1) of SGA 1979, 'the buyer under a conditional sale agreement is to be taken not to be a person who has bought or agreed to buy goods' (s 25(2)(*a*) of SGA 1979). It would appear that such conditional sales are governed by the CCA 1974. However, with respect to other conditional sales not covered by the 1974 Act, for example, if the total credit provided is in excess of £15,000, or if the buyer is a body corporate (s 189 of CCA 1974), s 25(1) still applies. Of course, this is of great importance for the lessor under a finance leasing transaction (see Chapter 12). Moreover, consignment sales, including sale or return transactions, are not covered by s 25(1) of SGA 1979 because the possessor is not a person who has agreed to buy goods, even though, in a certain sense, he has made a conditional contract of sale. This emphasises the continued existence in English law of legal form as a phenomenon triumphing over economic substance. This can also be seen in the context of sale or return transactions, which are sometimes referred to as consignment sales.

Consignment sales

Section 18, r 4 of SGA 1979 provides:

> When goods are delivered to the buyer on approval or sale or return or other similar terms, the property in the goods passes to the buyer:
> (a) when he signifies his approval or acceptance to the seller or does any other act adopting the transaction;
> (b) if he does not signify his approval or acceptance to the seller but retains the goods without giving notice of rejection, then, if a time has been fixed for the return of the goods, on the expiration of that time, and, if no time has been fixed, on the expiration of a reasonable time.

It is interesting that this does not refer to goods as being 'sold' but rather refers to delivery. It is clear that through this method Chalmers accommodated both 'a contract of sale' and an 'agreement to sell'. The latter analysis does not entirely fit conceptually the 'sale or return' transaction, that is, here there is an agreement to sell subject to the buyer adopting the transaction. Moreover, in the case of 'sales on approval' many of these are 'sales' (in the sense of property passing) subject to a right of rescission. The crucial question then is whether the buyer has engaged in an 'act adopting the transaction'. This was considered by the Court of Appeal in *Kirkham v Attenborough* [1897] 1 QB 201, where the plaintiff, a jewellery manufacturers, entrusted the jewellery to a rogue on a sale or return basis. The rogue pledged the goods with the defendant, but the Court of Appeal refused the plaintiff in his claim for the return of the goods on the basis that the rogue, by pledging the goods, had adopted the transaction (see also *Genn v Winkel* (1912) 107 LT 434).

The other criterion of determining approval of acceptance, the lapse of a reasonable time, cannot be stated in the abstract and much depends upon the facts in each particular case. In *Poole v Smith's Car Sales (Balham) Ltd* [1962] 1 WLR 744 this period was deemed to be three months where a car dealer had delivered a car to another dealer who had driven it for 1,600 miles, and it had been damaged as a result of an accident.

The question of what constitutes a true consignment sale is highly pertinent in that there is a natural judicial hostility to disguised security interests. A key consideration to the establishment of a true consignment as distinct from a security bill of sale is that, if a consignee is not obligated to pay the price of the goods until sale and can return unsold goods before sub-sale, this is a true agency relationship. The relevant factors are:
(a) reservation of title until sale;
(b) the consignor's right to demand return of the goods at will;
(c) the consignee's right to return unsold goods;
(d) the consignee's authorisation to sell the goods at a fixed price or above a 'floor';
(e) the consignee's obligation to segregate the goods from his own;
(f) the consignee's obligation to hold sales proceeds in trust and forward them to the consignor;

(g) a requirement that the consignee retain separate books and records;

(h) the consignor's right to inspect goods, books, records and premises; and

(i) all shipping papers being required to refer to the goods as consigned.

The determining feature of a 'false' consignment is whether the consignee is absolutely liable for the price of the 'consigned' goods with no right to return the goods unsold. Nevertheless, it has to be admitted that the tests identified are not always easy to apply because the consignment legal form seems so responsive to changing market factors that any test articulated is only going to be marginally useful.

Documents of title

Section 25(1) of SGA 1979 applies equally where the buyer is in possession of documents of title to the goods with the seller's consent. What if an unpaid seller transfers a bill of lading or other document of title before the buyer gets physical possession of the goods? In this event s 25(1) would appear to allow the buyer to resell the document of title so as to defeat any unpaid seller's lien or right of stoppage. However s 47(2) of SGA 1979 specifically provides for this eventuality and reproduces, in almost identical terms, s 10 of FA 1889. Section 47(2) provides:

> Where a document of title to goods has been lawfully transferred to any person as buyer or owner of the goods, and that person transfers the document to a person who takes it in good faith and for valuable consideration, then:
>
> (a) if the last-mentioned transfer was by way of sale the unpaid seller's right of lien or retention or stoppage in transit is defeated; and
>
> (b) if the last-mentioned transfer was made by way of pledge or other disposition for value, the unpaid seller's right of lien or retention or stoppage in transit can only be exercised subject to the rights of the transferee.

Section 47(2) apparently applies only where it is the same document which is transferred to the buyer and by the buyer to the third party (*DF Mount Ltd v Jay and Jay Co Ltd* [1960] 1 QB 159).

It should be noted that s 19(3) of SGA 1979 is subject to s 47, as is illustrated in *Cahn v Pockett's Bristol Channel Steam Packet Co Ltd* [1899] 1 QB 643. In this case, while goods were in the hands of the shipowners, the seller sent the bill of lading, together with a draft bill of exchange, to the buyer who promptly transferred the bill of lading to a sub-buyer who took it in good faith. This sub-sale left the original seller with no right of stoppage in transit when the first buyer failed to pay and became insolvent. The Court of Appeal held that, although the buyers did not accept the draft, this breach of s 19(3) did not deprive the plaintiffs of the protection given by s 47 of SGA 1979. In this regard, s 47 repeats the effect of s 25(1) by making it clear that the rights of the owner are overridden by the disposition.

Good faith and notice

The third party under s 25(1) must take the goods 'in good faith and without notice of any lien or other right of the original seller in respect of the goods'.

This provision is repeated in s 2(1) of FA 1889 and ss 23–25 of SGA 1979. It is sometimes said that s 47(2) is more favourable to the third party because it does not say anything about notice of the rights of the original seller. Before considering this point, it is important to draw a clear distinction between notice and knowledge. Notice is not necessarily knowledge since, essentially, the former is a mechanism by which the latter is attributed. Thus, the terms are not interchangeable since knowledge is a question of fact, whereas notice is a more expansive concept as it can anticipate knowledge being attributed to a person.

Although in its extreme form actual notice is co-extensive with knowledge in that the person with such notice has, as a matter of fact, conscious awareness, it should be recognised that notice is an aspect of a continuum and, on the other extreme, constructive notice is treated as being knowledge. Great difficulties have emerged in distinguishing actual notice from constructive notice. The modern approach is to eschew the evidence-orientated approach and concentrate rather on the question of whose actions are relevant. If the state of the mind of the party to be charged is relevant then this is a question of actual notice. Such is the case with s 47 and it is doubtful whether the absence of notice under this provision adds much to the good faith requirement. On the other hand, if the state of mind is irrelevant then the issue is whether a formal act has been properly performed by the party seeking to protect the prior rights. It follows that constructive notice is a question of form, whilst actual notice rests upon the consciousness of the relevant party.

The question of 'good faith' is defined in s 61(3) of SGA 1979 as follows:

> A thing is deemed to be done in good faith within the meaning of the Act when it is in fact done honestly, whether it is done negligently or not.

It is clear that negligence, when surrounded by other circumstances, will go to the question of knowledge. For the sake of convenience, knowledge may be categorised as actual, 'Nelsonian', ie wilfully shutting one's eye to the obvious, and 'naughty' knowledge where there has been an element of recklessness concerning circumstances which would indicate the facts to an honest and reasonable man (see *Heap v Motorists' Advisory Agency Ltd* [1923] 1 KB 577; *Pearson v Rose and Young Ltd* [1951] 1 KB 275). Nonetheless, the doctrine of constructive notice does not normally apply to commercial transactions (*Manchester Trust v Furness* [1895] 2 QB 539) and there is no general duty on the buyer of goods in an ordinary commercial transaction to make inquiries as to the right of the seller to dispose of the goods. Certainly, it would be anomalous to punish knowledge by the sub-buyer of the buyer's non-payment, especially since it is a common business occurrence for a seller to be paid for goods before he himself can pay for them. It would be unreasonable, in this respect, for a sub-buyer to be put on notice merely because of his knowledge of a retention of title clause, not least because there are so many types of retention of title clauses many of which include proceeds provisions (see Chapter 11). In the case where property has passed to the buyer, the sub-buyer's knowledge of non-payment cannot be described as bad faith because this can hardly be considered a right 'in respect of the goods'; it is merely a personal right in respect of the contract of sale. The principles were expanded by Neil J in *Feur Leather Corp v Frank Johnstone and Sons* [1981] Com LR 251 at p 253:

> . . . (2) For this purpose the court is concerned with actual notice and not with constructive notice. (3) In deciding whether a person in the position of the defendants had actual notice: (a) the court will apply an objective test and look at all the circumstances; (b) if by an objective test clear notice was given liability cannot be avoided by proof merely of the absence of actual knowledge; (c) a person will be deemed to have had notice of any fact to which it can be shown that he deliberately turned a 'blind eye' . . . (d) on the other hand, the court will not expect the recipient of goods to scrutinise commercial documents such as delivery notes with great care; (e) there is no general duty on a buyer of goods in an ordinary commercial transaction to make inquiries as to the right of the seller to dispose of the goods; (f) 'the question becomes: looking objectively at the circumstances which are alleged to constitute notice, do those circumstances constitute notice? This must be a matter of fact and degree to be determined in the particular circumstances of the case'. (4) The burden of proving a bona fide purchase for value without notice rests on the person who asserts it.

There may be some situations where the property in the goods sold will have passed to the buyer by virtue of documents of title having been delivered where the seller could still have a lien over the goods. With this in mind, the third party could invoke the good faith provision in s 9 of FA 1889 which refers to 'good faith and without notice of any lien . . .'. Moreover it seems that an unpaid seller might still retain his lien over the goods if possession has been given to the buyer for a limited period or temporarily. Even though possession of the goods may terminate the unpaid seller's statutory lien (see Chapter 13), the contract itself may create a special right in the seller analogous to a lien (as in the case of retention of title clauses).

The construction of s 9 of the Factors Act 1889 and s 25(1) of the Sale of Goods Act 1979

The reference to mercantile agent

In *Newtons of Wembley Ltd v Williams* [1965] 1 QB 560 the owners of a car sold it in return for a cheque, but it was expressly agreed that ownership should remain in the seller until the cheque was cleared. The rogue resold the car in Warren Street, London, a recognised market for second-hand cars. It was held that the sub-buyer prevailed since the rogue, as a buyer in possession, could transfer a good title by virtue of s 25(1) of SGA 1979. The Court of Appeal took a literal approach to the requirement of acting in the capacity of being a mercantile agent. In this respect, the resale by the rogue had been in circumstances (ie at an established secondhand car market) such that the sub-buyer could reasonably assume that he was buying from a mercantile agent in the ordinary course of business. Thus Pearson LJ pointed out:

> When the provisions of s 2 are applied to the s 9 position . . . this is the *prima facie* result: if the transaction is made by the person concerned when acting in the ordinary course of the business of a mercantile agent, the transaction is validated: on the other hand, if the transaction is made by him when not acting in

the ordinary course of business of a mercantile agent, the transaction is not validated. (p 578)

This *obiter* approach would, if unrestricted in its application, severely limit s 9 of FA 1889 and s 25(1) of SGA 1979. Moreover, it is difficult to understand the development of the hire purchase mechanism as a device to avoid s 9 if this indeed was the strict position. Certainly, the conventional legal position before the *Newtons of Wembley* case was that s 9 and s 25(1) were considered to validate a sale as if the buyer in possession were a mercantile agent, but did not include that he should act in such a way. To clarify the position, the 1966 Law Reform Committee 12th Report recommended that the law be amended to restore this position (para 23). Certainly, Clarke J in *Forsythe International (UK) Ltd v Silver Shipping Co Ltd* [1994] 1 All ER 851 appeared to champion the pre-1964 position while at the same time conceding that he was bound by *Newtons of Wembley*, although he did cite contrary Commonwealth authority (see *Gamer's Motor Centre (Newcastle) Pty Ltd v Natwest Wholesale Australia Pty Ltd* (1987) 163 CLR 236 at 259 per Dawson J).

Despite the fact that the buyer's possession in s 9 is 'fed' into s 2(1) of FA 1889 making it in fact wider than s 8 of that Act, it is doubtful whether the draftsman intended it to extend to theft. Indeed, the public policy issue of discouraging thieves may very well be the reason for the failure to implement the recommendation found in para 11 of the 12th Report of the Law Reform Committee. Here it was proposed that the market overt doctrine be abolished and replaced by a provision enabling a person buying in good faith at retail or trade premises, or at a public auction, to acquire good title. No attempt was made in the Report to consider the frequency of such an occurrence, as well as the degree to which the purchaser's right of action against the retailer under the right to sell provisions is insufficient to protect him.

The reference to 'sale, pledge or other disposition'

A precondition to the sub-buyer acquiring title under this provision is that he must fulfil the conditions imposed upon him under the terms of the disposition by the buyer. This issue becomes acute where in the original sale and also the sub-sale there is a retention of title provision. Thus, in *Re Highway Foods International Ltd* (1994) *The Times*, 1 November, meat was sold by a company called Harris subject to a reservation to title clause to the buyer Highway, which then sub-sold the meat to a sub-purchaser Kingfry also on retention of title terms. The goods were then delivered to the sub-buyer. It was held by Edward Nugee QC sitting as a Deputy High Court judge that until the sub-purchaser paid the buyer the price of the goods, the original seller could recover the goods on the basis that the nature of the contract between Highway and Kingfry was not a sale but only an agreement to sell. Whilst s 9 of the FA does refer to 'agreement to sell', the effect of this section, it was held, was only to render the buyer's agreement for sale valid as if it had been expressly authorised by the seller. Clearly, this could not be the case if the conditions for the passing of title under the buyer's agreement for sale to the sub-purchaser had not been satisfied.

The reference to 'seller', 'buyer', 'original seller' and 'owner'

There are bound to be real difficulties in a provision which uses four terms of identification. It could be argued that a literal approach to construing the section would allow a thief to pass good title by virtue of a strict interpretation of s 25(1). Such a result would not be confined to thieves, as it would naturally extend to situations where initial disposals of property were improper. An example is the removal of property from a church achieved without going through the proper procedure, for example, the confirmatory faculties heard before a Consistory Court (see *Re St Mary's, Barton-on-Humber* [1987] 2 All ER 861). The argument is that the thief's consent to his purchaser's possession could be treated as being equivalent to the consent of the owner. Nevertheless over the last 20 years certain Commonwealth decisions have equated 'seller' with 'owner' so that there can never be a 'seller', or at least 'original seller', where there has been a theft (*Elwin v O'Regan and Maxwell* [1971] NZLR 1124; *Avco Corp v Borgal* and *Brandon v Leckie* (1973) 29 DLR (3d) 633). This approach can be criticised on the basis that it departs from ordinary principles of construction in a way that the Court of Appeal refused to do in *Newtons of Wembley*

It may be that a literal construction of s 9 is contrary to a fundamental rule in the common law. Theft can hardly be considered a contractual defect because it constitutes a real vice which attaches to the movables themselves. This approach was evident in both the Court of Appeal and House of Lords' decisions in *National Employers Mutual General Insurance Assoc v Jones* [1987] 3 WLR 901, CA; [1988] 2 WLR 952, HL. In this case, the defendant had purchased a car from a motor dealer, neither party being aware that the vehicle had been stolen from a woman whose interest had subsequently been subrogated to her insurers. In the Court of Appeal, the majority held (Sir Denys Buckley dissenting) that the essence of 'sale' was the transference of the ownership or general property in goods from a seller to a buyer for a price. It was argued that the opening words of s 25(1) of the 1979 Act and s 9 of the 1889 Act lay down the condition precedent for the consequences provided by the later words of the section, which only contemplates a transaction in which the general property in goods has been acquired, or where it has been agreed that it should be acquired. This approach was summarised in *The Times* Law Report heading (6 April 1987) as follows: 'Innocent buyer has no title to stolen goods.' Interestingly, a similar argument was at one time employed in the context of negotiable instruments and bearer bills. It was maintained that no title passed on such a bill to a thief since the bill had not been delivered, and 'delivery' was equated with a genuine endorsement on the bill. This approach is impossible to maintain since an essential element of negotiability depends upon facts which can be ascertained by inspection of the instrument, ie who possesses it, what is written upon it, and who signed it (*Arab Bank v Ross* [1952] 2 QB 216).

The main objection to the Court of Appeal's approach in *Jones* (1987) is that it would seem to involve the consequence that a purported sale of stolen property is outside the provisions of the 1979 Act altogether. Furthermore, it undermines the relativity of title concept which permeates the structure of the Act.

This is confirmed by the House of Lords' decision in that case where *The Times* Law Report heading (25 April 1988) summarised the majority judgment as follows: 'Innocent buyer of stolen goods does not obtain *good title as against the owner*'. Consequently, s 9 does not, as a matter of construction, confer a good title on a purchaser if the mercantile agent from whom the goods had been purchased has come into possession of the goods from a thief. In this situation, the goods would not have been entrusted to the thief by the owner. As Lord Goff held in the House of Lords:

> In my opinion, s 9 of the Factors Act 1889 must be read as providing that the delivery or transfer given by the immediate transferor, B, shall have the same effect as if he was a mercantile agent in possession of the goods or documents of title with the consent of the owner, A, who entrusted them to him . . . The same construction must, of course, be placed on s 25(1) of the Sale of Goods Act 1979. (p 962)

In preferring the innocent owner, the thief rule distributes the loss onto the first purchaser from the thief. The second purchaser, if he has to yield the goods to the original owner, has an action against the first buyer for breach of the implied obligations under s 12 of SGA 1979 or related provisions in other supply contracts. As such, the chain of actions ends with the original purchaser from the thief because the latter will usually be judgment-proof. Despite this, the arguments for preferring the innocent owner where there has been theft over and above the good faith purchaser, are finely balanced. It could be maintained, for example, that the *bona fide* purchaser should be protected, not because of his praiseworthy character, but rather because such a rule makes buying more attractive. Indeed this rule will not require an elaborate investigation of property rights. This approach should be contrasted with the fault doctrine encapsulated in *Lickbarrow v Mason* (1787) 2 TR 63 which was applied by Simon Brown J in *Debs v Sibec Developments* (1989), discussed earlier (see p 192). The application of the fault formula is difficult since it is a Janus-faced formula, ie where the original owner gives up possession to another, without his act of delivery to the possessor, the wrong could not have been perpetrated, but equally indispensable is the act of the innocent purchaser who also trusts the possessor not to sell goods he is not authorised to sell. In the case of theft, these considerations cannot apply because they do not constitute a contractual defect. As such, a non-negotiability rule can be a constraint on theft in that it may increase the incentive for owners to attempt to recover stolen goods. It is wrong to underestimate the recovery of stolen goods by owners since, although the amount of stolen property that is recovered by the police is small, some stolen goods are easier to recover than others. If the non-negotiability rule were overturned, this would have a knock-on effect with regard to the exposure of sellers of stolen goods to actions based on implied-title warranties. Furthermore, the non-negotiability rule will give an extra incentive for the purchaser to take precautions in order to reduce the risk of surrender as he may have become familiar with the goods, and the cost of replacement could be high. This is anticipated in ss 24 and 25 of SGA 1979 in that the sale must be in the ordinary course of business, thereby introducing an objective standard in distinguishing between shady and non-shady circumstances.

The significance of possession as an indication of ownership

The dilemma posed by the conflict between security of property and the protection of purchasers can be conveniently illustrated in *Four Point Garages Ltd v Carter* [1985] 3 All ER 12, since it deals with the significance of possession as an indication of ownership.

The *Four Point Garage* case was brought before Simon Brown J in the Queen's Bench Division and was tried on affidavit evidence. The plaintiff sought a declaration of ownership concerning a new Ford Escort XR 3i sports car relating to events less than four weeks before the case came to court. The considerable speed with which this case was expedited demonstrates the importance attached to 'newness' in motor cars vis-à-vis their saleability and quality. The facts are fairly simple. The defendant desired to buy a new car, and after having made a number of inquiries primarily concerned with price from a number of garages, agreed on 2 October 1984 to purchase the car with accessories from Freeway (Cougar) Ltd for £6,889. Following the completion of independent financial arrangements, the defendant posted the necessary moneys to Freeway and arranged with the latter for delivery of the motor car on 10 October. The car was not in stock with Freeway, but they made arrangements to purchase a car of the same specification from the plaintiffs who believed that Freeway were engaged in the leasing and hiring business. On 9 October, the plaintiffs invoiced Freeway for the car to the sum of £6,746 and were persuaded before payment to deliver the car direct to the defendant. This they completed on 10 October, assuming the defendant to be a customer of Freeway rather than a sub-purchaser. The defendant, on the other hand, thought that delivery had been made to him direct by Freeway. Three days after delivery, notification was given to the plaintiffs that Freeway was going into liquidation. In response, the plaintiffs sought to recover the car relying on their contract of supply with Freeway which contained the following retention of title clause: 'The buyer is advised that title to the goods contained in this invoice remains with the seller until such goods are fully paid'. By establishing ownership, the plaintiffs would simultaneously establish the better right to possess and could then, presumably, resell the car. Clearly, as unsecured creditors, neither the plaintiffs nor the defendant were likely to recover their loss from the insolvent Freeway. In this respect, from the sub-buyer's perspective the case is the converse to the *Rowland v Divall* scenario (1923) discussed above (see p 193).

The court held in favour of the defendant, and one of the main strands to Simon Brown J's judgment was based on s 25(1) of SGA 1979. It was held that Freeway had constructive possession of the goods following *E & S Ruben Ltd v Faire Bros & Co* [1949] 1 KB 254, and could thereby pass good title to an innocent sub-purchaser. Nevertheless, it is difficult to see how the *Ruben* case applies here. This case was concerned with the buyer's right to reject and quite different policy considerations are involved in s 35 of SGA 1979 than those posed in s 25 (see Chapter 14). Moreover, in *Ruben* it was said that the buyers had acted inconsistently with the seller's ownership by taking constructive delivery at the seller's premises; contrastingly, in *Four Point Garage* the seller had expressly reserved title and sub-delivered the goods believing its ownership in the vehicle to be still subsisting. A further problem concerns the difficulty inherent with basing a decision on constructive possession. This expression is used in many different senses so that, for example, Salmond treats constructive possession as covering those cases where the law grants possession to one who is not in actual physical control (*Jurisprudence* (Fitzgerald, 1966) at p 286), whereas, Pollock and Wright in their seminal essay on Possession confine the expression to cases where there is a mere right to recover possession (*Possession in the Common Law* (1888) at pp 25–27). It is very difficult to determine a unitary concept of possession in English law, and Professor Stoljar has suggested that because possession is a ductile and intuitive concept, it should be rejected as even a foundation for any meaningful theory of bailment ((1935) 7 Res Judicatae 160).

Attempts have been made to elucidate a central core idea of possession, such as involving the present control of a thing on one's own behalf to the exclusion of all others. This is not a satisfactory approach because it fails to take into account divergent authorities which include the delivery of keys and the measure of control required for a finding of possession. Indeed, it may not be possible, *in abstracto*, to determine the meaning of possession, and Professor Hart suggests that we should avoid seeking elucidation of single words like possession ((1954) 70 LQR 37 at p 41). The word should rather be considered with sentences in which it plays its characteristic role, although this approach does beg the question as to what are typical sentences. However, it must be the case that the context in which possession appears within a statutory formula will have relevance and it is surprising, therefore, that no reference was made by Simon Brown J in his judgment to s 9 of FA 1889 which was the immediate precursor of s 25(2) of SGA 1893 (s 25(1) of SGA 1979). This could have been of assistance because, although no attempt is made in the SGA 1979 to define words like 'delivery', 'deliver', 'to possess', 'possession', s 1(2) of FA 1889 does provide that: 'A person shall be deemed to be in possession of goods or of the documents of title to goods, where the goods or documents are in his actual custody or are held by any other person subject to his control or for him or on his behalf'. It is evident that the question of actual custody is very important, which was confirmed in *Beverley Acceptances Ltd v Oakley* [1982] RTR 417. This case involved the pledge of two Rolls-Royce cars in return for a large loan; the pledgor having gained access from the pledgee to the locked parking lot showed the cars to a prospective purchaser. It was held that the purchaser was not protected since the eventual sale had taken place when any temporary possession obtained by the pledgor had lapsed, and s 2(1) of FA 1889 required an actual present possession in order to overcome the *nemo dat* rule.

The requirement of 'delivery' or 'transfer'

More recently doubt has arisen in respect of whether actual delivery is required for the purposes of s 25(1) SGA and s 9 FA despite the fact that this would seem to be implied in the criterion of 'receiving' the goods in good faith. In the celebrated decision of *Gamer Motor Center (Newcastle) Pty Ltd v Natwest Wholesale Australia Pty Ltd* [1987] 163 CLR 236, the High Court of Australia held that constructive delivery was sufficient where the character of the buyer's possession was transferred into a bailment. In this case, car dealers were in possession of stock on reservation of title terms but the dealers immediately 'sold' the vehicles to a finance company, but they retained possession of them for display purposes and they were authorised to sell the units on the finance company's behalf. Essentially, the approach of the court represents a policy decision of protecting the innocent third party purchaser arising out of the ostensible ownership of the seller or buyer in possession of the chattel in question, because following a sale the nature of the disposer's possession will necessarily change to that of being a bailment (compare *Nicholson v Harper* [1895] 2 Ch 415). Even so, the general approach adopted in *Gamer* was applied by Clarke J in *Forsythe International (UK) Ltd v Silver Shipping Co Ltd* [1994] 1 All ER 851. In this case the plaintiffs contracted with charterers to supply oil bunkers for a vessel which was on a time charter from the owners. The contract of supply contained a reservation of title clause. Before the charter expired the owners withdrew the vessel from the charterers for non-payment of hire. At this time the vessel was carrying bunkers for which the plaintiffs had not been paid. It was common ground that property in the bunkers had not passed to the charterers as they had not paid for them, but the owners of the vessel contended that they had acquired a good title to the bunkers by virtue of the buyer in possession exception to the *nemo dat* rule. The judge took the view that under s 25(1) there must be some voluntary act by the buyer in possession amounting to delivery. Mere inaction was not sufficient, and some holding out was necessary. Nonetheless in this case the contention of the owners of the vessel failed because there had been no voluntary transfer of possession, rather it had come about automatically as a result of the termination of the charterparty by the owners.

The significance of custody and the building law cases

The importance of custody is confirmed in the Scottish decision of *Archivent Sales and Developments Ltd v Strathclyde Regional Council* (1984) 27 Build LR 98. In this case, the plaintiff had sold to Robertson Ltd a number of ventilators for incorporation into a school building which the contractors were erecting for Strathclyde Regional Council. The conditions of supply included a simple retention of title clause linking property passage with payment. The Council paid the contractors the value of the ventilators but the latter became insolvent before paying the sellers. One of the issues before the court concerned s 25(1) of SGA 1979. It was conceded that the council were in good faith and that the contractors had obtained the ventilators with the consent of the sellers. Despite this, it was contended that by virtue of cl 14(1) in the contract between the contractors and the employers, the contractors never came into possession of the ventilators as they were always held by the contractors for the employers and were always in the employers' control. Clause 14(1) provided:

> ... unfixed materials and goods delivered to, placed on or adjacent to the works and intended therefor shall not be removed except for use upon the Works unless the Architect/Supervising Officer has consented in writing to such removal which consent shall not be unreasonably withheld. Where the value of any such materials or goods has, in accordance with cl 30(2) of these conditions, been included in any interim certificate under which the contractor has received payment, such material and goods shall become the property of the employer but subject to cl 20(b) or cl 20(c) of these conditions (if applicable), the Contractor will remain responsible for loss or damage to the same.

This ingenious argument was rejected by the court. It was held that since the goods had been delivered to the site which was occupied by the contractor who had issued a receipt acknowledging delivery, the latter was deemed to have possession. As Lord Mayfield held:

> The restriction on Robertsons [the contractor] was against removal from the site. In my view that is not inconsistent with possession. Indeed s 1(2) of the Factors Act 1889 states that a person shall be deemed to be in possession of goods or documents of title to goods where the goods or documents are in his actual custody. As to delivery there was clear evidence by the defenders' chartered surveyor that he had gone to the site and measured the goods on the defenders' behalf . . . the value of these goods was entered into the necessary certificates and payment made . . . In my view delivery took place when the goods came into the defenders' real control and ownership after they had been measured on the site by their chartered surveyor and not rejected . . . . (p 109)

The *Archivent* case provides an interesting contrast to *Dawber Williamson Roofing Ltd v Humberside County Council* [1979] CLY 212 as the facts are somewhat similar. In this case, the plaintiffs agreed to supply and fix roofing slates under a sub-contract with the main contractors subject to a reservation of title clause. The slates were never fixed as the main contractors went into receivership, thereby determining the main and sub-contracts. The defendants had paid the main contractor for the slates through an interim payment and they claimed title by virtue of s 25(1) of SGA 1979. This argument was rejected on the basis that the sub-contract was for the supply and fixing of the roofing materials to which, therefore, s 9 of FA 1889 and s 25(1) of SGA 1979 had no application (see s 2 of SGSA 1982). In the *Dawber* case, the court stressed that ss 21–25 of SGA 1979 provide an exception to the *nemo dat* doctrine and could not be extended into contracts of supply without express provision. As such, this approach upholds the security of property principle. By contrast, Simon Brown J in the *Four Point Garage* case through finding constructive possession or constructive delivery was in fact engaged in a policy decision of supporting the good faith purchaser.

It is a pity that Simon Brown J did not discuss the policy reasoning underlying his decision. To a large extent, the approach taken mirrors the French doctrine of *possession vaut titre* which does not represent the English legal position although an extension of this principle into English law was one of the options put forward for discussion in the much criticised DTI Consultation Paper,

Transfer of Title (January 1994). The effect of this general approach would have been to have destroyed the credit instalment industry in the UK. The existing law is that mere possession is not sufficient to raise an estoppel, but even if possession was a signal of ownership except when possession was in a thief, non-possession should warn the careful buyer not to buy goods he could not see. In the *Four Point Garage* case this is exactly what the defendant did. Even if one analyses the transaction as an aspect of commercial risk, it is by no means self-evident that Four Point Garage should have suffered the loss. It was clear that the sub-buyer had chosen Freeway having made several enquiries in other garages concerning the supply of the vehicle. Furthermore, he secured a keen discounted price for the car, which is reflected in the fact that Freeway's profit margin on the deal was less than 2.1 per cent, whereas the average profit for the sale of Ford motor cars exceeds 16 per cent. On the other hand, Four Point Garage acted under the assumption that they had successfully reserved title to the car, and that the car was not available for general circulation in the free flow of commerce since they thought that the nature of the business of the purchasers was that of hiring and leasing (see Chapter 12).

It has always been the case that under the factors' legislation, a mere bailee of goods without actual authority to sell or pledge does not come within the purview of the FA 1889 (*Helby v Matthews* [1895] AC 471). On the basis of this, it is difficult to justify Simon Brown J's holding that Four Point Garage were acting as agents for the purpose of delivery to sub-purchasers. Moreover, although it is well established that a seller in possession can attorn to his immediate buyer thereby putting the later in constructive possession, there was no 'holding out' that the buyer was owner here since it would have been contrary to an express provision, notably, the retention of title clause in the contract of supply.

Supplies of motor vehicles

Historical background

The strict common law *nemo dat* position would compromise purchases especially of secondhand vehicles. It was for this reason that the Molony Committee which reported in 1962 on *Consumer Protection* (Cmnd 1781) recommended reform but did not indicate which solution it favoured. Given the primacy of the *nemo dat* principle, it is little wonder that the first legislative proposal for reform encapsulated in the Hire Purchase (No 2) Bill 1963 included an elaborate system of notification in an attempt to balance the financier's ownership interest and also protect prospective purchasers of motor vehicles. These proposals were criticised by the finance industry as being too burdensome, which may explain why the Finance Houses Association (which represented the major financiers of motor vehicles) agreed to support an Opposition amendment to the original Bill that title should in any event pass to a private good faith purchaser without notice of a hire purchase or conditional sale agreement. Even though this approach was tantamount to a reversal of the traditional common law *nemo dat* doctrine, legislation to this effect was forthcoming, which was incorporated into Part III of the Hire Purchase Act 1964 and has since been substituted by the Consumer Credit Act 1974, s 192(2) and Sched 4, para 22.

Part III of the Hire Purchase Act 1964

This provides a special legislative regime in the context of dispositions involving motor vehicles. The general effect of this legislation is to champion security in transactions in non-motor trade dispositions.

The object of the legislation: motor vehicles

The conventional definition of 'motor vehicles' seen under road traffic legislation is adopted in Part III of the Hire Purchase Act 1964, so s 29(1) provides that: 'Motor Vehicle' means a mechanically propelled vehicle intended or adapted for use on roads to which the public has access. The courts have consistently adopted an expansive approach to this conventional definition. Thus in *Newberry v Simmonds* [1961] 2 QB 345 it was held that a motor car which had its engine removed was still a mechanically-propelled vehicle, and this reasoning has been extended to a vehicle being towed because of a defective engine (see *Cobb v Whorton* [1971] RTR 392). The question of the *scope* of the definition of 'motor vehicle' for the purpose of Part III revolves around the 'use on roads to which the public has access'. Plant or equipment may be mechanically propelled but they are not treated as motor vehicles because they are not 'intended or adapted for use on roads'. Consequently, dump trucks used in building works have been excluded on this basis, as would be, presumably, fork lift trucks used extensively in factory premises. On the other hand, in *Childs v Coghlan* (1968) 112 Sol Jo 175 a 'Euclid earth scraper' was held to be a motor vehicle; although its primary function was for use on building sites, because of its size it was not easily transportable and had to go on the roads under its own power to get from one site to another. The relevant test was laid down by Lord Parker CJ in the *Childs* case as follows:

> The real question is: is some general use on the roads contemplated as one of the uses? In the present case, if a reasonable person looked at the vehicle with the knowledge that it had to go from site to site and had to use the roads in so doing, and was capable of speeds of up to 45 mph it seemed clear that such person would have said that one of the users of the vehicles would be a road user.

Undoubtedly, the courts are rightly concerned to ensure that vehicles are covered by the safety requirements laid down by the Road Traffic Acts. However, while this approach is appropriate for promoting safety, there are different policy considerations applicable in legislation which is solely concerned with protecting consumers against asset financiers purely in a title dispute. In this context, it is conventional wisdom to distinguish between the type and kind of goods, that is, whether they are consumer goods, equipment or stock-in-trade. The point of substance here is that the unwieldy definition applied in Part III extends the protection accorded beyond the simple consumer context.

The parties affected: the debtor

Section 29(4) of the Hire Purchase Act 1964 (as amended) states:

> In this Part of this Act the 'debtor' in relation to a motor vehicle which has been bailed or hired under a hire purchase agreement, or, as the case may be, agreed to be sold under a conditional sale agreement, means the person who at the material time (whether the agreement has before that time been terminated or not) either—
> (a) is the person to whom the vehicle is bailed or hired under that agreement, or
> (b) is, in relation to the agreement, the buyer, including a person who at the time is, by virtue of section 130(4) of the Consumer Credit Act 1974 treated as a bailee or (in Scotland) a custodier of the vehicle.

The inclusion of the wording in brackets is obviously intended to cover *ipso facto* termination clauses so that nothing hinges upon the current contractual status of the debtor.

The main difficulty with the above approach is that it fails to distinguish between cases where the debtor is in possession of the vehicle from those situations where the finance company has repossessed the vehicle. As a matter of principle, repossession of the vehicle must terminate the ability to pass good title and, in any case, lack of possession should affect the *fides* of the disponee, given that the mischief of the legislation was to deal with the ostensible ownership problem of the hirer being in possession of the motor vehicle. It is significant that in ss 8 and 9 of the FA 1889 the ability to pass good title is dependent upon the giving up of possession through delivery.

A further dilemma is posed by the capacity in which the debtor is holding the motor vehicle. If the relevant agreement is illegal, this should not prejudice the ability of the debtor to pass title under Part III because the general effect of illegality is not render the contract totally void but merely to make it unenforceable. Where, however, the contract is voidable and has been avoided by the owner before the wrongful disposition takes place (for example, because of fraud or misrepresentation) then this will not be covered by Part III, which refers to termination of an agreement rather than *avoidance* of it. Misrepresentation allows for rescission, which is a powerful remedy providing for the restoration of the *status quo ante*, that is an *ab initio* avoidance of the transaction. This is potentially an important limitation of the scope of the consumer protection element in Part III.

The parties affected: the private purchaser

The provisions of Part III bite upon the contradistinction between a 'trade or finance purchaser' who does not acquire a good title, and a private purchaser who as a person in good faith and without notice can acquire a good title. The definition of 'trade or finance purchaser' in s 29(2) of the Act encompasses a purchaser who at the time of the disposition is involved in a business consisting wholly or partly:

(a) of purchasing motor vehicles for the purpose of offering or exposing them for sale, or
(b) of providing finance by purchasing motor vehicles for the purpose of bailing

> or (in Scotland) hiring them under hire purchase agreements or agreeing to sell them under conditional sale agreements . . .

The emphasis upon business suggests a degree of regularity and also the element of holding out. Thus in *Stevenson v Beverley Bentinck Ltd* [1976] 1 WLR 483, a tool inspector who had for less than two years bought and sold motor vehicles on a modest scale in his spare time was held to have been partly (not wholly) involved in the business of purchasing motor vehicles for the purpose of offering them or exposing them for sale and was, thereby, covered by s 29(2) of the Act. The fact that the plaintiff in this case was buying the motor vehicle in his private capacity was irrelevant since the Act draws the distinction between, as Browne LJ pointed out (at p 488), categories of persons, not between categories of transactions.

Undoubtedly, the mischief of the Act is geared towards the protection of the public who are not engaged in the motor business or involved directly in the financing of motor vehicles through credit sales or hire purchase. A private purchaser is defined in s 29(2) as 'a purchaser who, at the time of the disposition made to him, does not carry on [motor trade or motor finance] business'. Nevertheless the limitation of scope here has to be noted: Contract hire and leasing contracts which as a matter of legal form are not *sale* contracts will therefore not be covered by s 29(2) of the Act.

The transactions affected: dispositions

The Act applies to dispositions made by a debtor subject to a hire purchase or conditional sale arrangement. It would appear that Part III only applies in favour of a person who buys, agrees to buy, or takes the vehicle on hire purchase and that the disposition must be made by the debtor himself and not by any other party such as a bailee of the debtor. There is, however, a presumption in s 28(2) that it is the debtor who disposes of the vehicle. Even so, agency principles will apply, so in *Ford Motor Credit Co Ltd v Harmack* [1972] CLY 1649 the Court of Appeal held that a person who was the managing director and controlling shareholder of a company had actual and ostensible authority of the hirer company (which had taken a vehicle on hire purchase) to dispose of the car on behalf of the company and pass good title under s 27 of the Act.

It is clearly envisaged in the legislation that 'disposition' refers to sale and analogous defined transactions, namely, hire purchase and conditional sale. Consequently, 'disposition' does not cover a special property interest like pledge or lien and neither does it cover a gift, mortgage or assignment by operation of law, set-off or contractual assignments, for example, initiated by so-called vehicle transfer agencies. Particularly problematic in this context is the isue of exchange, which is not covered by legislation. It is often the case that consumers will 'swap' vehicles sometimes accompanied by a cash element, and the status of the transaction as being either sale or exchange is crucial to the protection provisions in Part III.

The transactions affected: hire purchase or conditional sale

The current definition of hire purchase can be found in s 189(1) of the Consumer Credit Act 1974 which states:

> 'hire purchase agreement' means an agreement, other than a conditional sale agreement, under which—
> (a) goods are bailed or (in Scotland) hired in return for periodical payments by the person to whom they are bailed or hired, and
> (b) the property in the goods will pass to that person if the terms of the agreement are complied with and one or more of the following occurs—
> (i) the exercise of an option to purchase by that person,
> (ii) the doing of any specified act by any party to the agreement,
> (iii) the happening of any other specified event.

Section 189(4) further provides that the agreement may be constituted in more than one document, that is to say, a hire agreement with a separate option provision. The developed English position constitutes a statutory reversal of *R v R W Proffitt Ltd* [1954] 2 QB 35, where it has been held that the relevant definition of hire purchase only applied where the bailee controlled the circumstances in which the property would or would not pass to him, and did not apply where the contingencies upon which the property was to pass were in the bailor's control.

A variation of the developed statutory position discussed above arose in the context of a conditional sale in *Dodds v Yorkshire Bank Finance Ltd* (1991) unreported (CA). The facts involved the disposition by a company director B of a Porsche car to the plaintiff which was still subject to an outstanding hire purchase agreement with the defendants. The relevant transaction was a conditional sale agreement by B to sell the vehicle to the plaintiff if he defaulted to pay back the plaintiff moneys advanced as part of an elaborate financing arrangement for B's ailing business. When B failed to pay back the money advanced by the plaintiff the condition precedent to the passing of property in the vehicle was satisfied. The fact that the condition for property passage was in the seller's control was irrelevant and, as such, is consistent with the position in hire purchase. There is no doubt that the Court of Appeal adopted the legal *form* of the transaction notwithstanding that as a matter of economic substance it is not possible to distinguish between an executory agreement to sell and a chattel mortgage.

Undoubtedly, Part III of the Hire Purchase Act 1964 (as amended) constitutes an important exception to the *nemo dat* principle. Even so, ownership interests are not lightly overturned and the statutory exception here refers to the necessity of the purchaser being in good faith and without notice of the ownership interest.

The pre-requisite for protection: good faith and without notice

The purchaser must act in good faith and without notice at the time of the disposition. The issue of good faith is not defined in Part III but s 29(3) of the Act defines 'without notice' as meaning that the purchaser 'has no actual notice that the vehicle is or was the subject of any hire purchase agreement'. From this it would seem to follow that actual notice of *any* hire purchase agreements prevents the purchaser being without notice. However, the Court of Appeal in *Baker v Bell* [1971] 1 WLR 983 held that there must be notice only of the *relevant* hire purchase or conditional sale agreement that had been supposedly paid off. The main judgment was given by Denning MR who explained his reasoning as follows (at p 986).

> If a car was originally let on hire purchase terms, the instalments have all been paid, or the settlement figure has been paid, that hire purchase agreement is entirely irrelevant: and I see no reason why notice of it should affect the purchaser's title. So far as the words 'or was' are concerned, they should not be construed so as to apply to a past agreement which is entirely irrelevant. They can be given a sensible meaning by restricting them to a case where there is a present hire purchase agreement (under which the owner now claims the car) which provides that, on an attempted sale or disposition of the car by the hirer, the agreement is automatically terminated. The words 'or was' do not apply to a past hire-purchase agreement which has been paid off. In short, a purchaser is only affected by notice if he has actual notice that the car is on hire purchase. He is not affected merely by being told that it was previously on hire purchase which has not been paid off.

There is no real symbiosis between good faith and notice. Thus for there to be bad faith in terms of notice mere carelessness is not sufficient—there must be conduct which evinces a deliberate design not to know more. The 19th Century authorities suggest that mere suspicion is not notice unless suspicion is taken a stage further, that is, where the actor resolved to see nothing which was contrary to his interests.

The definition of good faith which accords with the common law position at the end of the 19th Century is defined as we have discussed previously in s 61(3) of the SGA, namely, as when a thing 'is in fact done honestly, whether it is done negligently or not'. It follows that notice and good faith include implied or constructive notice. This is the point which emerges from *Heap v Motorists Advisory Agency Ltd* [1923] 1 KB 577, where Lush J held that the sale of a car which the plaintiff wished to sell at £210 but was eventually sold for £110 was at such a low price that it should have put the defendants on their guard. The defendant had failed to do what any reasonable man would have done by failing to discover more about the car when he bought it—it was this failure which was held to constitute notice on the part of the defendant of some want of authority on the part of the mercantile agent. Since the weight of authority is against constructive notice which, in any case, would render the good faith element unnecessary, it follows that the inclusion of this requirement ensures that the purchaser is protected where he is careless but not where he is wilful. Such an approach was confirmed in *Dodds v Yorkshire Bank Finance Ltd* (1991). In this case, the disposal of the vehicle subject to finance was part of an elaborate financing venture of the wrongful disposer's company. Undoubtedly, the plaintiff purchaser was suspicious and was concerned about the possibility of the vehicle being on hire purchase. In the Court of Appeal the question of good faith was treated as an aspect of honesty and the purchaser satisfied this test when she insisted that the disposer signed a receipt to the effect that the vehicle was not subject to hire purchase. The mere knowledge of the *possibility* of another's interest in the goods is not sufficient to constitute dishonesty.

The nature of protection: the title acquired

The basis for understanding the passing of property provisions in sale of goods is that of relativity of title. In the context of Part III of the Hire Purchase Act 1964 (as amended), what passes as a result of the disposition is the title of the financier to the hirer or the buyer under a conditional sale agreement. Herein, of course, lies a potential problem regarding the marketability of the motor vehicle, as there may be a shadow on the title thereby restricting the innocent purchaser's ability to dispose of the vehicle. The main difficulty is that s 12 of the SGA, in setting out the seller's implied contractual obligation relating to the nature of the title that the seller must invest in the buyer, refers to an implied condition that the seller has the right to sell and pass good title, that is, not merely a *power* to sell which is invested upon him by virtue of, for example, Part III of the Hire Purchase Act 1964 (as amended). As a matter of principle, a seller who by his action of selling the vehicle commits the tort of conversion cannot be said to have a 'right' to sell the goods. Even though a private purchaser in good faith does enjoy a good title by virtue of this exception to the *nemo dat* rule, it follows the breach of s 12(1) of the Sale of Goods Act 1979 which provides that the seller will have a right to sell the goods is merely technical, because the buyer is given what he bargained for, namely, a good title (see *Barber v NWS Bank plc* (Unreported) 17 November 1995 (CA)).

In the case of conditional sale account must be taken of the time factor for the right to sell under s 12(1) of the SGA 1979, which occurs 'when the property is to pass'. This would normally equate with the time when the buyer has completed his payment schedule. Where the buyer makes an accelerated payment, it could be argued, if the buyer is aware of the seller's difficulty in making title on early repayment, that the act of accelerated payment constitutes a waiver of this breach of condition. In a similar fashion, where there is a hire purchase agreement, s 8 of SOGIT 1973 equates 'right to sell' with when the general property is to pass, which coincides with when the hirer has completed his payments. The *purpose* of an executed sale transaction is to pass a perfect title and this is not the case with an executory contract of sale or hire purchase, at least until the time when property is to pass. Where there has been a technical breach of the right to sell or, in the case of a hirer under a hire purchase contract discussed above, this will only sound in a right to reject the goods where there has been a breach of the quiet possession warranty in s 12(2) of the SGA and s 8(1)(b) of SOGIT 1973. In this regard, the disturbance has to be substantial to justify repudiation, for example, the finance company as owner repossessing the vehicle or the buyer having to engage a solicitor to handle his affairs in defending his claim.

It is sometimes the case that a potential trade purchaser or motor dealer, when running a search of hire purchase interests with HPI plc, will discover the existence of the hire purchase or conditional sale agreement and will refuse to take the vehicle in part-exchange. As a consequence, the marketability of the motor vehicle is severely impaired because the private purchaser who shelters under the title protection provisions of Part III of the Act is compromised. The possibilities for the private purchaser will now be considered.

The acquirer's dilemma: keep the vehicle indefinitely

The effect of this is to take the car outside the stream of commerce, and is not, therefore, a realistic option because one of the features of commercial law is that it recognises the need for marketability of commercial assets.

The acquirer's dilemma: repudiate the original contract of sale

In many instances this is not a realistic option because the original fraudulent disposer will either be judgment-proof or beyond the reach of process. However, in the absence of this eventuality, for example, through the intervention of a financial intermediary in funding the disposition, there are considerable conceptual and practical problems associated with repudiation.

This point arose in *Barber v NWS Bank plc* (Unreported) 17 November 1995 (CA). In this case the appellant, Barber, financed the acquisition of a car from Kestrel Garages (Eastbourne) Ltd by means of a conventional conditional sale agreement with NWS. In fact the car was subject to a prior hire purchase interest and when Barber sought to sell the car to a motor trader in order to clear his debt with NWS, the sale was declined because of this prior interest which continued to be recorded on the outstanding finance register operated by HPI plc. Shortly afterwards Barber rescinded the agreement and it was held by the Court of Appeal in proceedings brought under Order 14A of the Rules of the Supreme Court 1965 (as amended) that he was entitled to recover the whole amount paid under the conditional sale agreement including the deposit paid by way of part exchange since the Court of Appeal determined that the dealer received this in its capacity as NWS's agent. The Court reinforced the view that an express term as to title is a condition so that Sir Roger Parker, who gave judgment on behalf of the Court of Appeal, held:

> In my judgment there can be no doubt but that the term was a condition. It was fundamental to the transaction that the Bank had the property [in the car] at the time of the agreement and would retain it until paid in full the monies due under the agreement.

At the time of the rescission NWS did not have the right to sell the vehicle (see below pp 249–50) although by the time of the application to the Court, NWS had settled the outstanding amount with the previous finance company owner. Had this occurred before rescission then it may be persuasively argued that the defect in title had been 'cured' and that the appropriate remedy should be damages (see below pp 324–5).

The acquirer's dilemma: sale to a private sub-buyer

In adopting this course of action the buyer runs the risk of liability for breach of the quiet possession warranty if the sub-buyer is disturbed at a later date, which is a question of assumption of risk. Herein lies the importance of the presumptions which operate to remove doubt as to the title of the good faith private purchaser. Thus s 28 of the Hire Purchase Act 1964 (as amended) lays out a system of rebuttable presumptions which operate in any proceedings (civil or criminal) relating to a motor vehicle. It is proved for the purpose of s 28(1):

    (a)   that the vehicle was bailed or (in Scotland) hired under a hire purchase agreement, or was agreed to be sold under a conditional sale agreement, and

    (b)   that a person (whether a party to the proceedings or not) became a private purchaser of the vehicle in good faith without notice of the hire purchase or conditional sale agreement (the 'relevant agreement').

The presumptions do not apply where the circumstances of the disputed transactions are fully known. This point emerges clearly in the judgment of Orr LJ delivering the judgment on behalf of the Court of Appeal in *Soneco Ltd v Barcross Finance Ltd* [1978] RTR 444 in the following terms:

> It is entirely clear from a reading of the Act as a whole that s 27 is dealing with the case, which is the present case, where all the relevant dispositions of the vehicle are known, whereas s 28 is dealing with cases where all dispositions of the vehicle are not known, and its ojective is to ensure that in such a situation a purchaser is not deprived of the relief granted by the Act, and for this reason s 28 provides that certain artificial assumptions are to be made in his favour . . . It is only, in our judgment, necessary to go on to s 28 where, as does not arise in the present case, there is a missing link in the history of the car, in which event the purchaser is given the benefit of the statutory presumptions in s 28. (pp 450–51)

It is clear that the claimant is only protected in these circumstances where there has been a break in the chain of title which would otherwise make it very difficult for a claimant in any dispute with the owner, as financier, who had let the vehicle to the fraudulent hirer to prove that he came within the shelter accorded by Part III.

The first presumption (s 28(2) HPA 1964) is that the disposition was made to the relevant purchaser who was a private purchaser from the debtor in good faith and without notice of the hire purchase or conditional sale agreement. If this presumption fails, the second may operate (s 28(3)), namely, that the debtor disposed of the vehicle to a private purchaser who was a purchaser of the vehicle in good faith and without notice of the relevant agreement and that the relevant purchaser is or was a person *claiming under the person to whom the debtor so disposed of the vehicle*. On the assumption that this presumption fails, the third will operate (s 28(4)), that is, the person who, after the disposition of the vehicle to the trade or finance purchaser in question first became a private purchaser who took in good faith and without notice and is or was a person claiming under the original trade or finance purchaser. Generally in order to invoke the presumptions in s 28, the claimant must show either that he himself had or he derived title from some other party in the chain of transactions. Thus, in *Worcester Works Finance Ltd v Ocean Banking Corp Ltd* (1972) unreported, where a motor dealer could not establish that any intermediate private purchaser was in good faith, it was held that the dealer could not by making a sale to a good faith private purchaser thereupon himself rely on the statutory presumption encapsulated in s 28 which could compromise the position of a subsequent private purchaser from the dealer (but see s 28(5) with regard to admissions made).

Even though the presumptions assist in establishing title, nonetheless the original buyer will still take the risk of quiet possession liability if the sub-buyer is disturbed by an earlier owner. Under s 12(2) of the SGA, the seller has to warrant that neither he personally nor anyone claiming under him will disturb the buyer's possession except insofar as this would be permitted under a disclosed or known encumbrance. It could be argued that any extension of the quiet possession warranty to include tortious acts of third parties would destroy the legal predictability of the warranty. However, the Court of Appeal in two cases has held the seller liable where the disturbance came from a third party and not from the vendor himself. In *Mason v Burningham* [1949] 2 KB 545 the buyer had to return a stolen typewriter to the owner, whereas, in *Microbeads AG v Vinhurst Road Marking Ltd* [1975] 1 WLR 218 the seller was held to be in breach of the quiet possession guarantee when the holder of a patent claimed that the buyer was using a machine in breach of this intellectual property right. A careful distinction should be drawn here with interference which is totally unconnected with that of the seller, for example, the actions of a thief. The significance of this analysis is that by taking such a strict approach to s 12(2) it would appear that a buyer will have an action if his possession is disturbed by a previous owner (financier) seeking to assert title. The actions of the owner (financier) can hardly be considered to be illegitimate in the sense as that of a thief who is totally unconnected with the seller. Given the complexity of the title issue in this context, the behaviour of the owner (financier) may be perfectly reasonable in view of the fact that the chain of title can only become clear in the light of legal argument and emergent facts. In this circumstance, in no sense can the financier's action be considered to be illegitimate so there is no policy issue here of confining the scope of s 12(2) to only legitimate interference with the title.

The quiet possession guarantee is certainly problematical for the seller. This is further compounded by the fact that he cannot exclude liability here because exclusion of the s 12 implied terms are void under s 6(1)(a) of the UCTA 1977. However, s 12(3) of the SGA does contemplate the possibility of the sale of a limited title and where this is the case, s 12(5) provides for a warranty that neither the seller nor any third person's whose title the seller is transferring by virtue of s 12(5)(c) nor 'anyone claiming through or under the seller or that third person' will disturb the quiet possession of the buyer. The dilemma here is that this does not cover the case where a previous owner (financier who loses out under the *nemo dat* exception in Part III wrongfully claims title because in law the seller's claim is not a limited one.

The acquirer's dilemma: disposal of the vehicle to another trade purchaser

There is natural reluctance on the part of a trade purchaser to accept a vehicle with a shadow on its title. This is compounded by the fact that a dealer cannot himself rely upon the presumptions laid down in s 28 of the HPA 1964 (as substituted). This analysis was confirmed by the Court of Appeal in *Barber v NWS Bank plc* (1995) where reference was made to s 27(6) of the Act which restricts trade or finance purchasers from benefiting from the provisions of the Act the mischief of which is to protect innocent *private* purchasers. Furthermore, the trade or finance purchaser does not derive a good title unless it is a derivative one, that is, where he derives title through the relevant good faith private purchaser, because otherwise the strict common law position applies. Significantly, s 27(3) of the Hire Purchase Act 1964 (as amended) protects only the first purchaser from the trade or finance purchaser so long as he is in good faith and has no notice of the hire purchase agreement. Therefore, there will be shadow on the title if the conduit pipe in this regard, the first private purchaser, is not in good faith.

Part III of the Hire Purchase Act 1964 (as amended) recognises the economic equivalence of different legal forms of transaction, namely, sale, conditional sale and hire purchase. Consequently, where a first purchaser is in good faith and without notice of the defect in title, so long as at the time of the *first* disposition to him he was without notice of the defect, good title will pass notwithstanding that when the hirer exercises his option to purchase by that time he had notice of the original hire purchase transaction. In this respect, s 27(4) of the Act provides as follows:

> Where, in a case within subsection (3) above —
> (a)   the disposition by which the first private purchaser becomes a purchaser of the motor vehicle in good faith without notice of the relevant agreement is itself a bailment or hiring under a hire purchase agreement, and
> (b)   the person who is the creditor in relation to that agreement disposes of the vehicle to the first private purchaser, or a person claiming under him, by transferring to him the property in the vehicle in pursuance of a provision in the agreement in that behalf,
> the disposition referred to in paragraph (b) above (whether or not the person to whom it is made is a purchaser in good faith without notice of the relevant agreement) shall as well as the disposition referred to in paragraph (a) above, have effect as mentioned in subsection (3) above.

There is an anomaly here, given that s 27(2) protects any purchaser in good faith and without notice. Where a disposition is effected by a trade or finance purchaser, and the first private purchaser takes the vehicle on hire purchase or conditional sale and the vehicle is repossessed and subsequently sold by the financer, the person to whom the vehicle is sold does not acquire a good title because he is not the first private purchaser. Furthermore, s 27(4) extends to hire purchase provided by a financier and does not apply where the vehicle is let to the private purchaser by the original debtor. Surely, this is a distinction without a difference given the access by both the dealer and the financier to the credit information reference agency, HPI plc?

Sale under common law or statutory powers

The SGA 1979 preserves other exceptions to the general rule of security of property. By virtue of s 21(2)(*b*), nothing in the Act shall affect 'the validity of any contract of sale under any special common law or statutory power of sale or under the order of a court of competent jurisdiction'. Many of the statutory powers of sale developed from the common law, for example, the right of a pawnee under ss 120, 121 of CCA 1974, those of a bailee of uncollected goods under ss 12, 13 of the Torts (Interference with Goods) Act 1977, and innkeepers' powers to sell guests' goods to meet unpaid hotel fees under s 1 of the Innkeepers' Act 1878. Other important statutory powers relate to insolvency and bankruptcy and are consolidated under the Insolvency Act 1986.

The High Court has significant statutory power to order sale if the goods are perishing or depreciating rapidly in value while litigation over them is proceeding (RSC Ord 29, r 4; County Courts Act 1984, s 38). In addition, rules of court allow for the sale of goods seized in execution where a claimant alleges that he is entitled to the goods by way of a security for a debt (RSC Ord 17, r 6; County Courts Act 1984, s 100).

Part IV

Security in Property and Personal Remedies

Chapter 11

Reservation of Title Clauses in English Law

The proprietary approach anticipated by ss 17 and 19 of SGA 1979, where the passing of property is an effect of contract rather than conveyance, means that third party interests, especially those of the buyer's creditors, will be adversely affected by the seller reserving title in the goods because *prima facie* these goods will be recoverable from the buyer on his insolvency. Such clauses have become very common in commercial contracts, and their profusion is symptomatic of the law's inability to protect trade creditors.

The characterisation and systematisation of the legal relations at different points in the sales process is particularly pertinent in the context of retention of title clauses. This is especially so if the seller's right is categorised as 'reserved' ownership and the buyer's right as 'conditioned' ownership, since this would indicate that both parties have some kind of ownership. In this respect, the analysis would be consistent with the doctrine of relativity of title (see Chapter 7). Furthermore, it cannot be the case that the buyer has no rights in the goods before the condition is fulfilled, as this would entail that the seller's right of ownership would remain unrestricted up to the point where the condition is fulfilled, ie payment of the price. Some of the rights that the buyer acquires have never belonged to the seller in the first place, most notably the cutting off of the seller's creditors. It would seem then that both seller and buyer have rights less than absolute (complete) ownership.

A retention of title clause is a sale subject to a condition precedent so that it constitutes a suspensive condition. In relation to such sales, property in the goods remains with the seller until (usually) the payment of the price, whereas the effect of a sale subject to a condition subsequent is said to impose only a personal obligation upon the buyer. Thus, in the situation where property in the goods passes to the buyer on or before delivery subject to the obligation of the buyer to return the goods, the effect of which is to revest the property in the seller or at a reasonable time thereafter, it has been held by Lord Sumner in *The Vesta* [1921] 1 AC 774 that: 'Even if the seller had such a right [an absolute right to require the buyer to return unsuitable goods] . . . this would be a personal right, the breach of which would sound in damages only' (p 783). Consequently different results are seen: on the one hand, the delivery of movable property under a retention of title clause is said to give the seller a right analogous to other real rights, such as his lien under the SGA 1979 (see

231

Chapter 13), whilst on the other hand, delivery subject to a first option clause gives the seller only a personal right against the buyer. This reveals a lack of consistency in logic in the law's present policy regarding the effects of delivery.

The emphasis on property reservation is that it allows the owner to seize the property should the debtor fail in one of his primary obligations. In a sense, virtually all extensions of credit give the creditor a contingent right to take property of the debtor in order to limit the extent of the indebtedness, ie after a court judgment the creditor can 'execute' or 'levy' on some of the debtor's property in order to satisfy the judgment. While the secured creditor has the right not enjoyed by the unsecured creditor to take property without the post-default consent of the debtor and without going to court, this may not be so valuable outside liquidation and even sometimes at liquidation, because a debtor's active objection will require the secured creditor to go to court as well. Nevertheless, since the purpose of the property retention is only to ensure priority, the supplier is not essentially retaining the asset himself but rather the right to use the asset to gain repayment of the debtor's debt to him. The secured creditor, it has been argued, is not entitled to any value derived from its continued use so that, for example, in the Court of Appeal in *Clough Mill Ltd v Martin* [1985] 1 WLR 111, Robert Goff LJ said *obiter* that the seller should retain the title to the material as trustee upon trust for sale accounting to the buyer for any surplus achieved. In contrast, the House of Lords in *Armour and Another v Thyssen Edelstahlwerke AG* [1991] 2 AC 339 held that where there is a valid retention of title clause the seller is not obliged following the failure of a condition precedent to account to the buyer for any part of the value of the goods repossessed (see pp 248–50, below).

The common law background

Typically, there are three parts to the reservation of title or '*Romalpa* clause' (*Aluminium Industrie Vassen BV v Romalpa Aluminium Ltd* [1976] WLR 676). The first part is concerned with reserving ownership in the goods themselves. This is satisfactory so long as the buyer remains in possession, but inadequate where, as so often happens, the buyer resells the goods to a third party who when acting in good faith will be protected by virtue of s 25 of SGA 1979. Hence, the second part of the clause concentrates not on the goods themselves, but the proceeds due to or received by the buyer in the event of resale, and seeks to create a trust in which the original buyer holds these proceeds on behalf of the original seller. The third part of the clause is concerned with the case where the goods having been delivered to the buyer are then used in the process of manufacture, and the device employed here is to declare the finished products as belonging to the seller.

Before embarking on a detailed survey of the cases, it is important to emphasise that each case revolved around the construction of their individual retention of title clause, and in each case this turned out to be defective in one way or another.

The question of construction

The Court of Appeal in *Romalpa*, the first modern English authority to deal with retention of title clauses, had to imply terms into the reservation of title clause in order to save the clause from being held void for uncertainty. In *Borden v Scottish Timber Products* [1981] 1 Ch 25, the contract, as a matter of simple construction, did not provide the plaintiff with the rights it was claiming. Essentially, what the claim amounted to was that any chipboard manufactured with 'their' resin was charged with payment to them of £320,000 and that all money representing the proceeds of the sale of chipboard were charged to the extent that they represented the resin. Contrastingly in *Re Peachdart Ltd* [1984] Ch 131, the Court disregarded the clear wording of such a clause, presumably on the basis of the doctrine of sham. This problem also presented itself in the seminal Court of Appeal decision in *Clough Mill v Martin* (1985). Occasionally, the retention of title clause has contradicted another term in the contract of supply, eg, the period of credit in *Hendy Lennox (Industrial Engines) Ltd v Grahame Puttick Ltd* [1984] 1 WLR 485:

The need for incorporation

In the *Romalpa* case, not only did the Court of Appeal have to imply terms into the retention clause, but there was the initial problem as to whether the clause itself had been incorporated into the contract of sale. The requirements for incorporation have been set out in a *Romalpa* context by Mervyn J in *Sauter Automation Ltd v HC Goodman (Mechanical Services) Ltd (in liquidation)* (1986) 34 Build LR 81. Incorporation may be established by any of the following means:

(a) through embodiment of the terms in a contract document signed by the buyer;

(b) through the embodiment of a term in an unsigned document which the buyer was aware contained contract terms even though he may not have been aware of their purport. In *Wavin Nederland BV v Excomb Ltd* (1983) 133 NLJ 937, Leggatt J held that the pattern of dealings between the parties had been so irregular that no course of dealing could be found through which to incorporate a reservation clause in the contract before him;

(c) embodiment is possible of a term in an unsigned document where the supplier has done all that is reasonably sufficient to bring the terms to his notice. Significantly, in *John Snow and Co Ltd v DBG Woodcroft and Co Ltd* [1985] BCLC 54, Boreham J held that although a quotation containing an extended type of retention of title clause was not in itself a contractual document, it was clear from the circumstances of the case that, where the quotation was given and the orders accepted by the plaintiff, this was subject to these terms and conditions. Interestingly, Boreham J considered that the retention of title was not so unusual as to require Lord Denning's 'red ink' treatment, ie that it was so unusually wide that attention should have been drawn to it in an explicit manner.

A related problem to the above is the so-called 'battle of forms' (*Butler Machine Tool Co Ltd v Ex-Cell-O Corp (England) Ltd* [1979] 1 WLR 401). In *Re Bond Worth* [1980] 1 Ch 228, the parties failed to take full account of the established contractual rule of offer and acceptance. Both parties thought that the contract came into being when Monsanto, the supplier, sent a confirmation note to Bond Worth of its order. However, Slade J held that each of the 29 contracts were concluded when the acrilan referred to in it was actually delivered and accepted by Bond Worth. This was due to the fact that each of the confirmation notes introduced additional terms beyond those proposed in Bond Worth's order note, thereby, constituting counter-offers which became binding only when Bond Worth signified its acceptance. The mishap was important because the time when the contract came into being affected the whole structure of the case. In particular, this arose in connection with the claim that the subject matter was 'future goods' and outside the ambit of the Bills of Sale Acts 1866–91 which require registration with the Registrar of Companies (see s 396(*b*) Companies Act 1985). It was also important as an indicator of who had 'created' the charge so that if the supplier was deemed to have done this, s 398(1) of the Companies Act 1985 would apply. It is anticipated here that, where a company acquires property which is subject to a charge of a kind which would be registrable if it had been created by the company after the acquisition of the property, the company shall register the charge. Under this section, non-registration only renders the company and its officers liable to monetary penalties, whereas, non-registration under s 399 of the Companies Act 1985 renders the whole transaction void as against the liquidator or creditor of the company.

There is no doubt that the issue of incorporation of the retention of title clause in the contract plays a very important role in the enforcement process of such clauses. This was highlighted in *New Zealand Forest Products v Pongakawa Sawmills Ltd* (1992) 3 NZLR 304 where a dispute arose in relation to logs processed by Pongakawa which had been supplied by the plaintiff. On 9 February 1989, the plaintiffs purported to include a retention of title clause in its terms and conditions of supply and backdate these to 11 January 1989. The issue was important because of the plaintiff's concern for the financial standing of the defendants. In the end this concern proved justified, in the light of the fact that of $267,891 worth of unpaid logs at the date of the receivership on 7 March 1989, $132,284 worth were delivered between 1 January and 9 February. On appeal from Henry J's view that the contract could be backdated, the Court of Appeal rejected the idea of retrospection and would not imply such a clause to cover that period. It would appear from this case that legal planning when formulating the contract is essential as is, of course, the need to ensure that the retention of title clause is incorporated in the finalised agreement and is not excluded by a buyer's acknowledgement slip of the supplier's invoice which includes an 'anti-*Romalpa*' clause, for example: 'Acceptance of the order will be deemed to exclude any of your [the supplier's] standard terms or conditions which purport to reserve ownership on any interest in goods supplied under this order'. Such a clause is an attempt to override the seller's terms of trade but the courts have so far not been required to deal with this issue, as the focus has centred upon the construction of retention of title clauses in particular cases.

The need for identification and proof of payment

Proof of payment is a difficult task, especially if there was a current account clause and the account had at any time been in credit. In such a case the supplier may be able to rely on the presumption of regularity and allege that goods received earlier were paid for earlier. This is the rule in *Clayton's Case* (1816) 1 Mer 572 and the full implications of this rule will be discussed in the context of tracing proceeds below. A possible course of action which a supplier may choose to follow in order to protect the proceeds owed, is to apply for a Mareva injunction (see *Mareva Compania Naviera SA v International Bulk Carrier SA* [1975] 2 Lloyd's Rep 509). In this respect, s 37(3) of the Supreme Court Act 1981 makes it clear that the High Court's power to issue Mareva injunctions exists whether the party restrained is or is not domiciled, resident, or present within England and Wales. The Mareva injunction is a useful tool to circumvent the possibility that the buyer may seek to avoid payment of the debt or perhaps to delay payment by removing assets out of England and Wales.

The onus is upon the supplier to show that the goods taken over by the buyer's trustee, such as an administrative receiver, belong to the supplier rather than a third party. However, the major difficulty here is that many insolvency practitioners regard retention of title clauses as being anathema to the speedy disposal of insolvencies, as well as eroding the debenture holder's position. Often this sentiment will be reflected in the administrative receiver adopting a blanket policy of no inspections shortly after appointment, thereby frustrating the supplier's attempt to identify the goods. Of course, there is nothing improper in the administrative receiver's action, especially in view of the fact that the first few days of a receivership are very hectic with the administrative receiver and his staff trying to conduct the 'cost and complete' exercise and make preliminary decisions about the company's future, as well as deciding the fate of the company's employees. At this point, the administrative receiver is unlikely to know which goods he needs. Each claim then is treated by the administrative receiver as providing a basis for negotiation, since he is in possession of the goods. The only instant relief that the formal law offers a supplier is that of an (interim) injunction, but this has only the effect of preserving the *status quo* by preventing the goods being used or disposed of until the claim is settled. Often an administrative receiver will provide the supplier with a joint deposit account arrangement if he wishes to use the goods. This proceeds arrangement will prove most satisfactory for the supplier since the invoice value of goods supplied is normally a far better recovery than the return of the goods themselves as it will represent the profit element. Also the return of the goods may be costly with regard to the collection process, as well as the possibility that the goods may deteriorate, not to mention the necessity of altering stock records, and the profit has still to be made.

If the administrative receiver refuses access, the supplier in an attempt to secure this can ask the High Court to grant him an Anton Piller order (*Anton Piller KG v Manufacturing Processes Ltd* [1976] Ch 55) which will have to be done quickly if it is to have any effect at all. Nevertheless, the costs associated with this may be prohibitive especially when coupled by the fact that the supplier cannot be sure of recovering the costs of the application from the administrative receiver, and there is no guarantee anyway that the goods are still on the premises. From the administrative receiver's perspective, the retention of title clause is seen as an individual creditor's remedy which makes other creditors, as a group, worse off. Furthermore, there is the cost in the expense and wastefulness of the individual remedies because the administrative receiver may spend valuable resources resisting the efforts of a *Romalpa*-type seller.

Undoubtedly, given the proliferation of retention of title clauses, they are important to suppliers. The position in the case law is very unsatisfactory and can present considerable dilemmas for the following reasons.

(1) Suppliers might find such clauses ineffectual.
(2) Persons extending credit face the reduction of their traditional priority.
(3) Liquidators or administrative receivers may be unclear as to the position where either the materials supplied or the proceeds of sale are mixed.
(4) Manufacturers may be compelled to accept such clauses which may adversely affect the bank's attitude towards loan facilities.

The form in which commerce adopts the reservation of title clause depends very much on the reception accorded to it by the judiciary and, as such, is an example of the impact of law on practice. Since each case turned on the construction of its individual reservation of title clause, the discovery of a valid form is elusive. It will be instructive, therefore, to consider the principal cases in greater detail.

The pivotal English cases

Aluminium Industrie Vassen BV v Romalpa Aluminium Ltd [1976] 1 WLR 676

Given the reception accorded to this decision by the legal community, it is curious that it was not officially reported in the Law Reports. One counsel referred to it as the most important case for 25 years and doubted whether any case decided this century has created a greater impact on the commercial world. In this vein, the decision has been welcomed by businessmen engaged in the international sale of goods, whilst others consider that the decision took us to a commercial precipice. The cynical explanation regarding the absence of the case from the Law Reports is that it was thought to be unreportable, although Roskill LJ did say that the decision turned on the construction of the particular contract: '. . . a rather simple contract not altogether happily expressed in the English language but [which] could not govern any other case'.

The facts are relatively simple. The defendants owed the plaintiffs (a Dutch firm) £122,000 and they possessed £35,000 in a separate account which represented the proceeds of sale of foil supplied by the plaintiffs. In addition, the defendants had in their possession unsold foil valued at £50,000. The plaintiffs relied on their reservation of title clause (number 13 in their contract of supply) in order to recover these assets which provided: 'The ownership of the material to be delivered by AIV will only be transferred to purchaser when he has met *all* that is owing to AIV, no matter on what grounds' Additionally, Romalpa was required to store the material in such a way that it could be identified as the property of AIV/Secondly, an assignment of future unascertained property was provided (ie the manufactured goods processed from the foil) as surety for AIV until full payment had been made. Lastly, a right was provided to sell the finished product with a transfer of all claims against the sub-buyers,

It is a pity that neither the first instance court nor the Court of Appeal in *Romalpa* considered the earlier Irish case of *Re Interview* [1975] IR 382 which was directly relevant. This case concerned a sale of electrical goods subject to a retention of title clause in those goods until all debts were paid, as well as an assignment 'by way of security' of all claims the purchaser had against the sub-purchaser. It was held by Kenny J that the unsold goods still in the possession of Interview Ltd (the buyer) on the date of the appointment of the receiver, belonged to the supplier, since crystallisation of the floating charge only operated as an equitable assignment of the goods owned by the company at the date of the appointment. As it was, in *Romalpa* the receiver conceded that the unsold foil belonged to AIV, a conclusion which was in accord with Kenny J's reasoning. Nevertheless, as far as the clause purporting to assign the debts of sub-purchasers was concerned, Kenny J held that this constituted a charge over book debts which was void for non-registration under the Irish equivalent of s 396(*c*)(iii) of the Companies Act 1985. What was intended was an assignment by way of security rather than an absolute assignment of book debts since this would have denied Interview Ltd any profit element in the transaction. Such an approach has more recently been confirmed in *Carroll Group Distributors Ltd v G and JF Bourke Ltd* [1990] ILRM 285.

In *Romalpa* at first instance, Mocatta J reasoned by analogy that, as the goods themselves were not owned by the buyer until payment, this must also apply to cash proceeds in the separate account opened by the receiver which represented the proceeds of the sale of the foil. The approach taken by Mocatta J, which was confirmed in the Court of Appeal, is difficult to sustain. To recognise a clause reserving ownership to secure payment of sums due on other transactions, some of which might be totally unrelated to the sale of specific goods (inherent in cl 13), seems to go far beyond the confines of the law on sale of goods. Moreover, in view of the fact that *Romalpa* was allowed to mix the money with its own, this would *prima facie* appear incompatible with a presently subsisting fiduciary relationship (*Re Nevill Ex p White* (1871) 6 Ch App 397; *Foley v Hill* (1848) 2 HL Cas 28; *South Australian Insurance Co v Randell* (1869) LR 3 PC 101; *Henry v Hammond* [1913] 2 KB 515). The difficulty with the position taken by the courts in *Romalpa* is shown in the first place by the fact that cl 13 reserved ownership in the foil until all indebtedness had been discharged. Since there was a 'running account' between Romalpa and AIV, it would have been very difficult to ascertain when Romalpa was in credit and free to deal with the money as they pleased, and when they were not. In addition, a 75-day credit period was provided for under the épitome of the General Conditions of Sale so that Goff LJ, in the Court of Appeal, enigmatically conceded the point of counsel for the defendants that this credit period would be destroyed if cl 13 was applied. The effect of this would have been to prohibit Romalpa from ploughing the profits they had made on sub-sale back into the business. Despite this fact, his Lordship felt compelled by the force of the plaintiffs' argument that the purpose of cl 13 was to protect the vendors from being left in the position of unsecured creditors:

> No doubt in practice as long as all went well the plaintiffs would allow the defendants to use the proceeds of sale in their business as indeed they did; but things ceased to go well and now one has to determine the strict rights of the parties . . . . (p 692)

Undoubtedly, what the Court of Appeal envisaged was a waiver of the terms of the general contract by the plaintiffs while the business was solvent. In itself this was not unusual given the policy of the law to uphold reasonable arrangements reached by businessmen and, as Roskill LJ conceded, the defendants would have been deprived of day-to-day finance, thereby suffering an acute cash-flow problem. Seemingly, the plaintiffs had conceded their security right for what counsel for the defendants argued was an ordinary contractual right against the defendants. Such a 'forbearance' would remain effective until made clear by notice or otherwise that the strict position under the contract was to be restored. The problem with the *Romalpa* case is that no indication is given whether AIV had intimated their desire to return to the strict legal position (see pp 39–40). Certainly, the restoration of the strict legal position could only have accelerated Romalpa's financial embarrassment, a fact which must have borne heavily on AIV's decision given that a creditor's prime interest is not his security but in receiving the money owed. A secured creditor's decision whether to return to the strict legal position is not similar, at least in its consequences, to the decision of a debenture-holder in appointing an administrative receiver. One of the latter's function is to generate sufficient cash flow to enable a company to meet its necessary outgoings, and a business sold as a 'going concern' produces a better realisation figure as well as maintaining employment. In contrast, a '*Romalpa* clause' prohibits the sale of stock-in-trade, or retains its proceeds, and is concerned with the determination of substantive rights (ownership) which exist outside the receivership/liquidation context. A fully secured creditor, as a person assured of full payment if the business were to stop, will tend to favour an immediate liquidation since he has nothing to gain from attempting to keep the firm intact.

A substantial objection to the approach of the courts in *Romalpa*, especially in relation to the goods already paid for where the contract is not severable, is that it is difficult to avoid the conclusion that the clause was void for total failure

of consideration since Romalpa had not received the supplier's property interest in the goods. Furthermore, the '*Romalpa* clause' itself was a somewhat
unlikely candidate for the role of establishing the legal respectability of reservation of title clauses. No evidence of Dutch law was given because Roskill LJ in
the Court of Appeal did not consider this point to be important: '. . . nor does it
matter, though it would have been interesting to have known what the position
was under Dutch law, as indeed it would have been interesting to know how a
Dutch lawyer would have construed some of those express terms' (p 684). It is
regrettable that this approach was taken particularly in the light of cl 30 of the
General Conditions of Contract which stipulated that Dutch law was to be given
exclusive jurisdiction. This must surely have made the matter more than one of
simple 'interest'. The point takes on further significance given the fact that the
Court had to work hard to save cl 13 from being held void for uncertainty. The
contra proferentem rule was discarded, and an implied power of sale was given
in relation to the sale of the aluminium foil. Indeed, Roskill LJ said: '[I]t would
be strange if the first part [of cl 13] were to afford no such security when the
second part is elaborately drawn to give such security in relation to manufactured or mixed goods' (p 690). It is not clear why *The Moorcock* ((1889) 14 PD
64) doctrine of implying terms into a contract to give it business efficacy should
have applied in this instance, particularly when the doctrine is said to be of
narrow application, and a last desperate expedient in a tenuous case.

It is unlikely that an implied power of sale gave business efficacy to the
agreement. Moreover, it probably only represented the true intention of the
parties in so far as what was attempted was a claim to the proceeds of resale
which included a future equitable assignment of a chose in action, namely, the
debt against the sub-buyer. The question of whether this constituted a charge
over book debts will be considered later (see pp 257–62). Clearly, if no power
of sale had been implied, Romalpa would have been liable in conversion and,
on waiver of the tort, this would have amounted to a personal claim for money
had and received thereby giving AIV no real rights to the proceeds. As it was,
the Court of Appeal construed Romalpa's relationship with AIV as being a fiduciary one with the result that proprietary tracing rights were available. The
problem of identifying the proceeds did not arise because the receiver had
opened a separate bank account. Nonetheless the question regarding the capacity of Romalpa in disposing of the goods reveals the difficulties inherent in the
approach taken by the Court of Appeal since the nature of the fiduciary relationship was never established. Indeed, the confusion was reflected in *Borden
v STP* (1981) where Bridge LJ having conceded that the defendants in *Romalpa*
were bailees, then proceeded to describe them as agents. This issue goes to the
heart of the legal recognition of the more extended type of clause and will be
considered later.

It is a pity that no evidence of Dutch law was adduced because under Dutch
law a contract to create future receivables creates only a personal obligation and
does not, by itself, vest the receivables in the hands of the transferee even after
they have come into existence. Since a reservation of title of future receivables
was invalid under Dutch law, why should a supplier enjoy the validity of such

a provision under English law? A more subtle variation of this problem arose before Lord Mayfield in the Scottish Court of Session in *Armour v Thyssen Edelstrahlwerke AG* [1986] SLT 452. In this case there was evidence that, as a matter of contract, a clause which is drafted so as to secure debts to or by other companies in the creditor's or debtor's 'group', is ineffective to retain title in German law. If in this case the proper law of the contract was Scots law, the question of the initial effectiveness of the clause would depend upon whether the 'all sums' clause is ineffective as a matter of contract, property or both. There are several Scottish cases dealing with choice of law in a *Romalpa*-type situation (see *Hammer and Sohne v HWT Realisations Ltd* [1985] SLT 21; *Zahnrad Fabrik Passau GmbH v Terex Ltd* [1986] SLT 84; *Armour v Thyssen* [1986] SLT 452). The conclusions arrived at in the cases can be justified along conventional choice of law analysis, namely, in Scots international private law the creation and extinction of real rights in corporeal movable property is governed by the *lex situs* at the time of the creation or extinction of such rights. The 'incidental question', ie real rights coming into being following the exercise of a personal right as seen in s 17 of SGA 1979 where property passes by agreement, is governed by the *lex causae*.

Re Bond Worth [1980] Ch 228

This case was decided three years after the *Romalpa* decision. The conditions of sale under which Monsanto, the plaintiffs, had supplied acrilan to Bond Worth for use in making carpets provided:

> Equitable and beneficial ownership shall remain with [Monsanto] until full payment has been received . . . or until prior resale, in which case [Monsanto's] beneficial entitlement shall attach to the proceeds of resale or to the claim for such proceeds. Should the goods become constituents of or be converted into other products while subject to [Monsanto's] equitable and beneficial ownership [Monsanto] shall have the equitable and beneficial ownership in such other products as if they were simply and solely the goods.

The reference to Monsanto's 'equitable and beneficial ownership' cannot be regarded as importing its usual meaning. Equity has never recognised that, where total ownership is vested in one person, he has a 'dual' ownership in the sense that he may transmit his equitable interest free of his legal dominion.

It is doubtful whether an equitable title in goods can subsist after the 1893 codification of the SGA, especially in the light of Atkin LJ's judgment in *Re Wait* [1927] 1 Ch 606:

> It would have been futile in a Code intended for commercial men to have created an elaborate structure of rules dealing with rights at law, if at the same time it was intended to leave, subsisting with the legal rights, equitable rights inconsistent with more extensive and coming into existence earlier than the rights so carefully set out in various sections of the Code. (pp 635–6)

On principle, it could be argued that if the conduct of the parties can produce a situation where the burdens of beneficial ownership pass to the buyer (*Sterns Ltd v Vickers Ltd* [1923] 1 KB 78), it is illogical that they should not also pass all of the corresponding benefits, for example, equitable ownership of the goods. Nevertheless, Atkin LJ in *Re Wait* does refer to legal rights and duties *dehors* the contract of sale which is the equitable charge or mortgage, and this was the approach taken by Slade J (as he then was) in *Bond Worth*.

The fact that Bond Worth had legal title whilst Monsanto claimed a beneficial title, should have strengthened the argument that there was a fiduciary relationship. Nonetheless, Bond Worth were at liberty to use the goods for the purpose of manufacture and Monsanto enjoyed no right to call for the redelivery of the goods. In addition, Bond Worth were not liable to account to Monsanto for the profit made on resale of the goods so that even if the buyers had been obliged to segregate the proceeds of sale, the sellers would only be entitled to an amount equal to the undischarged balance of the debt owed to him. From this Slade J concluded that this was a contract by way of security for the payment of a debt which conferred an interest in the property, and this was defeasible on the payment of the debt, thereby constituting a mortgage or charge over the different categories of assets (raw acrilan and proceeds of sale, products manufactured and proceeds). Seemingly, in order to avoid this conclusion, all of the proceeds would have had to be placed in an identifiable separate account ensuring that, if the buyer were in fact to mix the trust money with his own, the tracing remedy would then be properly available. Obviously, there are great practical difficulties in obtaining acceptance and observance of such a provision, especially as this would deprive the business of the proceeds of sub-sale, thereby affecting cash-flow. However, it can be argued following the approach of the House of Lords in *Abbey National Building Society v Cann* [1991] 1 AC 56 that no security was ever 'created' by Bond Worth requiring registration under s 396 Companies Act 1985, because at no stage was Bond Worth's interest as against Monsanto unencumbered, that is, it was always informed by the seller's equity in the goods (see below pp 257–9).

It is difficult to reconcile *Romalpa* and *Bond Worth*. The distinction drawn by Slade J in *Bond Worth* is hardly convincing, namely, that in *Romalpa* there was a fiduciary relationship (conceded by counsel) whereas in *Bond Worth* there was no such relationship. Undoubtedly, Slade J in *Bond Worth* felt constrained by the weight of precedent afforded by the Court of Appeal in *Romalpa*. No appeal was lodged against the decision in *Bond Worth* which may indicate an acceptance by the business community advisers of the legal reasoning adopted. In contrast, the *Borden* case (1981) went to the Court of Appeal as this was concerned with different facts, ie with goods mixed in the process of manufacture.

Borden (UK Ltd) v Scottish Timber Products [1981] Ch 25

Borden supplied Scottish Timber Products with urea formaldehyde resin which was used in the manufacture of chipboard. In the ordinary course, the chipboard resin was mixed by the buyers with certain hardeners and wax emulsion to form 'glue mix'. This was an irreversible chemical reaction, and the buyers generally did this mixing of the resin within two days of receiving it, the suppliers being well aware of this fact. The glue mix was then mixed with wood chippings and pressed to make chipboard.

The buyers went into liquidation with an outstanding debt to the sellers of £318,332. The retention clause on which they sought to rely provided:

> Goods supplied by the company shall be at the purchaser's risk immediately on delivery to the purchaser or into custody on the purchaser's behalf (whichever is the owner) and the purchaser should therefore be insured accordingly. Property in goods supplied hereunder will pass to the customer when: (a) the goods the subject of this contract; and (b) all other goods the subject of any other contract between the company and the customer which, at the time of payment of the full price of the goods sold under this contract, have been delivered to the customer but not paid for in full, have been paid for in full.

No stipulation was made in respect of a charge over the goods into which the chipboard resin had been consumed. Inevitably, the clause was a poor means of protection for Borden in view of the fact that the chipboard resin was never intended to remain for long in its original state.

At first instance ([1979] 2 Lloyd's Rep 168), Rubin J held that a fiduciary relationship existed giving rise to an equitable right to trace into the finished product and proceeds. This reasoning appears inconsistent because, although STP received the resin as bailees, to make commercial sense of the arrangement a term had to be implied giving STP a licence to use the resin in their manufacturing process. The Court of Appeal reversed this conclusion recognising, as Slade J did in *Bond Worth* (1980), what was involved here after the 'tearing away of the mask' was a sale since it was never intended that the resin be recovered either in its original or altered form. In particular, this attitude can be seen in the judgment of Templeman LJ who was wary of manipulating principles of equity in order to produce a new equitable tracing right having the same effect as a charge, but being immune from the requirements of registration.

The combined effect of *Bond Worth* and *Borden* was to limit the retention of title clause in *Romalpa* to its special facts. These two cases also appeared to limit the intrusion of equitable principles of trusts, fiduciary relationships and equitable tracing into contracts for the sale of goods. In subsequent cases, even the simple *in specie* clause was restrictively construed. One technique employed by the courts included construing the clause in the light of the doctrine of sham as in *Re Peachdart* (1984).

Re Peachdart [1984] Ch 131

Freudenberg Leather Co Ltd supplied leather to Peachdart Ltd for use in the manufacture of high quality leather handbags. On the latter's insolvency, Freudenberg sought to rely upon its retention of title clause incorporated into its standard conditions of sale to recover the outstanding debt of £16,200. Freudenberg claimed (a) the proceeds of sale of a stock of unused leather in the possession of Peachdart when the (administrative) receiver was appointed; (b) the proceeds of sale of handbags, some completely and some partly manufactured when the (administrative) receiver was appointed; and (c) the proceeds of sale of handbags which had been sold by the company before the (administrative) receiver was appointed but for which the company had not been paid. The clause provided *inter alia*:

> . . . ownership of the products shall remain with the seller who reserves the right to dispose of the products until payment in full for all the products have been received. . . . If any of the products are incorporated before such payment the property in the whole of such other goods shall be and remain with the seller until such payment has been made . . . . Until the seller is paid in full for all the products the relationship of the buyer to the Seller shall be fiduciary in respect of the Products . . . .

Counsel for the (administrative) receiver conceded that the property in the unused stocks of leather which came into the hands of the (administrative) receiver when he was appointed, remained with Freudenberg. As such, the case is similar to *Romalpa*. However, as far as the proceeds of sale of partly manufactured and completely manufactured handbags were concerned, Vinelott J came to the conclusion, despite the clear wording of the retention of title clause, that:

> . . . it is impossible to suppose that . . . the parties intended that until a parcel of leather had been fully paid for the company would remain a bailee of each piece of leather comprised in the parcel throughout the whole process of manufacture . . . and that on the sale of a completed handbag the company would be under an obligation to pay the proceeds of sale into a separate interest bearing account and to keep them apart from their moneys and not employ them in the trade. (p 142)

Although this approach is consistent with *Borden* (1981), and is also mirrored in the subsequent case of *Re Andrabell* [1984] 3 All ER 407, it may nevertheless be criticised as being difficult to reconcile with *Romalpa*. In *Re Peachdart*, Vinelott J not only felt unable to imply terms, as in *Borden*, he actually chose to disregard express contractual provisions. A better way, one would have thought, to reach this conclusion would have been by looking at the business operation in practice and demonstrating that this was totally at variance with the objectives of the clause.

Any hopes of claiming the manufactured and partly manufactured goods by virtue of the common law doctrine of *accessio*, whereby, the owner of a principal chattel (ie the leather) may claim ownership of it and the accession (for example, thread, buckles etc) in the absence of a contrary intention, were dashed by Vinelott J's finding that the parties had intended that, once Peachdart had appropriated a piece of leather to the manufacture of a handbag, the leather ceased to be the exclusive property of Freudenberg. It was also held that such a contrary intention could be implied since, in the absence of records, it would be impossible to ascertain whether those handbags made from the supplier's leather were sold before or after receivership. Obviously this would be important in determining whether the (administrative) receiver may have wrongfully disposed of the property after his appointment. This conclusion is difficult to understand given the previous concession in the case that it was possible to say for any given handbag whether or not it comprised the supplier's leather.

Hendy Lennox (Industrial Engines) Ltd v Grahame Puttick Ltd [1984] 1 WLR 485

This case revolved around the sale of engines which both parties envisaged would eventually be incorporated into diesel generating sets for sub-sale. Each engine remained identifiable by virtue of its serial number. Following the defendant's insolvency, the outstanding debt owed to the plaintiff sellers amounted to over £46,000, which was of little or no value since the buyers owed the debenture holders over £700,000 and the latter held a charge over the buyer's assets. The sellers sought to rely upon the retention of title clause incorporated in their standard conditions of sale which provided: '. . . all goods . . . shall be and remain the property of the Company [Hendy Lennox] until the full purchase price thereof shall be paid'.

The above clause contradicted the period of credit provided for under the conditions of sale, and the sellers conceded that the right to retake possession of and retain permanently any unpaid goods was only exercisable when the buyers were in default of payment, ie when the period of credit had expired (up to two months) and the price had not been paid. In addition, the sellers conceded an implied term in their contracts with the buyers that the latter were entitled to sell the goods in advance of paying the price thereof to the sellers. Four main groups of asset were identified:

    (a) a small quantity of spares which remained unused on the buyer's premises at the time of the receivership. These in fact had been paid for by the (administrative) receiver and were used in the process of manufacture;

    (b) invoices in respect of engines and spares totalling over £16,000 which had been incorporated into generator sets and delivered to sub-buyers before the receivership. Counsel representing the sellers conceded that the proceeds paid into Barclays Bank 'had sunk without trace into the buyer's overdraft'. The question regarding the propriety or otherwise of this concession will be discussed later;

    (c) invoices in respect of engines the property in which had passed to sub-buyers at the time of (administrative) receivership, and had been delivered to sub-buyers, but the price had not been paid until after the date of the receivership. These proceeds amounted to over £24,000 and were preserved in a joint bank account by virtue of an interlocutory injunction granted by Stocker J a few weeks after the (administrative) receiver's appointment in November 1980. These proceeds were now being claimed by the sellers;

    (d) invoices in respect of three engines still on the buyer's premises when the receiver was appointed. The sellers claimed a proprietary right to these engines, which became a direct claim to the proceeds of sub-sale by virtue of the interlocutory proceedings order to the effect that these proceeds be placed in a separate account.

Interestingly, the policy considerations evident in the Cork Committee Report on *Insolvency Law and Practice* (Cmnd 8558, (1982)) that insolvency procedures should be made more simple and just, and that ordinary creditors should be entitled to a bigger slice of the debtor's assets than at present are mirrored in Staughton J's *obiter* remarks in *Hendy Lennox* (at p 490):

> [I]f the seller's claim fails they will receive nothing or little as unsecured creditors. Equally I assume . . . that if the seller's claim succeeds, still the receiver will not go away empty-handed from his office. From what I was told it follows that the claims of employees for wages and of the revenue authorities for taxes will be met whatever I decide . . . . The dispute is simply as to which of the Sellers and Barclays Bank is entitled to salvage £28,988.01 from the wreck of the buyer's affairs which must be decided according to law. I have considerable sympathy with the sellers, in that they have become embroiled in expensive and protracted litigation in a field where the law is unclear. But I cannot award them compensation as such, for that misfortune.

Only with respect to one engine did Staughton J find that the sellers had a proprietary claim based on their retention of title clause. On the facts, it was held that this engine was not appropriated to any contract of sub-sale at the time when the credit period conceded by the sellers in their conditions of sale expired, thereby giving the sellers the right to reclaim the engine. Furthermore, by virtue of the interlocutory proceedings, the sellers had a derivative claim against the proceeds of sub-sale in substitution for the direct claim to retake the engine. With respect to the proceeds of sub-sale of the other generator sets, a debtor–creditor relationship was held to have intervened:

> . . . the implied term contended for here would have to relate to the proceeds of sale of generator sets which comprised more than the goods supplied by the sellers . . . the presumption of a fiduciary relationship . . . is neutralised by the agreement between the parties that the buyers should have credit for at least one month, and possibly two months. It is not easy to reconcile that with an obligation to keep the proceeds of resale in a separate account . . . . (p 499)

Undoubtedly, the purpose of the arrangement in *Hendy Lennox*, read as a whole, was a security device because the seller was only concerned with recovering the amount outstanding on the engines. Nevertheless, there is a substantial argument that *Romalpa* clauses covering sums due to the seller in excess of those relating to the contract of sale create valid security rights. This is especially so where there is an implied undertaking by the buyer/debtor to retransfer the relevant property, if it still exists, to the seller/creditor to hold it in possession. Many *Romalpa* clauses are, however, not easily susceptible to this construction since they would seldom become effective by such retransfer. Essentially, the point is that a *Romalpa* clause has a double function, ie it contains the elements of both sale and security which is a necessary consequence of the SGA 1979 approach whereby property passing is an aspect of contract rather than conveyance. This analysis is confirmed by the decision of the Court of Appeal in *Clough Mill*.

Re Andrabell Ltd (in Liquidation), Airborne Accessories Ltd v Goodman [1984] 3 All ER 407

The plaintiffs supplied travel bags worth nearly £29,000 to Andrabell Ltd, a firm which carried on business as retailers and exporters of travel bags but which went into liquidation before paying any of the money owed to Airborne Accessories Ltd. The contract of sale reserved title until payment, but allowed the buyer company 45 days' credit. The company resold the bags and paid the proceeds into its general bank account so commingling them with its other moneys. Shortly afterwards, the company went into liquidation.

The approach taken by Peter Gibson J in this case was similar to that adopted by Staughton J in *Hendy Lennox*, namely there was no express acknowledgement of a fiduciary situation. In the absence of a fiduciary relationship, the relationship was one of creditor and debtor and therefore the company was not under a duty to account to the plaintiff in respect of the proceeds of sale of the bags. The following indicia were considered crucial in the determination of the question of the establishment of a fiduciary relationship:

(1) There was no provision obliging the company to store the bags in a manner which manifested the plaintiff's ownership of the bags.

(2) The company was not selling as agent or on the plaintiff's account.

(3) There was no obligation on the company to keep the proceeds from the sale of bags supplied by the plaintiff separate from its own moneys.

(4) There was no duty to account for proceeds.

(5) During the 45-day credit period it was inferred that the company was free to use the proceeds received from the sale of the bags as it liked, which was not compatible with the plaintiff having an interest in the proceeds of sale.

It is significant that in both *Hendy Lennox* and *Re Andrabell* the provision of credit was considered inconsistent with an equitable duty to account. As such, it appears that the retention of title clause does not give protection in these circumstances. Nevertheless, this is not an inevitable consequence of a credit period because this could be construed as being subject to a duty to account for the proceeds of sale *on receipt*, thereby, reducing the buyer's price indebtedness. It follows that the existence of a credit period does not deprive of its effect the duty to account, as it merely postpones this to the end of the credit period except in relation to proceeds of sale received during that period.

Clough Mill v Martin [1985] 1 WLR 111

The facts involved four contracts relating to the sale of yarn by Clough Mill Ltd to Heatherdale Fabrics Ltd between December 1979 and March 1980. On the appointment of the (administrative) receiver, part of the purchase price on each of the four yarn contracts remained outstanding, although 375 kgs of unused yarn valued at £1,190 remained on the buyer's premises. Clough Mill sought to rely upon its retention of title clause (condition 12) incorporated into its standard conditions of sale. This provided as follows:

> However, the ownership of the material shall remain with the seller, which reserves the right to dispose of the material until payment in full for all the material, has been received by it in accordance with the terms of this contract or until such time as the buyer sells the material to its customers by way of bona fide sale at full market value.

If such payment is overdue in whole or in part the seller may (without prejudice to any of its other rights) recover or resell the material or any of it and may enter upon the buyer's premises by its servants or agents for that purpose.

Such payment shall become due immediately upon the commencement of any act or proceeding in which the buyer's solvency is involved.

If any of the material is incorporated in or used as material for other goods before such payment the property in the whole of such goods shall be and remain with the seller until such payment has been made, or the other goods have been sold as aforesaid, and all the seller's rights hereunder in the material shall extend to these other goods.

The (administrative) receiver refused to give up the yarn and instead allowed it to be used in a manufacturing process. An action was brought in conversion for damages against the receiver who, it was argued, remained personally accountable.

This case illustrates the dilemma posed by retention of title clauses to the administrative receiver. The latter's function is to generate sufficient cash flow so as to enable a company to meet its necessary outgoings, which is important since a business sold as a 'going concern' produces a better realisation figure as well as maintaining employment. In contrast, a retention of title clause will prohibit the sale of stock-in-trade or retain its proceeds. The approach taken at first instance in *Clough Mill* [1984] 1 WLR 1067 would appear to resolve the administrative receiver's dilemma. O'Donoghue J came to the conclusion that the prime purpose of the retention of title clause was a security device, and in reaching this conclusion a subjective test was applied. This involved construing the relevant clause as manifesting an intention to pass property immediately in the goods subject to a grant back by the buyer by way of a charge. Such a conclusion does seem at variance with the language used in the clause, namely that 'ownership of the material shall remain with the seller'. Indeed, O'Donoghue J's approach is startling since he maintained that because the right to repossess only arose on default, the supplier would 'seem' to have something less than ownership. The consequence of this approach would be to suggest that a bailor has less than an ownership right. Furthermore, the issue in *Clough Mill* involved the yarn in its original condition, whilst the proceeds of sub-sale of the yarn in its original or manufactured form was not in question. Despite this, O'Donoghue J formulated and applied a 'purpose and function' test: '[I]f the court is satisfied that this purpose was by way of security for the payment of unpaid purchase moneys then the transaction as a whole should be construed as a charge' (p 1076).

Essentially the conclusion arrived at first instance fails to recognise the distinction between form and function and what was involved was a policy decision. In construing the clause the way he did, O'Donoghue J was being no less formalistic than the parties themselves. The decision given by the court at first instance appeared to have left few of the *Romalpa* principles subsisting. The learned judge held that condition 12 of the supply contract (the retention of title clause) should be read as a whole, and that even the first part of the clause retaining title to goods *in specie* constituted a charge which was void for lack of registration under the Companies Act. This approach was in stark contrast to the previous cases where it had consistently been held that unsold goods supplied under a retention of title clause which were identifiable and still in the possession of the 'Romalpa-type' buyer on the date of the appointment of the receiver, belonged to the supplier, since crystallisation of a floating charge only operated as an equitable assignment of the goods owned by the company at the date of the appointment.

In a sense, the position adopted by the Court of Appeal which found in favour of Clough Mill, can be seen as a mere restatement of the conventional legal position regarding retention of title clauses. The concomitant of this was that there could be no question of a registrable charge being created by the buyer as this presupposes the grant of a security interest. Thus, Oliver LJ in distinguishing Re Bond Worth (1980) held:

> The operative word here, however, is 'confers' and the whole of Slade J's judgment in that case [Re Bond Worth] was based upon the fact, as he found, that the legal title to the goods had passed to the buyer. That was in the context of a clause which, in terms, sought to reserve only to the seller the 'beneficial' interest and to seek to apply it to the clause now under consideration is to assume the very thing that is sought to be proved. Of course, where the legal title has passed, security can be provided by a charge created by the new legal owner. But it is not a necessary incident of the seller's securing his position that he should pass the legal title. The whole question is, how has his position been secured? If in fact he has retained the legal title to the goods, then by definition the buyer cannot have charged them in his favour. (p 123)

This approach would suggest that the reservation of the legal title by the seller is necessarily inconsistent with the creation of a charge.

Armour v Thyssen Edelstahlwerke AG [1991] 2 AC 339

The facts in this case relate to the supply of steel strip by Thyssen (a German company) to a Scottish manufacturer (Carron) of metal, plastic and general engineering products. The conditions of supply included a retention of title clause which, when translated from the German, read as follows:

> All goods delivered by us remain our property (goods remaining in our ownership) until all debts owed to us including any balances existing at relevant times—due to us on any legal ground—are settled. This also holds good if payments are made for the purpose of settlement of specially designated claims. Debts owed to companies, being members of our combine, are deemed to be such debts.

In August 1982, Carron went into receivership. At this time, there was lying in Carron's work some 67,423 kg of steel strip, most of it being in the state in which it had been delivered. The invoice value of the steel was £71,769, no part of which had been paid.

Following the appointment of receivers, a dispute arose concerning the ownership of the steel strip. The receivers agreed that if Thyssen could establish an effective reservation of title clause, the steel strip would be returned or paid for if used. Litigation ensued in the Scottish courts; it raged for eight years and matters were not finally resolved until the recent House of Lords' decision. In a sense, the House of Lords restated the conventional legal position, namely, the reservation of title clause in a contract of sale does not constitute a security interest which may require registration of title rather than the grant by the debtor of an equitable interest in the form of a mortgage or charge. As Lord Keith put it:

> Can it be said that Carron obtained anything which gave it the capacity to retain an ultimate right to the goods? That could be so only if the contract of sale gave them the property in the goods but the contract of sale said that property in the goods was not to pass until all debts due to the appellants had been paid. We are here very far removed from the situation where a party in possession of corporeal movables is seeking to create a subordinate right in favour of a creditor while retaining the ultimate right to himself. It is true that by entering into the contract of sale Carron agreed that they should receive possession of the goods on delivery but should not acquire the property until all debts due to the appellants had been paid, and thus agreed that the appellants would in effect have security over the goods after they had come into Carron's possession. But at that stage Carron had no interest of any kind whatever in any particular goods. Carron was never in a position to confer upon the appellants any subordinate right over the steel strip, nor did it ever seek to do so. (pp 343–4).

An interesting problem that arises out of an 'all liabilities' retention of title clause, in relation to goods which have been repossessed by the seller, is whether a buyer can reclaim payments made to the seller in respect of those goods on the basis that there has been total failure of consideration. In order to succeed in this submission, the buyer will have to show that he received no benefit from the contract. The fact that the buyer has enjoyed mere possession of the goods does not constitute a benefit in this sense. This is because the essence of a sale contract involves the passage of general property in the goods (s 2(1) Sale of Goods Act 1979). As Atkin LJ put it in *Rowland v Divall* [1923] 2 KB 500:

> The whole object of a sale is to transfer property from one person to another, and I think that in every contract of sale of goods there is an implied term to that effect that a breach of the condition that the seller has a right to sell the goods may be treated as a ground for rejecting the goods and repudiating the contract notwithstanding the acceptance within the meaning of the concluding words of [the subsection] . . . (pp 506–7)

It should be noted that the seller in this case never acquired the right to sell the car, which was recovered from the buyer after four months' use. It seems from this that the crucial question is not whether the party to a contract has received any benefit at all, but whether he has received the benefit which he was entitled to expect under the contract. This is the point that arose in *Barber v NWS Bank plc* (1995) in relation to a conditional sale agreement (see p 223 above). Similarly, in hire purchase agreements, the question is whether the hirer has enjoyed both possession and a valid option to purchase. In *Karflex Ltd v Poole* [1933] 2 KB 251, it was held that despite the fact that the hirer had defaulted on his instalments under a hire purchase agreement, he was nevertheless entitled to repudiate the contract and recover his deposit because the finance company was not the owner of the car at the date of delivery. Nonetheless, in the case of a general supply of goods, it may be that where the contract is divisible, the court can treat each part individually so that one or more parts may be set aside for total failure of consideration notwithstanding that the other parts have been performed.

Retention of title: A triumph of legal form

It is the policy of the courts in England, where there is security with recourse to property which can be effected by means other than a transaction of loan or charge, not to treat it as registrable under s 396 of the Companies Act 1985. This is so even though the exact economic effect might be carried out through a transaction which in form was registrable as a security interest in the goods. As a matter of legal form the main distinction between a bill of sale (a chattel mortgage) and an executory agreement to sell (a retention of title clause) is that the first assumes an immutable debt or obligation for the performance of which the debtor's goods serve as a security. In this sense, ownership is divided, with legal title vested in the mortgagee and the beneficial ownership in the mortgagor who carries the burden of loss or damage, taxation and other costs. In the case of an executory contract of sale, there is no absolute debt—only a *promise* to pay. Nonetheless, it is simplistic to argue that the buyer obtains no interest in the goods, because how is it possible to maintain that the seller has full title in the goods where another has the right to acquire it by acts within his own control? It cannot be the case that the buyer has no rights in the goods before the condition is fulfilled, as this would entail that the seller's right of ownership would remain unrestricted up to the point when the condition is fulfilled, ie payment of the price. This is clearly not the position and in the case of *Stroud Architectural Services Ltd v John Laing Construction Ltd* [1994] 2 BCLC 276, it was held that a retention of title clause which additionally provided for a right of re-entry to recover the goods covered by the clause could not be effected without a notice of termination. Indeed, some of the rights that the buyer acquires have never belonged to the seller in the first place, notably, the cutting-off of the seller's creditors.

What suppliers are effectively striving to achieve is to draft the most advantageous retention of title instrument as far as legal consequence is concerned, namely, a superior, non-registrable security interest. However, s 62(4) of the SGA specifically excludes non-possessory security interests from the ambit of the Act. It reads:

> The provisions of this Act about contracts of sale do not apply to a transaction in the form of a contract of sale which is intended to operate by way of mortgage, pledge, charge or other security.

The difficulties involved in determining the 'true intentions' of the parties anticipated by s 62(4) were demonstrated in *Welsh Development Agency v Export Finance Co Ltd* [1992] BCLC 148, which concerned a company, Parrot Ltd, in which the Welsh Development Agency (WDA) was a principal shareholder. The company, by a debenture dated October 1985, charged its book debts and other property and assets in favour of the WDA. By May 1989, the company was insolvent and the WDA appointed receivers under the debenture.

bankrupt

The WDA claimed that by virtue of its charge, it was entitled to receive payment of all debts owed by overseas buyers in relation to goods exported to them by Parrot. However, the defendant (EXFINCO) claimed that it was entitled to receive payment of all debts on the basis of its agreement with Parrot, namely, that the selling of goods by Parrot was done on the basis of an agency relationship for EXFINCO. The merits of the scheme for EXFINCO were as follows: first, debts due under the contracts to sell goods to overseas buyers would never have been the property of Parrot but would have belonged to EXFINCO as undisclosed principal, so they would therefore not be subject to any prior floating charge over Parrot's debts or property; secondly, such a transaction would be a sale and not a secured borrowing and, as a result, the transaction would involve 'off balance sheet' accounting.

At first instance it was held that the transaction amounted in substance to a charge and was void for non-registration. This judgment was reversed by the Court of Appeal which upheld the arrangement as a genuine agency agreement. This was so despite the fact that the parties had constructed the agreement in such a way as to avoid all contact between the financier and the overseas buyer. Furthermore, the manufacturer's mandate to sell on behalf of the financier was limited to goods that complied with the sale contract, including the statutory implied terms of merchantable quality and fitness for purpose. This ensured that there would be no recourse against the financier for breach of contract. Nevertheless, the Court of Appeal held that an agent's authority to bind an undisclosed principal must have existed when the agent made the contract ostensibly as principal. As a matter of legal form the arrangement was categorised as a sale and not a charge on the debts. As the Privy Council noted in *Chow Yoong Hong v Choong Fah Rubber Manufactory* [1962] AC 209 at 216, 'There are many ways of raising cash besides borrowing. One is by selling book debts . . .'.

Classifying retention of title clauses

It is appropriate to consider the different ways in which retention of title clauses are framed in order to determine their validity on the basis of legal principle and authority. Broadly speaking, there is the primary clause reserving title to goods *in specie* followed by 'horizontal' extensions into debts; there are also 'vertical' extensions which seek to follow the goods supplied into a finished product or its proceeds.

Simple clauses

The seller retains ownership in the goods delivered as against the buyer until the full purchase price for the goods has been paid. The effectiveness of such a clause has been confirmed even in the context of branded goods, as seen in *Accurist Watches Ltd v King* [1992] FSR 80. In this case watches were sold and delivered, subject to a retention of title clause, to a registered user of the trade mark which later became insolvent. The issue before the court was whether the seller in repossessing and reselling the watches bearing the trade mark was infringing the rights of the trade mark owner. It was held that the seller was free to resell the watches and had a good defence under s 4(3)(a) of the Trade Marks Act 1938, namely, that the goods were connected in the course of trade with the registered user who had consented to the use of the mark. Significantly, Millett J pointed out that a contrary conclusion would destroy the value of retention of title clauses because it would deprive the supplier of the ability to sell unsold branded goods under the brand name.

Current account and money clauses

This is where the seller retains ownership in the goods delivered as against the buyer until all debts or other obligations owed by the buyer to the seller have been paid. The imprimatur here is the House of Lords decision in *Armour v Thyssen Edelstahlwerke AG* (1991) which upheld the following clause: 'All goods delivered by us remain our property (goods remaining in our ownership) until all debts owed to us including any balances existing at relevant times— due to us on any legal grounds—are settled'. It was acknowledged by Lord Keith (at 343) that this clause did 'in a sense give the seller security for the unpaid debts of the buyer. But it did so by way of legitimate retention of title not by virtue of any right over his own property conferred by the buyer'.

On the facts the issue of part payment did not arise, and as a matter of principle the clause is vulnerable for the simple reason that the buyer must be treated as the 'owner' of the goods when he has paid for them, otherwise the clause will be void for total failure of consideration. Whilst it is true that the buyer has received possession and use of the goods, the benefit bargained for is obtaining *property* in the goods which is a pre-condition for their sale as the contract mechanism in this context. Even though the clause can be set aside on the basis of total failure of consideration, this does not mean that the clause has no value in the insolvency context because of the requirement in the Insolvency Rules 1987, r 4.90 to set off in liquidation mutual credits, mutual debts or other mutual dealings between the parties. Thus, at the commencement of the winding-up proceedings, the supplier, whilst having to refund the purchase price for total failure of consideration, would have a claim against the buyer for non-payment of other indebtedness and the two claims should be offset against one another.

As a matter of logic, a problem of contractual construction can arise with a current account clause. An example of this phenomenon may be seen in the New Zealand case of *Reese Plastics Ltd v Inseson* (1990) unreported (see [1993] LMCLQ 382), where the clause in question provided as follows: 'Ownerhip in the goods is retained by the Plantiff company until payment is made for the goods and for all other goods supplied by the Company to the customer.' The clause would seem to suggest that where the seller had not been paid for the present goods supplied, title would not pass in the goods it had previously supplied even though they had been paid for. This conclusion was resisted on the facts, which involved a supply of fish crates, because there was no single on-going contract but rather a series of individual or severable contracts. As a matter of principle, the rule must surely be that title should pass when the goods have been paid for. It is significant that in the USA, the Uniform Commercial Code, art 9:107(a), in providing for a purchase money security interest, requires a specific correlation between the collateral in which priority is claimed and the specific obligation relating to that particular item of collateral.

Proceeds clauses

This extends a retention of title clause to the proceeds of resale of the goods supplied. As an equitable tracing right which arises by operation of law this is not registrable as a charge since such a right has not been conferred or created by the debtor company. Furthermore, if the traceable funds are mixed then equity may declare a charge on the mixed fund. The point of principle is whether a fiduciary relationship can be established in relation to the proceeds, which of course depends upon the categorisation of the relationship as one of principal and agent. In England, the general approach has been hostile to such clauses and there has been a reluctance to find for a fiduciary relationship, even where the obligee is under an obligation to separate the proceeds of sales from other moneys and pass on all the rights relating to the sub-sales to the seller. Thus, in *Tatung (UK) Ltd v Galex Telesure ltd* [1989] 5 BCC 325, Phillips J found that despite elaborate contractual provision having been made which effectively fettered the obligee's ability to deal with the proceeds, nevertheless this was categorised as a charge on the basis that the source of the plaintiff's rights was the contract and not equitable principles arising by operation of law. Such an approach does seem odd because it is tantamount to penalising the suppliers for being over-specific which would, if anything, suggest that they were acting as owners in relation to the process—it might have been thought that the fiduciary relationship argument would have been strengthened by these provisions in the contract (see also *Compaq Computer Ltd v Abercorn Group Ltd* [1993] BCLC 602).

A more recent English case tends to confirm the hostility of the English courts to proceeds clauses, because in *Modelboard Ltd v Outer Box Ltd* [1993] BCLC 623, Hart QC sitting as a Deputy High Court judge, held that a clause which provided that the buyers were entitled to resell only as 'agents and bailees', and a term that the proceeds were held 'in trust for the [seller]' was by way of charge. The judge was concerned by the apparent commercial consequences of upholding a proceeds clause, namely, had the buyer resold at a profit then the commercial sense of the arrangement had to be that the supplier after satisfying the outstanding indebtedness would be obliged to account to the buyer for the balance. However, this conclusion need not follow where the obligee is categorised as a commission agent, since the profit margin could be treated by the seller and the buyer as the buyer's agency commission. In large measure, this argument draws upon the approach of Jessel MR in *Re Smith, ex p Bright* [1879] 10 Ch App 566 who held:

> There is nothing to prevent the principal from remunerating the agent by a commission varying according to the amount of the profit obtained by the sale. *A fortiori* there is nothing to prevent his paying a commission depending upon the surplus which the agent can obtain over and above the price which will satisfy the principal . . . (p 570).

In New Zealand the courts have been less hostile to proceeds clauses, and there has been in some measure greater scrutiny of the alleged agency relationship. One example of this is *AM Bisley v Gore Engineering and Retail Sales Ltd* [1984] 2 NZBLC 103 where the plaintiff supplied agricultural equipment to the defendant for the purpose of resale and the retention of title clause provided as follows:

> It is agreed that property in any machinery or equipment covered in this agreement shall not pass until full payment thereof shall have been made, and until said payment shall have been made the dealer shall be bailee only of such goods.

At the time of receivership, the defendant owed $36,000 to the plaintiffs. Holland J found that there was no commission agency here and that the nature of the contract was that the defendant as the buyer was reselling the goods as the owner and passed a good title as of right, so that on sub-sale there was a simultaneous passing of title from the seller to the buyer thereby rendering the proceeds claim untenable. The designation of the buyer as a bailee was ignored by Holland J, on the basis that this was not the parties' intention. Thus, a distinction was drawn between goods sold 'on consignment' versus goods sold for resale. In the former instance, the dealer held the goods as 'fiduciary trustee only' but these words were missing from the retention of title clause. The treatment of these two devices was also differentiated in accounting terms in that goods sold on consignment were not debited until the actual time of resale whereas in the case of the goods sold for resale by the defendant, the plaintiff immediately debited the defendant's current account. The main problem for the plaintiff was that this account was at all material times in overdraft and that the only hope for the plaintiff was to argue that the bank 'knowingly received' funds paid in breach of a fiduciary relationship and was therefore liable as a constructive trustee.

The more recent case of *Peerless Carpets Ltd v Moorhouse Carpets Market Ltd* [1992] 4 NZBLC 102 upheld a proceeds clause in the context of a supply of carpets. The relevant clause provided as follows:

> 4(c) if any of the goods are sold or otherwise disposed of by the Purchaser before ownership and title pass the Purchaser shall hold the proceeds of each sale or disposition upon trust for Peerless and shall be accountable for such proceeds until the purchase price and other moneys owing by the Purchaser to Peerless in respect of the goods have been paid in full.

Serious debt occurred which amounted to over NZ $722,000. The plaintiff sought to recover the identifiable carpet in the defendant's possession (value $17,000) together with an unspecified sum representing proceeds. Despite the fact that there was no express obligation to store the goods separately and no express obligation to deposit proceeds in a separate account, the Court found for a fiduciary relationship on the basis that the defendant was to hold the carpet as 'bailee and agent' as well as hold the proceeds in trust and be accountable for such proceeds. The contemplation of the parties must therefore have been that an agency and fiduciary relationship was intended. The issue of a charge on book debts was dismissed by Williamson J on the basis that there was no creation but rather the clause stated boldly that the proceeds were to be held on trust. This approach would appear to be more broadly in line with that adopted by the Court of Appeal in the *Welsh Development Agency* case.

The commission agency arrangement in the *Romalpa* context would be seriously compromised if it fell within the terms of the Commercial Agents (Council Directive) Regulations 1993 (SI 1993 No 3053). This provides agents who sell by commission with levels of job security and compensation for loss of office comparable to those enjoyed by employees. In addition it imposes obligations upon principals as to payment of commission and also as to compensation at the end of the agency agreement. Such obligations do not reflect the commercial reality in a proceeds clause, and it is noteworthy that the Regulations do not apply to commercial agents dealing with property on their own account. In this respect, the analysis of the arrangement is crucial: there is nothing inconsistent between a proceeds clause and a contract for the sale of goods, because s 25(1) of the SGA 1979 provides that a buyer may 'agree to buy goods' and still pass a good title to a purchaser in good faith and without notice. Moreover, a commission agent does not establish privity between his principal and a third party and this internal agency arrangement is at the heart of Roskill LJ's judgment in *Romalpa*, that is, under the head sale, the seller and buyer could stand in any agency relationship but as between buyer and sub-buyers the buyer sold as a principal:

> I see no difficulty in the contractual concept that, as between the defendants and their sub-purchasers, the defendants sold as principals, but that, as between themselves and the plaintiffs, those goods which they were selling as principals within their implied authority from the plaintiffs view were the plaintiffs' goods which they were selling as agents for the plaintiffs to whom they remained fully accountable (p 690).

Aggregation clauses

This is where an attempt is made to 'retain' title in finished goods incorporating the goods supplied under a reservation of title clause. The obvious policy dilemma here is that of windfall, because the supplier would recover not only the buyer's processing efforts but also any new materials supported by third parties. Indeed, these considerations were alluded to by Robert Goff LJ in *Clough Mill* when he said (at p 119):

> Now it is no doubt true that, where A's material is lawfully used by B to create new goods, whether or not B incorporated other material of his own, property in the new goods will generally rest in B, at least where the goods are not reducible to the original materials (see *Blackstone Commentaries* (17th ed; 1830), vol. 2, pp 404–405).

Parties cannot by their contractual stipulations alone alter the application of the principles and rules of the law of property. It follows that if the supplier qualifies his interest in the finished product in order to avoid an unintentioned windfall for himself, this is tantamount to a security for the debt, that is, the arrangement will be categorised as creating a charge over the new goods. Nevertheless as Robert Golf LJ went on to point out in *Clough Mill*, it is possible for the parties to agree that title should pass in the new goods to the supplier under a retention of title clause. At common law, the assignment of future property is void unless it is completed by some 'new act' when the property later comes into existence and into the ownership of the assignor. The meaning of 'new act' is difficult to determine, although it is clear from *Lunn v Thornton* (1845) 1 CB 379 that seizure by the mortgagee of future goods is not sufficient: the question seems not to be whether there has been some completed act of apropriation by mutual assent from both parties. Even so, it could be maintained that the *Romalpa*-type buyer's separate storing of the finished product and its acknowledgement as belonging to the supplier would be a sufficient appropriation to the contract so as to satisfy the 'new act' doctrine. However, there would be practical difficulties in achieving this undertaking from the buyer, and the application of the 'new act' principle by itself is so uncertain that the courts may be reluctant, in this instance, to admit its possibility, especially since such a conclusion would prejudice other creditors of the buyer.

In general, the case law on retention of title has failed to grapple with aggregation clauses since the emphasis has been upon mixture of goods and the issue of identification which goes to the heart of proprietary claims at common law. The identification issue is usually solved by reference to the requirement in the retention of title clause to store the goods separately, and where this has not been done internal audit procedures become essential. In the Autralian case of *Ralph McKay Ltd v International Harvester Australia Ltd (Receiver and Managers appointed)* (1984) unreported, parts had been supplied to International Harvester for a long period of time on simple retention of title terms. Only some of the spare parts had been paid for, which therefore necessitated identification of the relevant goods. This was achieved only due to the fact that the stock-handling and documentation procedures of International Harvester were so precise that all chattels/stock could be attributed to individual shipments.

In more recent case law the question of continued identification of the goods is linked to the extent of the processing of them. Thus the House of Lords in *Armour* (1991) ignored the fact that steel strip supplied had been cut by the buyers and in a sense processed since it could still be identified as the original goods supplied. Similarly in *New Zealand Forest Products v Pongakawra Sawmill Ltd* (1991) it was held that title to logs supplied on reservation of title terms did not disappear when the logs had been converted by a process of saw-milling in a different form. The issue of windfall to the supplier was dismissed on the basis that title would pass once the price was paid, that is, the plaintiff supplier was not seeking the proceeds of the sawn timber ($300,000) but rather only the sale price of the logs delivered ($267,891). In contrast in the English case of *Modelboard Ltd v Outer Box Ltd* [1993] BCLC 623, it was held that as a result of processing the original cardboard sheets supplied subject to a retention of title clause, the boxes were no longer 'the goods' to which property could be retained, even though the product had not lost its essential physical identity. Clearly value enhancement is not always relevant and in *Modelboard* this was the case because printed cardboard for a dedicated merchant did not add value to the cardboard: in one sense this process diminished the saleability of the finished product elsewhere.

It may be possible to identify a trend in the Commonwealth to the effect that a change in physical properties does not preclude agreement between the parties about joint ownership in the new property. Thus in the New Zealand case of *Ahead Group Ltd v Downer Mining Ltd* (1991) unreported, the defendants supplied 20 loads of crushed metal to the plaintiff building company to resurface its timber yard. When the plaintiff went into receivership it owed in excess of NZ $13,500 to the defendants who, in reliance upon a simple retention of title clause which included a right of entry into the premises and also remove the goods supplied, proceeded to do so. In exercising the self-help remedy locked gates were lifted off their hinges and and an excavator was used to 'scoop' the surface material which included the crushed metal into waiting trucks. The plaintiff intervened after three truck loads were removed and applied for an interim injunction to restrain any further removal of surface material from its premises. In this case Wylie J found for the plaintiffs, basically because the defendant's recovery activities were likely to result in removing some of the plaintiff's material, that is, the original metal or soil and clay from the yard. No provision had been made for co-ownership here and so it was held:

> [T]here [was] an arguable case . . . that there ha[d] been such a degree of mixing that no removal of consequence could be safely effected without there being a risk of the removal of the plaintiff's property. If that be the case then there is an intermixture of property of two persons resulting, as I see it, in the loss of sole right of ownership reserved by the *Romalpa* clause to the defendant and in its place substituting an ownership in common according to the respective contribution of the plaintiff and the defendant . . .

The issue of co-ownership is discussed in greater detail in Chapter 7.

Retention of title clauses and registration of company charges

As we have noted above, a basic distinction is drawn in companies legislation between charges created by a company and charges existing on property which have been acquired by the company in question. Whilst both categories of charges are registrable, there is a significant difference as regards the consequences of non-registration. In the case of a charge which is already subsisting on property that is acquired by the company, non-registration does not lead to invalidation of this charge but merely to the imposition of a fine (Companies Act 1985, s 400(4)). By contrast, non-registration of a charge created by a company leads to avoidance of the charge against certain categories of person, notably insolvency practitioners (Companies Act 1985, s 395(1)). With this distinction in mind, the decision of the House of Lords in *Abbey National Building Society v Cann* [1991] 1 AC 56 is highly significant. In this case a son who had previously received help from his mother in buying a house and in return had been promised by him that she would always have a roof over her head, bought a house for occupation by her and also her eventual husband. The son bought the house with money obtained by means of a mortgage. He subsequently defaulted in payments under the mortgage and the building society sought to repossess the house. The mother and her husband claimed an overriding interest in the house arising by virtue of her occupation in it when the mortgage was created. The House of Lords held that when the son bought with the aid of a mortgage, the acquiring of the legal estate and the granting of the mortgage were one single transaction, that is, there was no *scintilla temporis* during which he held the legal estate free of charge and during which his mother's equitable interest could have attached. As Lord Oliver pointed out (at 92):

> [T]he acquisition of the legal estate and the charge are not precisely simultaneous but indissolubly bound together . . . the land is, from the very inception, charged with the amount of the loan without which it could never have been transferred at all and it was never intended that it should be otherwise.

As a result of this approach, the theoretical basis of the seminal judgment of Slade J in *Re Bond Worth* [1980] Ch 228 would seem to be undermined. In that case it was held that a clause retaining 'equitable and beneficial ownership' in fibre delivered could only mean that there was a sale of the entire property in the fibre to *Bond Worth*, which was then followed *eo instanti* by a security being granted to the original supplier by the (now) owner in the form of a chattel mortgage; that is, there was a *scintilla temporis* when Bond Worth became the owner of the fibre. The significance of the House of Lords decision in *Cann* is that it abolishes the *scintilla temporis* doctrine, so that the goods supplied under a retention of title clause are always impressed by the supplier's equitable and beneficial ownership and this is therefore not a charge 'created' by the company.

If full effect were to be given to the decision of the House of Lords in *Cann* then it could be persuasively argued that retention of title clauses which could be categorized as charges could be upheld against insolvency practitioners, for example, in relation to new products made from material sold. However, there are essential differences, not least in terms of commercial context, between a retention of title clause and a conveyance of land in conjunction with a mortgage. The whole purpose of a retention of title clause is to avoid the categorisation of the transaction as being one for security to which the charges regime relates and the relevant consideration is not the *scintilla temporis* doctrine but whether, in relation to the terms of the contract and the circumstances surrounding the contract, a charge has been created in the sense that property has passed to the buyer. This analysis was adopted in *Stroud Architectural Services Ltd v John Laing Construction Ltd* (1993) unreported, where a clause retaining 'equitable and beneficial ownership' in glazing units was construed by John

Newey J as a charge created by the buyer. Furthermore it was held that no *scintilla temporis* had occurred in *Bond Worth* since in that case Slade J had referred to the sale and charge back as occurring in *eo instanti*. Admittedly such an approach is a rationalisation and in a sense inductive reasoning, but as a matter of principle the general conclusion must be correct, since the commercial reality of (especially) the manufacture of products or their incorporation into finished products with inputs from others must be the creation by the buyer of a charge over what has not become its own finished product. In the context of sale of goods, the source of the security is not exclusively that of the seller as it is, for example, in cases involving mortgages of real estate.

The nature of charges created and proceeds clauses

The Court of Appeal judges in *Clough Mill* (1985) did expressly countenance the possibility of a charge having been created in manufactured products which comprised, in part, goods supplied by the seller. The relevant part of the clause read as follows:

> If any of the material is incorporated in or used as material for other goods before such payment, the property in the whole of such goods shall be and remain with the seller until such payment has been made . . . .

Unfortunately the nature of the charge was not considered. The other existing authorities are divided in this respect so that in *Borden* (1981) both Templeman and Buckley LJJ claimed that a charge over future property was a company bill of sale. This has now been replaced by s 396 of the Companies Act 1985 which states that registration requirements extend to 'a charge on goods or any interest in goods, other than a charge under which the chargee is entitled to possession either of the goods or a document of title to them'. On the other hand, Bridge LJ in *Borden*, as well as Slade J in *Bond Worth* (1980), considered the supplier's interest to be a floating charge. The resolution of this confusion is fundamental as it centres around the ability of a '*Romalpa*-type' buyer to treat the goods as unencumbered.

In *Specialist Plant Services Ltd and Another v Braithwaite Ltd* [1987] BCLC 1, the Court of Appeal considered that an extended clause was void for non-registration under s 395 of the Companies Act 1985, and it was held that the nature of the charge fell within the definition of a 'bill of sale' in s 4 of the Bills of Sale Act 1878. The facts of the case are as follows. The plaintiffs were two firms who carried on a mechanical repair business; a standard term of the contract for repairs was that, if the repairs involved the supply of parts which were incorporated into any article, ownership of that article was held by the plaintiffs as surety for what the customer owed for carrying out the repair. When the defendants went into liquidation and the administrative receivers were in the process of selling various machines which might have incorporated parts supplied by the plaintiffs when they repaired the equipment, the plaintiffs started proceedings claiming £8,800 and applied for an order that the administrative receivers be restrained from disposing of the machines. The question before the

Court of Appeal was whether there was a triable issue involved here sufficient so that the appellate court should interfere with the interlocutory injunction granted by Herod J at first instance. The Court of Appeal did not consider that there was a triable issue on the facts.

The above approach is regrettable since the nature of the charge created is not clearly determined in the case law. Indeed, counsel for the plaintiffs remarked that the charge is 'an animal of not clearly-defined nature' (p 7). In reply to this observation, Balcombe LJ held:

> I must respectfully dissent because it does seem to me that this clause, although by no means happily worded, is quite clearly a clause which creates a charge over the goods into which the items which the plaintiffs have used in the repairs have been incorporated, as security for payment of the costs of the repair. That is a charge which is the equivalent of an unregistered bill of sale. It is void . . . . (p 7)

Unfortunately, this argument fails to take into account one of the main purposes of retention of title clauses which is to allow the buyer freedom to deal with the property as he likes, the business being regarded both by the supplier and the buyer as a 'going concern'. The commercial reality of what the parties intend is to transfer the seller's lien from one bundle of assets, the goods supplied, to another, future property or book debts. This legitimate aim cannot be realised under English law without registration under s 396 of the Companies Act 1985 as a floating charge. Insofar as the Registrar of Companies has refused to register such retention of title clauses as company charges, it is clear, following the decision in *NV Slavenburg's Bank v Intercontinental Natural Resources Ltd* [1980] 1 WLR 1076, that lodging the prescribed particulars is sufficient to ensure validity. The practice of the Registrar of Companies is that *Romalpa* clauses are registered, but the specific nature of the charge is not identified.

The possibility of a retention of title clause constituting a charge over book debts was considered by Phillips J in *E Pfeiffer Weinkellerei-Weineinkauf GmbH and Co v Arbuthnot Factors Ltd* [1988] 1 WLR 150 and *Tatung (UK) Ltd v Galex Telesure Ltd* (1989), 5 BCC 324. In the *Arbuthnot Factors* case, the contract between the plaintiff supplier and Springfield Wine Importers Ltd set out comprehensively the nature of the interest which the plaintiff was to have by way of security in respect of debts created by sub-sales. The retention of title clause was (translated from the original German) as follows:

> All claims that [the importer] gets from the sale . . . with all rights including his profit amounting to his obligations towards [Pfeiffer], will be passed on to [Pfeiffer]. On demand the [importer] is obliged to notify the assignment of the claim to give [Pfeiffer] in writing all necessary information concerning the assertion of [Pfeiffer's] claims . . . . In case of cash sales, the money that has come from a third person immediately becomes [Pfeiffer's] . . . this money has to be separated from other money, it must be booked correspondingly, and must be administered until called for.

Springfield had agreed to assign to the plaintiff the future debts owed by the sub-purchasers to Springfield up to the amount of Springfield's outstanding indebtedness to the plaintiff. Subsequently, Springfield then entered into a factoring agreement with the defendant which amounted to an assignment of the future debts.

The approach taken by Phillips J is interesting in that he held that Springfield was not a bailee or any kind of fiduciary with respect to the plaintiff, and he found that the *Romalpa* case went the way it did because of the defendant's concession that it was a bailee of the plaintiff's goods. The normal implication, Phillips J considered, is that a buyer in possession, to whom title has not yet passed, when permitted to sub-sell in the ordinary course of his business does so for his own account. Such an approach is too extensive. The main objection against an agency relation is that the dealer is permitted to keep the profits on sub-sale. In *Bond Worth* (1980), Slade J cited *Re Nevill ex p White* (1871) 6 Ch App 397 as authority for this proposition. Nonetheless, it is important to recognise that the court in *Ex p White* was concerned with the substance of the relationship between the supplier and dealer. The court considered that, on the facts, the two-month credit period, together with the fact that the dealer was under no duty to account and could sell for whatever price he wished, pointed to a debtor–creditor relationship. Neither should a credit period count against beneficial ownership of the proceeds; the credit allows the dealer to extend a similar period of credit to a subsequent purchaser, although the dealer will have to account as soon as the proceeds are in fact received (compare *Re Andrabell* [1984] 3 All ER 407.

In contrast to the approach taken in the *Arbuthnot Factors* case, in the Irish case of *SA Foundries du Lion MV International Factors (Ireland) Ltd* (1983) ILRM 66, the court found (Barrington J presiding) that the plaintiff supplier had a valid proceeds clause which prevailed over the defendant's factoring arrangement. It is significant that in this priority conflict between a seller/supplier and a purchaser of proceeds, the former prevailed by virtue of the supplier's beneficial interest in the identifiable proceeds. In this respect, there can be no possible application of the rule in *Dearle v Hall* (1828) 3 Russ 1, since there is no competition between assignees of the same debt. The supplier is the equitable owner of the debt. This consideration did not arise in *Arbuthnot Factors* because of the finding that the proceeds clause created a charge by way of security over the book debts which, being unregistered, was void as against the dealer's creditors. However, the rule in *Dearle v Hall* was applied to the competition between the supplier's equitable interest in the proceeds by virtue of the supply contract and the interest of the factoring company under its factoring arrangement with the dealer. It is almost inevitable, through the application of the priority rule in *Dearle v Hall*, that the factor will prevail because factoring companies are geared up to giving notices of assignment which is not as likely to be the case with a supplier of goods subject to a *Romalpa* clause.

An important aspect of Phillips J's judgment in *Arbuthnot Factors* is the conclusion that a charge, by virtue of the proceeds clause, had been created over book debts which was registrable under s 396(*c*)(iii) of the Companies Act 1985 (as amended). The concept of 'book debts' suggests debts (*sed quaere* a single debt) due or to become due to the company in respect of services given, irrespective of whether in fact the debt was entered in the books of the business or not. It would seem that the better view is that 'book debts' refer both to existing and future book debts. Thus, in the leading case of *Independent Automatic Sales Ltd v Knowles and Foster* [1962] 1 WLR 974, Buckley J held:

> That it is competent for anyone to whom book debts may accrue in the future to create an equitable charge upon those book debts which will attach to them as soon as they come into existence is not disputed . . . . That such a charge can accurately be described as a charge on book debts does not appear to me to be open to question . . . . A charge on book debts, present and future, is not an unusual form of security in the commercial world, and it would seem to me strange if such a charge were registrable (as it undoubtedly is) and a charge confined to future book debts were not. I find nothing in the language of s 95 [of the Companies Act 1948] requiring me to read subsection (2)(*e*) in so restricted a way as to confine it to a charge on existing book debts. (p 985)

One further point that emerges from the *Arbuthnot Factors* case which is of considerable commercial significance is the possibility of a fixed charge on book debts. The importer was obliged to separate the proceeds of cash sub-sales from his other moneys and to administer the funds accordingly. These provisions do *prima facie* impose some manner of restriction on dealing with the books debts and the proceeds thereof. In *Siebe Gorman and Co Ltd v Barclays Bank Ltd* [1979] 2 Lloyd's Rep 142, a fixed charge was held to be created where a debenture granted to a bank not only prohibited the company from selling or charging its book debts, but required that they be paid into the company's account with the bank. Since the company was not at liberty to deal with the debts or their proceeds in the ordinary course of business, Slade J in a seminal decision held that each debt as it accrued was the subject of an equitable fixed charge. Of course, the elaborate and restrictive provisions concerning the collection of debts necessarily consequent on a fixed charge, are not going to be commercially acceptable. In this respect, on the facts of *Arbuthnot Factors*, since Springfield was free to assign or charge any book debts arising from sub-sales of the wine, it was unlikely that the requirements for converting a floating charge into a fixed charge had been achieved.

Tracing of fungibles and money

Tracing involves essentially an *in specie* claim to property to which the claimant has no property interest other than that which the right provides, and the property claimed is identifiably linked to the misappropriated property. The concept is restitutionary in the sense that it is premised on the principle of unjust enrichment, the 'unjust' element often being satisfied by the defendant's violation of his fiduciary duties. In the late 19th Century, Anglo–American courts declared that tracing claims reach all fiduciaries (*Re Hallett's Estate* (1880) 13 Ch D 696) who violate their duties, although the types of misappropriation that may give rise to tracing are varied including conversion, fraud, mistake, and where specific performance is available against breaches of contract. Tracing is most useful to a claimant when it provides him with a larger recovery than he would have received through a simple money judgment, for example, against an insolvent wrongdoer, or by allowing him to sue solvent third parties who have traceable property. Moreover, a claimant may trace an asset into the hands of an insolvent defendant when the asset is worth more than the claimant's actual loss.

Attempts have been made to restrict the reaches of the tracing doctrine, as in the case of 'innocent' converters through the Torts (Interference with Goods) Act 1977, and by reference to considerations of 'fairness' as is obvious in the dissenting judgments in *Boardman v Phipps* [1967] 2 AC 46. The arguments are often predicated upon the thesis that the defrauded person's recovery of the increased value of the trust *res* is a windfall. Interestingly, tracing analysis is still applied but this is restricted to the loss incurred. Tracing is essentially a rough doctrine of causation. The assumption is that the defendant has benefited at the claimant's expense, and that the amount of the benefit is the value of the traceable product. By contrast, if tracing is not available the court assumes that a wrongdoer has not benefited beyond receiving the value of the misappropriation. The dilemma of course is that essentially the inequity occasioned to victim one and victim two is the same, but the remedy depends upon the whim of the wrongdoer, ie whether he decided to use the proceeds to 'consume' or to 'invest'. It may be that the victim who cannot trace could maintain that the misappropriation enabled the wrongdoer to free-up and use other funds or assets to purchase a product. At least this approach goes some way to addressing the arbitrariness involved in tracing which overcompensates one victim, but creates distinctions between claimants on, for example, the basis of 'identifiability'.

In *Borden* (1981), Templeman LJ referred to the task before the court as one of: '. . . unearthing the unearthable, tracing the untraceable and calculating the incalculable' (p44). Similarly, Bridge LJ in that case posed the question whether the manufacturer of cattle cake who sells it to a farmer, who in turn feeds it to his cattle, can claim that the cow is a 'mixed fund'? The learned judge maintained that although the doctrine of tracing might apply where a bailee/trustee mixed goods of his bailor/beneficiary with goods of his own, this could not be the case where the mixing was between dissimilar items. If the *Borden* decision is seen as authority for the proposition that the problems in quantifying values and appropriate ratios make it impossible for there to be any tracing into the proceeds of a manufactured article, such a proposition is far too wide.

The tracing rules are not consistent and this can be easily demonstrated in the case of commingled funds. Money is an abstract means of dissolving all kinds of property into mere quantities and can serve as a medium of exchange as well as a store of value. The law of tracing assets may have some interest in these aspects which give money its economic functions and in a sense money might be equated with any fungible thing, for neither of them can be distinguished and earmarked so as to be recovered. Whether money is viewed as an actual object which serves as a medium of exchange or a unit of account by reference to which means of payment are denominated, the problem of fact with regard to identifiability arises.

The true limits of the common law right to trace into proceeds depends upon whether the proceeds are identifiable. The existence of a mixed fund does not necessarily thwart this (see *Lipkin Gorman v Karpnale Ltd* [1991] 2 AC 548). Nevertheless tracing at common law does not provide a supplier with priority on the insolvency of a '*Romalpa*-type' purchaser. This is because the seller's right to account at common law is a personal one only and is an unsecured interest. Moreover, when money is paid into a bank account, the bank's relationship with its customer is simply that of debtor–creditor (*Foley v Hill* (1848) 2 HL Cas 28). This debt, being a chose in action, is intangible and is, therefore, susceptible only to an equitable proprietary claim (*Space Investments v Canadian Imperial Bank* [1986] 1 WLR 1072). The position is different where the bank has not given value for money such as by not promising to repay on demand. In this case, an owner would have a direct claim for the money against the bank by reason of the latter's receipt of it as a tangible asset and not as a chose in action or debt. Furthermore, the common law duty of account will be important in a *Romalpa* situation where a '*Romalpa*-type' purchaser disposes of goods without the authority of the supplier, the payment of the goods being set-off against a previous loan owed by the '*Romalpa*-type' buyer to a sub-purchaser. In this situation, no equitable proprietary remedy is possible since this presumes the existence of a fund and it is difficult to see how a set-off can constitute this. As a matter of policy, the supplier in this instance should prevail (subject to the *nemo dat* exception in s 25(1) of SGA 1979) over the sub-purchaser. The latter should have no greater standing than a general creditor on the insolvency of the '*Romalpa*-type' buyer since he has received property which did not belong to his debtor.

In order for a plaintiff to trace in equity, it must be established that the defendant or a third party is in a fiduciary relationship to the plaintiff. It is anomalous that equity allows the tracing remedy where a fiduciary agent steals goods from his principal, but not where a total stranger steals from the owner. Despite objections to this fiduciary requirement, it still appears to be settled law, although the anomaly is ameliorated by the fact that the class of fiduciaries is very wide. An additional requirement is that the property must be identified. During the course of the 18th and 19th Centuries, equity developed a metaphysical approach to the identification of money. The argument for such a development happened in this way: no principal or beneficiary is interested to recover the very notes or coins which his fiduciary received on his behalf; the beneficiary is only interested in recovering an equivalent amount; if anybody is to be required to identify mixed money, it should be the agent or fiduciary who caused the whole difficulty to begin with. As such, this general approach does not contradict the economic function of money, but equity has employed technical and often irrational rules, such as the rule in *Clayton's* case (*Devaynes v Noble* (1817) 1 Mer 572), which the *Romalpa* clause has tended to highlight.

The Privy Council considered the issue of equitable tracing in *Re Goldcorp Exchange Ltd* [1994] 3 WLR 199. The claimants having failed in their submission that property in the bullion passed to them as an aspect of sale of goods law (see above, pp 124–7), an attempt was made to establish a proprietary claim in the remaining bullion based upon the various collateral promises made by Goldcorp relating to the ownership of the bullion; it was claimed that the bullion was therefore held on trust for the claimants or that Goldcorp was estopped from denying that title had passed to the claimants. In the alternative, it was also argued that title passed when Goldcorp subsequently purchased the bullion (see *Holroyd v Marshall* (1862) 10 HL Cas 191) and also that Goldcorp were fiduciaries or that there should be at least a constructive trust over the bullion which remained in Goldcorp's vaults. These arguments were doomed for the following reasons: first the nature of the relationship between Goldcorp and the claimants was not one by which they promised to create in the claimants an immediate interest in the fund of bullion which would inhibit further dealings in that bullion. As the Privy Council held:

> This is not a situation where the customer engaged the company as agent to purchase bullion on his behalf, with immediate payment to put the agent in funds, delivery being postponed to suit the customer's convenience. The agreement was for a sale by the company to, and not the purchase by the company for, the customer . . . There was nothing . . . which constrained . . . the company's freedom to spend the purchase money as it chose. (pp 218–19).

Neither did it help to label Goldcorp as a fiduciary, since Goldcorp's breach in terms of obligations went to the root of contractual obligations, that is, they had failed to honestly and conscientiously discharge their contractual obligations. No submission 'went beyond suggesting that by virtue of being a fiduciary the company was obliged honestly and conscientiously to do what it had by contract promised to do' (p 216). The estoppel argument was also flawed since the bank as the debenture holder was not privy to any estoppel that may have existed between Goldcorp and the claimants.

Having failed to establish title in the bullion itself an attempt was made to stake a proprietary claim in the money paid to Goldcorp under the contracts for sale. This was based upon the fact that the contracts had been initiated by mistake or misrepresentation or total failure of consideration so that the purchase monies paid could be traced. It was held that whilst the consideration did in the end fail, nonetheless until that time the claimants did enjoy the benefit of what they had bargained for, namely, a contract for the sale of ascertained goods. As for the other claims, all they were indicative of was a breach of contract and no more: whilst the contracts could have been rescinded for misrepresentation or mistake they had not been so in time before the bank's floating charge had crystallized.

In one respect the approach of the Privy Council is odd because whilst claiming that rescission had not taken place in time they pointed out another flaw, namely:

> Upon payment by the customers the purchase monies became, and rescission or no rescission remained, the unencumbered property of the company. What the customers would recover on rescission would not be 'their' money but an equivalent sum . . . [T]hey would have had a personal right to recover the sum equivalent

to the amount paid. But, even if they had chosen to exercise this right, it would not by operation of law have carried with it a proprietary interest. (p 221).

This approach fails to take into account the position in equity where following a false or fraudulent misrepresentation equitable title to the purchase money remained in themselves to support an equitable tracing claim (*Daily v Sydney Stock Exchange* (1986) 160 CLR 317). Of course it may be that the claim would fail because of the limits of tracing in equity, for example, where monies impressed by a trust are paid into an overdrawn account and ceases therefore to exist (see Re *Diplock* [1948] Ch 465).

One category of claimants in *Re Goldcorp*, the 'Walker & Hall' claims, did establish that there had been sufficient appropriation for there to be a shared interest in the pooled bullion because this was kept separate from the vendor's own stock. It was held that when Goldcorp absorbed this separated bullion into its own trading stock it wrongfully dealt with goods which were not its own. The difficulty, however, was that in applying conventional tracing principles of *Roscoe v Winder* [1915] 1 Ch 62, they could recover no more than the lowest balance of metal held by Goldcorp between the accrual of their rights and the commencement of the receivership. Unfortunately this balance was very low, so that an attempt was made to claim an equitable charge over all of Goldcorp's assets based upon the *dicta* of Lord Templeman in *Space Investments Ltd v Canadian Imperial Bank of Commerce Trust Co (Bahaman) Ltd* [1986] 1 WLR 1072. In that case it was held that if a bank trustee unlawfully borrows trust money for its own general purposes, then '[e]quity allows the beneficiaries to trace the trust money to all the assets of the bank to recover the trust money by exercise of an equitable charge over all the assets of the bank'.

In *Re Goldcorp* Lord Mustill (who gave the opinion on behalf of the Board which included Lord Templeman) avoided expressing any concluded view of the correctness of *Space Investments*, nonetheless the *dicta* were restricted in a significant way to cases where there is a 'mixed, not a non-existent fund'. In this way Lord Templeman's *dicta* have been restricted to assets acquired by the trustee after the unlawful borrowing as well as taking into account the restrictions on equitable tracing concerning overdrawn bank accounts. Furthermore, any concept of an equitable lien was rejected on the basis that it would be inequitable for the Walker & Hall claimants to enjoy this as they stood in a very similar position to the other claimants, since they had all received 'certification of ownership' and they were misled into placing their trust in Goldcorp.

The Privy Council resisted turning a breach of obligation into a claim of ownership. It would seem then that the parlous plight of unsecured creditors upon the insolvency of their debtors still remains, as does the policy issue of determining the point at which the equitable *in personam* right crosses over into the *in rem* proprietary right. In Canada the remedial constructive trust doctrine has emerged in this context and in *LAC Minerals Ltd v International Corona Resources Ltd* (1989) 61 DLR (4th) 14, La Forest J regarded the following factors as pointing to a restitutionary proprietary claim:
(a) whether giving the claimant a priority in bankruptcy, or value accrued to the disputed property while in the defendant's name, is 'appropriate';

(b) whether the defendant had intercepted property that the claimant would otherwise have acquired;

(c) the moral quality of the defendant's conduct, ie whether the disputed property was acquired through conscious wrongdoing;

(d) the uniqueness of the disputed property and difficulty in accurately valuing it.

Whilst it is true as the Privy Council stated that 'the doctrine is still in an early stage and no single juristic account of it has been generally agreed' (p 221) it is a pity that the Privy Council did not apply their learning to elaborate upon this phenomenon, especially in the view of developments in other Commonwealth jurisdictions.

Limits of equitable tracing

1. A fiduciary relationship must be established (*Westdeutsche Landesbank Gironzentrale v Islington Borough Council* (1993) *The Times*, 23 February).

2   The position established in retention of title proceeds cases is that a company cannot create a trust of money until it has segregated the money from its own money. In *MacJordan Construction Ltd v Brookmount Erostin Ltd* [1991] 56 BLR 1, Brookmount made interim payments to the plaintiffs in relation to construction work pursuant to an architect's certificate on the understanding that a percentage of this would be set aside in a separate trust account. All in all £109K ought to have been put aside but this had not been done before the defendant went into receivership, although there was about £157K in its bank account at that time. The Court of Appeal could not precisely determine which amount of Brookmount's money should have been set aside on trust for MacJordan so that the latter could not be treated as having an equitable interest in any specific part of the £157K. In this sense therefore the trust failed for uncertainty. Whilst it is true that it could have been argued that MacJordan had an equitable charge for value over the fund, this was not registered as a charge over the book debts and was therefore ineffective against creditors.

In *James Roscoe (Bolton) Ltd v Winder* [1915] 1 Ch 62, where a trustee mixed trust moneys with his own moneys in his general trading account, Sargant J held that when the drawing out of the account had reached such an amount that the whole of the trustee's own contribution had been exhausted, it followed that the rest of the drawings must have been against the trust moneys. If the trust moneys were exhausted or reduced to an intermediate balance before new money was paid in, Sergeant J held:

it is impossible to attribute to him that by the mere payment into the account of further moneys, which to a large extent he subsequently used for purposes of his own, he intended to clothe those moneys with a trust in favour of the plaintiffs.

This rule is at the heart of any form of tracing since this presupposes the existence of some fund. However, in the case of an overdrawn account, there is no longer any surviving property which it would be the object of tracing to identify. In such a case, equity would be as helpless as the common law. There is an additional reason why it is impossible to trace into an overdrawn account, namely that the bank which received the money in reduction of the customer's overdrawn account would normally be a *bona fide* purchaser for value without notice, at least in the absence of notice that the payment into the account was a breach of trust (not just that it was trust money).

The intermediate balance rule has more recently been applied by the Court of Appeal in *Bishopsgate Investment Management Ltd v Homan* [1994] 3 WLR 1270. There the court held that since MCC's accounts, into which pension assets under the management of BIM had been misappropriated, had subsequently become overdrawn, BIM could not trace. As regards a credit balance in MCC's account with Natwest, Dillon LJ said:

But in the absence of clear evidence to make good the depredations on BIM it is not possible to assume that the credit balance has been clothed with a trust in favour of BIM and its beneficiaries. (p 1277)

3. The rule of *Clayton's* case applies if it provides a convenient method of determining competing claims. If it would be impracticable or unjust, because for example, a small number of investors would get most of the funds or if it would be contrary to the express or implied intention of the claimants, it will not be applied so long as a preferable alternative method was available, for example, sharing rateably (see *Barlow Clowes International Ltd v Vaughan* [1992] 4 All ER 22. In this regard, for example the North American method of distribution seen in *The Ontario Securities Commission* (1986) 55 OR (2d) 673 is that each withdrawal from the mixed fund is attributed rateably to all depositors having money in the fund at the time of the withdrawal. This approach would however be impracticable where there are a large number of contributors.

Administration orders and the enforcement of retention of title clauses

The 1986 Insolvency Act envisages the appointment of an administrator as an interim step to save a business. Consistent with this goal, no steps can be taken to enforce a retention of title clause without the consent of either the court or the administrator (s 10(1) of the Insolvency Act 1986). The latter is given the power to dispose of property subject to a retention of title clause so long as one or more of the purposes specified in the administration order is satisfied. The administrative receiver will have to notify all known creditors of the company under s 21(b) of the Insolvency Act 1986, presumably advising them of his appointment and any claim they may have, for example by way of set-off or retention of title clause. Significantly under s 234(4) of the Insolvency Act 1986, personal liability is removed if the administrator, administrative receiver or liquidator *reasonably* believes and is not negligent that the goods belong to the insolvent company. Under this scenario, fault must be proven and this requires a higher standard of proof than that required for conversion, as seen in *Clough Mill v Martin* (1985). The supplier is in an invidious position because he will have to prove that his goods were on the premises at the time of the receivership. Moreover, even if the administrator or administrative receiver disposes of the goods negligently, s 234(4)(*b*) of the 1986 Act anticipates that he can retain a lien on the proceeds of disposal for his own expenses.

Neither the White Paper (*A Revised Framework for Insolvency Law* Cmnd 9175 (1984)) nor the 1985 and 1986 Insolvency Acts gave a discussion on reservation of title clauses, presumably because the approach of the Cork Committee on Insolvency Proceedings was deemed to resolve the matter. The Cork Committee recommended a moratorium of 12 months from the commencement of a receivership with regard to the benefit of enforcing a reservation of title clause (para 1650). Although bankruptcy proceedings promote the collective will, it is doubtful whether the repossession of collateral by the secured creditor should interfere with this bankruptcy goal, since if the secured party's collateral is worth more to the firm than to the third party, that collateral should end up back in the hands of the firm notwithstanding its repossession by the secured creditor in the interim. In practice though, there is no doubt that such repossession would hinder efforts to preserve the firm as a 'going concern', and there may be substantial costs involved in repossession and the subsequent repurchase. One way of balancing the tensions here is to substitute for a secured party actual substantive *rights*, a requirement that the secured creditor accept the equivalent *value* of those rights. There is nothing anomalous in this approach because if the firm is worth more as a going concern than if it is broken up, giving the secured creditor the benefit of his bargain should not prevent a firm from staying together. Indeed, a failure to recognise the secured creditor's rights in full would prejudice the bankruptcy goal of ensuring that the assets are used to advance the interests of everyone.

The above considerations are reflected in ss 10(1) and 11(3) of the Insolvency Act 1986. These sections provide for a statutory freeze procedure on the enforcement of real and personal rights against the company pending the hearing of a petition for an administration order and during the currency of any order that is made. The implication here is that there is nothing to prevent the seller terminating the agreement, but he cannot repossess the goods. This stems from the role of the administrator as the official corporate rescuer. One way of avoiding this conclusion is to provide in the contract of sale that payment should be made by the buyer not to the seller but to an associated company; in this way it would not come within the definition of a retention of title clause under s 251 of the Insolvency Act 1986, which anticipates a stipulation for payment to the seller. It is worth noting that Pt II of the Insolvency Act 1986 does not extinguish entitlements; it merely restricts enforcement to a substantial extent while the order remains in force. This was emphasised in the Practice Guidelines (Insolvency Administration) issued by the Court of Appeal following its decision in *Re Atlantic Computers* [1992] Ch 505. Leave to object to the moratorium sought by the administrator may be granted where it would cause significant loss to the applicant. In its assessment of this, the court would have regard to such matters as the company's financial position, the administrator's proposals, the period during which the administration order had been in force and was expected to remain in force, the effect on the administration if leave were given and upon the applicant if it were refused and lastly, the end result sought to be achieved by the administration with the prospects of it being achieved. However, at the same time s 27 of the 1986 Act provides that any creditor or member can apply to the court for relief on the grounds that the company's affairs, business or property are being, or will be, managed by the administrator in a manner unfairly prejudicial to the interests of some part of the members or creditors. In this event, the court may under s 27(4) discharge the administration order. Thus it would appear prudent for the administrator, when using the goods, to pay at least the use value of the goods. This action will prevent an application to the court by the seller on the ground of prejudice under s 27 of the Insolvency Act 1986. Even so in *Re Charnley Davies Ltd (No 2)* [1990] BCLC 760 it was held that a sale at a negligent undervalue was not sufficient without more to establish a claim for relief under s 27. In this respect Millet J held that whilst professional negligence would amount to misconduct this would not necessarily evidence unfairly prejudicial management in the light of the need to have proper regard for the interests of all the creditors.

One of the most important features of the Insolvency Act 1986 is s 15. What is anticipated here is that the administrator can dispose of the goods in the company's possession which are held on retention of title as if they were unencumbered by the company. This is achieved by applying for a court order to authorise disposal, and the court in making the order has to be satisfied that one or more of the purposes specified in the administration order will be satisfied. The purposes for which the order can be made are found in s 8 (see *Re Primlaks (UK)* [1984] BCLC 734). In this event, suppliers of goods under effective retention of title clauses will receive either the net proceeds of the sale, or if they are determined by the court to be less than the market value of the goods, sums will be provided to make up the market value by virtue of s 15(5)(*b*). Nevertheless, there are important limitations here. First, the court is under no obligation to view invoice value at the time of supply as 'market value' at the time of disposal. Secondly, there is no mechanism by which a supplier of goods on retention of title can object to disposal. In contrast, in the case of administrative receivership, although s 43 of the Act gives similar powers to those enjoyed by the administrator it would seem that retention of title clauses are excluded. This is because s 43 refers to the disposal of property which is subject to 'security' and this is defined as 'any mortgage, charge, lien or other security' (s 248(*b*)). Clearly, the reference here is to conventional security devices. Following on from this, it would seem that the validity of a retention of title clause has still to be determined. Thus, if the administrative receiver disputes the validity of the claim, the price of the goods will be paid into a joint deposit account, a practice which exactly mirrors the position of receiverships before the advent of the 1986 Act.

It is interesting that the approach taken under the 1986 Act concentrates upon economic substance rather than legal form. Consequently, the moratorium provisions discussed above extend to hire purchase agreements, chattel leasing arrangements (bailment of goods capable of subsisting for more than three months) and a retention of title clause. Strangely, the definition proffered for retention of title clause would have extended to all three credit instruments, viz an agreement for the sale of goods which does not constitute a charge on the goods but under which, if the seller is not paid and the company is wound up, the seller will have priority over all other creditors as respects the goods or any property representing the goods (s 251 of the Insolvency Act 1986). Here we find echoes of the accountant's approach to retention of title clauses. Soon after the *Romalpa* decision (1976), the Institute of Chartered Accountants in England and Wales recommended that the commercial reality of the situation should be accommodated in the accounts, ie it should be treated as a sale since this is the intention of both buyer and seller (see 'Accounting for Goods Sold Subject to Reservation of Title', *Institute of Chartered Accountants in England and Wales*, Statement V24, now Statement 2.207). The position is that provided a business shows all the signs of remaining a 'going concern', the sale of goods subject to reservation of title should be treated in the accounts of both the buyer and the seller in the same manner as an outright sale.

Drafting considerations with retention of title clauses

There exists a fine line between what is commercially acceptable and what is legally necessary in order to ensure priority. A retention of title clause, if it is not to be attacked on the basis of sham should provide the following:

(1) The possessor of the goods should be described as a commission agent in the case where resale of goods *in specie* is anticipated. Where this is not the case, the possessor should be described as a fiduciary bailee and agent.

(2) On resale, the commission agent should be described as selling as principal. There is no conceptual obstacle in viewing the agent as being both principal under the contract and at the same time as agent of the (undisclosed) principal in conveying the latter's title to the sub-buyer. Such an approach is consistent with relativity of title under sales law whereby the agent confers his own title on the buyer and also contracts to pass the principal's property to the third party (see Chapter 7).

(3) There should be an express obligation to account for all proceeds relating to the goods supplied, including insurance proceeds. Moreover, there should be included an obligation to keep the proceeds separate and identifiable.

(4) There should be an obligation to store the goods supplied in a proper fashion and that warehousing arrangements should ensure that the

goods are identifiable. Risk should be described as having passed whilst an obligation to insure should at the same time be imposed. Ancillary rights should also be incorporated, for example, a right of access to ensure against the charge of trespass. Such a right of entry should be associated with specific contractual contingencies, the most important being non-payment. Additionally, there should be a provision giving the supplier a right of removal. The problems associated here will be discussed in the next chapter in the context of finance leasing.

(5) In the case of fungible goods which are mixed with others, tenancy in common provisions should be incorporated (see Chapter 7).

(6) Where the possessor works through the application of labour or commingling in relation to the goods supplied, in order to avoid the possibility of a registrable charge, the nature of the relationship should be described in bailment for commodity processing terms (see especially pp 148–9 above).

Chapter 12

Equipment Leasing and Contracts of Hire

The essence of a lease, whether of goods or land, is to allow the lessee to acquire possession and use without paying the full capital cost. At the same time, the lessor can receive a return on its (in the case of a company) investment while retaining the title and security in the goods or land. The leasing of business and industrial equipment has become a popular and viable alternative to other methods of financing capital acquisition. In this respect, the volume of leasing business is increasing so that, for example, in 1983 new plant and equipment leased by members of the Finance Leasing Association, the national association for UK equipment lessors, totalled £2,894 million accounting for 12.9 per cent of fixed capital expenditure by British industry. By 1994, the value of leasing business exceeded £7,677 million accounting for 15.8 per cent of all fixed investment in plant and machinery in Britain. The leasing industry is wide-ranging encompassing 'big ticket' equipment leasing deals of aircraft engines for periods in excess of ten years, whilst a different lease or hire form will regulate the common phenomenon of car hire daily rental.

Problems of definition

The finance lease is one where the primary period rentals are sufficient for the lessor to recover the cost of the equipment, financing costs and overhead expenses, and also to earn a return on the investment in the lease. In contrast, the operating lease, as the standard contract of hire of plant and machinery, anticipates that the hirer rents the equipment for a period which is less than its useful life and for hire payments totalling less than the purchase cost of the item. Reliance is therefore placed on the realisation of a residual value on disposal or re-leasing of the equipment. Although the distinction between a finance lease and an operating lease is relatively easy to draw in abstract, it sometimes becomes blurred as, for example, in the case of a lease of a computer for a five-year primary period but which can be returned or traded in at any time subject to a minimum payment clause, and which will probably be released to another lessee on termination.

The distinction between the two different types of lease is often characterised as one of a conflict between a 'true' or operating lease, and a 'security' or finance lease. This reference to a finance lease is concerned with the ostensible ownership problem where there is a separation of ownership and possession. The argument here is that a person wishing to take a non-possessory property interest should bear the burden of 'curing' the ostensible ownership problem through a notice mechanism. In a dynamic commercial setting it may not be sensible to try and distinguish between a sale and a finance lease. However, insofar as a distinction is made, much will depend upon the attitude of the lessee. If he sees leasing as an alternative to buying the property, this will tend towards the finance lease, whereas an operating lease will arise when the lessee does not consider buying the property as a viable alternative.

Under the finance lease both the lessor and the lessee enjoy the 'benefits' and 'burdens' of ownership. Here the lessee will enjoy 95–99 per cent of the residual value of the *res* at the end of the lease term but will not enjoy an option to purchase, at least in the UK, since the lessee is still essentially selling its own tax depreciation to the lessor. At the same time, the lessor is exposed to both benefits and burdens because the term itself involves a risk, for example, if rental terms diminish or increase. This is particularly pertinent in the case of longterm leases (over five years) where the residual value at the end is small. Even if the lessor can retain the surplus realised by resale of the asset at the end of the lease term, it is obvious that because the opportunity and risk associated with the *res* can be separated from those associated with the use or possession of the goods, this would suggest that there is no tenable distinction between a lease and a security interest.

It is important to adopt a balanced approach. A distinction can be drawn between leases and conditional sales which represent a security interest, in particular where the leases are of short duration which do not contemplate the ultimate acquisition of the goods by the lessee. In this context, application to the true lease of the remedies traditionally associated with the conditional sale would do violence to the contract rights of the parties.

In many periodic payment transactions, it is difficult to determine which part, if any, of the total payments is 'principal' and which is interest. This demonstrates the difficulty of distinguishing between a lease/conditional sale/hire purchase transaction and sale. It could be argued that market conditions and other factors may prompt the transferee to agree to pay an amount equivalent to the value of the goods without the expectation of becoming owner. This approach is exceptional and it must be that the rental price will constitute a strong indication of the *nature* of the financing arrangement.

The English Accounting Approach seen in the Statements of Standard Accounting Practice SSAP 21, *Accounting for Leases and Hire Purchase Conracts*, distinguishes between finance leases and operating leases. A finance lease is one which transfers substantially all the risks and rewards of ownership of an asset to the lessee. There is a rebuttable presumption that such a transfer occurs when the present value of the minimum lease payments amounts to 90 per cent or more of the fair value of the asset. All other leases are operating leases. Hire purchase contracts are divided in a similar way to leases, ie between finance and operating contracts. In the case of a hire purchase transaction which is financial in character, the asset is depreciated over its useful life.

This recognises the economic reality of the transaction, notably that the hirer has, in effect, 'bought' the asset even though legally the title will only be transferred if the hirer exercises the option. For 'non-financial' hire purchase contracts, the treatment adopted is similar to that for operating leasing. The justification for this is that the exercise of the option is not regarded as automatic as it would be under a hire purchase finance contract.

Legal problems associated with finance leasing

In recent years the finance lease has been recognised as constituting a unique and asset-based financing device. Indeed even at the private international law level UNIDROIT, which has worked on the subject since 1974, recognises in its Leasing Rules the *sui generis* characteristic of the finance leasing transaction. The Rules attempt to reflect the economic reality of the transaction, as evidenced by the parties in their respective contracts, so as to facilitate the removal of certain legal impediments to the international financial leasing of equipment (see the Convention adopted on 28 May 1988, UNIDROIT News Bulletin 1988 N75/76). In a similar vein, art 2A to the American Uniform Commercial Code (UCC) recognises a finance lease as a unique kind of lease which is defined as follows:

> Finance lease means a lease in which (i) the lessor does not select, manufacture or supply the goods, (ii) the lessor acquires the goods or the right to possession and use of the goods in connection with the lease, and (iii) either the lessee receives a copy of the contract evidencing the lessor's purchase of the goods on or before signing the lease contract, or the lessee's approval of the contract evidencing the lessor's purchase of the goods is a condition to effectiveness of the lease contract.

A finance lease is unique because of the control that the lessee exercises in the selection, acquisition by the lessor, and approval of the equipment subject to the lease. We shall firstly consider the legal problems associated with the asset delivered to the lessee and then shall examine the remedies available to the lessor following the lessee's default.

Novation

Essentially, the ideal leasing arrangement involves the passing of property in machinery or plant to the lessor who, after taking delivery of the equipment, delivers it to the lessee pursuant to the terms of the lease. Of course, this presupposes that the lessee contemplated right from the very beginning that he intended to arrange for equipment to be acquired by a particular lessor according to terms and conditions mutually satisfactory for them. Inevitably, there will be instances where an order for equipment has been placed with a supplier by a potential lessee before entering into the lease arrangement. This will prove problematic for the finance lessor because property may have passed, and in order to qualify for tax allowances, the lessor must acquire title to new and unused equipment.

In order to circumvent the above problem, the finance lessor can, by means of a novation, substitute for the obligation of the original obligor (the lessee) a new contract by which in consideration of the supplier releasing the lessee from his obligation, the lessor agrees to assume responsibility for its performance. By virtue of the novation, the finance lessor will acquire title to new and unused equipment and qualify for tax allowances. Nevertheless, it will be necessary for the lessor and supplier to contract on the same terms with the lessor paying the cost of the equipment. Any similar sums already paid by the lessee will have to be returned which will show that the debt between the lessee and supplier has been extinguished, so providing consideration for the arrangement. It would follow that any exclusion clause governing the first agreement, for example, relating to the satisfactory quality provision, should be included in the novation if it is not to fail for absence of consideration.

Finance leasing and statutory implied terms

Due to the interrelated nature of the finance leasing transaction, it is clear that any breach of the supply agreement between the supplier and the lessor will ultimately affect the lessee who has chosen the equipment and has contracted for its use and possession. In many cases, it may be that a breach of the supply agreement by the supplier will in turn result in a breach of the leasing agreement as well. Inevitably the question arises as to whether the lessor, as primarily a financier, should be responsible for any defects?

The English position with regard to contracts of hire has been clarified in the SGSA 1982 (see Chapter 5). In particular, s 8 of that Act provides that goods under hire should correspond with description or sample and is analogous with the SGA 1979 in this respect. More difficult problems arise in relation to fitness for purpose and satisfactory quality. The common law did refer to the owner being under an obligation to hire out goods of a reasonable fitness, and quality or 'merchantibility' was included as part of this obligation. The appropriateness of this analysis is open to question in the context of finance leasing, as distinct from consumer hire or operating leases where the element of reliance can be great, and it may be necessary to highlight the distinction between satisfactory quality and fitness for a particular purpose. It is not unjust to expect the finance lessor to accept some responsibility for the quality of the goods supplied since the lessor has chosen the particular lease form as a financing venture. However, the fact that the hirer has inspected the chattel beforehand may be relevant in indicating that the agreement was to hire the chattel subject to all the defects and characteristics that were evident upon an inspection of the kind that had been made. No liability is envisaged against the finance lessor as far as the obligation to supply goods for a particular purpose is concerned where it is clear that the hirer had not relied, or that it was unreasonable for him to rely, on the owner's skill or judgment. It is for this reason that s 46(2) of the Consumer Protection Act 1987 deems that leasing and hire purchase companies are not categorised as suppliers for the purposes of that legislation.

In one important respect, the SGSA goes very far in the sense that s 9(4)(*b*) provides that:

. . . if a bailee expressly or by implication, makes known . . . to a credit-broker in the course of negotiations conducted by that broker in relation to goods sold by him to the bailor before forming the subject matter of the contract, any particular purpose for which the goods are being bailed [the bailor] is deemed to have knowledge of the purpose for which the goods are sought by the lessee.

Such a liability seems inappropriate as between commercial concerns bargaining at arm's length since it distorts the leasing transaction, and the finance lessor would be forced to shift its cost of insurance onto the lessee, thereby increasing the cost of leasing to him. This is recognised under s 9(6) of SGSA 1982. In any case, it is probable that this cost could be avoided through the provision of an exclusion clause expressly providing for this contingency. There is no reason why such a clause would be struck down as unreasonable or unfair because leasing contracts are notoriously flexible and may be modified to cover any particular asset or lessee's conditions. Furthermore, where there are many leasing companies, as well as other means of raising finance, it would appear that at least the guidelines for the application of the reasonableness test under Sched 2 of UCTA 1977 are satisfied.

Even if an extreme approach is taken in regard to freedom of contract analysis with finance leasing, there is no doubt that an essential aspect of the finance leasing transaction is quiet possession. This is reflected in s 7 of SGSA 1982 where the lessor impliedly warrants that the hirer will enjoy uninterrupted use and enjoyment of the goods for the period of the hire. This may prove problematical for a sub-lessee where the intermediary lessor (the finance lessee) had no right to sub-lease the goods. Use of the goods by the sub-lessee might amount to conversion. If the action is brought by the finance lessor after the subsidiary hiring term expired, it will be difficult to establish that such action creates an incursion upon the subsidiary hirer's quiet possession.

Contractual privity and finance leasing

The tripartite nature of the finance lease transaction introduces complex legal problems. The financing lessor is the intermediary who concludes a contract with the client and another contract with the supplier; it would seem that no contract is directly created between the client and the supplier. It cannot be that the supplier and client are total strangers since the object of the contract is for the use of the client and, in any case, it may be that the supplier was chosen by the client who laid down detailed specifications for the object sold. The interrelated nature of the contracts make it impossible to treat each contract separately or to view the contracts as one transaction between the supplier and the lessee. Treating the transaction as two independent contracts permits the supplier and the lessor to modify the supply agreement without notifying the lessee. Since the finance lessee will have negotiated the technical aspects of the supply agreement and will ultimately use the goods and be directly affected by their specifications, no changes should be made without the lessee's consent. This consent requirement flows from the principle that neither the lessee nor the lessor should act to jeopardise the rights of the other. Consequently, if the lessee sues the supplier directly for breach of the supply agreement, the supplier cannot raise the defence that the lessor modified the supply contract, making the lessee's sole recourse against the lessor.

Most lease domestic transactions are structured to minimise the privity problem posed in a finance leasing context. Thus, the lease agreement may assign to the lessee those warranties created in the supply agreement. However, this will not give the lessee adequate protection since it does not address those warranties given to the lessee in the supplier–lessee negotiations. Nonetheless, any such guarantee made by the supplier to the lessee during negotiations could be construed as an express warranty which will bind the supplier under a collateral contract, the consideration for which being the lessee entering into the main agreement (see *Shanklin Pier Ltd v Detel Products Ltd* [1951] 2 KB 854). The lessee, as the assignee of the warranties, may be limited to damages suffered by the lessor due to the supplier's breach rather than recovering for its own damages. The difficulty here is that the interests of the lessor and the lessee are not the same, nor are the damages suffered by each. In the case of a delay in delivery when payment is conditional upon delivery, the loss or damage to the lessor may be minimal. On the other hand, the lessee may have suffered huge consequential losses. The question is not one of transferring rights from the lessor to the lessee, but of giving the lessee an independent cause of action against the supplier. Significantly, in the absence of agreement, some US courts have allowed a direct action against the supplier on the basis of the latter's strict liability, the lessor bring regarded as merely performing a financing function (see *Citicorp Leasing Inc v Allied Inst'l Distribs Inc* (1977) 454 F Supp 511; *Atlas Indus v Nat'l Cash Register Co* (1975) 216 Kan 213).

In England, it is unlikely that the identity of object and the connection in fact between the lessee and the supplier will triumph over the principle of contractual privity. The privity doctrine is still entrenched and is applied, albeit reluctantly, by the courts as seen in Lord Scarman's approach in *Woodar Investment Development v Wimpey Construction (UK)* [1980] 1 WLR 277 (AC) at p 300:

> I respectfully agree with Lord Reid that the denial by English Law of a *jus quaesitum tertio* calls for reconsideration . . . If the opportunity arises, I hope the House will reconsider *Tweddle v Atkinson* and the other cases which stand guard over the unjust rule.

Many of the arguments used to justify privity are especially spurious in the finance leasing context. In this respect, privity is sometimes justified on the basis that the promisor would otherwise be subject to a double performance liability. This is not problematic in finance leasing because there is only *one* promise and once it is enforced by the promisee or the third party the promisor will have realised his liability. It is sometimes argued that third party intervention would inhibit or disallow the original parties from varying or rescinding their contract, but what is objectionable in this if this is indeed what the original parties bargained for? Furthermore, there is nothing gratuitous about the position of the third party since the lessor in the finance lease will have paid for the promise, and the lessee will have relied upon this by entering into the lease contract. The Law Commission's Consultation Paper, *Privity of Contracts: Contracts for the Benefit of Third Parties* (1991) Law Com No 121, at para 6.3 provisionally recommended a legislative initiative enabling a third party to sue on a contract made for his benefit where it is the intention of the contracting parties that he be given enforceable rights. The implementation of this recommendation would allow the finance lessee to sue upon the supply contract.

Remedies under lease and hire contracts

The law may not be satisfactory from the finance lessor's point of view since the case law turns on two unrelated principles of law: a lease of chattels is analogous to the lease of real property and therefore attracts some of the principles of landlord and tenant; and the rule against penalties developed in contract law applies.

Remedies available to the lessor while keeping the lease on foot

There is no doubt that the lessor may, upon default, leave the equipment in the possession of the lessee and recover the rental payment as it falls due. In addition, damages will be available for a specific breach of the contract such as a failure to insure the equipment or maintain it. At least two other approaches are available to the finance lessor.

Acceleration clauses

The lease contract may provide for rental payments being called up in full upon the lessee's default. Sometimes, the agreement will provide for automatic acceleration of liability on the occurrence of stated events. Such an approach is likely to prove inflexible in practice so creditors will often take powers to accelerate indebtedness on default only after notice has been given to the lessee. Where there is a 'true' lease, such a clause can be considered foreign to the lessor/lessee relationship because, unlike a defaulting buyer or borrower, a lessee is generally not obligated under the rules of damages to pay a specific predetermined sum to the lessor. Although the lessor will be entitled to damages for breach of contract, there is no certainty that those damages will be assessed to be the equivalent of all rental payments owing under the lease (discounted for early payment and also realisation of the chattel).

Under a finance lease where the lessor has no interest in the return of the asset, an acceleration clause is not foreign to the lease transaction. Indeed, an acceleration clause can be considered a natural and necessary part of the financing aspect of the transaction. It is obvious, in this circumstance, that the lessee is contractually obligated to make rental payments equivalent to the instalment purchase price of the chattel. The term of the lease dealing with default will provide for acceleration of all unpaid lease payments since it is the only way to guarantee the lessor recovery of his capital and a return on its investment. No question of penalty can arise in a contract where there is a stipulation that the entire rent be immediately due but the lessor agrees to accept payment of it by instalments, *debitum in praesenti solvendum in futuro*. Nevertheless, two Australian cases have demonstrated the difficulty of drafting such a clause (see *O'Dea v Allstates Leasing Systems (WA) Pty Ltd* (1983) 57 ALJR 172; *Amev-UDC Finance Ltd (formerly United Dominions Corp Ltd) v Austin and Anr* (1986) 60 ALJR 74). It has been held that an entitlement to this rent is fundamentally inconsistent with an early right to repossession on the basis that entitlement to the entire rent is consistent only with an affirmation of the contract of hire, whereas, entitlement to repossession is consistent only with its termination. Following on from this, there is no doubt that where the acceleration clause is combined with a right of repossession this will invite scrutiny on the basis of the court's jurisdiction to grant a hirer equitable relief from forfeiture.

Before a court will grant relief from forfeiture there would have to be a concession that rentals made were, in the case of hire purchase, payments on account of the purchase price and that therefore there had been a partial failure of consideration. In *Stockloser v Johnson* [1954] 1 QB 476, Denning LJ pointed out that there were two main criteria for the application of equitable relief. Firstly, the forfeiture clause had to be penal in nature and secondly, that it was unconscionable for the seller to retain the money (see *Goker v NWS Bank* (1990) TLR 393). There has been statutory interference in relation to regulated consumer credit agreements (see Chapter 2) so that s 132(1) of CCA 1974 provides:

> Where the owner under a regulated consumer hire agreement recovers possession of goods to which the agreement relates otherwise than by action, the hirer may apply to the court for an order that—
> (a) the whole or part of any sum paid by the hirer to the owner in respect of the goods shall be repaid, and
> (b) the obligation to pay the whole or part of any sum owed by the hirer to the owner in respect of the goods shall cease,
> and if it appears to the court just to do so, having regard to the extent of the enjoyment of the goods by the hirer, the court shall grant the application in full or in part.

Similar powers are also conferred on the court in the case of where an owner brings an action for repossession as distinct from recapture of the goods (s 132(2) of CCA 1974).

An acceleration clause in the case of a regulated consumer credit agreement is not considered void as being a restriction on the statutory right of the debtor to terminate the contract (see *Wadham Stringer Finance Ltd v Meaney* [1981] 1 WLR 39). This is because the sum payable under such a clause may be considered a 'final payment' for the purposes of s 99(1) of CCA 1974 which states:

> At any time before the final payment by the debtor under a regulated hire purchase or regulated conditional sale agreement falls due, the debtor shall be entitled to terminate the agreement by giving notice to any person entitled or authorised to receive the sums payable under the agreement.

It should be noted that under a regulated consumer credit agreement, s 93 of CCA 1974 protects the debtor against default interest, ie an increase in the rate of interest on default, and he is also granted the benefit of a seven-day notice period (ss 76(1)(*a*) and 87(1)(*b*) of CCA 1974).

Sub-leasing

Where the lessee has defaulted in his agreement with the lessor, in an attempt to sustain the lease and also to fulfil the duty imposed by the law of contract to mitigate the loss, the lessor may act as agent of the lessee and assign or sub-lease the equipment. Such an act by the finance lessor may be regarded as inconsistent with the continued existence of the lease, thereby releasing the lessee from his obligations under it and leaving the finance lessor with recovery only for breaches occurring before the date of release (see *Total Oil Great Britain Ltd v Thompson Garages (Biggin Hill) Ltd* [1972] 1 QB 318). However in *Highway Properties Ltd v Kelly Douglas and Co Ltd* (1971) 17 DLR (3d) 710, the Supreme Court of Canada showed that as dealings in commercial property developed, maintaining a theoretically pure approach to leases as executed contracts conflict with practical reality because once the tenant abandons the premises, the landlord can very easily resume possession and mitigate the losses. As Laskin CJ held:

> It is no longer sensible to pretend that a commercial lease, such as the one before this court, is simply a conveyance and not also a contract. It is equally untenable to persist in denying resort to the full armoury of remedies ordinarily available to redress repudiation of covenants, merely because the covenants may be associated with an estate in land. Finally, there is merit here as in other situations in avoiding multiplicity of actions that may otherwise be a concomitant of insistence that a landlord engage in instalment litigation against a repudiating tenant. (p 721)

This judgment represents Laskin CJ's attempt to bring property concepts into line with contract principles (see also *Progressive Mailing House Pty Ltd v Tabali Pty Ltd* (1985) 57 ALR 609). Such a reconciliation is both fairer and more efficient for society in the sense that a productive use will be made of the property, promoting activity and minimising waste. In repudiating the purported distinction between damages for breach of leases and damages for breach of other contracts, the *Highway Properties* case echoed the sentiments expressed in an American legal commentary written within the first quarter of the 20th Century ((1924–5) 23 Mich LR 211 at pp 221–2):

> Long after the realities of feudal tenure have vanished and a new system based upon a theory of contractual obligation has in general taken its place, the old theory of obligations springing from the relation of lord and tenant survives. The courts have neglected the caution of Mr. Justice Holmes, 'that continuity with the past is only a necessity and not a duty'. If one turns from a decision upon the conditions implied upon a contract for the sale of goods in instalments to one upon the obligation of the parties to a lease, one changes from the terms and ideas of the 20th century to those of the 16th. The notion of 'privity of estate' and its attendant rights and duties appears as quaint and startling as a modern infantryman with a crossbow.

If this approach were adopted in the context of finance leasing, the lessor's contractual rights under the lease would be protected. Consequently, a claim for any loss resulting from the sub-letting such as the difference in the rent received could be recovered.

Remedies available where the lease is not kept on foot

Self-help

The possibility of repossession of the equipment by the lessor is predicated upon the idea that the equipment is worth more than the costs involved with repossession. It may be possible for the finance lessor to insure against depreciation in the residual value of the equipment at the end of the lease term. Often the equipment will be unique and not easily marketable so that, for example, a lessor may have difficulty in recovering the cost of his investment in a film by seizing it if the film suffers at the box office. Therefore, as a matter of prudence the lessor should institute a thorough credit check on every prospective lessee. In this respect, sophisticated computer programs have been devised which assess such factors as the financial soundness of the lessee, the type of equipment to be leased, and the conditions of the leasing contract. Additionally, the lessor should monitor the lessee's creditworthiness throughout the term of the lease so that problems can be identified and acted upon as soon as possible.

Following a failure by the hirer or lessee to return the goods after a request by the owner, the latter is entitled to use reasonable force to recover the goods. Of course, the question of what constitutes reasonable force is a matter of degree so that if unreasonable force is used, this will amount to an assault (*Dyer v Munday* [1895] 1 QB 742). Moreover, there is the criminal offence of unlawful harassment of debtors encapsulated in s 40(1) of the Administration of Justice Act 1970 which provides:

> (1) A person commits an offence if, with the object of coercing another person to pay money claimed from the other as debt due under a contract, he—
>   (a) harasses the other with demands for payment such, in respect of their frequency or the manner or occasion of making any such demand, or of any threat or publicity by which any demand is accompanied, are calculated to subject him or members of his family or household to alarm, distress or humiliation.

The Act is notoriously imprecise in scope. It provides a defence for anything done by a person which is reasonable for the following purposes under s 40(3)(*a*): 'of securing the discharge of an obligation due, or believed by him to be due, to himself or to persons for whom he acts, or protecting himself or them from future loss;' or, under s 40(3)(*b*) 'of the enforcement of any liability by legal process'. The difficulty here is the precise determination of reasonableness within the meaning of s 40(3).

One alternative to recaption is repossession through court action on the basis of the hirer or lessee's neglect, or refusal to return the goods which is adverse to the owner's right to immediate possession. The forms of judgment available where goods are wrongfully detained can be found in s 3 of the Torts (Interference with Goods) Act 1977. The relief is as follows:

> (a) 'An order for delivery of the goods and for payment of any consequential damages' (s 3(2)(*a*)). This is a discretionary remedy (s 3(3)(*b*)) and criteria similar to those applicable to the remedy of specific performance will apply (see Chapter 14);

(b) 'An order for delivery of the goods, but giving the defendant the alternative of paying damages by reference to the value of the goods, together in either alternative with payment of any consequential damages' (s 3(2)(b)). Here delivery of the goods is anticipated within a period of time unless payment is made plus damages for their detention. The court does have the power under s 3(2)(a) and (b) to impose conditions requiring an additional allowance to be made to the owner where damages 'by reference to the value of the goods would not be the whole of the value of the goods' (s 3(6));

(c) 'Damages' (s 3(2)(c)). In this situation the owner cannot insist on the return of the goods but can seize the goods which still belong to him until the judgment is satisfied. In this last situation, the owner would be deemed to have waived his right under the judgment to their value.

Self-help and third party interests

The liquidation value of the equipment may be well in excess of the lessor's loss on the default of the lessee. However, if the equipment retains its value only if it is not removed from the premises, or if the equipment is 'attached' to the real estate or to other equipment in which others have an interest, the lessor may not be able to realise fully the equipment collateral. In this respect, it will be necessary for a lessor to determine in advance of funding what impact the various third party positions may have upon the collateral. Thus there is a presumption that a chattel fixed to realty is a fixture, though this may be displaced in the case of an equipment lease where the transaction would indicate that the chattel was only intended to be used for the period of the lease. The position may be otherwise in the case of hire purchase which might result in the presumption of permanent annexation on the basis of the hirer's option to purchase (*Vaudeville Electric Cinema Ltd v Muriset* [1923] 2 Ch D 74).

The leasing arrangement may contain an express provision entitling the lessor to enter the lessee's land on his default and recover physical possession of the equipment. Such a vested right in the lessor will constitute an irrevocable licence to enter and, in so doing, provides immunity from an action for trespass so long as there has been no breach of the peace (*Hurst v Picture Theatres Ltd* [1915] 1 KB 1). The issue of what constitutes a fixture does not depend solely on the intention of the parties but involves questions of law to which the degree of physical affixation will be highly relevant. Seemingly, as far as the finance lessor is concerned, if there is any possibility that the equipment may be considered a fixture, the best practice would be to assume that it will be and treat it as such. The primary rule governing fixtures is that they become the property of the owner of the land. The rigours of this rule have been ameliorated through the distinction drawn between chattels fixed by the tenant which he is not entitled to remove and those which he may remove, for example, trade fixtures. The right of the owner of a chattel to enter and seize the chattel on default by a lessee will also bind the lessee's landlord stemming, as it does, from Coke's dictum that:

[H]aving regard to strangers, who were not parties or privies thereunto, lest by a voluntary surrender they may receive prejudice touching any right or interest they had before the surrender, the estate surrendered hath in consideration of law a continuance. (Co Litt 388b)

This interest arises from the fact that the chattel owner stands in the same position as the tenant. On the expiration of the tenant's term, the owner's right to removal will therefore normally be exhausted. The interest is basically *sui generis* and is incapable of registration under the Land Charges Act 1925. It follows that the interest of a legal mortgagee who takes without notice of the chattel owner's prior equitable right will prevail (see *Hobson v Gorringe* [1897] 1 Ch D 182).

The legal position described above may be different where the legal mortgage was granted prior to affixation. This is because the legal mortgagee, by leaving the legal mortgagor in possession, may have impliedly authorised the mortgagor to carry on his business in the usual way. Often this will include the right to affix hired goods to the property and granting the owner of the goods a right to remove them on termination of the hiring contract (see *Gough v Wood* [1894] 1 QB 713). Nonetheless, the mortgage deed may negative the mortgagor's implied authority. From this it appears that the finance lessor's position is precarious. The situation is just as awkward where the hirer has sold the land on which the equipment is leased since a purchaser of a legal estate is entitled to all fixtures attached to the land at the time of the contract purchase. Several suggestions may be made to safeguard the finance lessor's position.

(1) A clause forbidding affixation without consent of the lessor.

(2) The lease contract should empower the owner to enter the hirer's premises and sever the chattel affixed.

(3) The agreement of the hirer's landlord to enter the premises and sever the chattel should be sought.

(4) Every attempt should be made to give the widest possible notice of the equipment lease, for example, markings.

(5) The hirer should enter into a covenant to give the lessor notice of his intention to create any interest in land. Of course, the finance lessor will not be bound by such interest unless it is a legal estate, ie a demise for a term of years absolute and the sub-tenant takes without notice of the finance lessor's equitable interest.

There are also various instances where the equipment may have no nominal value unless accompanied by certain other rights, for example, patents and trademarks. It may be necessary for the finance lessor to obtain these in order to make the equipment a 'saleable package'. Thus, an agreement should be concluded with the patent holder to assign the patent or the assumption of the patent by a buyer of the equipment. Additionally, an 'as is/where is' sale may be fine if the equipment is readily removable, but is of little use if this is not the case. In this situation, it will be necessary for the lessor to be able to offer the right to use the premises along with the equipment. This may be achieved either by the finance lessor owning the freehold, or where the lessee is a tenant an assignment of his rights under the lease along with the right to sell the lease-hold interest.

Third party interests, especially the repairer's lien, may prevail against the finance lessor on repossession. Since this lien arises by operation of law, it may be immaterial to the creation of a valid lien that the equipment owner is a stranger to the contract, or that the lessor without the repairer's knowledge has specifically prohibited the creation of the lien. The principles of agency apply here, so that even where there is no express obligation to repair, this may be implied when the object of the bailment, as in a finance lease, is to enable the bailee to use the goods where incidental to this use would be the need to repair (see *Tappenden v Artus* [1964] 2 QB 185). Even if the rights of the repairer are successfully excluded by an express clause in the leasing contract prohibiting repairs without the prior consultation and approval of the finance lessor, the repairer, in the absence of estoppel on the part of the finance lessor, may be able to take advantage of the innocent improver provisions under the common law. Thus in *Greenwood v Bennett* [1973] 1 QB 195, a person who mistakenly improved another's chattel was allowed a restitutionary claim against the owner. Since then, the Torts (Interference with Goods) Act 1977 provides in proceedings for 'wrongful interference with goods' an allowance to an inno-cent improver to the extent to which 'the value of the goods is attributable to the improvement'. No direct guidance is given in the Act as to what is the rel-evant time for assessing the value of the goods. If the conversion value is assessed as at the date of the conversion, which is the common law position, unless the improver commits a fresh act of conversion by selling the goods so improved, the improvement would normally be excluded from the award of damages. However, in *IBL Ltd v Coussens* [1991] 2 All ER 133, the Court of Appeal held that in appropriate circumstances, the owner might be entitled to be compensated for the value of converted goods at the date of judgment and not at the date of the conversion. Factors that will influence the court include whether the goods would have been kept by the owner, or whether he should have been obliged to replace them. If the goods would have been kept and it was decided that the plaintiff was not obliged to replace them, or would have been unable to do so, the damages would be assessed in the light of those find-ings probably by reference to their value at the date of judgment.

Undoubtedly, the wording of the 1977 Act is obscure. If it has reversed the common law rule so that a repairer's lien not only now arises where the repairer is in possession of the goods with the consent of the owner, the Act will have the effect of cutting across contractual boundaries, unjustifiably redistributing to the owner the burden of risks, for example the creditworthiness of a con-tracting party which the artificer assumed in his contract with the hirer. This was not the case in *Greenwood v Bennett* (1973) because the contract between the innocent improver and the rogue was one of sale. It follows from this that the innocent improver's restitutionary claim against the owner for the value of the repairs was independent of, and did not spring from, the contract of sale. If this approach were adopted in the context of finance leasing, the finance lessor would be able to avoid the repairer's lien.

Repudiation and termination

Where the lessee acts in such a way as to renounce his future obligations under the lease and the lessor accepts this repudiation, the agreement will be terminated. The classic statement of principle is that provided by Pollock and Wright, *Possession in the Common Law* (1888):

> Any act or disposition which is wholly repugnant to or as it were an absolute disclaimer of the holding as bailee, reverts the bailor's right to possession, and therefore also his immediate right to maintain trover or detinue even where the bailment is for a term or is otherwise not revocable at will . . . (p 132)

A failure to pay the agreed rental is a breach of contract which entitles the owner to sue for damages. Normally, a single lapse will not amount to repudiation, but where there is a persistent refusal, or where the agreement specifically provides for termination, in this event it will amount to repudiation of the contract. Here the lessor can claim damages in respect of loss of profit on further rentals to which it would have been entitled had the leasing run its full course (see *Yeoman Credit Co v Waragowski* [1961] 1 WLR 1124; *Yeoman Credit Co v McLean* [1962] 1 WLR 1312; *Overstone v Shipway* [1962] 1 WLR 117). Mitigation of damages will be a difficult factor where the leased chattel is unique. The rentals are discounted in order to allow for acceleration of payments. In the case of hire purchase, no account is taken of the hirer's right to terminate, which would militate against recovery of the whole hire purchase price (see *Union Transport Finance Ltd v British Car Auctions Ltd* [1978] 2 All ER 385). As against the hirer or his assignee, the courts have restricted the supplier to the outstanding balance of the hire purchase price. Of course in principle where the agreement has been terminated, the supplier should be entitled to the full value of the goods. The explanation here is that the hire purchase rule is *sui generis* (see *Belsize Motor Supply Co v Cox* [1914] 1 KB 244; *Belvoir Finance Co Ltd v Stapleton* [1971] 1 QB 210).

The effects of a repudiatory breach

One of the only English cases dealing with the effect of repudiation in a finance lease is *Lombard North Central Plc v Butterworth* [1987] QB 527. It is worth dwelling upon the facts. The plaintiffs, a finance company, leased a computer to the defendant for a period of five years on payment of an initial sum of £584.05 and 19 subsequent quarterly instalments of the same amount. Clause 2(*a*) of the agreement made punctual payment of each instalment the essence of the agreement, and failure to make such payments entitled the plaintiffs to terminate the agreement. Clause 6 of the agreement provided that following termination, the plaintiffs were entitled to all arrears of instalments and all future instalments which would have fallen due had the agreement not been terminated. When the sixth instalment was six weeks overdue, the plaintiffs terminated the agreement, and, having recovered possession of the computer, sold it for only £172.88. The plaintiffs brought an action against the defendant claiming the sixth unpaid instalment and the 13 future instalments, or alternatively, damages for breach of contract. Before the Court of Appeal, the defendant contended that he ought not to be held liable for more than the amount due and unpaid at the date of termination. The argument employed was that cl 6 of the agreement created a penalty and that the defendant's conduct had not amounted to a repudiation. The plaintiffs argued that cl 2(a) of the agreement entitled them to treat default in one payment as a repudiation of the agreement, thereby enabling them to recover their loss in respect of the whole transaction.

The lessor succeeded in the Court of Appeal and recovered for its loss of bargain under the general law of damages, irrespective of the fact that the liquidated damages provision could be struck down as a penalty. This conclusion was arrived at by the Court of Appeal somewhat reluctantly because, as Nicholls LJ pointed out, there was 'no practical difference' (p 23) between the terms of the contract in this case and the previous decision of the Court of Appeal in *Financings Ltd v Baldock* [1963] 2 QB 104. In the latter case, an owner had terminated a hire purchase agreement under an express provision entitling him to terminate for non-payment of hire. It was held that he was, in the absence of repudiation, entitled to no more than the amount of the hire unpaid at the time of termination. As Nicholls LJ said in *Lombard North Central* (at 546):

> There is no practical difference between (1) an agreement containing such a power [for termination] and (2) an agreement containing a provision to the effect that time for payment of each instalment is of the essence so that any breach will go to the root of the contract. The difference between these two agreements is one of drafting form and wholly without substance. *Yet under an agreement drafted in the first form, the owner's damages claim arising on his exercise of the power of termination is confined to damages for breaches up to the date of termination, whereas under an agreement drafted in the second form the owner's damages claim, arising on his acceptance of an identical breach as a repudiation of the agreement will extend to damages for loss of the whole transaction.* (emphasis added)

The reluctance of the learned judge in this case fails to take fully into account the following matters. First, merely because the parties refer to a term (time in this case) as a condition, this is not necessarily determinative of the question in so far as it describes the legal nature of the breach. Secondly, a finance lease is a financing venture where payment schedules go to the root of the contract because the lessor looks primarily towards the rental stream rather than repossession of the asset. Thus in this case there was a considerable risk of obsolescence, which is not so prevalent in the normal hire purchase transaction involving consumer durables.

Where the breach is not deemed repudiatory, the courts have in the context of hire purchase transactions taken into account the existence of the right to terminate as seen in *Financings Ltd v Baldock* [1963] 2 QB 104. In this case, Lord Denning enunciated a new general principle of law:

> I see no difference in this respect between the letting of a vehicle on hire and the letting of land on a lease. If a lessor under a proviso for re-entry, re-enters on the ground of non-payment of rent or of disrepair, he gets the arrears of rent up to the date of re-entry and damages for want of repair at that date, but he does not get damages for loss of rent thereafter or for breaches of repair thereafter. (pp 110–11)

What was awarded to the owner in the *Baldock* case having 'unreasonably terminated the agreement' was the two instalments of rent in arrears plus interest. The major objection to this is the failure to recognise that the lease in real property is both a conveyance and a contract and, usually, a minimum payment clause (indemnity) will govern termination of an agreement. More recently in *UCB Leasing Ltd v Holtom* [1987] RTR 362, the Court of Appeal refused to follow the approach of Holroyd Pearce LJ in *Yeoman Credit v Apps* [1962] 2 QB 508. In that case his Lordship held that if the hirer affirms the contract but the goods subsequently remain unfit, the continuing breach entitles the hirer to reject the goods. In *UCB Leasing*, the hirer did not reject the car until he had had it for seven months, and the court held that he had affirmed the contract by virtue of a lapse of a reasonable period of time (see pp 383–4). The owners were held entitled to all instalments due until rejection. The Court of Appeal applied *Financings v Baldock* (1963), namely, that the hirer by returning the car had not repudiated the agreement and the owners were therefore not entitled to payment in respect of the future instalments that had not fallen due before the owner's termination of the agreement. Interestingly, Balcombe LJ in *UCB Leasing* pointed out that, since the owner had made payment on time the essence of the contract, the owners were entitled to treat the contract as repudiated and, following *Lombard North Central* (1987), were entitled to compensation for loss of future instalments, subject to the hirer's counterclaim for damages (see *Charterhouse Credit Co Ltd v Tolly* [1963] 2 QB 683).

In *Amev UDC v Austin* (1986) 60 ALJR 74, the Australian High Court pointed out that there was nothing objectionable about an indemnity clause which anticipated the recovery of actual loss on early termination. Nevertheless, the majority held that where the indemnity clause was penal, it was not for the courts to rewrite the stipulation so as to limit it to what could be recovered as an indemnity. The court held that the lessor's claim should be limited to loss flowing from the breach which did not include loss of bargain where there was no repudiation. Such an approach is unduly restrictive in a finance leasing context because as Dawson J, dissenting, said in that case:

> For my part I am unable to see why the intention of the parties concerning payment of compensation upon termination should be disregarded merely because the provision which they make fails as a penalty. Just as actual loss is recoverable upon breach, even where there is a stipulation which is unenforceable as a penalty, there is no reason to my mind why actual loss should not be recoverable upon termination in the same circumstances. (pp 761–2)

Significantly, in *Robophone Facilities Ltd v Blank* [1966] 1 WLR 1428, Diplock LJ suggested (pp 1447–8) that a liquidated damages clause could properly include compensation for a loss which would normally be too remote. Such an argument is attractive in a non-consumer case such as *Lombard North Central* (1987), since businessmen should be expected to understand the terms offered in the contract of supply.

Lawful termination

In order to protect itself against loss in value through depreciation, the finance lessor will provide for payment of specific sums by the lessee on default. The difficulty here concerns the question of what actually constitutes a genuine pre-estimate of loss? In addition, to what extent is it possible to accommodate the doctrine of penalties in the context of finance leasing, bearing in mind the theoretical underpinnings of contract law? Occasionally, the agreement will represent neither, especially since both English and Australian courts have affirmed that a term will not be characterised as a penalty clause if it is expressed to take effect upon an event other than a breach of contract by the hirer. In *Campbell Discount Co Ltd v Bridge* [1962] AC 600, the House of Lords was divided on this question and Denning LJ pointed out that equity, by this method, commits itself to an 'absurd paradox' (p 629) appearing to grant relief only on breach of contract. Nevertheless, more recently, this reluctance has been overturned by the House of Lords in *Export Credit Guarantee Department v Universal Oil Products Co* [1983] 1 WLR 339. The reasoning here is that it has never been the function of the courts to relieve a party from a contract on the mere ground that it proves to be onerous or imprudent.

One important effect of this approach is that it allows a skilled legal drafts-man to avoid the rule against penalties. Ironically, a lessee who honours his obligations by terminating the agreement in a manner prescribed by the con-tract will be in a worse position than an irresponsible lessee who breaks the contract, and whose liability will be avoided because of the rule relating to penalties. Be that as it may, any attempt by a finance lessor to circumscribe the rule against penalties through mechanistically invoking an acceleration clause, and then proceeding to terminate the lease for default in payment of the accelerated rentals, is unlikely to succeed before the courts. Such conduct is similar to sharp practice making it inequitable to allow the finance lessor to retain the benefit of its full legal rights without allowing the lessee a *locus poenitentiae* under the rules against forfeiture (see *Barton Thompson and Co Ltd v Stapling Machines Co* [1966] Ch D 499). On the other hand, the exer-cise by the lessor of a contractual power of termination for breach is enforce-able.

Where a clause providing for automatic termination on insolvency is included in the leasing agreement, the lessor is seeking to recover the physical possession of the equipment only. Such a provision is a standard term in hire purchase agreements. In that context, where an option to purchase is provided, it would seem to be contrary to the principle of the equality of creditors, espe-cially if the trustee in bankruptcy offers to tender the balance of the hire pur-chase charges. Significantly, in *Re David Meek Plant Hire Ltd* [1994] 1 BCLC 680 it was held that goods let on hire purchase and physically in the possession of the company were subject to the restrictions imposed by the Insolvency Act 1986, for example, the moratorium provision in administration (see also *Re Piggin, Dicker v Lombank Ltd* [1962] 112 LJ 424).

Penalty clauses

In an attempt to protect its investment on the lessee's default, the finance lessor may invoke a 'minimum payment' clause. One of the main difficulties here concerns the genuineness of the pre-estimate of loss. Care has to be taken in drafting an adeemed repudiation clause so as to realistically limit the acts of default that would be deemed to constitute a repudiation to such matters as go to the root of the contract. Since finance leases will often contain a long list of events of default, for example, failure to insure or to repair, these very contractual provisions may run afoul of the rule against penalties. The courts may not consider all of these breaches of contract as being sufficiently serious so as to amount to repudiation by the lessee. Even so, the penalty clause will remain enforceable up to the amount of loss suffered, that is, the plaintiff's actual loss (see *Jobson v Johnson* [1989] 1 All ER 621).

All the relevant English cases to date have concerned minimum payment clauses with no realistic provision being made for the value of the repossessed equipment or for the acceleration of rentals. In *Bridge v Campbell Discount Co* [1962] AC 600, a clause which provided that a sum equalling to two-thirds of the hire purchase price together with expenses incurred by the owner should be payable, was considered not to be a genuine pre-estimate of liquidated damages. In spite of this, it is clear from the judgments given in the House of Lords that, had the default clause been properly drawn as a genuine pre-estimate of damages, it would have been enforceable. Despite this, such an ideal has proved elusive in subsequent cases. Thus in *Anglo-Auto Finance Co Ltd v James* [1963] 1 WLR 1042, the Court of Appeal considered a minimum payment clause which required payment of all monies in arrears and a sum equal to the amount by which the hire purchase price (less the deposit and monthly instalments already paid) exceeded the net amount realised by the sale of the vehicle to be penal. The judgments seem to indicate that, since in the *Bridge* case two-thirds of the hire purchase price recoverable under the minimum payment clause was held to be penal, a clause providing for 100 per cent of the purchase price had to be penal. Unfortunately, the judgments fail to take account of one essential difference: the clause in *Auto Finance* provided for the resale price of the car being deducted from the hire purchase price in computing the damages, but admittedly, it did fail to take into account a discount for acceleration of payment resulting from the disposal of the repossessed goods. Only in this latter sense could the clause be considered penal. As a matter of principle, there is nothing oppressive in a clause enabling the owner to place upon the lessee the risk of any deficiency resulting from repossession and resale from the discounted hire purchase price, except where the deficiency is increased as a result of the owner's negligence.

An example before the High Court of Australia of a liquidated damages clause being upheld can be seen in *Esanda Finance Corp v Plessnig* (1988) 166 CLR 131. In this case, the hire purchase agreement provided that if the hirer made default in any payment under the agreement, the owner would be entitled to retake possession of the goods, whereupon the hiring would terminate and the owner would be entitled to recover, as liquidated damages, an amount equal to the total rent payable under the agreement, less the deposit, any rentals paid, the value of the goods being the best wholesale price reasonably obtainable for them at the time of repossession, and a rebate of charges. This case confirms the possibility of drafting effective liquidated damages provisions that will not be struck down as penal.

In order to successfully draft a remedy clause, an allowance will have to be given to the lessee both for the value of the equipment repossessed and also for the accelerated payments given to the lessor. The difference between computing the owner's loss under a hire purchase agreement and that incurred under a finance lease is that in the case of the former, the full net proceeds of sale must be brought into account, whereas in the case of the finance lease, the owner would in any event have regained the goods at the end of the period. The finance lessor's potential gain, for which it will have to give allowance if the clause is not to be struck down as penal, will not equal the full proceeds of sale, but the amount by which this exceeds what would have been the value of the goods at the end of the hiring period. A useful summary of the damages formula is

(a) any past-due rentals; plus

(b) interest or delay damages; plus the present value of the future rent stream; plus

(c) the value of any insurance, maintenance and tax liabilities assumed by the lessee; plus

(d) the present value of the end-of-term residual value, adjusted for any loss due to abusive use; plus

(e) the additional costs and expenses of realisation.

There may be problems in determining the appropriate discount rate applicable. To the extent that the above formulation makes prior estimation of the loss by the lessor very difficult to assess, the court might favour a 'broad brush' approach. In *Robophone Facilities Ltd v Blank* [1966] 1 WLR 1428, it was held that a clause providing for the pre-estimate of damages involving the repudiation of an operating lease of telephone-answering equipment was not a penalty, even though it was not precise, because it was 'reasonably close' to the actual loss likely to be occasioned to the plaintiffs so far as it was capable of prediction. The clause required payment as liquidated damages of 50 per cent of the gross rents which would have been payable, and this was accepted by the court as a *via media* of the actual loss of the plaintiff which was estimated to lie within a range of 47–58 per cent of the gross rents for the unexpired term of the contract. Such a provision was commended by the court for its sound business sense in that it attempted to avoid the uncertainty of proving in a court the actual loss sustained. As Lord Diplock said:

> . . . the more difficult it is likely to prove and assess the loss which a party will suffer in the event of a breach, the greater the advantages to both parties of fixing by the terms of the contract itself an easily ascertainable sum to be paid in that event. Not only does it enable the parties to know in advance what their position will be if a breach occurs and so avoid litigation at all, but, if litigation cannot be avoided, it eliminates what may be the very heavy legal costs of proving the loss actually sustained which would have to be paid by the unsuccessful party . . .. (p 1447)

In applying the discount rate, credit should be given to the finance lessor for initial expenses incurred in setting up the transaction in the first instance. Of course, these initial expenses will figure prominently in the first few payments of the lease. In this respect, it would seem that a rebate on a straight apportionment may not do justice to the lessee, ie to treat the finance charge as evenly over the period of the lease.

Sub-letting of the goods

The difficulties involved in quantifying damages often lead the draftsman of the finance lease to include a right to sub-lease in the main leasing contract. This right to sub-lease will *prima facie* be limited to the duration of the main leasing agreement unless the sub-hirer can establish that the finance lessor held out the lessee as being the owner, or as being authorised to sub-let for a period not limited to the main hiring agreement. Such a conclusion is unlikely in the light of the fact that the courts, at least in hire purchase cases, have consistently held that the owner is not estopped from denying the hirer's authority to sell by mere delivery of possession unless there is some representation which can be spelled out from the owner's conduct (see *Lloyds and Scottish Finance Ltd v Williamson* [1965] 1 WLR 404). It normally follows that the termination of the main leasing agreement will automatically terminate the sub-lease. Indeed, if the sub-hirer refuses to deliver up possession he may be sued for 'wrongful interference' by virtue of s 3 of the Torts (Interference with Goods) Act 1977.

Clearly, the finance lessor will be interested in continuing the sub-lease on the insolvency of the lessee. The alternative of repossession will be costly, and full recovery of damages under a minimum payment clause or otherwise may be impossible where there are insufficient funds. The lessor will often release the goods on different terms to those in the original lease in order to satisfy the needs of the new lessee. Determining the fair market value of the lease in order to award market price damages will be extremely difficult when the only evidence of the secondary market is the release itself. Some leases set forth the anticipated value of the goods following the termination of the lease providing that upon breach, the lessee is liable for all future rentals plus the termination value minus the proceeds of any release. As an alternative, it is possible to set forth the depreciated value of the goods at given periods during the lease and provide that the lessee should have a credit against future rentals for the depreciation saved by early cancellation. If the figures in these schedules represent good faith approximations of the actual values, such clauses should be upheld.

The assignment of the benefit of the lease, for example the rights of the lessee under the sub-lease including the right to terminate or to accept termination by the sub-lessee, will only bind the lessee's liquidator if it was made before the commencement of the compulsory winding up of the company (compare *Re Atlantic Computers Systems plc* [1992] Ch 505). Such an assignment to the finance lessor of the sub-rentals due could be categorised as a charge of the lessee's book debts which will be void as against the liquidator unless registered (s 396(*c*)(iii) of the Companies Act 1985).

Leasing and the Consumer Credit Act 1974

Turning to the effect of the CCA 1974 on finance leasing it will be obvious, on any analysis, that the provisions of the Act will rarely extend to this form of commercial activity. The 1974 Act is concerned with consumer hire agreements, which consist of agreements made by a person with an individual for a bailment of goods which is not a hire purchase agreement, and is capable of subsisting for more than three months. 'Individual' is defined in s 189(1) as including 'a partnership or other unincorporated body of persons not consisting entirely of bodies corporate'. It follows that the CCA 1974 applies wherever the debtor is not a body corporate and would presumably apply to an unincorporated club, or charity, or trade union, or small business. Significantly, the government decided to amend the Act to take small businesses outside its ambit ((1987) 42 CC5/24). In any case, very many commercial leasing arrangements will usually involve sums over £15,000 which is outside the current credit limit for the application of the CCA 1974 (s 8(2); Consumer Credit (Increase of Monetary Limits) Order 1983 (SI 1983 No 1878)).

Some treatment of the Act is required in relation to the exercise by the lessor of any remedies under the lease contract. The exercise of the creditor's remedies are covered by the Act irrespective of the different forms of hiring agreement, for example, leasing, hire, contract hire, or rental, and any distinctions between them are regarded as purely functional and having little legal significance. Thus, a provision in the lease that the full balance shall immediately become payable is covered by s 76 of the Act which requires seven days' notice in prescribed form to be given by the owner to the hirer. By virtue of s 87(1), service of a default notice in accordance with s 88 is necessary before the owner can become entitled, following a breach by the debtor or hirer, to terminate the agreement or to demand earlier payment of any sum and recover the goods.

One of the most worrying aspects of the CCA 1974 from the finance lessor's point of view could have been the provision in s 101(1) enabling the hirer under a regulated consumer hire agreement to terminate the agreement by giving notice after 18 months. Of course, rental terms for equipment leases usually involve a time period of five years so the foregoing provision would have made small equipment leases to sole traders and partnerships uneconomic. It is for this reason that Parliament provided the s 101(7) exemption to three categories of lease:

    (a) where the minimum rental exceeds £900 per year (problematic in the case of balloon rentals);

    (b) where the goods are bailed to the hirer for the purposes of his business under a directly financed transaction;

    (c) where the hirer requires the goods for a sub-leasing business.

The underlying rationale here is questionable in the light of abuses associated in photocopier leases which in many cases have locked hirers into burdensome contracts for long periods of time where the total rental amounted to many times the value of the goods.

It is worth noting the powerful effect of s 132 of CCA 1974. This enables the court to order total or partial repayment of rentals to the hirer and release the hirer from all or part of any future liability under the agreement in any case where the hirer repossesses the goods, or obtains an order for their return whether this results from termination by the owner for the hirer's default or termination by the hirer himself. In addition, the court has a wide discretion as to time orders under ss 129 and 130 of CCA 1974 where no limitation is imposed on the court in allowing time for repayment by the hirer so long as the time does not go beyond the contract period of hire.

Termination of a regulated consumer credit agreement

The debtor under a regulated consumer credit agreement (see Chapter 2) has a right to repay early (s 94). There is also a further right to a rebate (s 95), the amount of which is determined by the Consumer Credit (Rebate on Early Settlement) Regulations 1983 (SI 1983 No 1562). The debtor, as distinct from a consumer hirer, has a statutory right on his written request to a written statement of the sum outstanding (s 97). He then may elect to make early payment of that sum (s 172) upon which he is is entitled to a statutory rebate in respect of future instalments.

In the all too common case where the debtor cannot repay, considerable protection is afforded by CCA 1974. Thus the debtor is given a statutory right under s 99 of CCA 1974 to terminate a regulated conditional sale or hire purchase agreement, except where he has sub-sold the goods (s 99(4) of CCA 1974). The general effect here is to assimilate hire purchase and conditional sale transactions. To meet the unusual case where the property has already passed to the conditional buyer before termination, for example, by operation of law in the case of *accessio* (see Chapter 7), s 99(5) provides that 'the property in the goods shall thereupon vest in the person (the "previous owner") in whom it was vested immediately before it became vested in the debtor'. Special provision is also made under s 99(5) for the situation where the 'previous owner' has died or become bankrupt in the meantime. The liability of the debtor outside of this is limited to a maximum of 50 per cent of the total price of the goods (s 100(1)), but if the agreement lays down a lower figure than this, the debtor can rely upon that (s 100(1)). The court is also empowered to prescribe a lower figure if this more accurately reflects the creditor's loss (s 100(3)).

There are important procedural safeguards which protect the defaulting debtor so effectively providing him with another opportunity to honour his agreement. Under s 87 of CCA 1974, the debtor must be supplied with a written default notice before the creditor can take any form of action. This provides as follows:

    (1)   Service of a notice on the debtor or hirer in accordance with s 88 (a 'default notice') is necessary before the creditor or owner can become entitled, by reason of any breach by the debtor or hirer of a regulated agreement,—
        (*a*) to terminate the agreement, or
        (*b*) to demand earlier payment of any sum, or

(c) to recover possession of any goods or land, or

(d) to treat any right conferred on the debtor or hirer by the agreement as terminated, restricted or deferred, or

(e) to enforce any security.

(Compare non-default notices under s 76(1) of CCA 1974 which deal with lesser terminations, such as the hiring element under a hire purchase agreement.) As expanded by regulations (Consumer Credit (Enforcement, Default and Termination Notices) Regulations 1983 (SI 1983 No 1561)), the notice must specify the nature of the alleged breach which must not have been waived by the owner, and the action required of the debtor or hirer. Such action will depend upon whether it is a remediable breach under s 88(1)(b), or an irremediable breach under s 88(1)(c). Moreover, s 88(5) makes it clear that a default notice may activate a provision in a regulated agreement that the agreement or hiring is terminable for arrears. It should be noted here that a default interest charge is prohibited in the case of consumer credit agreements (see above) but not in the case of consumer hirings (see (1989) 43 CC 6/17).

On receipt of the default notice in its prescribed form, the debtor or hirer is allowed at least seven days' grace (ss 76(1), 88(2), 98(1)). During this period, the debtor may seek relief from the courts where a time order may be granted in situations considered by the court to be just. In the case of hire purchase and conditional sale agreements, a time order can reschedule all remaining instalments so that it will not be confined to those instalments which have fallen due (s 130(2)). Additionally, the court may make a transfer order dividing the goods between the debtor and the creditor. Section 133 contains special rules to compensate the creditor for having to accept the return of used goods.

The consumer credit agreement may contain provisions relating to termination on death or insolvency. In these situations, the general rule still pertains so that no action can be taken without the giving of seven days' notice (s 76). The position on death is that the creditor must obtain a court order before taking action, but no action may be taken if the agreement is fully secured. Unfortunately, the distinction between fully secured and partly secured or unsecured is not defined under the Act. Section 189 defines 'security' as follows:

> 'security', in relation to an actual or prospective consumer credit agreement or consumer hire agreement, or any linked transaction, means a mortgage, charge, pledge, bond, debenture, indemnity, guarantee, bill, note or other right provided by the debtor or hirer, or at his request (express or implied), to secure the carrying out of the obligations of the debtor or hirer under the agreement . . ..

It is difficult to determine from this whether a hire purchase contract constitutes a 'fully secured' agreement. Although the creditor in this circumstance has the right to the return of his goods, has this right been 'provided by the debtor'? It would appear that an agreement is 'fully secured' if the debtor gives the creditor the right to take possession of the goods upon the termination of the agreement. Of course, the real problem here is the categorisation of security as the *granting* of an interest as distinct from the *retention* of title.

Repossession

Repossession, as the most dramatic illustration of self-help exercised by the creditor, is rigorously controlled by the CCA 1974 with regard to regulated hire or hire purchase or conditional sale agreements. Thus s 92(1) provides:

> Except under an order of the court, the creditor or owner shall not be entitled to enter any premises to take possession of goods subject to a regulated hire purchase agreement, regulated conditional sale agreement or regulated consumer hire agreement.

Further protection is afforded under such an agreement where the debtor has paid one-third or more of the total price of the goods. Following this circumstance, the goods are considered to be 'protected goods', and can only be repossessed by an order of court. In determining the one-third rule, special provision is made under s 90(2) for compulsory installation charges so that one-third of the total price is construed for this purpose as the aggregate of the installation charge and one-third of the remainder of the total price. Special provision is also seen in the case of successive linked agreements so that where the first agreement falls within s 90, both the old and new goods will fall within this section regardless of any amount paid.

A severe sanction attaches to wrongful repossession; the agreement is terminated under s 91 of CCA 1974 and the debtor can recover all the money he has paid out under it. However, 'protected goods' status is lost if the debtor has exercised his right of termination under s 90(5), or has consented to repossession at the time of recaption (compare s 173(3) of CCA 1974). To be effective consent, the debtor should be informed what his rights would be if he refused consent (*Chartered Trust v Pitcher* [1987] RTR 72). If the debtor has abandoned the goods, the creditor can seize them without contravening s 90 because he will not have seized them 'from the debtor'. This can be illustrated in *Bentinck v Cromwell Engineering Co* [1971] 1 QB 324, a case under the equivalent provision of s 90 of the Hire Purchase Act 1965. In this case the debtor, after having paid the deposit and a few instalments, badly damaged the vehicle in question and the credit payments fell into arrears. The car was left in a garage, but the debtor did not give orders to repair it. The finance company traced the car and sought to contact the debtor who had by then disappeared. After nine months, the finance company took the car and it was held that it had been abandoned by the debtor.

It should be noted that the protection of possession anticipated under s 90 is limited to the debtor, or his assignee, or authorised bailee since the goods will be deemed to be in the debtor's possession. It follows that such protection does not extend to a sub-buyer (see *Bentinck v Cromwell Engineering Co* [1971] 1 QB 324).

Extortionate agreements

This lies at the very heart of the CCA 1974. Indeed, ss 137–40, which relate to extortionate credit agreements, apply whether or not the agreement is regulated for the purposes of the Act. The court is empowered on application by the debtor or surety to reopen an extortionate credit agreement, and the burden of proving the contrary is placed upon the creditor (s 171(7)). The jurisdiction may only be invoked with regard to a credit agreement which is defined in s 137(2)(*a*) as, 'any agreement between an individual (the "debtor") and any other person (the "creditor") by which the creditor provides the debtor with credit of any amount'. It is obvious from this that consumer hire agreements will be excluded.

A credit bargain is extortionate if it requires the debtor or a relative of his to make payments which are 'grossly exorbitant', or in some other way 'grossly contravenes ordinary principles of fair dealing'. The relevant factors to be taken into account are fully set out in s 138 which states:

(1) A credit bargain is extortionate if it—
    (*a*) requires the debtor or a relative of his to make payments (whether unconditionally, or on certain contingencies) which are grossly exorbitant, or
    (*b*) otherwise grossly contravenes ordinary principles of fair dealing.
(2) In determining whether a credit bargain is extortionate, regard shall be had to such evidence as is adduced concerning—
    (*a*) interest rates prevailing at the time it was made,
    (*b*) the factors mentioned in subsections (3) to (5), and
    (*c*) any other relevant considerations.
(3) Factors applicable under subsection (2) in relation to the debtor include—
    (*a*) his age, experience, business capacity and state of health; and
    (*b*) the degree to which, at the time of making the credit bargain, he was under financial pressure, and the nature of that pressure.
(4) Factors applicable under section (2) in relation to the creditor include—
    (*a*) the degree of risk accepted by him, having regard to the value of any security provided;
    (*b*) his relationship to the debtor; and
    (*c*) whether or not a colourable cash price was quoted for any goods or services included in the credit bargain.
(5) Factors applicable under subsection (2) in relation to a linked transaction include the question how far the transaction was reasonably required for the protection of debtor or creditor, or was in the interest of the debtor.

When the court reopens a credit agreement, it has wide powers under s 139(2) to relieve the debtor or a surety from payment of any sum in excess of what is 'fairly due and reasonable'. The court may make the following orders under s 139(2):

In reopening the agreement, the court may, for the purpose of relieving the debtor or a surety from payment of any sum in excess of that fairly due and reasonable, by order—
    (*a*) direct accounts to be taken, or (in Scotland) an accounting to be made between any persons;
    (*b*) set aside the whole or part of any obligation imposed on the debtor or surety by the credit bargain or any related agreement;
    (*c*) require the creditor to repay the whole or part of any sum paid under the credit bargain or any related agreement by the debtor or a surety, whether paid to the creditor or any other person;

    (*d*) direct the return to the surety of any property provided for the purposes of the security; or

    (*e*) alter the terms of the credit agreement or any security instrument.

An order may be made under the above irrespective of the fact that it places 'a burden on the creditor in respect of an advantage unfairly enjoyed by another person who is a party to a linked transaction' (s 139(3)).

Chapter 13

Remedies of the Supplier for Misrepresentation or Breach

One effect of property passing is that the relationship between the seller and the buyer becomes that of debtor–creditor. Chapters 11 and 12 deal with the rise of contractual mechanisms designed principally to avoid this consequence, most notably retention of title clauses, finance leasing, contracts of hire and hire purchase. In this chapter we shall consider the statutory remedies available to an unpaid seller under the SGA 1979, as well as discussing the position of the ordinary supplier. The significance here is that, in appropriate circumstances, a buyer will not be entitled to possession of the goods by delivery irrespective of whether property has passed as an aspect of contract. The real remedies of the seller can only be exercised when the buyer has not paid the price for the goods and contain important innovative elements peculiar to the SGA 1979. We shall then proceed to consider the personal remedies available to the seller which are not restricted in their application to non-payment of the price. We have already discussed in Chapter 12 the remedies available to the owner or lessor following the default of the hirer or lessee.

Real remedies: the Sale of Goods Act 1979

The SGA 1979 confers upon the unpaid seller the following rights encapsulated in s 39:

  —(1)   Subject to this and any other Act, notwithstanding that the property in the goods may have passed to the buyer, the unpaid seller of goods, as such, has by implication of law—
  (a)   a lien on the goods or right to retain them for the price while he is in possession of them;
  (b)   in case of the insolvency of the buyer, a right of stopping the goods in transit after he has parted with the possession of them;
  (c)   a right of re-sale as limited by this Act.
  (2)   Where the property in goods has not passed to the buyer, the unpaid seller has (in addition to his other remedies) a right of withholding delivery similar to and co-extensive with his rights of lien or retention and stoppage in transit where the property has passed to the buyer.

The three rights enumerated above arise by implication of law, but they may be excluded by the express terms of the agreement between the parties.

Care should be taken to distinguish between the powers of the unpaid seller and his rights as against the first buyer. Thus it is easy to see that s 39(1) is geared towards conferring upon the seller not merely the power to deal with the goods, but also the right to do so as against the buyer. More difficulty is posed by s 39(2) which seems superfluous since the owner of goods has the power in any case of withholding delivery. Moreover it does not confer upon the unpaid seller a right to resell as against the buyer. Remarkably, an unpaid seller could, on this basis, resell where property had passed to the buyer, but could not do so where the property had not passed. The better view here is that s 39(2) ensures that a seller who has retained the property in the goods will be no worse off than one who has not done so with regard to his rights of lien and stoppage.

The real remedies afforded by the SGA 1979 are not of great practical importance for commerce. In large part this is due to the rise of the documentary letter of credit, and also the utilisation of the simple expedient of stipulating for prepayment. Often sales will be on credit terms so that both possession and property will pass to the buyer before payment. Section 38 of SGA 1979 makes it clear that the seller qualifies as being unpaid, and therefore entitled to exercise the real remedies under s 39, where the whole of the price has not yet been paid or tendered, or where conditional payment has been made by a negotiable instrument this has been dishonoured. Clearly, the real rights are not exercisable where both property and possession has passed unless the contract can be rescinded for misrepresentation. However, this will all too often be barred because of a resale by the buyer to an innocent third party (compare *Car and Universal Finance Co Ltd v Caldwell* [1965] 1 QB 525.

A wide definition is given to the term 'seller' for the purpose of exercising the unpaid seller's rights under Pt V of SGA 1979. The meaning of seller is explained by s 38(2) as follows:

> In this Part of this Act 'seller' includes any person who is in the position of a seller, as, for instance, an agent of the seller to whom the bill of lading has been indorsed, or a consignor or agent who has himself paid (or is directly responsible for) the price.

The conventional definition under s 61(1) defines a seller as 'a person who sells or agrees to sell goods' but here the concept is extended to include any person in the position of the seller, for example, his agent or assignee. Nonetheless, the definition does not extend to a buyer who has justifiably rejected the goods for non-compliance after paying the price (see *JL Lyons and Co Ltd v May and Baker Ltd* [1923] 1 KB 685). In this circumstance, the buyer should only reject the goods and sue for the price if he is satisfied as to the solvency of the seller.

The unpaid seller's lien and right of retention

At common law, a lien is possessory and presupposes that property in the goods has passed so a person cannot have, as Lord Wright pointed out, a lien over his own goods (see *Nippon Yusen Kaisha v Ramjiban Serowgee* [1938] AC 429 at p 444). However the purpose of s 39(2) is that an unpaid seller who has retained both property and possession should not have any less right than one who has merely retained possession. Thus, the unpaid seller's lien is a particular lien arising under the SGA 1979. It may be exercised only in respect of the price of the goods which are being retained (ss 39(1)(a), 41(1) of SGA 1979). No other charges are included within the scope of this lien, for example, charges for storing the goods which are only recoverable in a claim for damages (s 37 of SGA 1979). Of course, storage charges fall within the seller's lien if it is bargained for in the price.

The unpaid seller's lien is a qualification of the seller's obligation to deliver the goods found in s 27 of SGA 1979. Particular problems are posed by part delivery of the goods. The principle applied to this situation is s 42 of SGA 1979 which provides:

> Where an unpaid seller has made part delivery of the goods, he may exercise his lien or right of retention on the remainder, unless such part delivery has been made under such circumstances as to show an agreement to waive the lien or right of retention.

It appears here that the issue is whether delivery of the part was made in circumstances that showed an agreement to waive the lien. There is some difficulty because a waiver is not dependent upon an agreement but is a unilateral act. Clearly, where there is a series of contracts, a seller cannot claim a lien over part of the goods to be separately paid for and delivered. This would be equivalent to a general lien and although this may be conferred by contract, the SGA 1979 anticipates only a particular lien. Nevertheless, it does not follow that where goods are to be delivered and paid for by instalments that there is a series of contracts. On the contrary, the common law rule is that a contract for the sale of goods by instalments is one contract and the lien may be exercisable over the remainder of the goods (*Re Edwards, ex parte Chalmers* (1873) 8 Ch App 289).

The exercise of the lien

The conditions under which the lien is exercisable are set out in s 41(1) of SGA 1979:

> Subject to this Act, the unpaid seller of goods who is in possession of them is entitled to retain possession of them until payment or tender of the price in the following cases—
> (a) where the goods have been sold without any stipulation as to credit;
> (b) where the goods have been sold on credit but the term of credit has expired;
> (c) where the buyer becomes insolvent.

The first requirement is that the unpaid seller should be in possession of the goods. This is a difficult concept, especially since possession is not defined under the SGA 1979. Section 41(2) of the Act provides that the seller may exercise his lien, notwithstanding that he is in possession as agent or bailee for the buyer. The effect of this is that if the *seller* attorns, he will not necessarily lose his lien on the goods. Such was the common law position seen in *Grice v Richardson* (1877) 3 App Cas 319. In this case, the seller imported tea which he placed in his own bonded warehouse, and issued delivery orders in favour of the buyer who then became insolvent. It was held that the seller, although he held the goods as warehouseman to the buyer's order, still retained a seller's lien over the goods. The possession may be actual, constructive, or symbolic, such as where the seller is in control of the means of possessing the goods. Problems naturally arise where the goods are in the possession of a bailee, for example a warehouseman. The issue here is at what point in time did the bailee cease to possess the goods on behalf of the seller, and this is bound up with the question of attornment.

Attornment

To a great extent, attornment represents the legal solution to a dilemma caused by the dynamic nature of trade where ownership of goods will often be transmitted along a chain of successive vendors and purchasers. Attornment arises from a change in the *character* of possession without any change in the possession itself. In a sense, attornment reflects what Holmes, in his essay on *The Common Law* (1881), referred to as the materialism of the common law with its emphasis on 'actual receipt'. Thus, in *Farina v Home* 16 M & W 119, Baron Parke said that there could be no actual receipt 'until the bailee has attorned so to speak'.

The traditional pattern of an attornment envisages a triangular relationship arrangement with the seller drawing upon the warehouseman, issuing the delivery order to the buyer who then presents the document to the warehouseman/bailee. It follows from this that the bailee will have no better title than his bailor. The question of attornment against the owner or the person with the better right to possess is irrelevant because there is superiority of title. Nonetheless, in order to confer a proprietary right, the warehouseman must hold specific goods. It may be that the very act of attornment will constitute appropriation of goods to the contract, otherwise, the buyer can only have a personal claim against the warehouseman on the basis of estoppel. In this respect, it is irrelevant that the attornee has no title or a defective title in the goods (*Woodley v Coventry* (1863) 2 H & C 164), an approach which can be justified on the grounds of security in commercial transactions.

Clearly, it would be unfair to make a bailee liable for every change of ownership. In fact, attornment represents a dilemma for the bailee since, in recognising another's title in the goods, it is inconsistent with the bailee's position as against the original bailor. In the light of this, it is not surprising to find some difference of opinion among the authorities as to whether entry on the books of the warehouseman is sufficient to create an attornment. In the early case of *Harman v Anderson* (1809) 2 Camp 243, it was held that the mere presentation of the delivery order by the buyer was sufficient to bind the wharfinger to hold the goods for the account of the buyer. The facts are unclear; at first instance, the jury found that the bailees had made a transfer notation in their books, but at a later hearing Lord Ellenborough held: 'The delivery note was sufficient without any actual transfer being made in their books. From thenceforth they became the agents of Dudley, the bankrupt' (p 246). Most of the acknowedgement cases have involved some kind of *written* acknowledgement either in the form of a signature on the delivery, or some kind of notation on the books of the bailee.

Liens and credit sales

The seller is not entitled to a lien if the goods have been sold on credit. A seller can hardly be described as unpaid for the purpose of exercising his real rights over the goods if payment is not yet due. The effect of a period of credit in the parties' agreement prevents the operation of s 28 of SGA 1979 which, as a normal rule, makes payment and delivery concurrent obligations. Even where the seller has agreed to deliver in advance of payment, the unpaid seller's lien arises only when the term of credit expires, or where the buyer becomes insolvent. The right to retain goods where the buyer becomes insolvent arises whether or not the sale was one with a stipulation as to credit. As to the meaning of insolvency under the SGA 1979, s 61(4) provides:

> A person is deemed to be insolvent within the meaning of this Act if he has either ceased to pay his debts in the ordinary course of business or he cannot pay his debts as they become due.

The seller cannot be compelled to deliver in circumstances in which he will be reduced to claiming a dividend. On the other hand, insolvency by itself does not amount to a repudiation of the contract and it is open to the buyer's personal representative or a sub-buyer to tender the price and claim delivery.

Termination of the lien

The lien is lost when the seller obtains payment or tender of the price (s 41(1) of SGA 1979) simply because he will thereby cease to be an unpaid seller. It would seem that despite s 28, payment or tender is a condition precedent to the buyer's right to claim delivery. One way to reconcile these two contrasting provisions is to consider that the buyer's duty to tender the price is similar to the seller's duty of tendering delivery, but actual tender is not usually required because it is presumed that the buyer will perform his contract. There is a further express provision that the unpaid seller does not lose his lien merely by reason of his obtaining a judgment for the price of the goods (s 43(2) of SGA 1979).

The unpaid seller's lien is terminated in further circumstances which are set out in s 43(1) as follows:

> The unpaid seller of goods loses his lien or right of retention in respect of them—
> (a) when he delivers the goods to a carrier or other bailee or custodier for the purpose of transmission to the buyer without reserving the right of disposal of the goods;
> (b) when the buyer or his agent lawfully obtains possession of the goods;
> (c) by waiver of the lien or right of retention.

Delivery to a carrier is *prima facie* deemed to be delivery to the buyer (s 32(1) of SGA 1979) and unless the seller has reserved a right of disposal (s 19 of SGA

1979), the seller's lien is determined. However, the seller may still be able to exercise his right of stoppage in transit, although this is a more limited right confined to insolvency. The definition of right of disposal under s 19 is reservation of property, but it could be argued that to retain consistency with s 39(2) by which the seller's right to a lien is the same whether or not property has passed, the right of disposal should also extend in this context to possession.

Where the buyer or his agent lawfully obtains possession, the lien is given up. There has been some controversy as to the meaning of 'lawfully'. It is unlikely that 'lawfully' should be construed in terms of being in possession 'with the consent of the seller' as seen in s 25(1) of SGA 1979 and s 9 of FA 1889. This is because it is possible for a buyer to be in possession with the consent of the seller, even though this is obtained by fraud so that it would not be lawful for the purpose of s 43. The better approach is to construe 'lawfully' in terms of the absence of a trespassory taking by the buyer which could include criminal conduct on the buyer's part. Due to the nebulousness of the concept of possession, the seller may be deemed to retain possession in law in the above circumstance even though the buyer has possession in fact.

The lien of the unpaid seller may be waived expressly or by implication (s 43(1)(c)). Only in very rare cases will a waiver occur expressly; in the great majority of cases it will arise by implication from the circumstances. Obvious examples of this are where the buyer is given credit, or if there is estoppel (see *Knights v Wiffen* (1869–70) LR 5 QB 660). It is also said that the seller's lien is lost if he himself breaks the contract by some act that is inconsistent with his right to retain possession, for example, consumption (*Gurr v Cuthbert* (1843) 12 LJ Ex 309). In the case of credit and estoppel, it is possible where the unpaid seller is still in possession to go back on his waiver of the statutory lien. The Act itself envisages this where the credit granted has expired (s 41(1)(b), (c)) and in any case, the common law normally allows a party to resume the strict legal position following waiver after giving adequate notice (*Charles Rickards Ltd v Oppenheim* [1950] 1 KB 616).

The seller's right of lien is not affected by any sub-sale or other disposition unless the seller has assented to this. In the case of a buyer in possession of the documents of title or the goods themselves, transfer of the documents of title or the goods themselves to a good faith third party purchaser will defeat the original seller's lien (see Chapter 10). Lastly, it should be noted that the effect of a valid exercise of the unpaid seller's lien does not operate to rescind the contract of sale. The seller will still be able to sue for the price or damages, and an unpaid seller who has exercised his right of lien may be able to resell the goods to a third party and confer good title as against the original buyer (s 48(2) of SGA 1979).

The unpaid seller's right of stoppage in transit

An unpaid seller has the right to resume possession of the goods by preventing delivery to the buyer when they are still in the course of transit and the buyer has become insolvent (s 44 of SGA 1979). The right of stoppage is mostly of

theoretical interest as being an example of a right of recaption arising by operation of law. For obvious reasons, this right is only important where the transit
is a long one and is therefore mostly confined to international sales. Even here,
it has greatly reduced significance because of the widespread use of bankers'
confirmed commercial credits where there is little prospect of non-payment.

It makes no difference whether or not property has passed to the buyer
(s 39(2) of SGA 1979) so that the right of stoppage, as a matter of principle, is
an extensive one given that it entitles the unpaid seller to interfere not only in
the possession of goods, but also with the property in goods vested in another.
The right of stoppage does appear to be contrary to the *pari passu* principle of
distribution on bankruptcy, especially in the light of Lord Esher MR's remark
that the doctrine is always construed favourably to unpaid sellers (see *Bethell
v Clark* (1888) 20 QBD 615, at p 617).

The exercise of the right

The basic principle is set out in s 44 of SGA 1979 which states:

> Subject to this Act, when the buyer of goods becomes insolvent the unpaid seller
> who has parted with the possession of the goods has the right of stopping them in
> transit, that is to say, he may resume possession of the goods as long as they are in
> course of transit, and may retain them until payment or tender of the price.

The seller must be unpaid and the buyer must be insolvent. If the buyer is not
insolvent and the seller delays delivery by stopping the goods in transit, the
seller will be liable to the buyer for loss resulting from the delay in delivery
caused by the stoppage.

There is no doubt that the course of transit is one of the most thorny questions in this context. This is defined in s 45(1) as follows:

> Goods are deemed to be in course of transit from the time when they are delivered
> to a carrier or other bailee or custodier for the purpose of transmission to the buyer,
> until the buyer or his agent in that behalf takes delivery of them from the carrier or
> other bailee or custodier.

The right of stoppage only exists where the goods are in the hands of a third
party, and although it is presumed that there has been constructive delivery
when the goods are in the hands of the carrier (s 32(1)), for the purpose of stoppage the carrier is generally deemed to be neutral. Of course where the carrier
is the seller's agent, the seller can rely on his unpaid seller's lien and does not
need to invoke the less extensive right of stoppage. On the other hand, if the
buyer can show that the carrier was his agent then there can be no right of stoppage simply because the transit has never started (s 45(5)). Nevertheless, the
mere fact that the buyer is responsible for arranging shipping space, as in the
case of an fob contract means that transit does not end but continues until the
buyer or his agent acquires possession. This is a question of fact and s 45(5)
provides:

> When goods are delivered to a ship chartered by the buyer it is a question depend-
> ing on the circumstances of the particular case whether they are in the possession
> of the master as a carrier or as agent to the buyer.

The right of stoppage terminates following the carrier's attornment to the buyer (s 45(3)). This may be implied from the carrier's conduct, for example, where he follows instructions given to him by the buyer to carry the goods to a new destination. Even so, the seller retains his right to stop the goods until they reach their ultimate destination (see *Reddall v Union Castle Mail Steamship Co* (1914) 84 LJKB 360). If the buyer rejects the goods, the carrier or bailee is treated as if he were in continued possession of the goods by virtue of s 45(4). There is no difficulty in reconciling attornment and subsequent buyer rejection of the goods because clearly the attornment will only operate to transfer possession to the buyer provided that he has assented to this. Where there has been part delivery this may amount to a constructive delivery of the whole, but s 45(7) of SGA 1979 provides that the presumption is that it does not, and so the seller is enabled to stop what remains in the carrier's possession.

Interception of the goods before they reach their ultimate destination brings the transit to an end (s 45(2)). Thus in *Reddall v Union Castle Mail Steamship Co* the buyer intercepted the goods at the end of one stage of their transit. The goods were in the custody of a carrier who charged the buyer rent for warehousing costs, and Bailhache J held: 'Where the original transitus is interrupted by the buyers, the test is whether the goods will be set in motion again without further orders from the buyers; if not the transit is ended and the right to stop lost' (p 362). This exception recognises the fact that a carrier and buyer can agree to a different destination or form of disposal from that established by the seller and carrier. It may be, in this circumstance, the seller will have recourse against the carrier for breach of the contract of carriage by his compliance to the buyer's request. If the buyer wrongfully obtains possession, a strict reading of s 45(2) would suggest that the transit would terminate. Such an approach is consistent with s 45(6) which provides: 'Where the carrier or other bailee or custodier wrongfully refuses to deliver the goods to the buyer or his agent in that behalf, the transit is deemed to be at an end'. If it is the case that an arrangement between a carrier and consignee puts an end to the transit, it must also be the case that the buyer's wrongful taking of possession should have the same effect, not least because the wrongfulness of the act is directed at the carrier and not the seller.

The exercise by the unpaid seller of his right of stoppage may be through regaining possession or by giving notice to the carrier or bailee in possession (s 46). If, following this notice, the carrier or bailee in possession delivers the goods to the buyer he will be liable for conversion. On the other hand, if there is no right of stoppage, failure to deliver to the buyer will be wrongful and both seller and carrier or bailee in possession will be liable to the buyer in conversion. Clearly this is unsatisfactory for the carrier who, in an attempt to protect his position, may seek to be indemnified against the buyer for wrongful delivery, or against the seller for refusal to deliver.

When a notice of stoppage is given to the carrier or bailee in possession, the goods must be redelivered to or at the direction of the seller (s 46(4)). The expenses of such redelivery must be borne by the seller, and the carrier has a particular lien on the goods for his freight which prevails over the seller's lien.

As Lord Atkinson put it in *US Steel Products Co v Great Western Railway Co* [1916] 1 AC 189:

> The vendor's right to stop *in transitu* means not only the right to countermand delivery to the vendee but to order delivery to the vendor. It is subject to the possessory lien of the carrier for the charges due in respect of the carriage of the goods, but is not subject to any general lien which the carrier might have, as against the consignee of the goods, in respect of freight due on other goods. (p 203)

In addition, an unpaid seller who stops the goods in transit must provide the carrier with instructions as to their disposal or return, otherwise the carrier will be exonerated from any liability in this respect (see *Booth Steamship Co Ltd v Cargo Fleet Iron Co Ltd* [1916] 2 KB 570).

The exercise of the right of stoppage does not itself rescind the contract of sale. It follows that tender of payment by the buyer's personal representative obliges the seller to redeliver the goods in the absence of there being a repudiatory breach.

The right of resale

We have already seen that the effect of the unpaid seller's exercise of his right of lien or stoppage does not rescind the contract of sale (s 48(1)). Therefore, the seller may elect to rescind the contract and sue for non-acceptance damages. In this case, if property has passed to the buyer it will revert to the seller who can then transfer a good title to the sub-buyer. However, if the unpaid seller elects to affirm the contract, property will pass to the buyer and the seller can sue for non-payment of price and damages for non-acceptance, while perhaps maintaining his unpaid seller's lien. Where the seller subsequently resells the goods, s 48(2) of SGA 1979 confers a power of resale; the resale confers a good title on the new buyer though it does constitute a breach of the original sale contract. This remedy enables the seller to get rid of unwanted possession of goods and it is for this reason, unlike s 24 of SGA 1979 and s 8 of FA 1889, that there is no requirement that the buyer acted in good faith and without notice of the original sale.

Where goods have been delivered and property passed, the seizure and resale of the goods will be a tortious act. In the absence of one of the exceptions to the *nemo dat* doctrine applying, good title will not pass. Section 48 of SGA 1979 deals with two situations in which the unpaid seller may resell the goods without breaking his contract with the original buyer. Section 48(3) states:

> Where the goods are of a perishable nature, or where the unpaid seller gives notice of his intention to resell, and the buyer does not within a reasonable time pay or tender the price, the unpaid seller may resell the goods and recover from the original buyer damages for any loss occasioned by his breach of contract.

No mention is made as to whether the effect of resale is to rescind the original contract. This situation contrasts with s 48(4) of SGA 1979 which provides:

> Where the seller expressly reserves the right of resale in case the buyer should make default, and on the buyer making default resells the goods, the original contract of

sale is rescinded but without prejudice to any claim the seller may have for damages.

It was suggested in *Gallagher v Shilcock* [1949] 2 KB 765 that the effect of s 48(3), where property had passed to the buyer, was that the seller was reselling the buyer's goods as a quasi-pledgee and would therefore have to account to the latter. This approach was rejected by the Court of Appeal in *RV Ward Ltd v Bignall* [1967] 1 QB 534. The argument here is that the seller, in reselling the goods, is accepting the buyer's repudiation of the contract. The effect of s 48(3) is to make the time of payment stipulation of the essence of the contract where goods are perishable, or when notice of resale has been given. In this respect, the right of resale is an aspect of the seller's ownership which revests on termination. Such a right arises by operation of law, but if the seller had stipulated in the contract of sale that he should have a right of resale, the effect of s 48(4) is that it makes it clear that the contract is brought to an end. It follows that the reason for the contrast between s 48(3) and (4) is not because the former subsection is intended to have a different result, rather, the express provision of rescission, in the sense of termination of the contract (compare *Johnson v Agnew* [1980] AC 367), is not necessary under s 48(3).

The effect of resale under s 48(3) and (4) is that the seller is acting in his own capacity and should therefore be entitled to any profits which accrue on resale. Thus, where there is a retention of title clause linking property passage with payment of the price, if the supplier recovers the goods for failure of the contract it is clear that the buyer cannot claim any surplus profit made on resale. However, the Court of Appeal in *Clough Mill Ltd v Martin* (1985) suggested that it was possible for such a resale to take place without rescission (see pp 246–8). This approach is anomalous in the light of s 48(4) which would appear to insist that such a sale contract will be rescinded in this circumstance. Of course, where the transaction is categorised as creating a security interest for the seller, it is perfectly proper for the buyer to be entitled to any surplus gained on resale on the basis that property will have passed to him.

Contracts of supply

The transferor may have real remedies like those of the unpaid seller under the SGA 1979. In the case of work and materials contracts, the lien is analogous to that of the artificer's lien which applies by operation of law so long as the work done improves the goods (*Re Southern Livestock Producers Ltd* [1963] 3 All ER 801). Sometimes particularly fine distinctions arise which as a matter of legal logic may be criticised. In this respect, whilst maintenance work on cars is not considered to amount to an improvement, a lien can attach when a car is actually repaired since this is considered to constitute an improvement (see *Hatton v Car Maintenance Co Ltd* [1915] 1 Ch 621). As a species of particular lien, it entitles the lienee to retain the goods against payment for services only provided in relation to them.

One important difference between unpaid transferors and sellers is that s 48(2) of SGA 1979 empowers the unpaid seller to sell the goods without terminating the contract and confer a good title upon the third party. This power was an innovation of the SGA 1893. It follows that an unpaid transferor has no power of sale as opposed to a right of resale on termination of the contract. However, the sophisticated argument applied by the Court of Appeal in *RV Ward Ltd v Bignall* (1967) (discussed above), will be pertinent in this context with respect to products of a perishable nature. In other cases, the general position is that a disponee will be held liable in tort for conversion if the transferee subsequently tenders performance and by doing so obtains an immediate right to possession. Of course, in the case of a bailment at will, the very act of disposition will go to the root of the bailment thereby entitling the bailor to repossess the goods (*Cooper v Willomatt* (1845) 1 CB 672).

Personal remedies

In addition to the real remedies over the goods discussed above, the unpaid seller has personal contractual remedies against the transferee himself.

Action for the price under the Sale of Goods Act 1979

It is the duty of the buyer to pay for the goods according to the terms of the contract of sale. Payment must usually be made at the seller's place of business, subject to a contrary intention expressed in the contract. It is normally the duty of the buyer, as any other species of debtor, to ensure that payment is tendered to the seller and he will take the risk of this failing to occur. We have already seen that time is not normally of the essence in a contract of sale (s 10(1) of SGA 1979). This reflects the fact that in a commercial transaction the most the seller is likely to lose is his interest payment on monies received, and repudiation here would be a penalty disproportionate to the loss suffered by the seller through non-payment.

Unless otherwise agreed, delivery of the goods and payment are concurrent conditions (s 28). The duty to pay the price is remediable by an action for the price. Breach of the duty to pay the price can result in the exercise by the seller of both real and personal remedies where the goods are still in the possession of the seller, ie before acceptance. If there has been acceptance by the buyer followed by non-payment, only a personal remedy may be pursued. The basic remedy with respect to the action for the price is dealt with in s 49 of SGA 1979. The analogy here is with the remedy of specific performance which has significance for two reasons. First, there will often be a difference between the price of goods and damages received for breach, and secondly, in an action for the price the seller is under no obligation to mitigate his loss.

Complications arise because property passing in English law is linked to contract rather than conveyance. Section 49(1) of SGA 1979 states:

> Where, under a contract of sale, the property in the goods has passed to the buyer and he wrongfully neglects or refuses to pay for the goods according to the terms of the contract, the seller may maintain an action against him for the price of the goods.

On the other hand, s 50(1) of the SGA provides that, 'Where the buyer wrongfully neglects or refuses to accept and pay for the goods, the seller may maintain an action against him for damages for non-acceptance'. It appears to be essential that property should have passed, and it is not enough that property would have passed if the buyer had co-operated, unless the buyer is estopped by his conduct from denying that property has passed. Thus in *Colley v Overseas Exporters Ltd* [1921] 3 KB 302, the facts involved a sale of unascertained goods sold fob, but which were not put on board a ship because of the buyer's failure to nominate a suitable ship. It was held that the seller's remedy was in damages and not for the price because, as McCardie J pointed out, there was no ground for establishing an estoppel merely on the basis that the buyer had failed to act as he ought to have done under the contract.

The seller is placed in a somewhat invidious position where the goods have not been delivered. If he maintains that property has passed and sues for the price, the court could maintain that, on the facts, property has not passed and restrict the seller to damages for non-acceptance where he will have a duty to mitigate his loss. On the other hand, if the seller does attempt to resell the goods, the court could take the view that this is an acceptance by the seller of the repudiation of the contract by the buyer, so that an action for the price will no longer lie.

The requirement that property should have passed is dispensed with in one situation contained in s 49(2) of SGA 1979:

> Where, under a contract of sale, the price is payable on a day certain irrespective of delivery and the buyer wrongfully neglects or refused to pay such price, the seller may maintain an action for the price, although the property in the goods has not passed and the goods have not been appropriated to the contract.

The assumption here is that by separating payment from delivery the parties are impliedly making it independent also of the passing of property. There are definitional problems associated with the meaning of 'a day certain' and the maxim *certum est quod certum reddi potest* may be relevant in this context. Although in *Workman Clark and Co Ltd v Lloyd Brazileno* [1908] 1 KB 968, the Court of Appeal decided that s 49(2) applies to instalments payable on a day certain, a strict construction is applied to cases where the price is payable by a day certain so that the time for payment must be fixed and determinable in advance, irrespective of an action by either party to the contract or third person (see *Shell-Mex Ltd v Elton Cop Dyeing Co Ltd* (1928) 34 Com Cas 39).

In the case of advance payments made to the seller, there may be difficulties with the application of the strict distinction drawn by the House of Lords in *Johnson v Agnew* (1980) between mere termination as a result of breach, and rescission of a contract *ab initio*. It has been suggested that if the price is payable before termination, this can be retained or recovered by the seller even if he has not delivered the goods (see *Hyundai Heavy Industries Co Ltd v Papadopoulos* [1980] 1 WLR 1129). This approach cannot be correct insofar as it applies to sale of goods contracts because the duty to pay will normally be conditional on the other party's performance. Moreover, the effect of termination in sale of goods does have a retrospective element in that if property has already passed to the buyer it will revert in the seller (s 48(4)). Equally, it could be said that the non-delivery amounts to a total failure of consideration.

Special damage claims

Where the buyer neglects to take delivery, the seller in addition to his right to claim damages for non-acceptance or an action on the price, can sue under s 54 for any special loss incurred. Furthermore, s 37 provides:

(1) When the seller is ready and willing to deliver the goods, and requests the buyer to take delivery, and the buyer does not within a reasonable time after such request take delivery of the goods, he is liable to the seller for any loss occasioned by his neglect or refusal to take delivery, and also for a reasonable charge for the care and custody of the goods.

(2) Nothing in this section affects the rights of the seller where the neglect or refusal of the buyer to take delivery amounts to a repudiation of the contract.

This allows the seller to claim for further loss resulting from incidental costs such as care and custody of the goods. In any case, these costs will figure in a damages action as a matter of course.

As a matter of principle, linking the action for the price with the question of whether property has passed is too simplistic. The spectre of property passing covers too many classes of buyer and seller for it to be a meaningful concept in this context. The issue would be better resolved by reference to whether, as a matter of commercial practice, the buyer or the seller should have the responsibility of reselling or otherwise disposing of the goods.

Termination and damages

Once property and possession has passed to the buyer, the seller cannot terminate the contract for non-payment because this is not repudiatory conduct. The reasoning here is that if the buyer has received the full benefit of the contract and wants to keep the goods, this can only be treated as an affirmation rather than a repudiation of the contract. Conversely, if the buyer wants to give up the goods and is unwilling to pay for them, this is a repudiation which the seller can accept by repossessing the goods.

We have already seen that by virtue of s 50(1) of SGA 1979, where the buyer wrongfully neglects or refuses to accept and pay for the goods, the seller may maintain an action against him for damages. This action can be brought irrespective of whether or not property has passed. Damages for non-acceptance can now be awarded in a foreign currency where this is appropriate (*The Despina* [1979] AC 685). The rule is applied in such a way as to produce a just and appropriate result. In *Miliangos v George Frank (Textiles)* [1976] AC 443, reversing its earlier decision in *Re United Railways of Havana and Regla Warehouses* [1961] AC 1007, the House of Lords held that an English court did have the power to order that a defendant in an action of debt should pay the sum owing in a foreign currency (Swiss francs) rather than in pounds sterling. In determining the date for payment, the House of Lords settled for 'the date when the court authorises enforcement of the judgment in terms of sterling' (*per* Lord Wilberforce at p 468). Such an approach favours the creditor in the face of swift changes in the value of sterling.

Part payments and deposits

The buyer's misconduct may amount to repudiation entitling the seller to rescind the contract and he will be absolved from liability for failure to deliver. In such a case can the buyer recover the prepayment? The general rule is that where there is a part payment the sum is recoverable (*Dies v British and International Mining and Finance Co* [1939] 1 KB 715). However, as was noted above one effect of the analysis of the House of Lords in *Hyundai Shipbuilding and Heavy Industries Co Ltd v Papadopoulos* [1980] 1 WLR 1129 is that where it is clear from the contract that the payee will have to incur reliance expenditure before completing the contract then the part payment will not be recoverable in the absence of an express stipulation to the contrary.

Where the payment constitutes a deposit being in the nature of a preliminary contract guaranteeing completion, this is not returnable (see *Howe v Smith* (1884) 27 Ch D 89). A critical limit upon the ability of parties to stipulate for excessive deposits was established by the Privy Council in *Workers Trust and Merchant Bank Ltd v Dojup Investments Ltd* [1993] AC 573 where it was held that earnest money should be restricted to what is reasonable. There is of course no objective benchmark but in this case a deposit of 25 per cent of the purchase price was held to be unreasonable. Moreover the Court was not prepared to rewrite the terms of the contract by inserting a 'reasonable' deposit which on the facts taking into account custom and commercial practice the Privy Council considered to be 10 per cent.

It may be that equity may offer relief against forfeiture of the deposit. In *Stockloser v Johnson* [1954] 1 QB 476 both Denning and Somerwell LJJ stated that a deposit may be recoverable in equity if the forfeiture clause was of a penal nature and if it was unconscionable for the innocent party to retain the money. In contrast, Romer LJ stated that the jurisdiction of the court was confined to allowing late completion by the defaulting party and did not extend to ordering the repayment of a sum which had been paid in accordance with the contract and which, on breach, was stated to be forfeit. As a result the position is uncertain but the general policy is clear, namely, that this equitable relief is only used in exceptional cases (see *Goker v NSW Bank plc* (1990) TLR 393). However, in the case of a prospective regulated consumer credit agreement, a preliminary contract will be void under s 59 of CCA 1974 so that the deposit will be recoverable for total failure of consideration.

Measure of damages for non-acceptance

Non-acceptance denotes rejection of the goods, which is repudiatory conduct at least as to the part of the contract relating to the goods in question. A careful distinction should be drawn between non-acceptance and refusal to take delivery since the latter may simply denote that the buyer is not yet ready to receive the goods.

The measure of damages for non-acceptance is provided by s 50(2) and (3) in the following terms:

    (2)   The measure of damages is the estimated loss directly and naturally resulting, in the ordinary course of events, from the buyer's breach of contract.

    (3)   Where there is an available market for the goods in question the measure of damages is prima facie to be ascertained by the difference between the contract price and the market or current price at the time or times when the goods ought to have been accepted or (if no time was fixed for acceptance) at the time of the refusal to accept.

The object of s 50(2) is to include the first rule in *Hadley v Baxendale* (1854) 9 Ex 341 in the SGA 1979. The effect is to distinguish normal, foreseeable consequences of a breach for which damages are recoverable, from abnormal, special or particular loss which does not come within the scope of recoverable damages. It would seem that the underlying test for recoverable damages, as in *Victoria Laundry Ltd v Newman Industries Ltd* [1949] 2 KB 528, is that of reasonable foresight. This approach was generally approved by the House of Lords in *The Heron II* [1969] 1 AC 350, although a higher degree of probability of occurrence was anticipated in this case (see Chapter 14). The second rule in *Hadley v Baxendale* (1854) finds expression in s 54 which applies where the guilty party has knowledge of some special circumstance which increases the loss naturally arising from his breach.

Having set out in s 50(2) the general rule for calculating the measure of damages in actions for non-acceptance, the SGA 1979 provides in s 50(3) a *prima facie* rule for the computation of damages. There are several problems flowing from this which will now be discussed.

Available market

Where there is an available market, the presumption is that the seller will go into that market and resell the goods. The question whether there is an available market is a question of fact and also of degree. Thus in *Garnac Grain Co v HM Faure and Fairclough* [1968] AC 1130, it was held that there was a market even though it was not possible to buy the contract quantity in one amount for immediate delivery. Evidence that similar goods are disposable will suggest that there is an available market. In general, the courts take a broad view of this question.

The significance of the market price attached to the available market concept should not detract from the fact that the supplier will be compensated for any special damage incurred (s 54 of SGA 1979). An example of this would be the cost of return carriage, although this must be offset against any rise in the market price after the due date for acceptance. The onus of proving the price obtainable in the market at the time of acceptance is on the seller so that if this is below the contract price, the seller is *prima facie* entitled to the difference between the two (s 50(3)). Where the market price or value is difficult to establish, the actual resale price may be evidence of it.

The market rule is really an abstract concept since it is based upon the supposed activity of reselling by the seller at the time of non-acceptance as part of of his duty to mitigate his loss. Thus, if the seller delays the resale, he can still only recover the difference between the contract price and the market price at the time of non-acceptance. In *Campbell Mostyn (Provisions) Ltd v Barnett Trading Co* [1954] 1 Lloyd's Rep 65, the seller retained goods after the buyer's breach and Somervell LJ quoted with approval Lord Wrenbury's dictum in *AKAS Jamal v Moolla Dawood* [1916] 1 AC 175, a Privy Council decision dealing with shares:

> If the seller retains the shares after the breach the speculation as to the way the market will subsequently go is the speculation of the seller, not of the buyer; the seller cannot recover from the buyer the loss below the market price at the date of the breach if the market falls, nor is he liable to the purchaser for the profit if the market rises. (p 179)

In a more recent case, it was held by Webster J in *Shearson Lehman Hutton Inc v Maclaine Watson and Co Ltd (No 2)* [1990] 2 Lloyd's Rep 441, that the measure of damages payable by the defaulting buyer is the difference between the contract price and the market price at the date of breach, irrespective of any characteristics of the seller which may have led to a lower price being obtained. This approach stresses the element of certainty and objectivity in s 50(3), which does not require scrutiny of whether the seller has behaved reasonably. The question of 'available market' was linked to whether there was, in the case of an actual sale, one actual buyer at the date of breach at a fair price. On the other hand, in the case of a hypothetical sale, the test is whether on the relevant day there were in the market sufficient traders so as to enable the seller if he so wished to sell the goods. In determining a fair price where there is no actual sale, this is not confined to the price obtainable assuming that the seller sold them on the relevant date; rather in large-scale commodity contracts, the court can take into account the price which would be negotiated within a few days with persons who were members of the market on that day, and who could not be taken into account as potential buyers on the day in question only because of difficulties of communication.

The courts have shown reluctance in applying s 50(3) to cases of statutory price fixing. In *WL Thompson Ltd v Robinson (Gunmakers) Ltd* [1955] Ch 177, it was shown that the supply for the type of car in question exceeded demand, and it was held that the seller was able to recover the full sum because they had lost a profit they would otherwise have made. At this time, resale price maintenance was strictly in force in relation to cars and there was rarely any difference between the contract price and the marked (fixed retail) price. On the other hand in *Charter v Sullivan* [1957] 2 QB 117, where demand exceeded supply, it was held that the plaintiff could only recover nominal damages because he had lost no profit.

No available market

There may be no available market for the seller where the supply exceeds demand. Where a chattel is unique, the rule in s 50(3) is not applied, as seen in *Lazenby Garages Ltd v Wright* [1976] 1 WLR 459. In this case, the contract was for the sale of a second-hand car which the buyer later wrongfully refused to accept. It was held by the Court of Appeal that the 'available market' rule was not one to invoke as there was no market for second-hand cars. In contrast, where the seller could show, as in the case of a new car, that he had sold one car less than he would otherwise have done, the seller would then be allowed the loss of profit on the car.

The problem of how to assess damages where there is no available market was considered by the Court of Appeal in *Re Vic Mill Ltd* [1913] 1 Ch 465. In this case a company ordered machines, which it later did not accept, but parts had been purchased by the seller in preparation for the manufacture of the machines. Following the repudiation of the contract by the buyer, the seller modified these parts and sold them to another customer. The Court of Appeal held that the seller had lost the opportunity of making two sets of profit: one from the defaulting buyer and the other from the actual buyer. If no such opportunity had existed, the sellers could not have claimed loss of profit on the sale since the sellers would have made that profit through a substituted customer. The Court of Appeal held that the customer in this case was an additional and not a substituted customer. It is for this reason that the House of Lords in *Hill and Sons v Edwin Showell and Sons Ltd* (1918) 87 LJKB 1106, permitted a buyer to show that the seller could not have earned more as a result of acceptance by the buyer because the seller could not have dealt with more than one order at a time.

As a matter of principle, the rule allowing recovery for loss of profit on the extra sale can be criticised. For example, although it can be shown that the seller had the capacity to meet the different orders, this should not be determinative of the issue, especially since the manufacture of the two orders may have been prevented by other factors, for example, industrial action. Moreover, it is simplistic to equate the loss sustained with the full profit given up from the defaulting sale because each unit of stock carries its own overhead expenses for the supplier, and there may be considerable savings here resulting from the buyer's termination. At least some discount should be considered in order to take into account the possibility that the second sale would have been less profitable than the broken contract.

The duty to mitigate loss

Where the buyer is in default, it is the duty of the seller to mitigate his damages. Generally, the standard required for mitigation is a low one, although it has been held to be unreasonable for a plaintiff to decline an offer by the defendant to enter into a fresh contract on cash instead of credit terms (*Payzu Ltd v Saunders* [1919] 2 KB 581), or to refuse an offer for late delivery (*The Solholt* [1983]

1 Lloyd's Rep 605). A problem which has arisen is whether a seller is obliged, in fulfillment of his duty to mitigate, to spend money upon goods in order to render them fit for resale. In this respect, it was held in *Jewelowski v Propp* [1944] KB 510 that where the expenditure is speculative, a plaintiff's duty to mitigate cannot be taken so far as to make it necessary for him to spend money.

The overriding issue concerning the duty to mitigate loss is whether or not the seller's conduct is reasonable having regard to the character of the goods and the demand for them. This is also pertinent in determining where there is an available market for disposal of the goods. The relevant criterion is not where a substitute sale is to be made but whether a seller can reasonably find a substitute purchaser. It is for this reason that English courts take a broad and commonsense view of what is an available market.

One problem that emerges with respect to mitigation is that of anticipatory breach. The seller may elect to accept the anticipatory breach and will be under the ordinary duty to mitigate, or alternatively, affirm the contract and so increase his loss. With regard to the former, the assumption is that the seller will wait until the due date of acceptance before reselling the goods and thereby mitigate his loss (*Millett v Van Heeck* [1921] 2 KB 369). Any profit or loss made by the seller through selling the goods before the due date is ignored. Such an approach is odd and seems inconsistent with the literal words used in s 50(3) which refer to the relevant time as being when the buyer refuses to accept the goods (compare s 2:706 of the US Uniform Commercial Code).

Rescission of the contract

When a contract has been induced by misrepresentation, the innocent party may be able to rescind the contract *ab initio*. The most common event giving rise to a right of rescission in this context will be the buyer's fraud, for example, where he misrepresents his identity (*Lewis v Averay* [1972] 1 QB 198; compare *Ingram v Little* [1961] 1 QB 31). The right to rescission will be lost if an innocent third party acquires an interest in the goods so the seller will have to act swiftly if rescission is to be effective (see *Car and Universal Finance Co Ltd v Caldwell* [1965] 1 QB 525).

There has been some discussion in the case law as to whether the remedy of rescission of a contract of sale of goods for innocent misrepresentation has survived the SGA 1893. Despite some Commonwealth authority to the contrary (see *Riddiford v Warren* (1901) 20 NZLR 572), the Court of Appeal has on several occasions assumed that rescission is available for contracts of sale of goods (see *Leaf v International Galleries* [1950] 2 KB 86; *Long v Lloyd* [1958] 1 WLR 753; *Goldsmith v Rodger* [1962] 2 Lloyd's Rep 249). The remedy of rescission is a powerful one and is available even if both property and possession have passed to the buyer, irrespective of the latter's solvency.

Chapter 14

Remedies of the Transferee for Misrepresentation or Breach

A buyer or á hirer has a series of remedies available to him if the supplier is guilty of a breach of contract or misrepresentation. Indeed, in large measure the complexity of the law is due to the multiplicity of the remedies available to him. Of particular significance is the right of the transferee to reject the goods tendered and rescind on the grounds of defective performance. However, this right may be lost where the buyer or hirer has accepted the goods as this will be treated as an election to affirm the contract.

Loss of the right to reject

Even though the seller has been guilty of a breach of condition which will *prima facie* give the buyer the right to reject the goods, he may in certain circumstances lose this right and be relegated to a claim for damages. Section 11(4) of SGA 1979 provides:

> Subject to section 35A below, where a contract of sale is not severable and the buyer has accepted the goods or part of them, the breach of a condition to be fulfilled by the seller can only be treated as a breach of warranty, and not as a ground for rejecting the goods and treating the contract as repudiated, unless there is an express or implied term of the contract to that effect.

Acceptance in contracts of sale

The issue of acceptance is crucial to the loss of the right to reject. The seller must afford the buyer a reasonable opportunity to examine the goods (s 34) (see Chapter 8). Acceptance is an interrelating rule to this right of examination and is defined in s 35(1)–(3) as follows:

(1) The buyer is deemed to have accepted the goods |subject to subsection (2) below—
   (a) when he intimates to the seller that he has accepted them, or
   (b) when the goods have been deliverd to him and he does any act in relation to them which is inconsistent with the ownership of the seller.
(2) Where goods are delivered to the buyer, and he has not previously examined them, he is not deemed to have accepted them under subsection (1) above until he has had a reasonable opportunity of examining them for the purpose—

(a) of ascertaining whether they are in conformity with the contract, and
(b) in the case of a contract for sale by sample, of comparing the bulk with the sample.

(3) Where the buyer deals as consumer or (in Scotland) the contract of sale is a consumer contract, the buyer cannot lose his right to rely on subsection (2) above by agreement, waiver or otherwise.

From this it appears that the buyer will lose his right to reject in the following circumstances.

Express acceptance

As the buyer has a statutory right to examine the goods, in order to bar his right to reject it must be shown that the buyer has elected to accept the goods delivered as conforming with the contract. This could amount to a complete waiver of all claims arising under the sale or supply contract. Particularly problematic in this context is the acceptance note signed by a buyer before he has had an opportunity to examine the goods. This is the logic of s 35(3), so that a consumer is now not deemed to have accepted goods without reasonable examination even if he were to intimate acceptance to the seller.

Inconsistent act

It is difficult to understand what is meant by an act 'inconsistent with the ownership of the seller'. If the property has passed to the buyer, this can only mean an act which is inconsistent with the reversionary interest of the seller (*Kwei Tek Chao v British Traders and Shippers Ltd* [1954] 2 QB 459). The commonest example here would be sub-sale by the buyer (see *Graanhandel T Vink v European Grain* [1989] 2 Lloyd's Rep 531). However, it is important not to be dogmatic as it is difficult to see how the original seller's reversionary interest would be prejudiced, even on sub-sale, where the sub-buyer rejected the goods. Essentially, it is a question of fact to be decided in each case as to what sort of use the buyer has made of the goods, and then relating this to the seller's continuing reversionary interest, for example, by pledging or mortgaging the goods. In *E Hardy and Co v Hillerns and Fowler* [1923] 2 KB 490, it was held in the Court of Appeal that there was an act inconsistent with the seller's ownership when the buyers took delivery of part of a cargo and sent it to the sub-buyers. As a matter of principle, it is questionable whether the buyer should have lost his right to reject in this situation if he can restore the goods to the seller.

There are two main strands of authority. The first relates to where the buyer has destroyed, damaged or used the goods or incorporated them into another product so that they cannot be returned to the seller in good order. The second strand is where the buyer has acted in such a way as to show that he did not intend to reject the goods, notably by delivering them to a third party following a sub-sale. The SGA as amended deals with the latter and in the same way acceptance is not deemed to have taken place simply by virtue of asking or agreeing to a repair of goods. Section 35(6) provides:

> The buyer is not by virtue of this section deemed to have accepted the goods merely because—

(a) he asks for, or agrees to, their repair by or under an arrangement with the
     seller, or
(b) the goods are delivered to another under a sub-sale or other disposition.

In this way an informal cure mechanism can be found in the amended SGA (see
Chapter 8).

If the buyer is unable to restore the goods in substantially the same condition as when they were delivered, this can be considered inconsistent with the
interest of the seller. Moreover, if the goods are damaged albeit accidentally by
the buyer, he will be precluded from rejecting the goods on the basis that *restitutio in integrum* is not possible which, as a common law bar to rejection, is
specifically preserved by s 62(2) of SGA 1979. On the other hand, where the
goods are damaged without the fault of either the seller or buyer, the latter does
have a *prima facie* right to reject. The issue is one of risk, and it would seem
following *Head v Tattersall* (1871) that the risk of loss in this circumstance falls
on the seller.

Lapse of time

If the buyer has not rejected the goods, s 35 provides that he is deemed to
have accepted them if he retains them beyond a reasonable time. The issue is
one of fact and the court must balance the interests of the parties. Clearly, if the
market is a fluctuating one or is seasonal, protection of the seller's interest
requires a speedier notification of rejection than when the market remains constant.

The amended SGA makes it clear that a buyer will not be deemed to have
accepted the goods until he has had a reasonable opportunity to examine them
to ascertain whether they conform with the contract or to compare the bulk with
the sample (s 35(5)). However the new Act does little to remedy the problem
seen in *Bernstein v Pamson Motors Ltd* [1987] 2 All ER 220 where a consumer
lost the right to reject a defective new car despite the fact that he had owned it
only for 27 days and had driven it for 141 miles before it had a serious break-
down. This was so even though there was no means of discovering the defect
(a piece of sealant in the lubrication system) through a reasonable examination.
The only way the buyer could have discovered the sealant would have been to
dismantle the engine, but given the nature of the problem, the engine could have
seized up at any time. However, the loss of the right to reject was linked by
Rougier J with a sufficient time to give the car a *general* trial. The right to reject
is, therefore, not lost on account of any dereliction on the part of the buyer.

The question that arises is as to the nature of the interest of the seller that is
being protected. It can only be that as a result of the passage of time the seller
would have been adversely affected, for example, the seller could have found
it difficult to raise the money which he has paid for the goods. This is unlikely
in the case of a new car dealer where there exist sophisticated floor plan financing techniques. The general point here is that the buyer's loss of the right to
reject is not necessarily tied to any prejudice on the part of the seller, and this
suggests that even the amended law provides a crude mechanism for the balancing of the respective interests of the parties. It may have made sense in the

19th Century for businessmen whose main interest in the goods was a financial one, as articles of commerce, and where the defects in the goods were perhaps more readily discoverable, as with agricultural products or simple machinery. It makes little sense in the case of a complex product in which faults take time to emerge, and where the buyer is a consumer who is interested in the goods as articles to be used, not as items of commerce to be bought and sold.

Of course, much depends upon the nature of the goods. This approach is confirmed in *Simpson Nash Wharton v Barco Graphics Ltd* (1991), unreported. In this case the plaintiffs were a firm of packaging and design consultants and they ordered from the defendants a computer system of hardware and software which they had specifically created to meet the requirements of designers. The system cost in excess of £225,000 and it proved to be unsatisfactory in that it was not commercially usable. The plaintiffs had not repudiated the contract for breach of the merchantable quality and reasonable fitness for purpose provision until 40 weeks had elapsed from the date of delivery and installation. Taking into account the nature of the goods it was held that there had been no deemed acceptance and that it was irrelevant that, within a month, part of the system was put right and was operable. In this respect Judge Rivlin QC maintained that the plaintiffs:

> . . . could not have had a crystal ball at that time |the time of rescission| which would have enabled them to look into the future to see that at one time in the future further developments to this particular system would be made which would ensure that those who purchased it would be satisfied with it.

In addressing the reasonableness of time issue for the purpose of acceptance, the principles were helpfully set out by the learned judge as follows:

> In my view, in all the circumstances the plaintiff had not retained the goods longer than the time necessary to give them a reasonable opportunity to examine the goods for the purpose of ascertaining whether they were in conformity with the contract. I arrive at that view having regard to all the circumstances of this case, including in particular the highly sophisticated nature of this equipment, and the many promises that were made to them throughout the relevant period to the effect that shortly the equipment would be put right to the point where they would achieve complete satisfaction with it. Reference has been made to a number of authorities in this regard, and in particular to the case of *Bernstein v Pamson Motors (Golders Green) Limited* |1987| 2 All ER 220. In that case the learned judge was faced with the problem which the defendants sought to pose in this case as to just when it was reasonable for the plaintiffs to rescind this contract. At page 230 the learned judge says: In my judgment, the nature of the particular defect, discovered '*ex post facto*', and the speed with which it might have been discovered, are irrelevant to the concept of reasonable time in section 35, as drafted. That section seems to me to be directed solely to what is a reasonable practical interval in commercial terms between a buyer receiving the goods and his ability to send them back, taking into consideration, from his point of view, the nature of the goods and their function, and from the point of view of the seller the commercial desirability of being able to close his ledger reasonably soon after the transaction is complete. The complexity of the intended function of the goods is clearly of prime consideration here. What is a reasonable time in relation to a bicycle would hardly suffice for a nuclear submarine.

It would appear from this case that the period for acceptance does depend upon the nature of the goods. Thus in *Burnley Engineering Products Ltd v Cambridge Vacuum Engineering Ltd* (1994), unreported, the facts involved a sophisticated electron beam welding machine for the aerospace industry valued at over £1m, and it was held that a period of about a year for 'bedding in' of the machine after the installation and signature of the acceptance certificate was appropriate, and that the buyer had a right to reject up to that point of time.

The *Bernstein* case (1987) shows that the remedies of rejection and rescission are often quickly lost in contracts of consumer sale. Only defects likely to be discovered quickly will permit rescission. There is a greater chance of a minor defect such as a cosmetic blemish being spotted quickly than a latent defect that may take a few hundred miles to emerge. Indeed this is specifically recognised in the definition of 'satisfactory quality'. Stronger remedies are likely to be available in the case of a minor defect, but may well be lost before major mechanical or structural problems surface. Of course, the buyer has a remedy in damages if necessary to cover the cost of selling and replacing the vehicle. Nonetheless, such action would not always be justified and, anyway, why should the buyer bear the burden and inconvenience rather than the seller? Damages may be appropriate where the buyer's interest in the goods is a purely financial one, but it is less appropriate when the buyer is interested in using the goods. Even so, the Law Commission in their Report No 160 rejected a single arbitrary fixed period as an indication of what is a reasonable time. If an attempt had been made to deal meaningfully with the concept this would have necessitated an examination of specific market context, for example the so-called 'lemon laws' enacted in some States in the USA. In some respects this has not been necessary in the UK by virtue of self-regulation, seen notably in motor manufacturers' various exchange schemes.

Part acceptance

Before the 1994 Act, a buyer under a non-severable contract had the right under s 30(4) to reject goods that did not correspond with their description while accepting those that did. In a new s 35A this right of partial rejection is extended so that whatever the nature of the breach, the buyer has three options: (a) he can reject all the contract goods; (b) he can accept all the contract goods; or (c) he can reject some of the goods and accept others, so long as he accepts all the goods that conform with the contract. Section 30(4), now redundant, has been repealed. Where an instalment contract is involved and, under s 31(2), the buyer has the right to reject all the goods under the contract, then he is given this same right of partial rejection. Where the buyer has the right to reject only goods contained in a particular instalment, the right of partial rejection operates with reference to that instalment alone. This does not prejudge whether there is, in any case, a right to reject. It is worth setting out the examples of the right to partial rejection as elaborated in the Law Commission Report No 160, at 6.16:

   (a)   If the buyer is a non-consumer and orders 100 objects, of which only 1 is defective (the breach being 'slight' or 'non-material'), he may not reject any but may claim damages. If the buyer were a consumer, he could keep them all, reject them all, or keep 99 and reject 1 (and in all cases claim damages).

(b) If the buyer orders 100 objects of which 50 are defective, he may reject 100, keep 100, or keep the 50 conforming objects and reject any or all of the 50 defective objects (and in all cases claim damages).

(c) If the buyer orders 100 objects and all are defective, he may reject all or any of them and claim damages.

(d) If the 100 objects in the previous examples comprised an instalment of a larger order, the result would be exactly the same as regards that instalment; the partial rejection rules do not affect any rights the buyer may have as regards other instalments.

This new general right of partial rejection has necessitated making s 11(4) subject to the new s 35A. However, if matters were left like this it would allow buyers to break up goods forming one unit. To prevent this a new concept is introduced by s 35(7) which provides as follows:

> Where the contract is for the sale of goods making one or more commercial units, a buyer accepting any goods included in a unit is deemed to have accepted all the goods making the unit; and in this subsection 'commercial unit' means a unit division of which would materially impair the value of the goods or the character of the unit.

This definition draws upon art 2:105(6) of the American Uniform Commercial Code. In its Report the Law Commission provides the following examples of the 'commercial unit' phenomenon:

(i) A buyer who accepted part only of a set, such as a single volume of an encyclopaedia which is sold as a set, would normally be deemed to have accepted the whole set.

(ii) A buyer who accepted part only of a sack or other unit (whether measured by weight or in some other way) by which goods of the type in question are customarily sold in the trade would be deemed to have accepted the whole unit. The buyer would not be restricted if it was merely the seller (and not the trade in general) who chose to sell goods in that particular way.

(iii) A buyer who accepted one shoe of a pair would be deemed to have accepted the pair; but he would be entitled to accept one of a number of identical articles, even if more than one at a time was commonly bought, if each was in fact a self-contained unit.

Acceptance in contracts of supply

The SGSA 1982 does not purport to regulate the exercise of the transferee's remedies. The issue concerning the loss of the right to reject is determined by the common law, although there is no substantial divergence from the position under the SGA 1979. There is no doubt that the right to reject lapses after a reasonable time in contracts of hire purchase (*Jackson v Chrysler Acceptances Ltd* [1978] RTR 474). It was argued that in the case of a contract of hire purchase, the supplier must supply goods which remain fit to be used throughout the period of hire on the basis of the theory of continuous breach. This approach was firmly scotched by the Court of Appeal in *UCB Leasing Ltd v Holtom* [1987] RTR 362.

The question of acceptance in contracts of hire purchase is construed widely, the courts taking into account factors such as the conduct of the hirer and seller, attempts at repairs, negotiations for a settlement and the discovery of latent defects. Thus in *Porter v General Guarantee Corpn* [1982] RTR 384, the plaintiff acquired a secondhand car from the defendants, a finance company, under a hire purchase agreement dated 26 January 1980. The agreement was negotiated by third party dealers who had been informed by the plaintiff that he wished to use the car as a taxi. They informed him that it would be suitable for such use. On delivery, the car was found to be defective in many respects. Repairs, negotiations and inspections continued over a period of two months with the plaintiff continuing to use the vehicle. Finally, the contract was repudiated on 20 March. On the question of whether the plaintiff had lost his right to repudiate by continuing to use the car when he was aware of the defects, Kilner Brown J, stated: 'I think it was reasonable to continue negotiation to see whether or not the third party would pay for the work done at the plaintiff's behest and on his own terms. If he was unreasonable in his demands this does not go to affirmation' (p 394). The plaintiff was allowed to reject the car, the judge indicating that he would be liable for an outstanding instalment under the agreement representing his use of the car over a month during which he was in a position to repudiate. Undoubtedly, following this case, the relevant factor determining the affirmation issue is that of knowledge of the defect and lack of satisfaction with the product. This can be summarised by Lord Denning's approach in *Farnworth Finance Facilities v Attryde* [1970] 1 WLR 1053 where, despite the concession that the hirer had used the motor cycle (the object of the hire purchase contract) for four months and had ridden it for 4,000 miles, it was held:

> A man only affirms a contract when he knows of the defects and by his conduct elects to go on with the contract despite them. In this case the hirer complained from the beginning of the defects and sent the machine back for them to be remedied . . . But the defects were never satisfactorily remedied . . . The hirer was entitled to say then: 'I am not going on with this machine any longer. I have tried it long enough.' After all it was a contract of hiring. The machine was not his until the three years had been completed . . . .. (p 1059)

It would appear that where the goods contain a latent defect the customer is better off in a non-sale case since he does not lose his right to terminate until he becomes aware of it.

In *Woodchester Equipment Leasing Ltd v Marie* (1993) unreported, a drinks vending machine was installed at the defendant's hairdressing salon, but there was a hire agreement between the plaintiff finance company and the defendant (which had come about following a sale by the suppliers of the equipment which was then leased back to the defendant). The vending machine was faulty although it was still held to be merchantable by the Court of Appeal, so the defendant was confined to setting off a sum of money representing her damages against the sum which would otherwise have been the plaintiff's entitlement. As Russell LJ found:

> The equipment was still in the possession of the defendant and still being used no doubt to her advantage, albeit a limited advantage, for a considerable period of time after defects first came to the notice of the defendant.

In some situations where there is a breach which goes to the root of the contract the damages awarded to the defendant may be sufficient to extinguish its liability to the plaintiff. The case in point here is *UCB Leasing Ltd v Holtom (trading as David Holtom and Co)* [1987] RTR 362. This was a case where the judge found at first instance that the defect in a motor car hired to a customer was so serious as to be a breach of a fundamental term. The argument therefore followed that the hirer, once the agreement was brought to an end (as it was) by the leasing company in consequence of the failure of the hirer to pay instalments, was entitled to contend that but for the fundamental defect he would, for the rest of the period of the agreement, have had to hire an alternative vehicle, hypothetically at all events at the same cost to him. By that process, as the Court of Appeal found, the claim by the hiring company in respect of a long period after the vehicle was returned to them was extinguished by the notional loss occasioned to the hirer.

No recommendation was made by the Law Commission in their Report No 160 to harmonise sale and supply contracts here, and a distinction was drawn between hire contracts and sale. In the case of the former, there is a continuing relationship between the parties and in a very real sense in operational leases the goods belong to the owner who may have a continuing obligation to repair and replace hired goods. Furthermore, in hire there is a convenient method of valuing use and enjoyment of the goods, namely, the hire charge itself. In the case of sale no principles on the use and enjoyment of goods have emerged. It could be argued, however, that leasing and hire purchase are devices established to finance the acquisition of goods and it is purely a matter of legal form; the fact that legal rights will be different from sale should be considered to be unsatisfactory. However, the Law Commisison pointed out at 5.46:

> It is true that hire purchase is a device for financing what in the end will amount to a sale. We are, however, not persuaded that this means that the acceptance rule of sale contracts should also apply to hire purchase. A pattern of rights and duties has grown up and we do not think this pattern should be disturbed unless there are compelling reasons to do so.

Rejection and total failure of consideration

In *Rowland v Divall* [1923] 2 KB 500, the Court of Appeal held that the buyer of a car was entitled to reject it for breach of s 12(1) of SGA 1979 despite the fact that he had resold the car and the sub-buyer had had four months' use of it. There is nothing wrong in legal logic with recognising a limited notion of 'curing' a title defect (see Chapter 10). Indeed, this is illustrated by *Butterworth v Kingsway Motors Ltd* [1954] 1 WLR 1286 where the hirer of a car under a hire purchase agreement sold it but continued to pay the instalments as they fell due. After almost a year's use, the plaintiff was notified by the finance company that the car was on hire purchase and he promptly terminated his contract with the defendant. Within a very short time, the hirer paid her final instalment, and it was held that this 'fed' the titles of the intermediate buyers. Thus, although the plaintiff could recover the full price, all the intermediate buyers who had not terminated before their titles were 'fed' could only recover damages for breach of contract (compare *Barber v NWS Bank plc* (Unreported) 17 November 1995 (CA) discussed at p 223).

It is not surprising that the reasoning of Atkin LJ in *Rowland v Divall* (1923) has been restricted in other contexts. For example, it could be applied for breach of s 13 where what is tendered is something different from what was agreed on. One explanation for the reluctance to extend the reasoning in *Rowland v Divall* to other contexts is the recognition that title is so important that any act on the part of the buyer must be without prejudice to his right to reject for breach of s 12(1). It is noteworthy that in *Rowland v Divall* the seller never acquired the right to sell the car and could not, therefore, be regarded as having accepted the goods. As Atkin LJ put it: 'In fact the buyer has not received any part that which he has contracted to receive — namely the property and the right to possession' (p 507).

The action for damages

A buyer or hirer may have at his disposal an action for damages available against his supplier or third party for breach of the supply contract, or for some collateral contract otherwise concluded. As an alternative, there is no reason why the buyer or hirer should not be able to treat the collateral warranty as a misrepresentation and rescind the contract. Where there has been a fraudulent misrepresentation, the supplier will be liable in tort for deceit. For negligent misrepresentation, damages are available at common law when the misrepresentation results in physical injury, or where there was a breach of a fiduciary duty, or a duty created by a special relationship (*Hedley Byrne and Co Ltd v Heller and Partners Ltd* [1964] AC 465). A right to damages is now expressly provided by s 2(1) of the Misrepresentation Act 1967.

Damages for misrepresentation

Where a misrepresentation is fraudulent at common law, then damages may be recovered in the tort of deceit. The aim of an award of damages in deceit is to put the plaintiff in the position which he would have been in had the tort not been committed (*Doyle v Olby* [1969] 2 QB 158). In addition, all damage directly flowing from the fraudulent inducement and which is not too remote in the light of the plaintiff's own conduct is recoverable. In the case of negligent misrepresentation, at common law damages are awarded which put the plaintiff in the position he would have been in had the tort not been committed. The representor will be liable for all losses which are a reasonably foreseeable consequence of the misrepresentation (*The Wagon Mound (No 1)* [1961] AC 388). If the representee has also been at fault then the damages payable may be reduced on the grounds of contributory negligence (Law

Reform (Contributory Negligence) Act 1945, s 1; *Gran Gelato Ltd v Richcliff (Group) Ltd* [1992] Ch 560).

Section 2(1) and 2(2) of the Misrepresentation Act 1967 also make provision for the recovery of damages for misrepresentation. The measure of damages under s 2(1) is to put the plaintiff in the position which he would have been in had the representation not been made. Damages are assessed as if the representor had been fraudulent (see *Royscot Trust Ltd v Rogerson* [1991] 2 QB 297) so that the remoteness rules applicable are those pertaining to the tort of deceit, not the tort of negligence. It has also been held that damages payable under s 2(1) may be reduced on the basis of the representee's contributory negligence (see *Gran Gelato Ltd v Richcliff (Group) Ltd* (1992)). This approach does seem somewhat incongruous since in *Royscot* it was held that the appropriate analogy was with the tort of deceit, where contributory negligence does not apply (see *Alliance and Leicester Building Society v Edgestop Ltd* [1994] 2 All ER 38).

At common law the traditional rule was that damages were not available for innocent misrepresentation. However, this strict approach has been mitigated by s 2(2) of the Misrepresentation Act 1967 so that the courts now have a discretion to award damages in lieu of recession. We have already discussed the limits of s 2(2) (see pp 32–4) and at this point all that has to be mentioned is that the measure of damages compensates the plaintiff for the loss suffered on account of the innocent misrepresentation and is therefore the contract measure (see *William Sindall plc v Cambridgeshire CC* [1994] 1 WLR 1016).

Breach of contract

The general rule is that the measure of damages constitutes the difference between the price paid, or if it is lower, the market value of what was contracted for, and the market value of what was obtained (see *White Arrow Express Ltd v Lamey's Distribution Ltd* (1995) *The Times*, 21 July). The quantification of the measure of damages has been confirmed recently by the House of Lords in *Ruxley Electronics and Construction Ltd v Forsyth* [1995] 3 WLR 118, where Lord Mustill held that this relates to 'the loss truly suffered by the promisee' (p 127). In quantifying this loss the court will have regard to the 'consumer surplus' element, that is the sum by which the value of the promise to the promisee exceeds the financial enhancement of his position which full performance would secure. The House of Lords appears to have sanctioned an *ex post facto* objective valuation of the promisee's expectations so that where the expenditure is out of all proportion to the benefit to be obtained by curing the defect, the appropriate measure of damages is not the cost of reinstatement but the diminution in the value of the work occasioned by the breach. In the sale and supply of goods context, the conventional scenarios for the action for damages for breach may take one of two forms, (a) an action for damages for non-delivery, or (b) an action founded on a breach of a term(s) in the contract of supply.

Damages for non-delivery

Sale

In the case of non-delivery constituting a repudiation of the contract, the buyer can treat it as being at an end and recover payments made on the basis of total failure of consideration. As an alternative, the buyer can sue for damages for non-delivery. If the failure does not constitute repudiation, or the buyer chooses not to accept it, the contract continues in force for the benefit of both parties. In this circumstance, the buyer will be able to claim damages for non-delivery.

The measure of damages for non-delivery

The counterpart to the seller's action for non-acceptance (s 50 of SGA 1979) is the buyer's action for non-delivery under s 51 of SGA 1979. This section provides as follows:

(1) Where the seller wrongfully neglects or refuses to deliver the goods to the buyer, the buyer may maintain an action against the seller for damages for non-delivery.

(2) The measure of damages is the estimated loss directly and naturally resulting, in the ordinary course of events, from the seller's breach of contract.

(3) Where there is an available market for the goods in question the measure of damages is prima facie to be ascertained by the difference between the contract price and the market or current price of the goods at the time or times when they ought to have been delivered or (if no time was fixed) at the time of the refusal to deliver.

As can be seen, the so-called first rule in *Hadley v Baxendale* (1854) 9 Exch 341 is set out in s 51(2). The second rule is referred to in s 54 which denotes damages for loss not as a result of some natural consequence of the defendant's breach, but from some special circumstance which the plaintiff must demonstrate ought reasonably to have been within the defendant's contemplation at the time of the loss. Section 51(3) sets out the normal measure of damages available by reference to whether there is an available market.

Where there is an available market

The onus of proving the buying price in the available market is upon the buyer. The *prima facie* measure of damages is the amount by which the market price exceeds the contract price at the stipulated date and place of delivery of the goods or documents of title. If delivery is to be by instalments, the market price is fixed separately for each instalment at the time when it is due (*Roper v Johnson* (1873) LR 8 CP 167). Where a contract expressly provides for a period during which delivery is to be made, the seller is not in breach until the last day of the permitted period. Similarly, if the time of delivery has been extended at the request of the seller, the market price is taken at the postponed delivery date (*Ogle v Earl of Vane* (1868) LR 3 QB 272). Although the buyer has a duty to mitigate his loss, it is unrealistic to maintain that the buyer would be able to buy goods in the market on the very day which the seller fails to deliver. The buyer is therefore entitled to a reasonable time within which to ascertain the seller's intentions after a failure to deliver, for example, to examine the possibility of a postponed delivery date.

The market rule is of overriding significance and is not easily displaced. It does not matter that the buyer does without the goods, or that having gone into the market he has bought goods of the same description at a lower price. The reasoning here is that the buyer has lost the benefit of two bargains. A distinction should be drawn here with the facts in *Pagnan and Fratelli v Corbisa Industrial Agropacuaria Limitada* [1970] 1 WLR 1306. In this case, the buyer lawfully rejected the goods, and following negotiations between the parties, the buyers agreed to buy the same goods from the sellers at a reduced price which were then resold by the buyers for a profit. It was held that there was a connection with the original contract which could not be ignored, otherwise it would be tantamount to giving the buyers damages for a fictitious loss when they had in fact made a profit. Nevertheless, the general rule is not easily displaced, even if the buyer has already contracted to resell the goods to a third party at a price higher (*Williams Bros Ltd v ET Agius Ltd* [1914] AC 510) or lower (*Rodocanachi v Milburn* (1886) 18 QBD 67) than the market price at the date when delivery should have been made. The reasoning here is that the buyer will always have the option of obtaining the goods from the market place in order to fulfil the subcontract.

The question of the determination of the date of the market price is highly relevant in the case of anticipatory breach. In these circumstances, the concluding words of s 51(3) do not apply. The difficulty is that where no fixed time for delivery has been set, following the approach of the House of Lords in *White and Carter (Councils) Ltd v McGregor* [1962] AC 413, and the Privy Council decision in *Tai Hing Cotton Ltd v Kamsing Knitting Factory* [1979] AC 91, the buyer can keep the seller's obligations alive by refusing to accept the repudiation. If the buyer elects to hold the contract open, the duty to mitigate is deferred. The criticism is that this rule encourages economic waste because the mitigation of damages principle will only apply upon termination. However, the courts may view the matter differently if the innocent party has no legitimate interest in the continuing performance of the contract, as can be illustrated in *The Alaskan Trader (No 2)* [1984] 1 All ER 129. In this case, charterers in breach of contract refused to take the ship back after repairs. The owners kept the vessel at anchor and fully crewed, ready to sail for the rest of the charter. It was held that the owners had no legitimate interest in so behaving and could not recover the entire rent due under the charter because this would be tantamount to the court enforcing gross economic waste.

Where the buyer elects to accept the repudiation, he comes under an immediate duty to mitigate. Provided the buyer acts reasonably, he is entitled to damages assessed by reference to the price at which he purchases, irrespective of the market value at the due delivery date (*Melachrino v Nickoll and Knight* [1920] 1 KB 693).

Where there is no available market

This may be the case where demand exceeds supply, or no reasonable substitute for the goods was available. In such cases, s 51(3) is inapplicable and here the measure of damages payable is by way of compensation for loss of bargain, the object being to put the buyer as nearly as possible in the position he would have been had the contract been performed. The rule in *Hadley v Baxendale* (1854) requires consideration of whether the loss could reasonably have been contemplated by the seller as flowing from his breach, a question which is bound up with the extent to which the buyer's intended application of the goods should reasonably have been present in the seller's mind.

The cases are not easy to reconcile and much depends upon the non-remote purpose for which the goods were required. Thus, in the case of a wholesale supply, the buyer's loss will be determined as the normal trade mark up on subsale (*Koufos v Czarnikov Ltd (The Heron II)* [1969] 1 AC 350). In other circumstances where there has been sub-sale, the loss to the buyer will *prima facie* be the amount by which the value at the date of breach exceeds the contract price, ie the buyer is able to recover for his lost profit (*Household Machines Ltd v Cosmos Exports Ltd* [1947] 1 KB 217). The sub-sale price is not necessarily conclusive evidence of the goods' value, which will primarily depend upon the circumstances of the case: for example, where the sub-sale contract had been concluded a long time before the due date of delivery, it would be anomalous to visit upon the seller the risk of a falling market (*The Arpad* [1934] P 189).

Particular difficulties arise in defining the circumstances in which a buyer is entitled to claim damages in respect of lost sub-sales. In order for the buyer to recover for this consequential loss, he must show that he purchased the goods for resale and that he had committed himself, or intended to do so, with respect to delivering the same goods (not merely an equivalent amount) to a sub-purchaser. Furthermore, the seller should be aware of these facts, or they ought reasonably to have been within his contemplation at the time of entering into the main contract. The main decision is that of *Re R & H Hall Ltd and WH Pim and Co* (1928) All ER Rep 763. In this case, there was a standard term trade association contract with respect to the supply of wheat which expressly contemplated resale along a string of contracts, these being supplemented by subsidiary agreements. The case involved the sale of a cargo of wheat at 51s 9d per quarter which the buyer resold at 56s 9d per quarter. When the seller refused to deliver, the market price was 53s 9d per quarter and the seller argued that he should only be liable for the difference between the contract and market price, ie 2s per quarter. The House of Lords held the seller liable for the difference between the contract and resale prices (5s per quarter), a decision influenced by the original sellers' sharp practice of trying to defer their breach of contract so as reduce their damages on a falling market.

The crucial factors in the above case were that there was a sale of specific cargo, on an identified ship, which had been resold, and this was specifically anticipated in the original contract of sale. As a string contract, there was no available market simply because the resale contract would not allow the buyer to buy a substitute. Everything turns on what the seller could have foreseen under the rules of remoteness, the loss being confined to ordinary loss of profit on sub-sale unless the seller was aware of a specially lucrative contract lost because of his failure to perform (see *Victoria Laundry Ltd v Newman Industries Ltd* [1949] 2 KB 528). It also follows in a non-remote sub-sale that the seller should be liable for any compensation which the buyer has to pay his sub-buyer by way of damages or indemnity (see *Household Machines Ltd v Cosmos Exporters Ltd* [1947] KB 217).

The buyer may not in every case seek to recover damages. As an alternative, he may elect the recovery of expenditure incurred in connection with the transaction. The aim here is restoration of the position the buyer occupied before entry into the contract. This must be distinguished from special damage which is recoverable in any case for breach, for example, where the buyer has to pay for freight despite the non-delivery of the goods (*E Braude (London) Ltd v Porter* [1959] 2 Lloyd's Rep 161). Expenditure which would not have been incurred but for the breach, including consequential loss, is recoverable in addition to damages for loss of bargain, such as extra freight, or insurance charges in connection with the acquisition of substitute goods.

Contracts of supply

In the case of a simple contract of hire or hire purchase, the measure of damages for failure to deliver should be the difference between the contract hire or hire purchase rate and the market rate for such transactions. As a matter of consistency in logic, this should also be the case where a hirer lawfully terminates the contract and rescinds. This situation should be distinguished from the case where the hirer has accepted delivery but has subsequently rejected on the basis of continuous breach. In such circumstances, it was held in *Yeoman Credit Ltd v Apps* [1962] 2 QB 508 that the hirer can recover by way of damages the reasonable sum necessary to repair the object bailed. Of course, this is open to the objection that the measure of damages relates to breach of warranty rather than rescission. The theoretical incongruity here in no small measure contributed to the demise of the continuous breach doctrine (see *UCB Leasing Ltd v Holtom* [1987] RTR 362), so the measure of damages is confined where the hirer affirms the contract following a reasonable opportunity to discover the defect.

Damages for breach of condition or warranty

Where there has been a breach of warranty in a contract of sale, s 53(1) of SGA 1979 provides as follows:

> Where there is a breach of warranty by the seller, or where the buyer elects (or is compelled) to treat any breach of a condition on the part of the seller as a breach of warranty, the buyer is not by reason only of such breach of warranty entitled to reject the goods; but he may—
> (a) set up against the seller the breach of warranty in diminution or extinction of the price, or
> (b) maintain an action against the seller for damages for the breach of warranty.

Insofar as this reflects the common law position, it will also be relevant to other contracts of supply.

It is clearly envisaged in s 53(1) that the buyer in an action by the seller for the price may counterclaim the seller's breach by way of defence. In addition, s 53(1) anticipates that the buyer can maintain an action in contract or tort for breach. Where the buyer's loss exceeds the price, s 53(4) states:

> The fact that the buyer has set up the breach of warranty in diminution or extinction of the price does not prevent him from maintaining an action for the same breach of warranty if he has suffered further damage.

As far as remoteness of damage is concerned, s 53(2) sets out the first rule in *Hadley v Baxendale* (1854), whilst the second rule is referred to in s 54.

Defects in title

The implied term as to title is a condition the breach of which entitles the buyer or transferee to treat the contract as being repudiated. In addition, the buyer will be able to recover for loss of bargain, or in the alternative, recover any payment made on the basis of total failure of consideration (*Rowland v Divall* (1923)). The transferee may also recover any consequential loss which the supplier ought reasonably have contemplated would flow as a result of the breach. If the transferee affirms the contract this is similar to when the transferor's repudiation is accepted, and the *prima facie* level of damages is the purchase (or hire purchase) price, including expenses, since the transferee has not enjoyed the essential benefit contracted for (*Warman v Southern Counties Car Finance Corp Ltd* [1949] 2 KB 576).

Delay in delivery

Where time is of the essence, late delivery is treated as a breach of condition. The effect of this is that where a late tender is made, the buyer's lawful rejection makes the case one of non-delivery. In the case of a delay in delivery which the transferee cannot rescind (in a case where time is not of the essence) or he elects not to rescind, the action for damages is akin to a breach of warranty. As such, the contract continues and this has an impact on the transferee's duty to mitigate his loss. Thus, in the case where goods are bought for resale, where there is an available market, the *prima facie* measure of damages is the amount by which the market value at the contractual time for delivery exceeds the market value at the actual time of delivery. In this respect, resales by the buyer should be ignored because there is no reason why the original seller should gain from a providential sale by his buyer. In this respect, the Privy Council decision in *Wertheim v Chicoutini Pulp Co* [1911] AC 301 can be criticised, and it is submitted that the decision in *Slater v Hoyle and Smith Ltd* [1920] 2 KB 11 is to be preferred where the below-market price realised by the buyer on resale was ignored.

Where there is no available market, the measure of damages is the amount by which the contract price exceeds the actual value at the contractual time for delivery. In the case where goods are bought for resale, since the seller has intimated that he is willing to perform, there is no reason for the buyer to mitigate his loss by buying replacement goods on the due delivery date. This explains why damages are measured not by reference to the price at which the buyer could have bought substitute goods on the due delivery date, but by reference to the price at which he could reasonably be expected to sell them on the actual delivery date (*Kwei Tek Chao v British Traders and Shippers Ltd* [1954] 2 QB 459).

Contracts of hire or hire purchase contain a prohibition of sale by the hirer so there is, by definition, no available market. This will also be the case where goods are bought for use, and the measure of damages here relates to the deprivation of the use of the asset for the period of delay. It follows that where the asset is of an income-producing kind, the transferee should be able to recover for the loss of profit that the transferor could reasonably have contemplated as flowing from the breach. This can be illustrated in the famous case of *Victoria Laundry (Windsor) Ltd v Newman Industries Ltd* (1949) where the defendants were late in supplying a boiler required by the plaintiffs for their laundry and dyeing business. It was held that the plaintiffs were liable for loss of normal profits resulting from the plaintiffs' loss of business, but not for additional losses relating to the special contracts entered into on particularly lucrative terms as these could not have been foreseen by the seller. Of course, the transferee is under a duty to mitigate his loss where he can, for example, by hiring substitute goods pending delivery.

Defects in quality: sale

Where non-conforming goods are tendered by the seller, the buyer may reject the goods, and if the seller cannot or is unwilling to re-tender the goods in due time, the buyer can treat the contract as repudiated. There are two other possible courses of action available to him: firstly, he can seek to recover the price paid on the basis of total failure of consideration; secondly, he may accept the goods and sue for breach of warranty. In this case, s 53(3) of SGA 1979 provides:

> In the case of breach of warranty such loss is prima facie the difference between the value of the goods at the time of delivery to the buyer and the value they would have had if they had fulfilled the warranty.

It appears from this that the *prima facie* measure of damages is the amount by which the warranted value of the goods exceeds the actual value of the goods delivered and accepted.

There is no doubt that s 53(3) of SGA 1979 reflects the common law position (see *Jones v Just* (1868) LR 3 QB 197). This may be displaced where the goods are consigned and delivered to sub-buyers. In *Van den Hurk v Martens and Co Ltd* [1920] 1 KB 850, it was held that the goods should be valued at the time and place of delivery to the sub-buyer, provided that the seller should have foreseen that the goods might be delivered without examination. The general rule is that the market price of the goods is irrelevant to an action of damages of this kind. There may be evidence of an actual value of the goods to a hypothetical buyer with knowledge of the breach, and this may be applied by the court especially in consumer sales (*Jackson v Chrysler Acceptances Ltd* [1978] RTR 474). Where the actual value cannot be determined, damages may be awarded on the basis of bringing the goods up to the requisite contract standard (*Minster Trust Ltd v Traps Tractors Ltd* [1954] 3 All ER 236).

It would seem, following s 53(3), that the market price is irrelevant except insofar as it may be taken to be the value which the goods should have had. Where the buyer has lost the opportunity of rejecting the goods before he has become fully aware of a defect, in cases involving shipping documentation, the courts have awarded the buyer the contract price less the fallen market price (*James Finlay v NV Kwik Hoo Tong* [1929] 1 KB 400; *Kwei Tek Chao v British Traders and Shippers Ltd* [1954] 2 QB 459; compare *Proctor and Gamble Philippine Manufacturing Corp v Kurt A Becher GmbH* [1988] 2 Lloyd's Rep 21). In principle, there is no reason to apply these cases in ordinary contracts of sale. It would be anomalous to allow a buyer who accepts goods which he is entitled to reject, the right to be placed in the same financial position as he would have been in if he had rejected the goods. It is otherwise where there has been a misrepresentation since this may render it unjust to apply the *prima facie* rule encapsulated in s 53(3) (see *Naughton and another v O'Callaghan (Rogers and others, third parties)* [1990] 3 All ER 191).

Defects in quality: contracts of supply

In the case of contracts of hire, the measure of damages should be the difference between the warranted hire rate and the amount which the hired goods could command in their actual state. With contracts of hire purchase, an allowance should be made for the option to purchase and account should be taken of the possibility that the hiring may be determined. No general rule can be laid down, but in *Charterhouse Credit Co Ltd v Tolly* [1963] 2 QB 683, Upjohn LJ suggested (at pp 711–12) that in the absence of the owner terminating the hire purchase contract, the hirer would have been entitled to the amount required to put the vehicle in a proper state of repair as well as damages for loss of use.

Damages for distress and inconvenience

The courts remain reluctant to award damages to compensate a plaintiff for his 'subjective losses'. The principles for recovery of damages for distress and inconvenience were confirmed by the Court of Appeal in *Alexander v Alpe Jack, Rolls-Royce Motor Cars Ltd* (1995) *The Times*, 4 May. The facts involved the sale of a second hand Rolls-Royce which was held to be of not merchantable quality because at the time of sale it had a defective gear box and torque converter and a worn fridge compressor, worn camshaft and tappets, all of which needed replacement. It was held by Beldam LJ that the general rule is that damages for distress, inconvenience or loss of enjoyment are not recoverable for breach of an ordinary commercial contract. This is so even in relation to a computer hardware and software design package which was intended to remove the drudgery of production away from the plaintiff purchasers leaving them more time to be creative and give them peace of mind and freedom from stress. Damages of this kind are not appropriate in purely commercial contracts (see *Hayes v James and Charles Dodd (A firm)* [1990] 2 All ER 815.

The leading authority is the Court of Appeal decision in *Watts v Morrow* [1991] 1 WLR 1421, where the plaintiffs claimed damages for distress and inconvenience consequent upon the purchase of a property relying on a negligent survey and report. The Court held that in such a case general damages were recoverable only for distress and inconvenience caused by the physical consequences of the breach of contract, including a modest sum for the amount of physical discomfort endured. The general position was summed up by Bingham LJ (at p 1445):

> A contract-breaker is not in general liable for any distress, frustration, anxiety, displeasure, vexation, tension or aggravation which his breach of contract may cause to the innocent party. This rule is not, I think, founded on the assumption that such reactions are not foreseeable, which they surely are or may be, but on considerations of policy. But the rule is not absolute. Where the very object of a contract is to provide pleasure, relaxation, peace of mind or freedom from molestation, damages will be awarded if the fruit of the contract is not provided or if the contrary result is procured instead. If the law did not cater for this exceptional category of case it would be defective. A contract to survey the condition of a house for a prospective purchaser does not, however, fall within this exceptional category.

On the basis of this approach it was held in the *Alexander* case (1995) that a breach of contract to repair even a very prestigious car like a Rolls-Royce does not give rise to a liability for damage for distress and inconvenience or loss of enjoyment in the use of the car. As Beldam LJ held:

> I do not doubt that it was the appellant's object to enjoy to the full the ownership of this Rolls-Royce car, but it by no means follows that every time it was submitted for service or repair to those who undertook the work but failed to carry it out with proper care and skill that they would be answerable in damages for any distress, frustration and anxiety or lack of pleasure caused by the owner.

Contributory negligence

Where the defendant has broken a contractual obligation which is expressed in terms of taking reasonable care but which does not correspond to a common law duty of care, it is unclear whether the provisions of the Law Reform (Contributory Negligence) Act 1945 apply. However, where the defendant is sued for the breach of a strict contractual duty, then the 1945 Act is inapplicable and damages cannot be reduced on the ground of contributory negligence (see *Forsikringsaktieselskapet Vesta v Butcher* [1989] AC 852). In this respect the plaintiff may be overcompensated as no reduction is made to reflect the plaintiff's contribution to the loss which has arisen (see Law Commission Report, *Contributory Negligence as a Defence in Contract* No 219 (1993)).

Consequential loss

Consequential loss claims may well arise upon the acceptance of goods which prove to be defective. The rules in *Hadley v Baxendale* (1854) provide a sound and rational basis for paying due regard to the normal and foreseeable results which flow as a result of breach of contract. Nonetheless, there are difficulties with constructing a single formula which expresses the degree of foreseeability necessary. In *The Heron II* [1969] 1 AC 350, the House of Lords seems to have settled on 'not unlikely' as expressing the degree of foreseeability. The problem here is that it may not be just always to impose liability for foreseeable consequences, especially as other factors may be relevant. Thus, in the case of sale of goods, the price of the goods will normally reflect the scarcity value of them. An illustration of this is provided in *Victoria Laundries v Newman Industries* (1949) where the sellers were selling a boiler for laundry use at a time when laundries were in great demand. This affected the price at which the boiler was sold so it was reasonable in that case to treat the seller as liable for normal lost profits.

A dramatic illustration of the difficulties posed by the foreseeability test can be seen in *H Parsons (Livestock) v Uttley Ingham and Co Ltd* [1978] QB 791. In this case, the defendants supplied and installed a large hopper for holding animal foodstuffs for the plaintiff, a pig farmer. A ventilator at the top of the hopper, which could not be seen from the ground, was left closed with the result that some of the food became mouldy. The pigs became ill and subsequently a more serious condition was triggered off by the first illness with the result that many of the pigs died. The farmer recovered for all his lost and diseased pigs on the basis that this was foreseeable. There does seem to be an air of unreality about the foreseeability test here because it would seem that the only events which can be regarded as unforeseeable, following this case, are those in which the train of events has been interrupted by conscious human intervention. This seems to go too far.

If the buyer or hirer does not take the normal precautions with a view to discovering any patent or latent defect concerning goods delivered, this may be a *novus actus interveniens* preventing the supplier being liable for the consequences of his breach. Thus in *Lambert v Lewis* [1982] AC 225, a farmer who continued to use a coupling which he knew or ought to have known was defective could not claim an indemnity from the seller in respect to the farmer's liability to the plaintiff, who was injured when the coupling gave way. However, where the goods have been put to their contemplated use and the defect amounts to a breach of the contract of supply, it has been held that the buyer may recover for personal injury as well as injury to other property (*Bostock and Co Ltd v Nicholson and Sons Ltd* [1904] 1 KB 725). Damages are also available, in appropriate cases as discussed above, for inconvenience and disappointment (see *Jackson v Chrysler Acceptances Ltd* [1978] RTR 474; compare *Kemp v Intasun Holidays* [1987] 2 FTLR 234).

Particular dilemmas have arisen where defective goods are of an income-producing kind. It is clear that the hirer or buyer cannot claim both the diminution in the warranted value at the contract delivery date and the full loss of profit resulting from the nonconformity of the goods as this would allow him to duplicate his compensation. The problem is that there are several ways of calculating loss of profit. In the troublesome case of *Cullinane v British 'Rema' Manufacturing Co* [1954] 1 QB 292, the Court of Appeal held that the buyer could not split his claim as between capital loss and income loss. This was an indefensible position and it is hoped that in future the decision will not be followed. Of course, this does not mean that the plaintiff should be free to split his claim in an arbitrary fashion. Reference must surely be made to what a reasonable buyer would do to mitigate his loss, for example by hiring substitute goods in appropriate cases. The problem of double recovery can be seen in *George Mitchell (Chesterhall) Ltd v Finney Lock Seeds Ltd* [1983] AC 803, where a seed merchant sold defective seed to a farmer with the result that the latter's crop failed. It was said that the damages included 'all the costs incurred by the [farmer] in the cultivation of the worthless crop as well as the profit [he] would have expected to make from a successful crop if proper seeds had been supplied' (p 812). In this regard the reference to 'profit' must refer to the proceeds of a successful crop less the cost of cultivating this type of crop and this cost of course might well be lower than the cost of attempting to cultivate an unsuccessful crop.

Where the goods are bought for resale, the seller will be liable for loss if it can be shown that the resale was not too remote. The buyer's burden of proof is lighter here than where he claims damages for non-delivery; he need only show that the sub-sales were a reasonable probability in order to recover under s 54 of SGA 1979. Nevertheless, to claim damages it has to be demonstrated that the sub-sale was on substantially similar terms, as it would be anomalous to visit upon the seller liability for a more onerous sub-contract. If the sub-sale is not on the same terms, the buyer can still claim damages paid to the sub-buyer in respect of defects for which the seller would have been liable (*per* Devlin J in *Biggin and Co Ltd v Permanite Ltd* [1951] 1 KB 422 at p 434, reversed on other grounds). Where there has been a settlement of a claim, it is open to the seller to contest the amount and demonstrate that the sum paid was excessive in relation to the breach of contract. The legal costs incurred in reasonably defending the sub-buyer's claim will also be recoverable (*Hammond and Co v Bussey* (1887) 20 QBD 79), as will the loss of repeat orders from the sub-buyer where this is within the contemplation of the parties (*GKN Centrax Gears Ltd v Matbro Ltd* [1976] 2 Lloyd's Rep 555). Nonetheless, the courts have rejected a claim in respect of loss of a business connection (*Bostock and Co Ltd v Nicholsons and Co Ltd* [1904] 1 KB 725).

Damages in tort

Where the transferor has property and an immediate right to possession, he may sue for wrongful interference with goods. Certainly, if a seller under a conditional sale agreement refuses to deliver the goods to the buyer, the latter will have a cause of action in conversion. Where the buyer is suing a third party, the measure of damages is *prima facie* the value of the goods at the date of conversion. As between the parties to the contract, suing in tort has no advantages and is rarely used (*The Arpad* [1934] P 189). Moreover, by suing in tort the transferor cannot obtain an order of specific restitution where he could not have obtained a decree of specific performance of the contract (*Cohen v Roche* [1927] 1 KB 169).

Specific performance

The Divisional Court in *Re Wait* [1926] Ch 962 DC (reversed) concluded that the court ought to grant a decree of specific performance and not leave the sub-purchasers 'to the doubtful remedy of proof for damages in bankruptcy' (*per* Lawrence J at p 974). Counsel argued that there should be specific performance of the contract for the sale of 500 tons of wheat by virtue of s 52 of SGA 1893. This section replaced s 2 of the Mercantile Law Amendment Act 1856 which itself was an enabling provision for the decree of specific performance to be awarded by the common law courts. Indeed, the tenor of the 1856 Act reflected the majority view of the Second Report of the Mercantile Law Commissioners published in 1855, which was that the civilian approach to specific relief be adopted. The generous treatment to the availability of this remedy under civil law may be seen in Scotland where there is a presumption in favour of granting specific performance, unless there is a good ground in equity for refusing it.

As we have seen, s 52 of SGA 1893 (now the 1979 Act) was intended to enlarge the jurisdiction of the courts. Significantly, whereas s 2 of the 1856 Act referred only to 'specific goods', s 52 of the 1979 Act gives the court a discretion to order a decree of specific performance in any action for breach of contract to deliver 'specific or ascertained goods'. Nevertheless, the majority in the Court of Appeal in *Re Wait* adopted a restrictive approach to s 52 and Lord Hanworth MR maintained that:

> [The operation of s 52] remains limited. It is not possible to overlook the original purpose and scope of its predecessors which was to meet the difficulty and hardship suffered by a buyer in respect of specific goods, and the section reproduces the old law in a codifying statute. It has not changed the law. (p 617)

This conclusion does seem odd as a matter of statutory interpretation, because why should Chalmers, the draftsman of the SGA 1893, bother to use two synonymous concepts where one would do, unless a different treatment was intended?

In the Divisional Court it was held that the property in the 500 tons of wheat had not passed to the sub-purchasers, but that the goods were specific goods within the meaning of s 52 as 'being identified and agreed upon at the time of the contract'. Despite this, in the Court of Appeal, Atkin LJ interpreted 'ascertained' to mean:

> . . . identified in accordance with the agreement after the time a contract of sale is made . . . It seems to be beyond dispute that at the date of this contract there were no goods identified and agreed upon; and I think it equally clear that at no time were there any goods ascertained. (p 630)

The reasoning evident in the Court of Appeal is one of determining policy. It would seem that the court, as a matter of policy, relegated a purchaser who pays merely on the strength of an invoice in favour of the seller's creditors. Even if specific performance is not available under s 52, there seems to be no reason in principle why specific performance should not be decreed outside of s 52, for example in the case of a long-term supply contract as in *Sky Petroleum Ltd v VIP Petroleum Ltd* [1974] 1 WLR 576.

The difficulty with the above approach is that it contradicts the judgment of Atkin LJ in *Re Wait* (which was not cited in *Sky Petroleum Ltd*) where the argument employed was that, as a matter of commercial convenience, the Code was meant to be exhaustive. However, this objection is not fatal because the judgment itself undermines s 62(2) of SGA 1979 (the common law saving provision) thereby making the Act appear internally inconsistent. In fact, it is anticipated under the Act that the rules of common law apply, save insofar as they are inconsistent with the express provisions of the Act. The Code does not carefully set out the circumstances in which specific performance is available, for example, there is no reference to injunctive relief and it is, in any case, restricted to suits brought by the buyer, the seller only being given an action for the price under s 49 of SGA 1979. This is certainly the position in the USA where equity and common law are unified. Thus, although the *Commentary to the US Restatement of Contracts* (2 edn) recognises the 'adequacy of damages' formula, it goes on to say, in para 359,: '. . . the modern approach is to compare remedies to determine which is more effective in serving the ends of justice . . . Doubts should be resolved in favour of the granting of specific performance . . .'. Moreover, the Official Comment 2 accompanying art 2:716(1) maintains that uniqueness is not the sole basis of the remedy which may also be granted in 'other proper circumstances'. Similarly, in England, it has been persuasively argued that specific performance should be decreed if it is an 'appropriate' remedy (see Jones and Goodhart, *Specific Performance* (1986)).

The English courts have taken a restrictive view of the availability of specific performance, especially where damages may not compensate a plaintiff for the entire loss which he has suffered because it is too remote (see, for example, *The Stena Nautica (No 2)* [1982] 2 Lloyd's Rep 336). Such an approach is particularly seen with the court's insistence that the chattel must have some unique attribute. However, the courts have not been consistent with their application of the 'uniqueness' test; it is difficult to understand why specific relief was refused in respect of a set of Hepplewhite chairs in *Cohen v Roche* [1927] 1 KB 169, but was granted in respect of an Adam-style door as in *Phillips v Lamdin* [1949] 2 KB 33.

The courts tend to start from the assumption that damages will usually compensate the complainant. From this perspective, the 'uniqueness' test for the assumption of the specific performance remedy is a classic example of money damages failing to compensate adequately. Where goods are not unique, information acquired in searching for the goods is very likely to have an independent usefulness which will survive a breach by the promisor. Moreover, where there is substantial information in a particular sale environment, the risk of undercompensation by the court is not great since information on substitutability will be readily available. On the other hand, where there is no established market and/or few transactions, the risk is substantial. With this in mind, it could be argued that the great attraction of the 'uniquenes' test for specific performance is that this is what the parties would have agreed *ex ante* had they been engaged in a hypothetical bargaining process. An extension to this approach is that where a creditor seeks a secured interest contract, this should be considered unique for the purpose of ordering a decree of specific performance. In this context, the question of adequacy of damages does not arise and this factor has weighed heavily in cases involving the specific enforcement of agreements to mortgage chattels: *Taylor v Eckersley* (1876) 2 Ch D 302; *Clements v Matthews* (1883) 11 QBD 808. Compare *Buckland v Hall* (1803) 8 Ves 92; *Neale v Mackenzie* (1837) 1 Ke 474. The argument here is that where a party has attempted unsuccessfully to create a security interest, this may demonstrate that damages *per se* are not an adequate remedy principally because if the defendant is insolvent he will not be able to satisfy a judgment for damages. A better approach might be to draw a distinction between the *risk* of insolvency and *actual* insolvency. As Goulding J said in *Anders Utkilens Rederi v Lovisa Stevedoring Co* [1985] 2 All ER 669: 'Commercial life would be subjected to new and unjust hazards if the court were to decree specific performance of contracts normally sounding only in damages simply because of a party's threatened insolvency' (p 674).

It is important to weigh up the position of the promisee and other creditors. In theory, third party hardship should not prevent the granting of a decree of specific performance to a plaintiff who is *prima facie* entitled to it, although it will be a factor in the exercise by the court of its discretion. The policy issue confronted here goes to the heart of the distribution problem among creditors on insolvency. It can hardly be said that the objection to applying specific performance is to avoid private abuse of a powerful and intrusive remedy, since the 'servitude' which is imposed is no greater than that confronted by secured credit generally. Essentially, the basis of the creditor's case for ordering specific performance is that he had bargained to be preferred and is, therefore, in a different class from the ordinary creditors who had advanced their money or goods without bargaining for such protection.

It is clear that s 52 applies whether or not property has passed. Nonetheless, where property has passed, the buyer has an option of claiming a decree of specific restitution under s 3 of the Torts (Interference with Goods) Act 1977. As an equitable remedy, its availability rests within the court's discretion and there has been a tendency in recent years for the principles governing the application of equitable remedies to be relaxed (compare *CN Marine Inc v Stena Line (No2)* [1982] 2 Lloyd's Rep 336).

It may be possible for the transferee to be granted injunctive relief. This will be important to restrain a supplier from delivering the goods in breach of contract to another client. In *Redler Grain Silos Ltd v BICC Ltd* [1982] 1 Lloyd's Rep 435, it was held in these circumstances that it was no defence for the sellers to show that damages would be an adequate remedy, an approach which appears to be wider than that seen with specific performance.

Index